Edward Gibbon

Private Letters of Edward Gibbon (1753-1794)

Vol. I.

Edward Gibbon

Private Letters of Edward Gibbon (1753-1794)
Vol. I.

ISBN/EAN: 9783337016647

Printed in Europe, USA, Canada, Australia, Japan

Cover: Foto ©ninafisch / pixelio.de

More available books at **www.hansebooks.com**

PRIVATE LETTERS

OF

EDWARD GIBBON

(1753–1794).

WITH AN INTRODUCTION BY

THE EARL OF SHEFFIELD.

EDITED BY

ROWLAND E. PROTHERO,

BARRISTER-AT-LAW, SOME-TIME FELLOW OF ALL SOULS' COLLEGE, OXFORD.

VOL. I.

LONDON:

JOHN MURRAY, ALBEMARLE STREET.

1896.

LONDON :
PRINTED BY WILLIAM CLOWES AND SONS, LIMITED,
STAMFORD STREET AND CHARING CROSS.

INTRODUCTION BY THE EARL OF SHEFFIELD.

THE centenary of the death of Edward Gibbon (died January, 1794, aged fifty-six) was recorded by a public commemoration held in London in November, 1894, at the instance of the Royal Historical Society. The distinguished committee of English and foreign students, who were associated on that occasion, invited me to become their President, as representing the family with which Gibbon had been so intimately connected, and which still retained the portraits, manuscripts, letters, and relics of the historian. The exhibition of these in the British Museum, and the commemoration held on November 15, reawakened interest in the work and remains of one of the greatest names in English literature ; and a general desire was expressed that the manuscripts should be again collated, and that what was yet unpublished might be given to the world.

As is well known, it was my grandfather, the first Earl, who made the historian almost his adopted brother, gave him a home both in town and in country, was his devisee and literary executor, and edited and published the famous Autobiography, the letters, and remains. All of these passed under Edward Gibbon's will to Lord Sheffield ; and, together with books, relics, portraits, and various mementos, they have been for a century preserved by my father and myself with religious care and veneration in Sheffield Park. The original autograph manuscripts of the *Memoirs*, the *Diaries*, *Letters*, *Note-books*, etc., have now become the property of the British Museum, subject to the copyright of all the unpublished parts which was previously assigned to Mr. Murray. And it is with no little pleasure and pride that

I have acceded to the request of the publishers that I would introduce these unpublished remains to the world, and thus complete the task of editing the historian, to which my grandfather devoted so great a portion of his time, not only as a testamentary duty, but as a labour of love.

The connection of the historian with my grandfather, his early friend, John Holroyd, and the members of the Holroyd family, forms one of the pleasantest and also most interesting passages in literary history. It was in no way interrupted by Lord Sheffield's public and official duties; it was continued without a cloud to obscure their intimacy, until it was sundered by death; and the Earl, who survived his friend so long, continued to edit and to publish the manuscripts left in his hands for some twenty years after the death of the historian.

By a clause in the will of Edward Gibbon, dated July 14, 1788, his papers were entrusted to Lord Sheffield and Mr. John Batt, his executors, in the following terms :—

" I will that all my Manuscript papers found at the time of my decease be delivered to my executors, and that if any shall appear sufficiently finished for the public eye, they do treat for the purchase of the same with a Bookseller, giving the preference to Mr. Andrew Strahan and Mr. Thomas Cadell, whose liberal spirit I have experienced in similar transactions. And whatsoever monies may accrue from such sale and publication I give to my much-valued friend William Hayley, Esq., of Eastham, in the County of Sussex. But in case he shall dye before me, I give the aforesaid monies to the Royal Society of London and the Royal Academy of Inscriptions of Paris, share and share alike, in trust to be by them employed in such a manner as they shall deem most beneficial to the cause of Learning."

In pursuance of the directions contained in the will and of many verbal communications, Lord Sheffield, in 1799, published the *Miscellaneous Works of Edward Gibbon, with Memoirs of his Life and Writings*, in 2 vols., 4to. A third volume was added in 1815, and a new edition of the whole, with additions, appeared during the same year in 5 vols., 8vo. In 1837 another edition, in one large 8vo volume, was published.

By a clause in his own will, Lord Sheffield directed that no further publication of the historian's manuscripts should be made.

"And I request of my said trustees and my heirs that none of the said manuscripts, papers, or books of the said Edward Gibbon be published unless my approbation of the publication be directed by some memorandum indorsed and written or signed by me. And I also request the person entitled for the time being to the possession thereof not to suffer the same to be out of his possession or to be improperly exposed."

This direction has been strictly followed by my father, the second Earl, and by myself; and it is believed that no person has ever had access to any of the manuscripts for any literary purpose, excepting the late Dean Milman, who, when editing his well-known edition of the *Decline and Fall*, in 1842, was permitted to inspect the original manuscripts of the Autobiography, on condition of not publishing any new matter.

The commemoration of 1894, however, again raised the question whether such an embargo on giving to the world writings of national importance was ever meant to be, or even ought to be, regarded as perpetual. Whilst persons named in these papers or their children were living, whilst the bitter controversies of the last century were still unforgotten, whilst the fame of Edward Gibbon had hardly yet become one of our national glories, it was a matter of good feeling and sound judgment in Lord Sheffield to exercise an editor's discretion in publishing his friend's confession and private thoughts. Now that more than a hundred years have passed since his death, no such considerations have weight or meaning. And the opinion of those whom I have consulted, both professionally and as private friends, amply corroborates my own conclusion, that it is a duty which I owe to my own ancestor and to the public to give to the world all the remains of the historian which for more than a century have been preserved in the strong room of Sheffield Park.

The unlocking of the cases in which these manuscripts were secured was quite a revelation of literary workmanship, and has

led to a most interesting problem in literary history. The manuscripts of the historian are all holographs—the text of the famous
Memoirs being written with extraordinary beauty of calligraphy,
and studied with the utmost care. · But, singularly enough, none
of the texts are prepared for immediate, or even direct, publication.
The historian wrote, at various intervals between 1788 and 1793,
no less than *six* different sketches. They are not quite continuous ;
they partly recount the same incidents in different form ; they
are written in different tones : and yet no one of them is
complete ; none of them seem plainly designed to supersede
the rest. There is even a small seventh sketch, from which one
of the noblest and most famous passages that Gibbon ever wrote
has been excised, and inserted in the published Autobiography.

Lord Sheffield executed his editorial task with extreme
judgment, singular ingenuity, but remarkable freedom. He was
assisted in preparing the manuscripts for publication by his wife
and by Lady Maria Holroyd, his eldest daughter, who became by
marriage the first Lady Stanley of Alderley. This very able and
remarkable woman, of whose abilities the historian expressed in
letters his great admiration, evidently marked the manuscripts
in pencil handwriting (now recognized as hers) for the printer's
copyist. These pencil deletions, transpositions, and even additions,
correspond with the Autobiography as published by Lord Sheffield.
Quite a third of the whole manuscript is omitted, and many of
the most piquant passages that Gibbon ever wrote were suppressed
by the caution or the delicacy of his editor and his family.

The result is a problem of singular literary interest. A piece,
most elaborately composed by one of the greatest writers who
ever used our language, an autobiography often pronounced to be
the best we possess, is now proved to be in no sense the simple
work of that illustrious pen, but to have been dexterously pieced
together out of seven fragmentary sketches and adapted into
a single and coherent narrative. The manner and the extent of
this extraordinary piece of editing has been so fully explained
in the address of November 15, published by the Centenary
Committee, that it is not necessary for me to enlarge upon it
further.

No sooner had the discovery of the process by which Gibbon's *Autobiography* had been concocted been made public, than a general desire was expressed to have the originals published in the form in which the historian left them. It was no case of incomplete or illegible manuscripts, nor of rough drafts designed only as notes for subsequent composition. The whole of the seven manuscripts are written with perfect precision ; the style is in Gibbon's most elaborate manner ; and each piece is perfectly ready for the printer—so far as it goes. It was impossible to do again the task of consolidation so admirably performed by Lord Sheffield. Nothing remained but to print the whole of the pieces *verbatim*, as the historian wrote them, not necessarily in the order of time of their apparent composition, but so as to form a consecutive narrative of the author's life.

The reader may now rest assured that, *for the first time*, he has before him the Autobiographic Sketches of Edward Gibbon in the exact form in which he left them at his death. The portions enclosed in dark brackets are the passages which were omitted by Lord Sheffield, and in the notes are inserted the passages or sentences, few and simple in themselves, which Lord Sheffield added to the original manuscript. For various reasons it was found impracticable to print the six sketches in parallel columns ; but the admirers of the historian and all students of English literature will find abundant opportunity for collating the original texts with each other, and with the text as published by the editor, and now for a century current as one of the masterpieces of English literature.

The *Letters* of the historian, the bulk of which were addressed to Lord Sheffield and his family, were published in part by my grandfather in one or other of the editions of *The Miscellaneous Works of Edward Gibbon*. But in this collection many letters were omitted, and most of them were printed with some omissions and variations. These omissions have now been restored ; and the *Letters*, like the other papers of our author, are now for the first time given to the world in the form in which they were composed.

I cannot pretend to any rivalry with my grandfather in the

matter of the skill with which he performed the task of editing
and selecting for publication the remains of his friend. But
I can assure the reader that *every piece contained in this volume as
the work of Edward Gibbon is now printed exactly as he wrote it
without suppression or emendation*. And in transferring these
literary treasures to the nation, and in giving them to the world,
I feel that I am fulfilling the trust which the historian reposed
in my grandfather, and am acting in the spirit of the lifelong
friendship that bound him to my family.

I cannot conclude these prefatory remarks without acknowledging to the fullest extent the obligation I am under to Mr. Frederic
Harrison for the assistance he has given me in the preparation
and composition of this Preface.

EDITOR'S PREFACE.

This collection of Gibbon's correspondence, extending as it does from 1753 to 1794, practically covers the whole of the historian's life, and contains his observations on society, literature, and politics during a period which includes such momentous events as the Seven Years' War, the War of American Independence, and the French Revolution.

By far the greater number of the letters now appear for the first time ; but portions of the correspondence, marked in this edition with asterisks, were printed by Lord Sheffield shortly after Gibbon's death. These published portions were treated by the editor with great tact and more freedom. Lord Sheffield was giving to the world letters which discussed recent events and criticised living persons ; it was, therefore, necessary for him to suppress some allusions and conceal many names. Jealous of his friend's literary reputation, he corrects errors in spelling or grammar, gives a dignified turn to the more homely phrases, and omits as trivial the petty details of domestic life. Sometimes, also, Lord Sheffield's editorial methods pass beyond the exercise of these more or less legitimate powers. In order to concentrate the interest of the correspondence, he culls a few lines from one letter, chooses a sentence from a second, extracts a passage from a third, and prints his patchwork as a genuine letter from Gibbon's own hand.

In this edition the letters are printed as they were written. For the blanks which conceal the identity of persons are substituted the real names ; the suppressed passages are restored ;

the spelling and grammar of the original are preserved; the language is left as Gibbon wrote it. If the Memoirs give us Gibbon in the full dress of a fine gentleman of letters, the correspondence reveals to us the man as he was known to his valet and his housekeeper.

The letters have the case and freshness of conversations with intimate friends, and, considering the character of the century in which they were written, they present one feature which deserves special notice. Only one short sentence has been omitted as too coarse to be printed. With this solitary exception, the reader knows the worst as well as the best of Gibbon, and there are scarcely a dozen phrases, scattered over 800 pages, which will offend good taste or good feeling.

The notes must speak for themselves. Though some points on which information is needed remain obscure, it is hoped that, so far as they go, they may be found useful. In their correction and revision, valuable aid has been given by Mr. G. H. Holden, Assistant Librarian at All Souls' College, Oxford.

ERRATA.

Vol. I. page 185, note, last line, *for* "Roslyn" *read* "Rosslyn."
,, ,, 314, note 2, line 7, *for* "Madame du Barry" *read* "Madame du Barri."
,, ,, 386, note 2, *for* "Wibraham" *read* "Wilbraham."
Vol. II. page 4, note 1 (twice), *for* "Bushy" *read* "Bushey."

GIBBON'S CORRESPONDENCE.

1753–1794.

On June 8, 1753, Edward Gibbon, then sixteen years of age, and an undergraduate of Magdalen College, Oxford, was received into the Roman Catholic Church by a Jesuit named Baker, one of the chaplains to the Sardinian Embassy. His change of religion led to his removal from the University, and decided his father to place him under the care of M. Pavillard, a Calvinist minister at Lausanne. Escorted by M. Frey, a Swiss gentleman of Basle, Gibbon left England on June 19, 1753. His first letter announces his safe arrival.

1.

To his Father.

[Lausanne], July 30th, 1753.

Dear Sir,

I must beg you to excuse my not having wrote till now, but knowing that Mr. Frey had given you an account of my safe arrival by the first post, I chose to stay some time, that I might be able to give you a more exact account of my present situation. After a pretty tiresome journey of eleven days, I got safe to Lausanne. Mr. Frey, when he had delivered me into Mr. Pavilliard's hands, left the place and went to Geneva. I have now been with him a month, and during the whole time have been treated by him with the greatest civility imaginable. I read French twice every day with him. I already understand almost all that is said, and can ask for any common things I want. With regard to other things, the people here are extremely civil to strangers, and endeavour to make this town as agreeable as possible. The English here are Mr. Townshend, nephew to the present Lord Townshend, Lord Huntingtower, Mr. Crofts, and Mr. Umberstone. I have also been introduced to the Earl of Blessington, who resides here now with his family, as well as to Madame de Brissoné, to whom you gave me a letter of recommendation, and who is an extremely agreeable woman. This is the chief I have to say of the place. As to the climate, I have reason to think it will agree extremely well with me. When I was at Calais my books were seized and sent to Paris to be examined, but a friend there, whom Mr. Frey has wrote to, is to send them to Lausanne. I must beg my sincere compliments to Miss Ellison.

I am, dear Sir,
With the greatest respect and sincerity,
Your most obedient and most dutiful son,
EDWARD GIBBON.

2.

To his Aunt, Miss Catherine Porten.[1]

February, 1755.

" Pray remember this letter was not addressed to his mother-in-law, but his aunt, an old cat as she was to refuse his request." [2]

DEAR MADAM,

*I have at length good news to tell you ; I am now a good Protestant, and am extremely glad of it.[3] I have in all my letters taken notice of the different movements of my mind.

---

[1] Judith Porten, the mother of Edward Gibbon, was the third and youngest daughter of Mr. James Porten, a merchant of London. She died in December, 1747, leaving the maternal care of her son to her sister, Miss Catherine Porten, the " Aunt Kitty " of the later correspondence, to whom this letter is addressed. After her father's commercial ruin, Miss Catherine Porten opened a boarding-house for Westminster School, in College Street. Under her care Gibbon spent the two years which he passed at Westminster. He entered the school in January, 1748, and was placed in the second form.

[2] This endorsement is in the handwriting of his stepmother, the second Mrs. Gibbon.

[3] " M. Pavilliard has described to me the astonishment with which he gazed on Mr. Gibbon standing before him; a thin little figure, with a large head, disputing and urging, with the greatest ability, all the best arguments that had ever been used in favour of popery." [Lord Sheffield.]

Entirely Catholic when I came to Lausanne, wavering long time
between the two systems, and at last fixed for the Protestant,
when that conflict was over, I had still another difficulty.
Brought up with all the ideas of the Church of England, I could
scarce resolve to communion with Presbyterians, as all the people
of this country are. I at last got over it in considering that, whatever difference there may be between their churches and ours in
the government and discipline, they still regard us as brethren,
and profess the same faith as us. Determined, then, in my design,
I declared it to the ministers of the town assembled at Mr.
Pavilliard's, who, having examined me, approved of it, and permitted me to receive the communion with them, which I did
Christmas Day, from the hands of Mr. Pavilliard, who appeared
extremely glad of it. I am so extremely myself, and do assure
you feel a joy pure, and the more so as I know it to be not only
innocent but laudable.*

Could I leave off here I should be very glad, but I have
another piece of news to acquaint you with. Mr. Pavilliard has
already hinted it in the letter you have, I suppose, already
received, and which I have translated into English. Let me tell
you the whole fact as it is really past.

One evening I went to see Mr. Gee, one of the English now
here. I found him in his room, playing at Pharaon with some
other gentlemen. I would have retired, but he desiring me to
stay, I took a chair and sat down by the fire. I continued to look
at the gamesters about half an hour, till one of them going away,
Gee desired me to take his place, and I refused; but on his
assuring me that I might punt as low as I would, at last complied,
and soon lost about half a guinea; this vexed me, and I continued
upon my word. The play warmed, and about three o'clock the
next morning I found I had lost only forty guineas. Guess my
situation (which I did not dare communicate to any one); such
a loss, and an utter impossibility of paying it. I took the worst
party I could. I demanded my revenge; they gave it me, and the
second meeting was still worse than the first. It cost me 1760
francs, or 110 guineas.

Never have I felt a despair equal to that I had then. I was
a great while hesitating upon the most violent parties. At last I
resolved to go seek my money in England, not doubting to be able
to raise that sum at London. I had not forgot that step would

expose me to all the indignation of my father, but I shut my eyes on all those considerations, to reflect that it was my only resource to pay my debt and to disengage my word ; in pursuance of this, I bought a horse, a watch, and some other things of Mr. Gee himself, payable with the rest in England, and set out proposing to sell those things to carry me on my journey. Was successful as far as Geneva, but there the difficulty I found to dispose of my horse having stopped me some days, Pavilliard, who had perceived my evasion, ran after me, and half entreaties, half force, brought me back to Lausanne with him.

I am there at present, not knowing what to do ; the term given me almost out, and my creditors extremely pressing. What party can I take ? Should I acquaint my father with it ? What first-fruits of a conversion should I give him ? I have then no other resource than you. Tell me not you are poor, that you have not enough for yourself. I do not address myself to you as the richest, but as the kindest of my relations ; nor do I ask it you as a gift, but as a loan. If you could not furnish me the whole sum, let me have at least a part of it. I know you have thoughts of doing something for me by your will ; I beg you only to anticipate it. I shall make no use of any other prayers than this plain recite of my situation ; if it produces no effect on you, nothing else would. Remember only that my term finished March 15. I tremble for your answer, but beg it may be speedy. I am too much agitated to go on. I will tell you something of myself in my next, *i.e.* very soon.

I am, dear Kitty,

Your unfortunate nephew,

E. GIBBON.

P.S.—I have enclosed a *carte blanche*—write there a promise for what you send me ; it may serve you with my father in case of my death.

P.S.—You may inquire for Grand and Wombwell, bankers, who will give you bills upon Mr. Grand, banker, at Lausanne for as much as you will.

3.

To his Father.

March 1st, 1755.

DEAR SIR,

As Mr. Pavilliard writes to you at present, I will not let slip the occasion of sending my letter by the same post. Give me leave, sir, to demand of you, once more, and to demand of you with the last earnestness, the return of your paternal tenderness, which I have forfeited by the unhappy step I have made. I hope to merit that return by my behaviour. Give me leave, too, to repeat my former demands of some masters, as for the *manége* for fencing and for dancing. With regard to the last, I own that Mr. Pavilliard, overcome by importunities, and imagining you would not disapprove of it, gave me leave to take it about three months ago, and I actually learn. My health still continues good, and I continue my studies in the same manner I have already described to you. The only news I have to tell you is that the famous Mr. de Voltaire[1] is come to spend, as he says, the rest of his days here. He has bought an estate near Geneva, where he proposes to spend the summer, and to pass the winter at a country house he has hired near Lausanne.

Give me now leave, dear Sir, to finish, repeating the demand of your former affection. If I could hope to hear from you I should think myself completely happy.

I am, dear Sir,
Your most obedient and most dutiful son,
E. GIBBON.

4.

To Miss Catherine Porten.

September 20th, 1755.

DEAR MADAM,

In compliance with your request, I answer the very day I have received it. I own you had vexed me ; not so much in refusing me the money I asked you, as by revealing the thing to my father. But what is done cannot be undone, and as my father

---

[1] Voltaire lived from 1755 to 1758 at *les Délices* near Geneva, and within Genevan territory.

has forgiven me, I think I may do as much for you. I consent,
then, to the renewal of our correspondence with all my heart. I
shall begin by the tail of your letter. My whole debt was not
with Gee ; a great part was with a person of this town, who has
heard reason easily enough. He has consented to receive a note
by which I own the debt, and promise to pay him when I can.
Gee has not been so easy. After having obliged him to take back
the watch and the mare, the debt was still at fifty guineas. I
bought him for twenty another watch, paying (as I do still) two
guineas a month to the watchmaker, and which Mons. Pavilliard
and I contrive to retrench out of my other expenses. Gee left us
about four months ago. Have you a mind to know his destiny ?
Yes. Hear it, then. His parents had ordered him forty guineas
for his journey, but as they had allowed him to stay a fortnight
at Paris, he was to take twenty more in that place. Gee quits
Lausanne in this manner. Suppose him at Lyons. He goes
immediately to the correspondent of his banker, for whom he had
a letter of recommendation. "Sir," says he, in accosting him, "I
have a letter for you from your correspondent, Mons. Grand of
Lausanne. You will find in it that he desires you to pay me
twenty-five guineas at sight." The banker puts on his spectacles,
reads the letter, but finds nothing in it about money. Upon
which he tells Gee that certainly there is some mistake, and he
cannot give him a farthing before it is cleared up. Gee replies
that he must be at Paris a certain day, and that without money
he cannot go. In a word, for I hate long stories, the banker
gives him the money, but writes to his correspondent at Paris to
stop Gee's twenty guineas. He, having some wind of the affair,
runs post, day and night, arrives at Paris four hours before the
letter, and draws the money. Gee's adventures at Paris would
take up a volume, as he played a great deal. Once he had a
hundred and fifty thousand livres, French money, in his pocket
(£6700), but a week after he was 1500 guineas in debt, thanks to
the famous Mr. Taff [1] and some others of much the same stamp.

[1] It is probable that this was the Mr. Taaffe who, with Mr. Wortley
Montagu and Lord Southwell, invited a Jew named Abraham Payba to
dine with them at Montagu's lodgings in Paris, in September, 1751. Having
made him drunk, they won from him in less than an hour eight hundred
louis d'or. Their debtor paid them with drafts which he knew would be dis-
honoured. Finding themselves outwitted, Taaffe and Montagu broke into
Payba's house, and possessed themselves of a considerable sum of money and

The end was *that his mother, though extremely poor, paid all his debts*, and sent him into England, where he is now, having lost his commission, having hardly any other resource than his Majesty's highway. So much for Gee.

A tear to poor Nell; she really deserves it. Am glad Nemmy is well married. Would write to my aunt Hester,[1] but know not what to say to her. You tell me Snell and Milton are gone; where? Compliments to Bett Gilbert and to the Darrels[2] since you are at Richmond. I hurry over; but, à propos, who directed your letter, for it is not your hand? I hurry over all these things to come to my father's marriage.

About a fortnight ago I received a vastly kind letter from my father of the 18th of August (inquire the day of his marriage). He forgave me in it all my past faults, promised never to speak of them again to me, provided only I kept the promises I had made him about my future behaviour; allows me to make a little tour about Switzerland, which I had asked him, and tells me that, after having completed my studies and my exercises, he would make me make that of France and Italy. But not a syllable about his marriage.[3] Three days after I heard of it by the canal of a certain Mr. Hugonin, whose father is our neighbour in Hampshire, but without any particularities either of name or anything else. Guess my surprise; you know he had always protested that he never would marry again—at least, had he done it in the time he was angry with me, I should have been less struck; but now what can he mean by it? What frightens me most is what I remember you told me; if my father married again, by my grandfather's will the estate went to the children of the second

a quantity of jewellery. For this offence they were imprisoned for three months in the Grand Châtelet (Nichols' *Literary Anecdotes of the Eighteenth Century*, vol. iv. pp. 629-634).

[1] Miss Hester Gibbon died unmarried in 1790, at the age of eighty-six, at King's Cliffe in Northamptonshire. William Law, the author of the *Serious Call*, originally her brother's tutor at Putney, afterwards her almoner, spiritual adviser and guide, died at her house in 1761. In the tomb which she caused to be built for him, she was also herself buried. Hester Gibbon is stated to have been the Miranda of the *Serious Call*; but her age at the date when the book was published (1728) makes this doubtful.

[2] The second daughter of Mr. James Porten married Mr. Darrel of Richmond, and left two sons, Edward and Robert.

[3] Gibbon's father married his second wife, Miss Dorothea Patton, in 1755.

bed, and that I had only 200 a year, provided the second wife
had more fortune than my mother, who had only £1500. You
may easily guess the anxiety that has put me in. I have wrote
to a friend in England, who I think I can trust to get me a copy
of that will out of Doctors' Commons; but though sure of his
discretion, I do not know whether he will care to serve me.
Could you not do it YOURSELF? and inquire whether my father
has not taken care of me by his marriage contract.

You say that Mrs. Gibbon (Miss Patton) has set my father
against the Mallets.[1] I do not know if 'tis so very good a sign.
Since she was intimate with him when I was under Ward's[2] hands,
I should think you must have heard something of her. Do make
some inquiries about her and send them me. I wonder what will
become of my poor cousin. She will be sold at last. Since they
are in France, and that the war is going to break out, what if
they should come to Lausanne?

*Now for myself. As my father has given me leave to make a
journey round Switzerland, we set out to-morrow. Buy a map of
Switzerland, 'twill cost you but a shilling, and follow me. I go
by Iverdun, Neufchâtel, Bienne or Biel, Soleure or Solothurn,
Bâle or Basil, Bade, Zurich, Lucerne, and Bern. The voyage will
be of about four weeks; so that *I hope to find a letter from you
waiting for me*. As my father had given me leave to learn what I
had a mind, I have learned to ride, and learn actually to dance
and draw. Besides that, I often give ten or twelve hours a day
to my studies. I find a great many agreeable people here; see
them sometimes, and can say upon the whole, without vanity,
that, tho' I am the Englishman here who spends the least money,
I am he who is the most generally liked. I told you that my
father had promised to send me into France and Italy. I have
thanked him for it. But if he would follow my plan, he won't do

---

[1] David Mallet, or Malloch, poet, playwright, and miscellaneous writer
(1705-65), is best known for his ballad of *William and Margaret*, his
unsubstantiated claim to the authorship of *Rule Britannia*, and his edition
of Bolingbroke's works. Bolingbroke, said Dr. Johnson, had "spent his life
in charging a gun against Christianity," and "left half-a-crown to a hungry
Scotchman to draw the trigger." Mallet was "a great declaimer in all the
London coffee-houses against Christianity," and the obtrusion of his sceptical
views made his household unpleasing to David Hume. To his house Gibbon
was taken after his reception into the Church of Rome.

[2] A well-known doctor of the day.

it yet a while. I never liked young travellers ; they go too raw
to make any great remarks, and they lose a time which is (in my
opinion) the most precious part of a man's life. My scheme
would be, to spend this winter at Lausanne—for tho' 'tis a very
good place to acquire the air of good company and the French
tongue, we have no good professors—to spend (I say) the winter
at Lausanne ; go into England to see my friends a couple of
months, and after that, finish my studies, either at Cambridge
(for after what's past one cannot think of Oxford), or at a university in Holland. If you liked the scheme, *could you propose it to
my father by Metcalf, or somebody else who has a certain credit
over him ?* I forgot to ask you whether, in case my father writes
to tell me his marriage, would you advise me to compliment my
mother-in-law ? I think so. My health is so very regular that I
have nothing to say about it.

I have been the whole day writing you this letter ; the preparations for our voyage gave me a thousand interruptions.
Besides that, I was obliged to write in English. This last reason
will seem a parradox, but I assure you the French is much more
familiar to me.* *À propos*, do you know anything of my Lord
Newnham ?[1] I heard he was in Germany.

I am, dear Kitty,
Your affectionate nephew
(*Not your grave, obedient, humble servant*),
E. GIBBON.

5.

To his Father.

10 juin 1756.

MON TRÈS CHER PÈRE,
Je reçus hier votre lettre avec beaucoup de plaisir, mais
qui ne fut pas tout-à-fait sans mélange d'Inquietude. Je craignois
vous avoir encore offensé par quelque nouvelle faute. Vous savez
combien une affection vive et sincère prend facilement l'allarme
aux plus grandes minucies. Je fus frappé en ouvrant votre lettre
de voir votre style ordinaire de Dear Edward changé en un froid

---

[1] George Simon (1736-1809), Viscount Nuneham, afterwards second
Earl of Harcourt, eldest son of the first earl. He was remarkable for his
affectation of French manners and fashions.

Monsieur. Il est vrai que la suite me rassura; j'y voyois un Père tendre qui vouloit bien entrer dans mes peines, les soulager, et me delivrer de toutes mes craintes, en m'assurant que, si je me conduisois toujours d'une façon conforme à mon devoir, le nouvel engagement qu'il avoit pris ne me porteroit aucune prejudice. J'espère que je me connois assez à présent pour pouvoir regarder cette condition comme une promesse absolue. En effet si je m'en écartois, avec quels yeux pourrois-je me regarder moi-même après m'être coupable d'une aussi noire ingratitude pour tant de bonté? Ce trait dont vous me faites part au sujet de votre nouvelle épouse, me la fait déjà aimer d'avance. Je n'aurai pas beaucoup de peine à considérer comme ma mère celle qui, ne pouvant pas me donner la vie, me l'a au moins rendu. J'aurai l'honneur de lui en faire mes très humbles remerciemens, et de l'assurer des vœux qui je fais pour son bonheur. Pour vous, mon très cher Père, je puis vous protester dans la sincerité de mon cœur que tous ceux que je fais à votre sujet ont pour unique but votre felicité mutuelle. Puissiez-vous gouter tous les agreémens d'une Union fondée sur l'amour et l'estime, et puisse je vous réiterer ces mêmes souhaits pendant une longue suite d'années.

Vous me demandez compte de mes études et de mes exercises. Pour vous en rendre il faut nécessairement que j'entre dans un certain détail. Vos questions la-dessus peuvent se rapporter : 1. à mon François. Je sais qu'il s'en faut de beaucoup que je ne possède cette langue aussi bien que je pourrois le faire. Mais j'ose dire pourtant, sans craindre d'en être démenti par Monsieur Pavilliard, que je la sais mieux que la plupart des Anglois que j'ai vu à Lausanne. 2. Mes Langues mortes. Vous savez mieux que personne ma faiblesse par rapport au Latin lorsque j'ai quitté l'Angleterre. Il n'y avoit alors point d'auteur que je pusse lire avec facilité ni par conséquent avec plaisir. A present il n'y en aucun que je ne lise coulamment. J'en ai lu plusieurs depuis quelque peu de tems, tels que la plus grande partie des ouvrages de Ciceron, Virgile, Saluste, les Epitres de Pline deux fois, les comédies de Terence autant, Velleius Patercule, et je me propose de les lire tous avec le tems. Pour ce qui est du Grec comme je n'ai commencé à l'aprendre que depuis un mois, ou six semaines, vous sentez bien que j'en suis encore aux Premiers Principes. 3. Ma Philosophie. J'ai achevé la Logique de Monsieur de Crousaz laquelle est fort estimée dans ce pays-ci, en partie avec

Monsieur Pavilliard et en parti dans mon Particulier. Je vais lire pour la seconde fois L'Etendement Humain, et, aussitôt que je l'aurai fini, je commencerai l'Algèbre que vous me recommandez tant. 4. Ma Danse et mon Dessein. Je crois que vous ne serez pas mécontent de mes progrès dans la dernière de ces choses. Pour ce de la première je fais tout ce que je puis. Monsieur Pavilliard me rendra la justice de dire je ne suis pas fort dissipé. Je ne sors pas beaucoup et alors même ce n'est que pour aller dans les compagnies de la ville.

Je suis bien fâché, mon très cher Père, de voir que ces malheureux mots de Mons. Hugonin, lachés et rapportés si mal à propos, ne sont pas encore effacés de votre esprit. Je vous en demande sincèrement excuse, et je vous prie de les oublier totalement. Pour ce qui est de mon . . .[1] que j'avois parlé à ma Tante, je voudrois n'en avoir jamais parlé puisqu'il vous déplait. J'avoue pourtant que l'ayant mûrement reconsidéré je n'y ai point pu decouvrir l'Incongruité dont vous me parlez. Comme ma Tante vous a montré mes lettres je ne repeterai point ce que j'y ai dit. Je remarquerai seulement qui ce même Locke dont vous me conseilliez tant la Lecture, pense tout comme moi au sujet des voyages prematures.

J'ai, l'honneur d'être,

Mon très cher Père,

Avec un profond respect et une affection sincère,

Votre très humble et très obéissant serviteur et fils,

E. GIBBON.

P.S.—Si j'osois je prierois de m'envoyer par un des voituriers qui vont si souvent de Londres en Suisse, la Bibliothèque Oriental d'Herbellot qui est parmi mes Livres.

6.

To his Father.

4 juin 1757.

MON TRÈS CHER PÈRE,

Je me hate de vous assurer encore une fois de mes sentimens. Je ne crois pas qu'ils vous soient inconnus, mais je me plais à les repeter ; heureux si les expressions de mon cœur ne vous deplaisent pas.

Quand pourrois-j'esperer de vous les temoigner, ces sentimens

---

[1] Word omitted in original.

en Angleterre ? Quatre ans se sont déjà écoulés depuis qu'un arret de votre part m'a fixé dans ce pays. Ils m'ont paru autant de siècles. Ce n'est pas que je me plaigne du pays même ni de ses habitans. Je leur ai des obligations essentielles. Je dois au séjour que j'y ai fait mon gout pour la culture de mon esprit, et les progrès quelqu'ils soient que j'ai fait dans quelques genres d'études. Je me suis même acquis un petit nombre d'amis qui meritent mon estime, et dont le souvenir me sera toujours cher. Mais ces amis que sont-ils au prix d'un père à qui je dois tout, d'une mère qui a autant de droit sur ma reconnoissance que sur mon respect, d'une Tante que j'aimai dès que je la connus, et qui je connus aussitôt que moi-même ? Je ne repasserai pas toutes les raisons dont je me suis déjà servi, pour faire voir que, quelques soient vos intentions, un plus long séjour à Lausanne ne me peut être que nuisible. Je vous les ai proposé, c'est à vous à les peser. Mais permettez-moi, mon très cher Père, de vous prier de réfléchir serieusement quel effet le différent emploi de mes plus belles années peut avoir sur le reste de ma vie. Je ne fais point entrer en ligne de compte mon propre agrément, c'est un objet trop leger pour être mis à coté de ceux-ci. Au moins, quelques soient vous resolutions, ne m'accablez pas par le silence. Que je les apprenne de vous, ce sera toujours pour moi une sorte de consolation.

Mais si des raisons que je n'ai gardé de blamer vous engagent à me laisser plus longtems dans ce pays ; adoucissez au moins ma situation. Je vous ai souvent demandé la liberté de prendre un Domestique. Je vous le demande encore comme le douceur qui me seroit le plus sensible. Comme je sais, mon cher Père, que vous n'aimez pas beaucoup à écrire des lettres, si après six semaines ou deux mois, je regarderai votre silence comme un consentement.

Je n'ai rien de nouveau à vous dire sur ma santé ni sur mes études. Celle-la est passable ; je fais tout ce je puis pour qu'on puisse dire quelque chose de plus de celles-ci.

Assurez ma chère mère (c'est avec bien du plaisir que je lui donne ce titre) de tous les sentimens que ce nom sacré emporte avec lui. J'ai l'honneur d'être, mon très cher Père, avec le plus profond respect et le plus tendre devouement

Mon très cher Père,

Votre très humble et très obeissant Serviteur et fils,

E. Gibbon.

7.

To his Father.

Lausanne, 26 Octobre, 1757.

MON TRÈS CHER PÈRE,

Dois-je me flatter que vous m'aimiez encore ? Si j'en croyois mes propres sentimens, je me dirais sur le champ que j'aime mon père avec une tendresse si vive et si vraie qu'il est impossible que je ne sois pas payé de retour. Si j'ai bien entendu ses paroles, ajoutais-je à moi-même. Ce père, ci-devant si rempli de bonté, m'a daigné assurer que tout étoit oublié et qu'il me rendoit son ancienne affection. Je ne dois donc plus en douter. Il m'aime, je suis heureux. Cependant d'un autre coté mille Idées facheuses s'offroient en foule à mon esprit. Je lui ai écrit plusieurs fois, je lui ai demandé des graces que je croyois raisonnables, et que j'esperois d'obtenir. Il se tait cependant. Un silence si cruel m'afflige, m'épouvante, me fait envisager le plus grand des malheurs : la perte de son amitié. Ne croyez pas, mon très cher Père, qu'il entre le moindre reproche dans ces plaintes, le respectueux attachement que j'aurai pour vous m'en interdit jusqu'à l'apparence. Vous avez sans doute vos raisons, et quand même elles me paroitroient pas tout à fait suffisantes, mon devoir, et, plus encore, mon cœur feroient taire ma faible raison et vous assureroient d'une obeissance libre de tout murmure.

Lorsque vous me permettez, il y a deux ans, de faire le tour de la Suisse, de peur de faire une depense trop forte, nous laissâmes Genève pour une autre fois. Je viens de faire ce petit voyage actuellement. J'y ai passé trois ou quatre semaines que j'ai taché de mettre à profit. Ma depense pendant ce tems là est allée à seize Louis neufs. J'espère, mon très cher Père, que vous ne la désapprouverez pas. Je ne l'aurois pas fait sans préalablement demander votre permission, mais le tems pressoit. Une troupe de Comédiens François étoient à Genève en passant. Il étoit bien naturel de saisir une occasion de prendre quelque Idée du Théâtre François, et cette occasion (vu la Guerre) étoit presque unique. De retour à Lausanne, j'ai repris mes anciennes occupations avec une ardeur nouvelle. Assurez, s'il vous plait, madame votre epouse de mon sincère Attachement, et faites moi la justice de me croire avec une tendresse et un respect sans bornes

Mon très cher Père,

Votre très Humble et très obeissant Serviteur,

E. GIBBON.

8.

To his Father.

Lausanne, March 29th, 1758.

DEAR SIR,

It is with the greatest pleasure that I see the time approach in which I may hope to enjoy what I have so long desired, your presence and the view of my native country. With regard to the road, the war[1] renders all roads almost impracticable. However, after having consulted the persons most used to travelling, they all agree that that of France will be the least dangerous. I shall pass for a Swiss Officer in Holland. I shall have Dutch Regimentals, and a passeport from the Canton of Berne. I am pretty sure that my Tongue won't betray me. I think of setting out the 8th or 10th of next month, and if I stay a few days in Holland to look a little about me, I may be in London the 2nd or 3rd of May, where I hope to meet you. I return you beforehand my most hearty thanks for your condescendance in concurring with my impatience. Tho' you think I shall not relish Beriton, I can assure you that the prospect of passing the summer in yours & Mrs. Gibbon's compagny, dividing my time between successive study, exercise, and ease, is the most agreable one I can conceive. I shall punctually follow your directions about money, and shall not abuse of the confidence you have in me. Be so good as to assure Mrs. Gibbon of all the sentiments Esteem and duty can inspire. As I run post I cannot bring her the Arquebuzade Water myself, but I shall remit to a waggoner, who will be at London almost as soon as I, several bottles of the very best I can find.

I am, Dear Sir, with the greatest respect and the truest affection,

Your most obedient humble Servant and Son,

E. GIBBON.

---

[1] The Seven Years' War, 1756-63.—" A war," says Horace Walpole, "that reaches from Muscovy to Alsace and from Madras to California" (Horace Walpole to the Earl of Strafford, June 12, 1759).

9.

To his Father.

The Hague, April the 29th, 1758.

DEAR SIR,

After a journey pretty tiresome, but in whitch I have not run the least risk, I am arrived safe at the Hague. Holland is certainly a country well worth the curiosity of a stranger, but as I have not the time to examine it as it deserves, I choose rather to put off that pleasure, than to enjoy it imperfectly. Perhaps my desire to see you soon deceives me, perhaps that desire is the only true source of my great haste. However it be, I intend to embark at Helvetsluys next Wednesday, and if the wind is good I may be in London Saturday or Sunday, where I hope to have the pleasure of seeing you and Mrs. Gibbon.

I am, Dear Sir,

Your most obedient humble Servant and Son,

E. GIBBON.

10.

To his Aunt, Miss Hester Gibbon.

Beriton, July the 20th, 1758.

DEAR MADAM,

Tho' the public voice had long since accustomed me to think myself honoured in calling Mrs. Gibbon my aunt, yet I never enjoyed the happiness of living near her, and of instructing myself not less by her example than by her precepts. Your piety, Madam, has engaged you to prefer a retreat to the world. Errors, justifiable only in their principle, forced my father to give me a foreign education. Fully disabused of the unhappy ideas I had taken up, and at last restored to myself, I am happy in the affection of the tenderest of fathers. May I not hope, Madam, to see my felicity compleat by the acquisition of your esteem and friendship? Duty and Inclination engage me equally to solicit them, all my endeavours shall tend to deserve them, and, with Mrs. Gibbon, I know that to deserve is to obtain. I have now been in England about two months, and should have acquitted myself much sooner of my duty, but frequent journeys to London scarce left me a moment to myself, and since a very ugly fever my father has had, engrossed all my thoughts. He is now entirely recovered, and desires his love and service to you, Madam, as well as to Mr. Law.

I am, Dear Madam,

With the sincerest esteem and most profound respect,

Your most obedient humble servant and dutiful nephew,

E. GIBBON, JUNIOR.

11.

To his Father.

London, October the 24th, 1758.

DEAR SIR,

The Chevalier and myself, after a pretty tedious journey, which his conversation did not render less so, arrived in town Sunday evening. We have got our old lodgings in Charles Street. Hugonin arrived a few minutes afterwards, tired of the country, and he seems to be now tired of the town. I have not yet got the lottery tickets. I shall certainly buy yours, but my forgetfulness of leaving money in my bureau may perhaps hinder me from buying my own myself. We have no great news in town, but that, one day, Sir George Elkin, a man of family and fortune, has married Miss Roach, a woman of the town. Everybody pities him. He is but eighteen : unluckily they were married in Scotland. She stayed five days with him, the sixth she ran away and came up to London. I beg you would assure Mrs. Gibbon of my respects. I hope to see you the latter end of the week.

I am, Dear Sir,

With the greatest respect,

Your most obedient servant and dutiful son,

E. GIBBON.

12.

To his Stepmother.

November, 1758.

DEAR MADAM,

I arrived in town between four and five o'clock safe and well, though almost frozen.—Turton[1] was not to be found, but

---

[1] Dr. John Turton (1736–1806) was in 1782 appointed physician to both the King and Queen. He attended Goldsmith on his death-bed. His progress to fame and fortune was very rapid, and when he died he left his

I will endeavour to see him to-morrow ; though I believe that
change of air and scene will be of greater benefit to me, than any
prescriptions he can order me.—I write from Mrs. Porten's,[1]
who begs to be remembered to you in the kindest terms. She is
totally ignorant of *forms*, but will see Mrs. Darrel to-morrow
morning and endeavour to settle everything. Let me entreat you,
my dearest Mrs. Gibbon, to try to divert thoughts, which cannot
be suppressed, and believe me that I can only be easy as I have
reason to think that you are so.

I am, Dear Madam,

Most truly yours,

E. G.

Dean's Yard. Tuesday Evening. Nine o'clock.

My sincerest compliments wait on Mr. and Mrs. Bayley. I
wish they would recollect anything in which I could be useful to
them in town.

13.

To his Father.

New Bond St., December the 14th, 1758.

DEAR SIR,

I must begin by the most disagreeable news I have to
tell you. All our tickets have come up blanks.[2] All our visionary
plans of grandeur are disappointed, the dream of those who have
had the ten thousand pounds will last a little, but perhaps, not
much longer.

I am settled at last in a very good lodging ; I say at last
because I lived a day and a half at Mrs. Porten's in the middle of
hurry and noise and measles. My aunt desires her compliments
to you and Mrs. Gibbon. We eat the leveret together. Pray did
you not send her a hare some time ago ? I know not what

---

widow £9000 a year in land, and £60,000 in the funds. " The bulk of his
great fortune he has bequeathed, after the death of his wife, to her Royal
Highness the Princess Mary, their Majesty's fourth daughter" (*Annual
Register*, April 15, 1806).

[1] Miss Porten had now removed from College Street to a large boarding-
house which she had built in Dean's Yard, Westminster.

[2] The lottery began to be drawn November 14, 1758; the last ticket was
drawn December 12, when "No. 72,570 in the present lottery was drawn a
prize of £10,000."

happened, but she never received it. I saw at her house Dr. Maty's son,[1] a little odd cur, and by an unexampled generosity I tipped the boy with a crown and the father with a coal of fire. Last night I was at the King's Scholars play, and, proper allowances being made, was very well entertained. All spoke justly enough and some (one or two) promised a good deal. Harry Courtenay was one of these, but he disappointed me before the end of the play. He came on with ease and entered well into his character (an old man in the Phormio), got safe over the dreadful first scene. From thence he sunk gradually tho' encouraged by repeated claps, dragged himself through the last scenes in the most dead and lifeless manner. My expectations were deceived more than they ever were in my whole life. I am just come from Madame Cilesia's.[2] She received me in a dirty white linnen gown, no rufles ; in a word, a *negligé qui n'alloit pas le mieux du monde, à sa Majesté Corse.* She received me, however, like an old fellow-sufferer. Not that we talked at all of the M . . . . . s, tho' on the brink of it several times, but neither of us broke the ice. I do not think her pretty, something sweet enough in her face, *mais enfin voilà tout.* I am to dine there to-morrow. To-day I dine in state at home, and after dinner shall go to Cleone,[3] though generally disliked.

I lodge in New Bond Street at a linnen draper's, a Mr. Steward, and I have a very good first floor, dining-room, bed-chamber and light closet with many conveniences for a guinea and half a week. I believe I shall keep to it. Lee is very serviceable to me, he has got me a very handsome chair for twenty-seven shillings.

---

[1] Matthew Maty, born near Utrecht in 1718, settled in England as a physician in 1741; in 1756 he was appointed an under-librarian at the British Museum, and in 1772 succeeded Gowin Knight as chief librarian. His *Journal Britannique* (1750-55), published in French at the Hague, contains a bi-monthly review of English literature. He died in 1776. If the son, whom Gibbon "tipped," resembled the father, this passage may confirm Dr. Johnson's description of Maty as a "little black dog." For Gibbon's relations with Maty, see note to Letter 15.

[2] Dorothea Mallet, Madame Celesia (1738-1790), a poet and dramatist, eldest daughter, by his first wife, of David Mallet. She married Pietro Paolo Celesia, a Genoese gentleman, who was ambassador to this country from 1755 to 1759, and was afterwards ambassador to Spain. Madame Celesia's drama of *Almida*, an adaptation of Voltaire's *Tancrède*, was brought out at Drury Lane in 1771, and published in the same year.

[3] Dodsley's tragedy of *Cleone* was then being played at Covent Garden.

I beg you would present my best compliments and true respects to Mrs. Gibbon.

I am, Dear Sir,

With the greatest regard,

Your most *faithful*, humble servant and son,

E. GIBBON, JUNIOR.

P.S.—I have not yet been able to do your commissions.

14.

To his Stepmother.

London, December, 1758.

DEAR MADAM,

How many thanks have I to return you! I shall wait upon Sir William Milner [1] as soon as he is in town, and do not doubt of liking that family, at least the lady : to say she is your friend is a sufficient enconium.

But, Madam, I am really concerned my father has not sent me a draught. I am really distressed for money. I have hardly a guinea left, and you know the unavoidable expences of London. I have tryed to borrow of Mrs. Porten and of Harvey, my father's lawyer. But without success. Could not you send me a bank-note by the Hastings Post of Monday? I would run all the risks of its being lost; for upon my word I shall hardly know what to do in three or four days.

Will you admit my excuse? I am just going to see Garrick, *alias* Sir John Brute.[2] It will be a *vilaine bête*.

I am, Dear Madam,

Yours most sincerely,

E. GIBBON.

P.S.—The author of Eurydice [3] (who greeted me at the Smyrna

---

[1] Sir William Milner, Bart. (1719-1774), for many years receiver-general of the Excise, married Elizabeth, youngest daughter of the Hon. and Rev. George Mordaunt, brother of the third Earl of Peterborough. She died a year after her husband.

[2] Sir John Brute, the surly, drunken husband of Lady Brute in Vanbrugh's play of *The Provoked Wife.*

[3] Mallet's tragedy *Eurydice*, written in 1731, was revived in 1759. The Smyrna Coffee-house in Pall Mall stood on the site now occupied by Messrs. Harrison, the booksellers. It was famous in the days of the *Tatler* and the *Spectator.*

Coffee-house) asked much after you and my father. What can you mean about Miss Allen ?

15.

To his Father.

London, December the 21st, 1758.

DEAR SIR,

I am afraid you will be angry at seeing a letter instead of me, but indeed I knew not how disagreeable it was, travelling in this season. I am besides invited to Mrs. Wray's and Mr. Darrel's for next Monday and Wednesday. Do you think these reasons sufficient ? (I beg you would tell it me freely.) If you do not I will endeavour to come down the latter end of next week ; as I suppose my being there Christmas Day is of no consequence.

I have seen Dr. Maty. *La La.* He made little or no excuse for having deferred writing, but has already criticised it with sense and severity. He finds it as I hoped ; good, in general, but many faults in the detail.[1]

I have dined once with M. Cilesia, with whom I am extremely pleased ; he has wit and learning, and speaks French like a Parisian. But pray have you heard the shocking pretensions of Mlle. de Vaucluse ? A prior marriage with him, or at least a promise of Marriage with a vast forfeiture. I do not know the particulars, but she pushes the affair vigorously at Genoa, and disperses a Memoire, which I hope to see. If she is not an Imposture, how criminal it makes the husband and how unhappy the wife.

I believe it is needless to assure Mrs. Gibbon of my sincerest love and regard. Pray tell her Sir W. Milner is in town. I shall execute all her and your commissions.

I am, Dear Sir,
With the greatest regard,
Your most obedient and affectionate servant and son,
E. GIBBON.

---

[1] On his return from Lausanne Gibbon completed his *Essai sur l'étude de la Littérature*, his first published work. The manuscript was submitted to Dr. Maty in 1758, and by his advice partly rewritten and wholly revised. It was published in French, with a letter to the author from Dr. Maty, in 1761. The essay is printed in *The Miscellaneous Works of Edward Gibbon* (ed. 1814), vol. iv. pp. 1-93.

16.

To his Father.

New Bond Street, December the 30th, 1758.

DEAR SIR,

Your illness really alarmed me. To be taken in so sudden and violent a manner. If you had not assured me that you was so much better, I would have set out immediately for Beriton. I hope you have had some advice better than Harvey's. I hope too that Mrs. Gibbon tries to hinder you from going out in the cold. I say tries, because I know that with regard to going out you are a most ungovernable patient.

At last Maty and I have downright quarrelled. He behaved so very contemptuously to me. Never made the least excuse for having eked out two weeks into two months, left two letters I wrote him since, without any answers, never came near me, that at last I desired him to send back my manuscript. He did so. I then wrote him a letter to explain my behaviour. He answered it by another politely bitter. So *tout est fini!*

I return you, Dear Sir, my sincerest thanks for telling me of my faults. I shall always consider it the truest proof of your affection for me. I hope you do not impute my not writing to Mrs. Gibbon to the least want of regard for her. I should be the most ungrateful of men, if I did not love and respect her like my own mother. But I really thought that in a union like yours, writing to one was writing to both. However, dear Sir, it is enough that you think it an omission, for me to repair it by the very next post.

I endeavour to see no company in town but such as you yourself would approve of. Mrs. Cilesia's and Mrs. Hayes's are the two houses I frequent the most. The former has promised to introduce me to Lady Harvey's [1] Assembly, where ('tis true though wonderful) there is no card-playing, but very good company and very good conversation. I am also to meet

---

[1] Lady Hervey, the beautiful " Molly Lepel," daughter of Brigadier-General Nicholas Lepel, was the widow of John, Lord Hervey, the " Sporus " of Pope's Prologue to the *Satires*, and the Boswell of George II. and Queen Caroline. Married in October, 1720, she was the mother of four sons, three of whom in succession became Earl of Bristol. She died September 2, 1768.

at Mrs. Cilesia's the great David Hume. I shall seek his acquaintance without being discouraged by Maty.

I have answered Bordot's letter. He desires a present relief, a quick release, and a good place in England. The first alone is in my power. I beg you would give him Five Guineas and deduct it upon the Christmas quarter of my Allowance. I do not doubt but you will do something for him, as I really think his situation deserves pity. This cessation of the prisoner's allowance shows, I think, better than fifty monitors to how low an ebb the French are reduced. I cannot help pitying them too. I do not think it necessary to have no compassion, in order to be a good Englishman. My unfashionable politicks are that a war can hardly be a good one, and a peace hardly a bad one. My sincerest love and regard wait upon Mrs. Gibbon.

I am, Dear Sir,

With the highest regard and best wishes for your health
Your most affectionate son and humble servant,

(E.) GIBBON.

P.S.—The Barometer was broke on the road. You will lay it upon me. I lay it upon François, and François upon Henry who packed up the things. Shall I buy another? Numbers 15553, 15554 Blanks.

17.

To his Father.

1760.
DEAR SIR,

*An address in writing, from a person who has the pleasure of being with you every day, may appear singular. However, I have preferred this method, as upon paper I can speak without a blush, and be heard without interruption. If my letter displeases you, impute it, Dear Sir, only to yourself. You have treated me not like a son, but like a friend. Can you be surprized that I should communicate to a friend all my thoughts, and all my desires? Unless the friend approve them, let the father never know them; or, at least, let him know at the same time, that however reasonable, however eligible, my scheme may appear to me, I would rather forget it for ever, than cause him the slightest uneasiness.

When I first returned to England, attentive to my future interest, you were so good as to give me hopes of a seat in Parliament. This seat, according to the Custom of our venal country, was to be bought, and fifteen hundred pounds were mentioned as the price of the purchase. This design flattered my vanity, as it might enable me to shine in so august an assembly. It flattered a nobler passion ; I promised myself that by the means of this seat I might be one day the instrument of some good to my country. But I soon perceived how little a mere virtuous inclination, unasisted by talents, could contribute towards that great end ; and a very short examination discovered to me, that those talents were not fallen to my lot. Do not, Dear Sir, impute this declaration to a false modesty, the meanest species of pride. Whatever else I may be ignorant of, I think I know myself, and shall always endeavour to mention my good qualities without vanity, and my defects without repugnance. I shall say nothing of the most intimate acquaintance with his country and language, so absolutely necessary to every Senator. Since they may be acquired, to alledge my deficiency in them, would seem only the plea of laziness. But I shall say with great truth, that I never possessed that gift of speach, the first requisite of an Orator, which use and labour may improve, but which nature can alone bestow. That my temper, quiet, retired, somewhat reserved, could neither acquire popularity, bear up against opposition, nor mix with ease in the crowds of public life. That even my genius (if you will allow me any) is better qualified for the deliberate compositions of the Closet, than for the extemporary discourses of the Parliament. An unexpected objection would disconcert me ; and as I am incapable of explaining to others what I do not thoroughly understand myself, I should be meditating, while I ought to be answering. I even want necessary prejudices of party, and of nation. In popular assemblies, it is often necessary to inspire them ; and never Orator inspired well a passion, which he did not feel himself. Suppose me even mistaken in my own Character ; to set out with the repugnance such an opinion must produce, offers but an indifferent prospect. But I hear you say It is not necessary that every man should enter into Parliament with such exalted hopes. It is to acquire a title the most glorious of any in a free country, and to employ the weight and consideration It gives in the service of one's

friends. Such motifs, tho' not glorious, yet are not dishonour-
able; and if we had a borough in our command, if you could
bring me in without any great expence, or if our fortune enabled
us to dispise that expence, then indeed I should think them of
the greatest strength. But with our private fortune is it worth
while to purchase at so high a rate, a title, honourable in itself,
but which I must share with every fellow that can lay out Fifteen
hundred pounds ? Besides, Dear Sir, a merchandize is of little
value to the owner, when he is resolved not to sell it.

I should affront your penetration, did I not suppose you now
see the drift of this letter. It is to appropriate to another use
the sum you destined to bring me into Parliament ; to employ it,
not in making me great, but in rendering me happy. I have
often heard you say yourself, that the allowance you had been so
indulgent as to grant me, tho' very liberal in regard to your
estate, was yet but small, when compared with the almost necessary extravagances of the age. I have indeed found it so, notwithstanding a good deal of œconomy, and an exemption from
many of the common expences of youth. This, Dear Sir, would
be a way of supplying these deficiencies, without any additional
expence to you.—But I forbear.—If you think my proposals
reasonable, you want no entreaties to engage you to comply with
them ; if otherwise, all will be without effect.

All that I am afraid of, Dear Sir, is, that I should seem not so
much asking a favour, as this really is, as exacting a debt. After
all I can say, you will still remain the best judge of my good, and
your own circumstances. Perhaps, like most Landed Gentlemen,
an addition to my annuity would suit you better than a sum
of money given at once. Perhaps the sum itself may be too considerable. Whatever you shall think proper to bestow upon me,
or in whatever manner, will be received with equal gratitude.

I intended to stop here ; but as I abhor the least appearance
of art, I think it will be better to lay open my whole scheme
at once. The unhappy War which now desolates Europe, will
oblige me to defer seeing France till a peace. But that reason
can have no influence upon Italy, a country which every Scholar
must long to see ; should you grant my request, and not dis-
aprove of my manner of employing your bounty, I would leave
England this autumn, and pass the winter at Lausanne, with
M. de Voltaire and my old friends. The armies no longer

obstruct my passage, and it must be indifferent to you, whether I am at Lausanne or at London during the winter, since I shall not be at Beriton. In the spring I would cross the Alps, and after some stay in Italy, as the war must then be terminated, return home thro' France, to live happily with you and my dear Mother. I am now two or three and twenty ; a tour must take up a considerable time, and tho' I believe you have no thoughts of settling me soon, (and I am sure I have not) yet so many things may intervene, that the man who does not travel early, runs a great risk of not travelling at all. But this part of my scheme, as well as the whole, I submit entirely to you.

Permit me, Dear Sir, to add, that I do not know whether the compleat compliance with my wishes could encrease my love and gratitude ; but that I am very sure, no refusal could minish those sentiments with which I shall always remain, Dear Sir, your most dutiful and obedient son and servant,*

E. GIBBON, JUNIOR.

18.

To his Stepmother.

Winchester Camp,[1] Monday Morning,
[in pencil] '61 ?

DEAR MADAM,

I have got four dozen of Franks for you from Sir Gerard Napier, which I shall send you by return of the waggon. In return I must beg the favor of a book. It is Greek, but don't be frightened ; you may easily find it. It is a short but very thick folio, bound in parchment, the title on the back in large letters, either Strabo, or Strabonis Geographia, printed in two

---

[1] In June, 1759, Gibbon and his father joined the Hampshire regiment of militia as respectively captain and major. The South battalion, to which they belonged, was kept "under arms, in constant pay and duty," from the date of its enrolment till December 23, 1762, when it was disbanded as a permanent force. The battalion was at Winchester Camp from June 25 to October 23, 1761, and from the latter date to February 28, 1762, at "the populous and disorderly town of Devizes" (see next letter). His *Autobiography* shows that Gibbon found that "a camp," as Johnson wrote to Mrs. Thrale in October, 1778, "however familiarly we may speak of it, is one of the great scenes of human life," and that, partially at least, he agreed with Lord Chesterfield, that "courts and camps are the only places to learn the world in."

columns, one Greek, the other Latin. I am pretty sure it is
upon the couch. I hope you like the Devizes; the place is good,
& I think the neighbourhood to Bath no objection. I hope soon
to meet you there, and am,

Dear Madam,

Yours most affectionately,

E. GIBBON, JUNIOR.

19.

To his Stepmother.

Devizes, February the 14th, 1762.

DEAR MADAM,

Knowing you as I do I can easily judge of the effect
my father's accident must have produced upon you. Besides, I
can guess at it by the impression it made upon me, though I
heard of the danger and the escape at the same time. I thank
God it was no worse. I hope my father is now thoroughly
recovered. I shall remember the Arquebusade this week.

Of myself and my situation at the Devizes I have little to say,
and that little not very agreeable. A great deal of noise and no
conversation, a great many people and no society, a most excessive
familiarity and no friendship; in a word, the usual scene, only I
think we are not so quarrelsome as we used to be.

I wrote to my father who by this time must have received my
letter. However I must just mention to him two or three things
relative to the battalion. He will see by the enclosed return, our
strength and what we have done, which is nothing to what we
might do had we money. The Blacks[1] now grow so numerous
that I think they must drive us out of town, they desire it so
strongly, & Lord Shelbourne[2] has such powerful interest. I believe
Sharrock[3] will get an ensign, one Hall,[4] near this place, a very

---

[1] The Black Musqueteers of Colonel Barré were raised in 1761-2 as
the 106th Regiment of Foot (or Black Musqueteers.) See List of General
and Field Officers for 1763, p. 175.

[2] William, Lord Fitzmaurice, M.P. for Chipping Wycombe, afterwards
Prime Minister (1782), and first Marquess of Lansdowne, succeeded his father
as second Earl of Shelburne in the spring of 1761. He acted as the go-
between in the negotiations between Bute and Fox, which led to the cessation
of the Seven Years' War and the Treaty of Paris.

[3] Robert Sharrock was a captain in the South Battalion of the Hampshire
Militia.

[4] James Hall received his commission as ensign in February, 1762.

pretty lad of sixteen with a good qualification, though not in our county. He expects an answer from Durnford, who, by the bye, has not yet wrote either to Harrison [1] or me.

How does your pupil go on ? I hope soon to have an account of him, as William is very clamourous for a new livery.

You say nothing of your brother. I hope he is sailed. Surely it must by this time be determined. I beg you would present my love and duty to my father, and believe me,

Dear Madam,

Most affectionately yours,

E. GIBBON, JUNIOR.

20.

To his Father.

Boulogne, January the 25th, 1763.

DEAR SIR,

*You see by the date of my letter where I am. I arrived here in company with the Duke of Bridgewater,[2] the Marquis of Tavistock,[3] Lord Ossory [4] and a Mr. Leigh, about three in the afternoon, after a tedious but pleasant passage of about nine hours. We were forced to come in here, not being able to make Calais. I have hired a chaise, & propose setting out to-morrow, but alone, as the road will not supply horses for our number. I hope to be at Paris either Thursday or Friday. Writing in the

---

[1] John Butler Harrison, lieutenant in the South Battalion, was Gibbon's chief friend in the regiment. In his journal Gibbon speaks of the disagreeable society in which he was compelled to live. "No manners, no conversation, they were only a set of fellows, all whose behaviour was low, and most of whose characters were despicable. I must, however, except Sir Thomas and Harrison out of this society. Harrison is a young man of honour, spirit, and good nature. The virtues of his heart make amends for his having none of the head."

[2] Francis Egerton, third and last Duke of Bridgewater (1736-1803), with the assistance of Brindley, developed the canal system of the north of England.

[3] The Marquis of Tavistock, who married, in June, 1764, Lady E. Keppel, was killed in the hunting-field in 1767.

[4] John, second and last Earl of Ossory, married, in 1769, the Duchess of Grafton. Anne Liddell, daughter of Lord Ravensworth, married to the Duke of Grafton in January, 1756, was separated from her husband in 1765. Her daughter by Lord Ossory was born in 1768; her divorce from the duke, and her marriage with Lord Ossory, took place in March, 1769.

midst of noise and hurry & being just ready to go to supper, you will excuse my ending abruptly.*

I am, Dear Sir,

Yours most affectionately,

E. GIBBON.

21.

To his Stepmother.

Paris, February the 12th, 1763.
DEAR MADAM,

You remember our agreement; short and frequent letters. The first part of the treaty you have no doubt of my observing : I think I ought not to leave you any of the second. *A propos* of treaty,[1] our definitive one was signed here yesterday, and this morning the Duke of Bridgewater and Mr. Neville[2] went for London with the news of it. The plenipotentiaries sat up till ten o'Clock in the morning at the ambassador of Spain's ball, and then went to sign this treaty which regulates the fate of Europe.

Paris in most respects, has fully answered my expectations. I have a number of very good acquaintances which encrease every day, for nothing is so easy as the making them here. Instead of complaining of the want of them, I begin already to think of making a choice. Next Sunday for instance I have only three invitations to Dinner. Either in the houses you are already acquainted, you meet with people who ask you to come and see them, or some of your friends offer themselves to introduce you. When I speak of these connections, I mean chiefly for dinner & the evening. Suppers, as yet I am pretty much a stranger to, and I fancy shall continue so : for Paris is divided into two Species who have but little communication with each other. The one who is chiefly connected with the men of letters dine very much at home, are glad to see their friends, and pass the evenings till about nine in agreable and rational conversation. The others are the most fashionable, sup in numerous parties, and always play or rather game both before and after supper. You may

---

[1] The Treaty of Paris was signed February 10, 1763.

[2] Mr. Neville arrived in London with the Definitive Treaty, February 15, and at once had an audience of the king, which he describes in a letter printed in the *Bedford Correspondence*, vol. iii. p. 199.

easily guess which sort suits me best. Indeed, Madam, we may
say what we please of the frivolity of the French, but I do assure
you that in a fortnight passed at Paris I have heard more conversation worth remembering, and seen more men of letters
among the people of fashion, than I had done in two or three
winters in London.

Amongst my acquaintance I cannot help mentioning M. Helve-
tius,[1] the author of the famous book *de l'Esprit*. I met him at
dinner at Madame Geoffrin's,[2] where he took great notice of me,
made me a visit next day, & has ever since treated me not in a
polite but a friendly manner. Besides being a sensible man an
agreable companion, & the worthiest creature in the world He
has a very pretty wife, a hundred thousand Livres a year and one
of the best tables in Paris. The only thing I dislike in him is
his great attachment to and admiration for Stanley,[3] whose
character is indeed at Paris beyond any thing you can conceive.
To the great civility of this foreigner, who was not obliged to
take the least notice of me, I must just contrast the behaviour of

[1] Claude Adrien Helvétius (1715-1771) published his materialistic book,
De l'Esprit, in 1758. He married Mademoiselle de Ligneville, who survived
him more than a quarter of a century.

[2] Madame Geoffrin (1699-1777), a woman of humble origin, the widow of
a wealthy ice-merchant, opened her *salon* to philosophers and men of letters.
Madame du Deffand called her *la mère des philosophes*, also *la reine mère de
Pologne* for her intimacy with Stanislas Poniatowski. She affected to despise
the influence of Madame Geoffrin. When some friend spoke to her of her
rival's *salon*, she exclaimed, "Voilà bien du bruit pour une omelette au lard."
Gibbon owed his introduction to Madame Geoffrin to Lady Hervey.
Writing to Lady Hervey in October, 1765, Horace Walpole says of Madame
Geoffrin, "she has one of the best understandings I ever met, and more
knowledge of the world." Yet his account of her, on the whole, confirms
Lord Carlisle's opinion that she was "the most impertinent old brimstone"
(Lord Carlisle to George Selwyn, December 26, 1767). Gibbon speaks in his
Autobiography of her "capricious tyranny." In a letter to Gray (January 25,
1766) Walpole paints an elaborate portrait of her and her rival, Madame du
Deffand.

[3] The Right Hon. Hans Stanley, of Paultons in the New Forest, was
a grandson of Sir Hans Sloane. He was a distinguished diplomatist, a
Fellow of the Royal Society, a Trustee of the British Museum, Cofferer of
the Royal Household, and M.P. for Southampton. Walpole speaks of him
as "deep in the secrets of the peace of Paris." He committed suicide at
Althorpe on January 13, 1780. Gibbon knew him through Stanley's connection with Hampshire and the Isle of Wight. Stanley was twice Captain
and Governor of the Island, 1764-66 and 1770-80.

the D. of B.[1] I could not see him (on account of his gout) till
last Sunday. I was then introduced to him & presented my letter
from the D[uke] of R[ichmond].[2] He received me civilly,
desired I would apply to him whenever I wanted his assistance,
and thus dismissed me. I have not heard of him since. Indeed
I have often blushed for him, for I find his stateliness and
avarice make him the joke of Paris. Instead of keeping any
thing of a publick table, he hardly ever asks any body; while
the Spaniard[3] gives balls every week, the magnificence of which
is only exceeded by their politeness & elegance. Neville who is
exactly Mr. W. Patton[4] received me very well, but seemed to
laugh both at Mallet & his letter of recommendation.

I beg my duty to my father to whom I propose writing next
week, and my most sincere compliments to the two Gentlemen.

I am, Dear Madam,

Most affectionately yours,

E. GIBBON, JUNIOR, *alias* DE GUIBON.

22.

To his Stepmother.

Paris, March the 25th, 1763.

DEAR MADAM,

I am afraid (as dates are stubborn things) that I have
been rather too lazy. As you love truth, and know me, I will not
attempt an awkward apology, but shall only say, that I will
endeavor such a delay shall not happen a second time. My

---

[1] John, fourth Duke of Bedford (1710–1771), to whom Gibbon had a
letter of introduction from the Duke of Richmond, was in 1756 appointed
Lord Lieutenant of Ireland, Keeper of the Privy Seal in 1761, and in 1762
ambassador to France, where he signed the preliminaries of peace with France
and Spain. " The Duke of Bedford," writes Horace Walpole in September,
1762, " is gone in a fury to make peace, for he cannot be even pacific with
temper."

[2] Charles, third Duke of Richmond, born 1735; ambassador at Paris,
1765; Secretary of State, 1766; Master of the Ordnance, 1783; died 1806.

[3] The Marquis Jeronymo Grimaldi, a member of an illustrious Genoese
family, was at this time the Spanish ambassador. He negotiated the family
compact of 1761 between France and Spain.

[4] Mrs. Gibbon's youngest brother.

father has more extensive priviledges, and indeed he seems to be very well acquainted with them.

I still continue to like Paris, as well as I expected. You know that is saying a great deal. In two months I am acquainted with more, (and more agreable) people, than I knew in London in two years. Indeed the way of life is quite different. Much less play, more conversation, and instead of our immense routs, agreable societies where you know and are known by almost every body you meet. I have added several families to those I have already mentioned to you, and I find my conquests multiply every day. With regard to Mrs. M.'s son,[1] I am glad to see that for once she has not exagerated ; indeed she hardly could in speaking of him. We are now very intimate, & I think I begin to know his character. It is astonishing for a young French officer of the Guards. He is as reserved, as little a man of the world, and as awkward as I can be. But he has a fine natural understanding, improved upon almost every subject, a clear un-prejudiced head, and a heart which seems to be full of the noblest sentiments of honor, probity and friendship. I will not decide too hastily, but I believe and hope that I am forming a connection which will last as long as my life. We see one another very often, and in most of my visits of curiosity he generally accompagnies me. These parties are of service to us both. I improve by the communication of his remarks, and he has occasion to see twenty places which he would perhaps not have seen for the too common reason, that they were in the place he had passed all his life in. The only unlucky circumstance is, that he has no women in his family. A Wife or a sister are, you know, most usefull and con-venient things to bring friends together, whereas we are both single ; he in his cousin's house, I in a lodging ; and in this great town, are both obliged to get our living, which prevents our meeting so often as we could wish. Madame Bontems[2] is a very good sort of a woman, agreable and *sans pretensions*. She seems to have conceived a real motherly attachment for me. I generally sup there three or four times a week quite in a friendly way.

[1] M. d'Augny.

[2] Marie Jeanne de Chatillon, Madame Bontemps. Gibbon had met her son, who was acting as private secretary to the Duc de Nivernois in London, at Mallet's house in November, 1762. She translated Thomson's *Seasons* into French prose in 1759.

I have nothing new to say of his Excellency. I have not seen him since my last letter, and but once in all. Not a single invitation either general or particular, and tho' I have made it a rule to leave my name at the door, at proper intervalls, I have never been lett in. The behavior is so very singular (especially with *such a recommendation as mine*) that I am sometimes tempted to think, some ill offices must have been done me. Not that I am conscious of any thing wrong or even imprudent in my behaviour. On the contrary, whenever I have heard the D.'s manner of living here blamed and laughed at, I have always thought it right to try to justify him, even against my own conscience. Indeed I am sorry, for the honor of my country to see how contemptible a figure he makes amongst our late enemies and constant rivals. My only comfort is that the National character is as much revered as his is despised. What Cromwell wished is now litterally the case. The name of Englishman inspires as great an idea at Paris as that of Roman could at Carthage, after the defeat of Hannibal. Indeed the French are almost excessive. From being very unjustly esteemed a set of pirates and Barbarians, we are now, by a more agreable injustice, looked upon as a nation of Philosophers and Patriots. I wish we would consider this opinion as an encouragement to deserve a character, which I am afraid we have not yet attained. I could add many things (some curious enough) with regard to the reigning politicks and publick affairs ; but I have no occasion to say *why* it is much better to talk them over in your Dressing room some time hence. Perhaps I have even said too much already.

With regard to Paris itself, I mean the houses and buildings, you know very well that their people of fashion are incomparably better lodged there than in London. Their vast Hotels, courts, stables, gardens, are very magnificent as well as convenient. A striking proof of the difference is the situation of our Embassador. He is full as well if not better lodged, in the Rue St. Dominique, than in Bloomsbury Square. However, his own house is reckoned one of the very best in London, and his hired one here is, both as to size, beauty and price, far inferior to a great many, even of that class, at Paris. Indeed I take the article of house rent to be much higher than in London. Did you ever hear of seven and eight hundred and even a thousand pounds a year being given for a house unfurnished.

There are instances of it here. But as to the middling people, even those of fashion, I like a London house better. Without a regular porter to answer at the door, our little street-doors are more convenient. A fine large court is a very agreable thing, but a dark nasty gate-way is a very disagreable one. When you get up stairs you generally meet with two rooms. If we sat as much in our bed-chambers as they do, we have as many. They have indeed besides, an ante-chamber ill fitted up, and much littered, which the servants inhabit all day, except at noon and night that it serves for an eating parlour.

I have just seen here two families, the one my father's acquaintance, the other your's. The first was Mr. Prowse, who only passed thro' Paris, in his way for Tours, to which place he was going, with all his family, for his health. I dined with him at Mr. Foley's[1] & went about with him to several places the next day. In consequence of some little civilities of that kind, he asked me to dine with him the day after. He is a very agreable sensible man, but a strange being in France. The second is your good friend Mrs. Poyntz,[2] whom I met by accident. She talked of you, whom she adores, asked me a hundred questions in a breath, told me all her own affairs, her tradesmen, her house-rent, her daughter, Lord Spencer, &c. &c. &c. &c. &c. &c., and insisted upon my calling upon her.

My love and duty to my father. I shall write to him next post and hope to hear from him sometimes. I have been obliged to draw for another hundred pounds. I do assure you I study the œconomical art.

> I am, Dear Madam,
> Most affectionately yours,
> E. G.

23.

To his Father.

Paris, April the 5th, 1763.

DEAR SIR,

I received your last letter with pleasure, because every thing that comes from you gives me pleasure ; but I must own it

---

[1] The English banker at Paris.

[2] Mrs. Poyntz, wife of Stephen Poyntz, of Midgeham, Berkshire, was mother of Lady Spencer and grandmother of Georgiana, the beautiful Duchess of Devonshire.

afflicted me very much, as I see there are several things in which
I have had the misfortune to displease either you or some other
of my friends. I must endeavour to justify myself, and I think I
can easily do it upon most of those heads.

Lord Litchfield[1] is angry at my writing to him. I am sorry
for it and surprized at it at the same time. I could discover
many reasons why he might not serve me, none that He could be
angry at my application to him, especially as that application was
made with all the decency and moderation, I could put into my
letter. I should with pleasure have communicated it to you, and
known your sentiments, but as we imagined here that the D. of
B. would go away very soon, I was afraid that delay might
destroy the very small hopes I had. Indeed I thought it the less
necessary as I knew already your opinion both as to the eligibility
of the thing, and the propriety of an application to the Noble
Lord. I own the giving him no direction was not a happy
specimen of my Secretarial acurracy.

As to my friends, Mallets, Worsleys,[2] Portens, &c. &c. &c. &c.,
I must plead guilty, very guilty indeed to the indictment. I will
not take up my time and yours in vain excuses, my best and only
excuse ought to be and shall be, more exactness for the future.
Notwithstanding Mrs. M.'s outrageousness she is the person I
trouble my head the least about. However I propose writing to
her to-night tho' with great repugnance and difficulty. I neither
·chuse to go to the Bastille for sending her observations upon the
French government, nor to fill my letter full of romantick protestations of attachment and friendship, which I do not feel for
her, and which she feels for nobody. As to La Motte I cannot

---

[1] George Henry Lee (1718-1772), who succeeded his father as third Earl
of Lichfield in 1743, was one of the leaders of the Jacobites. He came to
court, however, on the accession of George III. "Lord Lichfield and several
other Jacobites have kissed hands; George Selwyn says, 'They go to St.
James's, because now there are so many *Stuarts* there'" (Walpole to Montagu,
November 13, 1760). Lord Lichfield became in 1762 Chancellor of the
University of Oxford, which may explain his reception of Gibbon's letter.

[2] Sir Thomas Worsley, Bart., Lieut.-Colonel of Gibbon's battalion of the
Hampshire regiment, succeeded his father, Sir James Worsley, of Pilewell
in Hampshire, and Appuldurcombe in the Isle of Wight. He married the
eldest daughter of the Earl of Cork, by whom he had a son and a daughter.
He continued a collection of notes on the Isle of Wight, commenced by his
father and completed by his son, Sir Richard Worsley, the author of the
History of the Isle of Wight (1781). He died September 23, 1768.

forgive him his complaints, when I have so much juster ones to make of him. Follow his advice I most certainly did not, since he never would give me any, tho' I asked him several times in as intelligible terms as I could properly make use of. I was forced to have recourse to my other friends, to Madame Bontems, to M. d'Anguey and to M. de Mirabeau,[1] and their directions have been very usefull to me. La Motte always shewed me such a dryness, such an unwillingness to connect himself at all with me, that I have been at last obliged to drop him almost entirely.

Do you think, dear Sir, that I would have stood upon the formality of a visit with the great Duke? Besides I had no occasion to do it. He returned mine the very next day. Since that time I have presented myself at his door once every week or ten days without being ever let in or hearing a syllable from him. What can I do more than sit down quiet and wonder at his behavior?

I have enquired into Mr. Thos. Bradley's affair. Mr. Taaffe is no longer at Mr. George Woolfe's. He is in a much safer place, in the Châtelet, a prison of Paris for debt. He has settled with his English Creditors and given up his estate at Jamaica for the payment of his debts. He wants to compromise with his other Creditors who are very numerous, (but as they are convinced he wants to cheat them and that he only offers the same estate after the other debts are cleared, which cannot be in less than ten or fifteen years) they will hear of no compromise. All that Mr. Bradley could do, would be to join with those Creditors in case they should at last agree to his proposals. Mr. Taaffe's scheme is to keep another estate at Jamaica clear of his creditors. They on their side want to starve him into giving up that likewise. If Mr. Bradley thinks it worth his while to push the affair, it will be attended with some trouble and expence. He must impower somebody at Paris to act in his name, and in order to do so a journey to London will be necessary where he must find out Mr. Benjamin Bobbin an Attorney beyond the Royal Exchange,

---

[1] The Marquis de Mirabeau (1715–1789), father of the famous orator and political leader, belonged to the school of Economists. In 1760 his *Théorie de l'Impôt* had lodged him in the Bastille, and made him the fashion in Paris. Gibbon speaks of him in his Journal (February 24, 1763): "Il a assez d'imagination pour dix autres, et pas assez de sens rassis pour lui seul." He met him at a supper-party in the house of Madame Bentemps.

who does all that kind of business, and who will draw up a letter of attorney in French for him, and get it certified by the French ambassador ; a formality absolutely necessary to give it weight in this country. As to his Attorney at Paris, the necessary delays of the Law will render it proper to have a man who is established at * * *

I cannot therefore offer myself, (which I should otherwise do with great pleasure,) and I should hope Mr. Foley would be willing as he is certainly able to undertake it. I wish I could give Mr. Bradley a better account, but this seems to be the true state of the case.

My losses at Play have not been very considerable since I have been here, they amount to seven Livres lost one night at Picquet. It is indeed rather my good luck than my prudence that saves me. All my Societies are houses where I never see a card, so that I do not fall because I have no temptation. I find Paris however very expensive. One article which, tho' it encreases my draughts at present, will diminish them hereafter is cloathes, ruffles, silk stockings, &c., which after serious deliberation, I thought I had better make a provision of at this Capital of the Fashionable world. However as I begin to have pretty well seen Paris, I propose (if you have no objection) setting out about the eighth of next month, & going thro' Dijon and Besançon to Lausanne to pass two or three quiet and cheap months with my old friends there on my way to Italy. Adieu, Dear Sir, my paper fails me and I would avoid a cover.

I am, Dear Sir,
Yours most affectionately,
E. G.

24.

To his Stepmother.

Besançon, May the 18th, 1763.

DEAR MADAM,

You will give me leave according to an article of our treaty, to write you only three lines, just to tell that I am well and where I am.

Upon my arrival at Besançon I saw Mr. Acton[1] directly.

---

[1] Dr. Acton was a cousin of Gibbon. He married, "renounced his country, and settled at Besançon, and became the father of three sons, the

He has received me with a degree not only of civility but of friendship which astonished me, insisted upon my taking an appartment in his house, and since my seeing him, himself and his three sons (our Southampton friend is one) have been only taken up in procuring me every kind of amusement, in carrying me to all my father's friends here who have all enquired much after him, in seeing publick places, and in parties at home and abroad. The only inconvenience is that I have not an instant to myself and that I am forced to write this scrawl at half an hour after one in the morning. The day after to-morrow I set out for Lausanne, where I shall be a little quieter. The Acton family desire to be remembered to my father.

I am, Dear Madam,
Yours and my father's with the truest affection,
E. G., JUNIOR.

25.

To his Father.

Lausanne, May the 31st, 1763.

DEAR SIR,

I staid four or five days at Besançon longer than I intended, so that I got here only the 25th. It was even with some difficulty that I could disengage myself so soon from Mr. Acton's civilities. Indeed nothing could exceed them. Not only they insisted upon my lodging in the house, but during the time I passed in it, the sole business of the family seemed to be finding out amusements for me. They carried me to the best houses in the place, showed me whatever was worth seeing, and made several parties for me in the country. What I saw of Besançon pleased me so much, that, could I have stayed there without being an inconvenience to them, I should have liked to have stayed a few days or even weeks longer. Mr. Acton is the best sort of man in the world, and is bent on doing everything most agreable. He has a great deal of business, many friends and a very high reputation. He has indeed unluckily been too long out of England to remember his own language, and not long enough in

eldest of whom, General (afterwards Sir John Francis Edward) Acton, is conspicuous in Europe as the principal minister of the King of the Two Sicilies." He was the grandfather of the present Lord Acton.

France, to have learnt that of the country. He talked a vast
deal of you, and tho' it is so long since you have been there, I
have found your memory very fresh & many people who have
enquired after you. The two sisters in particular of your *écuyer*
(I have forgot their names) talked to me by the hour of their old
friend Monsieur de Guibon. As to Acton's wife, you know the
character Mrs. Darrel gives of her, and I was sorry to find it
is pretty well established at Besançon ; but she is certainly a very
agreable and sensible woman, and I should have taken her for
a very good-natured one. If she is a termagant I never saw
such a Wolf in sheep's cloathing.

At last, Dear Sir, I am got to Lausanne and established very
agreably among my old acquaintance, and in a way of life I like
extremely, a moderate mixture of society and study. News from
a place so very quiet and obscure you cannot expect. I have
however seen an old friend of ours who has just left us ; Sir
Willoughby Aston.[1] He had been here about a twelfmonth with
Lady Aston and his numerous [family], and are just gone to
Tours in France. Nobody could guess why. They lived very
cheap here ; Lady Aston had as many rubbers of Whist, and Sir
Willoughby as many bottles of wine every day as they wanted.
What could they have more ? Sir Willoughby asked much after
you, and was glad to see me to talk over Winchester camp and
Reading court martial.

A propos of our militia, I have seen that of Switzerland.
Their General review (of the Lausanne Battalion) was last Monday, Tuesday and Wednesday. I attended all three from beginning to end, and making all proper allowances saw them with
great pleasure. They are only exercised twelve days in the year,
and tho' many of them have been in foreign services, yet you
know, Dear Sir, how very easy it is for a soldier to forget. They
went through the manual, fired by divisions and platoons, formed
the column, and square, a General discharge and charge : all very
decently, and some (especially the Grenadiers) very prettily. I
do not compare them to our militia. As we were embodied two
or three years, the comparaison would be an affront.

---

[1] Sir Willoughby Aston was returned M.P. for Nottingham in 1754, and
was appointed Colonel of the Berkshire Militia in 1759. Lady Aston was a
Miss Pye, of Farringdon, Berks. His " numerous " family consisted of his
only son and successor, and of six daughters. He died August 24, 1772.

I took credit from Mr. Foley upon a Lausanne banker, who is likewise a brother captain of Grenadiers. I have not made use of it yet, and when I do, it shall be as sparing as possible. I have got a few books together, and am busy upon the ancient Geography of Italy and the reviewing my Roman history and antiquities. If you have no objection to leaving me here till the spring, I should like it very much and think it might be of use to me. But I submit the thing entirely to you.

You will be so good, Dear Sir, as to present my sincerest love and duty to Mrs. Gibbon, and my most affectionate compliments to her brothers, and to believe me

Most truly yours,

E. GIBBON, JUNIOR.

26.

To his Stepmother.

Lausanne, June the 18th, 1763.

DEAR MADAM,

If my own laziness did not deprive me of any right to complain, I should say perhaps that it was a great while since I had heard either from you or my father. I have indeed the satisfaction of knowing my father was well the 26th of May, and I hope he is by this time one of the Honorable Verdurers of the forrest of Beer. Pray, a propos of English and county news, who is our Lord Lieutenant? I had the mortification of seeing in the paper that the Duke of Bolton was turned out (I mean had resigned) and that the Marquis of Caernarvon was appointed in his room. *I hope* it is not true.

You have often heard me talk of Lausanne and of the pleasure I should have in seeing it again. Our imagination generally improves upon those agreable prospects; but I can assure you, my ideas had not heightened any part of this. A beautifull country, great leisure for study, and a very agreable society, make me pass my time very much to my satisfaction. I have found all my old friends here very glad to see me, and my countrymen, who only know the outside of the companies, are amazed at the number of family parties I am asked to every day. Those countrymen (whom I do not reckon as a very important

part of my happiness) consist only in a Mr. Sidney and a Mr.
Guise.[1] The former (Mrs. Perry's son) is a meer boy, and the
second (a Sir John Guise of Gloucestershire's son) is a very sensible
well-bred man. Pavillard and I were really glad to see one
another. He shewed me his snuff-box which he always carries in
a wooden case for fear of spoiling it. I was at first uneasy about
my lodging. I did not chuse to see the leg of mutton roasted a
second time with a gash in it, and yet I was afraid of disobliging
my old friend. Luckily he had got into a new house and had no
room for me ; so that he himself assisted me in settling in a very
agreable family which I was very well acquainted with before.
The Husband[2] who is much of a gentleman keeps the Academy,
his wife is a charming woman ; and the apartments and table are
both cheap and good. I should like extremely to pass the winter
here, if my father would give me leave. Give me leave to add
(for I am sensible you may have suspicions) that no woman is
the least concerned in my desire, and that as to any old inclinations,[3] they are so far from subsisting that no one can be more

[1] William (afterwards Sir William) Guise, subsequently M.P. for
Gloucestershire, only son of Sir John Guise, Bart., died without issue,
April 6, 1783.
[2] M. de Mesery.
[3] In Gibbon's Journal at Lausanne, in June, 1757, occurs the entry: "I
saw Mademoiselle Curchod—*Omnia vincit amor, et nos cedamus amori.*"
He was, in fact, shortly afterwards engaged to Suzanne Curchod, daughter
and only child of the Minister of Crassy, a hamlet at the foot of the lower
slopes of the Jura, between Geneva and Lausanne. Both the lovers were
born in 1737, and were in their twenty-first year. At Lausanne, at the
Société du Printemps and the *Académie de la Poudrière*, of which Suzanne
Curchod was the founder and the president, she frequently met Gibbon,
and the attachment, on her side at least, was strong and genuine ; on his it
seems to have always had a touch of affectation. The account given by Julie
von Bondeli (E. Bodemann, *Julie von Bondeli*, pp. 217, 218 : Hanover, 1874)
of Gibbon's passion has the exaggeration of unreality. He was seen, says
this friend of Wieland and Rousseau, stopping the country people near
Lausanne, and demanding, at the point of a naked dagger, whether a more
adorable creature existed than Suzanne Curchod. Gibbon wrote her several
letters, some of which are quoted by M. d'Haussonville in his *Salon de
Madame Necker*, and addressed to her indifferent verses. The following
lines seem to be an expansion of the entry in his Journal :—

> " Tôt ou tard il faut aimer,
> C'est en vain qu'on façonne ;
> Tout fléchit sous l'amour
> Il n'exempte personne,

opposite to them at present than myself. This I assure you of upon my word of honor. I hope after that I need say nothing more.

> Car Gib. a succombé en ce jour
> Aux attraits d'une beauté
> Qui parmi les douceurs d'un tranquil silence
> Reposait sur un fauteuil," etc., etc.

They became engaged, and Gibbon implored her to marry him without waiting for the sanction of his father. This, however, she refused to do. When Gibbon left Lausanne in 1758, she wrote to him once; then all correspondence between them seems to have ceased, though Gibbon says that he wrote to her twice on his journey and once on his return to England. He also sent her his *Essai* with a dedicatory letter in 1761. In August, 1762, he wrote to break off the engagement, on the ground of his father's opposition, in a letter quoted by M. d'Haussonville (*Le Salon de Madame Necker*, pp. 57, 58). In 1763 Gibbon came to Lausanne, and there received from Mademoiselle Curchod a letter in reply, which showed, so far as words could prove anything, that she had never ceased to love him. Her friend, the Pastor Moultou, endeavoured to interest J. J. Rousseau in the story, and to make him speak to Gibbon on the subject. But Rousseau declined to interfere, saying that Gibbon was too cold-blooded a young man for his taste or for Mademoiselle Curchod's happiness. In Gibbon's unpublished diary, he thus comments on the receipt of this letter, September 22, 1763 : "J'ai reçu une lettre des moins attendûes. C'etoit de Mademoiselle C. Fille dangereux et artificielle ! Elle fait une apologie de sa conduite depuis le premier moment, qu'elle m'a connû, sa constance pour moi, son mepris pour M. de Montplaisir, et la fidelité delicate et soutenue qu'elle a cru voir dans la lettre où je lui annoncois qu'il n'y avoit plus d'espérance. Ses voyages à Lausanne, les adorateurs qu'elle y a eû, et la complaisance avec laquelle elle les a ecouté formoient l'article le plus difficile à justifier. Ni d'Eyverdun (dit elle), ni personne n'ont effacé pendant un instant mon image de son cœur. Elle s'amusoit à Lausanne sans y attacher. Je le veux. Mais ces amusements la convainquent toujours de la dissimulation la plus odieuse, et, si l'infidelité est quelquefois une foiblesse, la duplicité est toujours un vice. Cette affaire singulière dans toutes ses parties m'a été très utile; elle m'a ouvert les yeux sur le caractère des femmes, et elle me servira longtemps de preservatif contre les seductions de l'amour." Mademoiselle Curchod came to Lausanne in February, 1764, and again met Gibbon; "Elle me badine sur mon ton de petit maître. Elle a du voir cent fois que tout étoit fini sans retour." "Nous badinons," he says again in the same month, "trés librement sur nôtre tendresse passée, et je lui fais comprendre tout clairement que je suis au fait de son inconstance." Gibbon's continued coldness at length convinced Mademoiselle Curchod that his affection for her was entirely extinguished, and she took her leave of him in an indignant letter, quoted by M. d'Haussonville, as she undoubtedly thought, for ever. In this farewell letter she repudiates the suggestion of her inconstancy: "Si l'on vous a dit que j'aie écouté un seul moment M. d'Eyverdun, j'ai ses lettres, vous connoissez sa main, un coup d'œil suffit pour me justifier." Mademoiselle Curchod married, at the end of 1764, Jacques Necker, and became the mother of Madame de Staël-Holstein.

I have just drawn a bill of fifty pounds sterling upon my father. I shall do my utmost to endeavour at Economy, and I hope here my endeavours will be successfull.

Present, Dear Madam, my love and duty to my father and my sincerest compliments to your brothers. Pray let me hear from you or my father soon.

I am, Dear Madam,

Most affectionately yours,

E. Gibbon.

27.

To his Stepmother.

Dear Madam,

Lausanne, August the 6th, 1763.

I hope I need not assure you how agreable your letters are to me. Letters such as you write would be highly pleasing from an indifferent person, judge of the pleasure they must give me when I receive them from a friend and a mother : I put the friend first and I believe you will not blame me for it. I should be very glad to hear somewhat oftener from my father ; But tho' his dislike to letter-writing is *inconceivable* to me, I see I must be contented with hearing from you that he is well. At this time especially I have no hopes. He must be now (according to my reckoning) in the very midst of Harvest, and I am very sensible, that

When Harvest is in the case
All other business must give place.

You will hardly expect news from me. We are buried in a quiet Solitude, and seem separated from the rest of the universe by a Wall of mountains, whose summits are at this instant covered with snow. I have found most of my old friends well, and made some new ones, and between the society of both, I lead a very agreable life. I could talk to you with great pleasure about them did I not know how very uninteresting an account of people you know nothing of must be to you. I should be glad to know soon whether my father has any objection to my passing the winter here. I do not dissemble that my inclination would make me desire it ; but I have a much better tho' as real a motive to alledge to him ; a considerable work I am engaged in, which will be a most usefull preparation to my tour of Italy and which I shall not be able to finish sooner. It is a Description of the ancient Geography of Italy, taken from the Original writers. If I go into Italy with a work of that kind tolerably executed, I shall carry every where about with me an accurate and lively idea of the country, and shall have nothing to do but to insert in their proper places my own observations as they tend either to confirm, to confute, or to illustrate what I have met with in books. I should not even despair, but that this mixture of study and observation, properly digested upon my return to England, might produce something not entirely unworthy the eye of the publick on a subject, upon which we have no regular or compleat treatise.

I made a little excursion some days ago to Geneva, not so much for the sake of the town which I had often seen before, as for a representation of Monsieur de Voltaire's. He lives now entirely at Fernay, a little place in France, but only two leagues from Geneva. He has bought the estate, and built a very pretty tho' small house upon it. After a life passed in courts and Capitals, the Great Voltaire is now become a meer country Gentleman, and even (for the honor of the profession) something of a farmer. He says he never enjoyed so much true happiness. He has got rid of most of his infirmities, and tho' very old and lean, enjoys a much better state of health than he did twenty years ago. His playhouse is very neat and well contrived, situated just by his Chappel, which is far inferior to it, tho', he says himself, *que son Christ est du meilleur faiseur de tout le pays de Gex.* The play they acted was my favourite Orphan of China. Voltaire himself acted *Gengis* and Madame Denys *Idamè;* but I do not know how it happened : either my taste is improved or Voltaire's talents are impaired since I last saw him.[1] He appeared to me now a very ranting unnatural performer. Perhaps indeed, as I was come from Paris, I rather judged him by an unfair comparaison, than by his own independent value. Perhaps too I was too much struck with the ridiculous figure of Voltaire at seventy, acting a Tartar Conqueror with a hollow broken voice, and making love to a very ugly niece of about fifty. The play began at eight in the evening and ended (entertainment and all) about half an hour

---

[1] At Monrepos in 1757-58, when Voltaire was living at *les Délices,* Gibbon had heard him in his tragedies of *Zaïre, Alzire, Zulime,* and his sentimental comedy *L'Enfant Prodigue.* Voltaire settled at Ferney in 1758.

after eleven. The whole Company was asked to stay and set Down about twelve to a very elegant supper of a hundred Covers. The supper ended about two, the company danced till four, when we broke up, got into our Coaches and came back to Geneva just as the Gates were opened. Shew me in history or fable, a famous poet of Seventy who has acted in his own plays, and has closed the scene with a supper and ball for a hundred people. I think the last is the more extraordinary of the two.

You may imagine how glad I am to hear of the fall of our Tyrant[1] and the accession of a just and righteous prince. Lord [2] was always our utmost wish, and I have so very good an opinion of him as to believe he will not even plague our enemies to oblige us. I am very glad to hear the battalion addressed him, as you style it, and as I could not sign the general letter, I apprehend a particular compliment to his Lordship cannot displease him. I have accordingly wrote to him this post. My father had formerly some thoughts of resigning the Majority to me. It is a matter of great indifference at present, but if he has a mind to provide against a future storm, I suppose it would be very easily settled at present, and that my friend Poussy (who has never answered me any more than Sir Thomas[3]) would have the Company of course. I wish my father would consider too, whether changes of much greater consequence might not be effected, such as the incorporation of both battalions, &c. But these are only hints.

Present, Dear Madam, my love and duty to my father, my sincerest Compliments to your Brothers, and believe me ever

Most affectionately and entirely yours,

E. Gibbon, Junior.

[1] Charles Paulet, fifth Duke of Bolton, who committed suicide in 1765, was succeeded in the Lord Lieutenancy of Hampshire by James Brydges, Marquess of Carnarvon. Lord Carnarvon resigned the post in 1764, because Mr. Stanley was appointed Governor of the Isle of Wight (*Grenville Correspondence*, vol. ii. pp. 399–403).

[2] Name illegible. Probably Lord Northington.

[3] Sir Thomas Worsley, Bart.

28.

To his Father.

Lausanne, September the 10th, 1763.

DEAR SIR,

This morning I received your letter, and according to your desire prepared myself immediately to answer it.

I hardly thought it possible, any letter of yours could have given me so much uneasiness. I am very sensible how many obligations I have to you, and that in this affair you continue to act with your usual goodness to me. If there is any fault it is partly my own and partly that of unhappy circumstances. My expences have been too great for our fortune. I was afraid of it at the time; and tho' I cannot yet see that relative to my situation of travelling and being at Paris I have launched into any extravagancy, the consequences are equally disagreable. But what is past cannot be recalled. With regard, Dear Sir, to the proposal mentioned in your letter; if your own ease or happiness had depended upon it, I should not have hesitated an instant, but as the advantages resulting from it relate only to me you will give me leave to canvass it freely.

I need not say any thing of the great inconvenience of mortgages nor how much they eat up an estate piece meal. We feel it but too sensibly : Sir T. R.'s is particularly disagreable, since he has it in his power to distress us whenever he pleases by calling for his money. I own the thought of increasing it hurts me very much.

The advantages for me would be, your being able to bring me into Parliament, increasing my annuity and enabling me to continue my travels. Give me leave to say, Dear Sir, that the first has very little weight with me. I find my ambition diminish every day, and my preference of a quiet studious life to hurry and business grow upon me. Besides I should imagine the thing almost impossible in the middle of a parliament and at such an interesting period :[1] and if I was in, what could I do ? Whether

---

[1] On April 7, 1763, Lord Bute resigned, and was on the same day succeeded by George Grenville, as First Lord of the Treasury. During the autumn recess, George III. opened negotiations with Pitt to take Grenville's place. But no change was made, and Grenville was preparing to meet Parliament in November, 1763, as Prime Minister.

I consulted principle or prudence, every thing seems so unsettled that I might find myself very soon at the tail of an opposition ; (and as a total change seems to be the modern maxim of every new Ministry,) in case I had got any thing, I should be reduced to my former situation, with the additional mortification of having just tasted a little more power and plenty. The encreasing my annuity would be certainly very agreable, but as it would be only the difference of passing four or six months every winter in London, I should not think it equivalent. The continuing my travels is the great object. When I am just in view of Italy, to be obliged to give up a scheme which has been always a favourite, would afflict me to the greatest degree.

Would it not be possible, Dear Sir, to think of another scheme ? One has come into my head which would set me entirely at my ease without costing you a shilling. It would be to change my annuity into a perpetual rent charge upon the Estate : this I would sell immediately for an annuity upon my own life, which would certainly give me Six hundred pounds a year, would enable me to travel (at least with a small addition) and to live afterwards in a very agreable manner in England. I think I may venture to say I shall never marry, and even supposing that possibility and afterwards the possibility of children ; Would this scheme hurt them more than the other ? But I submit it entirely to you. In case this proposal should be disagreable to you, you have my full consent to the other. Only give me leave, Dear Sir, to mention one thing. I should be a monster, If I could distrust either your honor or your goodness to me ; but I am afraid (excuse the freedom) that Œconomy is not the virtue of our family. A variety of schemes would offer, old incumbrances would appear, and you yourself would be the first surprised to find the sum almost sunk to nothing. I should think that the dividing it might equally suit us both. I should have a fund for my extraordinary expences, which I should be the more interested to husband, as I should know that I could have no pretence to ask for any thing more. You on the other hand, Dear Sir, would be likewise at a certainty with regard both to your expences and mine.

I shall end here, Dear Sir ; for I am too much agitated to talk of any thing else : only begging you to excuse the liberty I have taken. Your goodness has encouraged me to it and I think our mutual interest requires it. In case you should approve of my first proposal, I suppose my going over in the Spring will be sufficient. Otherwise, I should be glad to hear from you as soon as possible, that I might set out before winter.

My love and duty are always Mrs. Gibbon's and my sincere compliments wait upon the Brothers.

I am, Dear Sir,
With the greatest affection sincerely yours,
E. GIBBON, JUNIOR.

29.

To his Father.

Lausanne, October the 15th, 1763.

DEAR SIR,

Give me leave to begin with the part of my letter which has given you the most uneasiness, and which is entirely owing to a mistake. As I have no copy of my letter, I cannot exactly recollect my expressions, tho' I am perfectly sure of my meaning. When I mentioned *unhappy circumstances* I meant only that my expences, tho' not excessive in themselves, appeared great, and were in fact more than what the *unhappy circumstances* of our estate allowed you to support. That I assure you, Dear Sir, was my only meaning; if my expression was doubtfull, attribute it solely to the agitation of spirits I was in when I wrote. When I reflect on my expences, I do not see, that were I to live last winter over again at Paris, I could, according to the almost necessary extravagance of the age, spend less than I have done. I do not pretend to say that a man of a more exact economy might not have done sometimes the same things for less money, but I am sure there was no one blamable or ridiculous expence. Play in particular, Dear Sir, must have occurred to you, tho' you do not mention it. I give you *my word of honor*, that since I have left England I have not lost twenty pounds.

I will say no more of my scheme, since you disaproove of it. I own I thought it might have made me very easy without any additional expence to you. But you do not mention, Dear Sir, my other proposal supposing we borrowed the five thousand ; that of giving me half of it, and making no addition to my allowance

whatsoever.   Unless you want the whole sum, I should still think
it must be more, or at least as eligible to you as any other.   I own
it would be highly agreable to me, to have always a sum of money
lying by me, besides my income ; for I do assure you, Sir, that
it is much more a scheme of economy than of expence.   I should
employ about seven or eight hundred of it to encrease my annuity
during a year and a half and to enable me to travel agreably.   The
remainder I should put into the stocks, and spend only the
interest, reserving the Capital, for any uses that might appear
to both of us worthy of it, for I would promise, Dear Sir, not to
touch any part of it without your knowledge and consent.   In
case you want the greatest part of the sum, I should beg at least
that, instead of the two Hundred a year you design adding to my
annuity, you would only add one hundred a year and a thousand
pounds.   If the whole is necessary, I am far from contesting it
with you, Dear Sir, but after thanking you for the very handsome
encrease of my annuity, you must give me leave to say that six
hundred pounds a year will not enable me to travel.   In this age,
it would be almost impossible for me to do it under 9 or 8 hundred ;
every thing is much altered since you were abroad, and I believe
if you consult those who have travelled lately, they would name
scarcely less than a thousand.   After the experience I have had,
it would be deceiving both myself and you to talk in another
strain.

I own the thoughts of a mortgage frighten me.   The diminution of the estate, the weight of the interest, the uncertainty of
paying which we have already felt in the old one, give me the
greatest repugnance to encreasing it.   Tho' it would hurt me
excessively, I could wish we could avoid it.   I would return to
England and wait for a more favorable opportunity.   This I
speak merely for myself.   If it is necessary to make you easy,
I have nothing more to say.

At all events, Dear Sir, you may depend upon my being in
England a few days before the 30th of December.   As I should
be glad to return to this place as soon as the business is over (in
case you still chuse it) I was thinking that so short an apparition
might set the world a talking and guessing at the reasons, and as
it would be better they should know nothing of them, it might be
as well if I came over incognito.   I could see you and Mrs. Gibbon
in London, appear very little in publick and go back immediately.

But as I can hear from you again before my departure, you will settle every thing as you please.

I am surprised that Mrs. Gibbon has not received the Arquebusade water I sent her four months ago, tho' I forgot to mention it.—A propos upon reflexion, I directed it to Becket and neglected giving him any directions about it. If you will write a line to him, I dare say it lies at his shop, near Somerset house in the Strand. I shall endevour to get you some Lucerne myself, unless you chuse to stay till next [autumn].

I beg my love and duty to Mrs. Gibbon and sincere compliments to all friends.

I am, Dear Sir,

Most affectionately and most sincerely yours,

E. GIBBON, JUNIOR.

30.

To his Stepmother.

Lausanne, December the 7th, 1763.

DEAR MADAM,

I am afraid I have made you wait a little. But let me tell you without any reproach that I have imitated your example in proclaiming the arrival of my letter about two months before it really begins its march. I must acknowledge your letters deserve waiting for better than mine. However I flatter myself you are as well pleased with hearing from me as I can be in hearing from you, and that is saying a great deal.

After having assured you how much I love and respect you, Dear Madam, which I hope you are convinced of without my saying it, I should give an account of my method of passing my time here, but the happiness the most difficult to be described is perhaps the truest in reality. If I was in a place where I could fill pages with accounts of balls, reviews, Court assemblies, &c., the conclusion would perhaps be only that I had spent a great deal of time and money with very little genuine satisfaction. Here every day is an agreable mixture of books and good company, & consequently every day resembles the day that preceded it ; I have passed six months at Lausanne, but tho' the sum of my pleasures has been very pleasing I cannot pick out any single event that I think worthy your attention. You would hardly be

entertained with minute characters of people you are not acquainted with & will probably never see.

We have some English here ; most of them raw boys just
escaped from Eaton. Mr. Guise—I do not reckon him in the
number of them. He is about my age, has seen a good deal of
the world, & without being a profound scholar is far from wanting either parts or knowledge. As far as I can judge of him he
seems to be a prudent worthy young man. If I can go into
Italy with him I should like it extremely. Lord Palmerston[1]
passed thro' some time ago. He seems to have a very right
notion of travelling and I fancy will make very great improvements.

As we have the English papers here, we are by no means
strangers to what passes at home, and many an insignificant piece
of news which we should not have minded in England, gives us
great pleasure at this distance. I was very glad to hear of my
friend Wilkes's deserved chastisement,[2] and if the law could not

---

[1] Henry Temple, second Viscount Palmerston (1739-1802), a man of
artistic tastes, and, in after-years, a frequent resident in Italy. He was at
this time M.P. for Hastings. He married, as his second wife, January 3,
1783, Miss Mee, by whom he was the father of the Prime Minister, born 1784.

[2] In Gibbon's Journal for September 23, 1762, written at Southampton,
occurs the following entry which explains the words " my friend Wilkes : "—
" Colonel Wilkes of the Buckinghamshire Militia dined with us, and renewed
the acquaintance Sir Thomas and myself had begun with him at Reading.
I scarce ever met with a better companion ; he has inexhaustible spirits,
infinite wit and humour, and a great deal of knowledge : but a thorough
profligate as well in principle as in practice ; his character is infamous, his
life stained with every vice, and his conversation full of blasphemy and
bawdy. These morals he glories in, for shame is a *weakness* he has long
since surmounted. He told us himself that, in this time of public dissension,
he was resolved to make his fortune. Upon this noble principle he has
connected himself with Lord Temple and Mr. Pitt, commenced a public
adversary to Lord Bute whom he abuses weekly in the *North Briton*, and
other political papers in which he is concerned. This proved a very debauched day ; we drank a good deal both after dinner and supper, and when
at last Wilkes was retired, Sir Thomas and some others (of whom I was not
one) broke into his room and made him drink a bottle of claret in bed."
Wilkes had been challenged by Mr. Samuel Martin, M.P. for Camelford,
formerly Secretary of the Treasury under both the Duke of Newcastle and
Lord Bute, for speaking of him in the *North Briton* as a low fellow and dirty
tool of power. Wilkes was dangerously wounded in the duel, which was
fought in November, 1763. In the preceding April he had been arrested
under a General Warrant on suspicion of being the author of No. 45 of the
North Briton. He applied for a writ of Habeas Corpus, and the case came

punish him, Mr. Martin could. After all the noise of faction, the numbers in the first division seem to have shewn that the court still preserves a very great superiority.

Will you be so good, dear Madam, as to assure my father of my constant love and duty, and to acquaint him that I have just drawn a bill of a hundred pounds upon him. I beg my best compliments to the brothers. I hope poor David has destroyed his old enemy the gout. As to Billy [Patton] (do not tell it to him) I hope he is no longer at Beriton, and that he has got the better of a enemy still more dangerous—*Laziness*.

I am, Dear Madam,

Ever yours most affectionately,

E. Gibbon.

31.

To his Father.

Lausanne, February the 1st, 1764.

Dear Sir,

I had the pleasure of your letter last saturday, & found with great satisfaction that you & Mrs. Gibbon were very well, and that everything went on as usual in our part of the world. I am very proud of my new dignity,[1] tho' I have not as yet communicated my promotion to my countrymen here. We have three or four honest regulars in the house with whom I am in a constant state of war, which I have tolerably maintained as yet notwithstanding their great superiority of number : I hope you continue to be well-pleased with our Lord Lieutenant, and that he is in every thing the reverse of his predecessors.

I am much obliged to you, Dear Sir, for your goodness in paying the bill I drew upon you in December last, but am sorry to find you are so much dissatisfied at my expenses, which I endeavour to moderate as much as I can : keeping up the kind of figure which you would desire your son should. In case I leave this place about the end of next month, I am afraid that

before Lord Chief Justice Pratt in the Court of Common Pleas. He was discharged from custody, the judges unanimously holding that the arrest was a breach of his privilege as a member of Parliament.

[1] Gibbon refers to his promotion to the rank of major in the Hampshire Militia.

reckoning the several bills I have to pay, the purchase of a chaise, and some money to carry me on to the next place, I shall want about two Hundred pounds more, or at least one hundred and fifty. I am very much concerned I have already drawn for above half your income, and the more so, as I see no possibility of my expences being less when I am moving about in Italy. We have here a young Englishman and his governor, who is a very sensible sedate man. I have questioned him very much about Italy; he has assured me that it was not possible for an Englishman to keep good company in Italy, and to go thro' the country in an agreable manner, under 800 or at the lowest under 700 pounds a year. If it was possible for you, Dear Sir, to make such an effort for *only one year*, I should consider it as an obligation which it ought to be my study to repay by the most exact œconomy upon all other occasions, and by coming (if necessary) into any schemes which might be thought of to make us both easy. But in case you cannot do it, I had rather give up a scheme (I have indeed always set my heart upon) than it should be the occasion of perpetual uneasinesses and inconveniences to us both.

Upon reading over what I have wrote, I am afraid, Dear Sir, you will suspect me of murmuring and being out of humor. Such sentiments are far from me. I am convinced there is nothing occasions your complaints but your not being able to support it, and in that case, tho' I cannot lessen my expence, I can put an entire stop to it. May I beg, Dear Sir, your speedy directions for my conduct. If I am to pass the mountains (which I wish and hope still) I must not wait for the month of April as it is the very worst in the year.

I beg my love and duty to Mrs. Gibbon. I shall write to her very soon, though I have little more to say than what I have just said. My Aunt Porten—— Indeed I am much in the wrong, but I will not be so longer, and I hope very soon to clear score with all my friends. Sr Thomas is the only one with whom I have a C^t account; creditor indeed in more than one sense of the word. If he and George Dux, my other creditor, would pay me, it would be a little help.

I am, Dear Sir,

Most affectionately yours,

E. GIBBON, JUNIOR.

32.

To his Stepmother.

Lausanne, February 17th, 1764.

DEAR MADAM,

You are very good to take notice of my owing you a letter. I am afraid I am too apt to depend upon my friends knowing me, and upon their being convinced that there is not the least connection between my regard for them and my putting pen to paper to assure them of it.

My laziness as to writing is but too natural to me ; but no place is so apt to encourage it as this, where my way of life is so agreable but at the same time so uniform, that a month or two are elapsed before I know any thing of the matter. Pleasant weather, (I am forced to draw the curtain this moment to exclude the sun) study in the morning, and company in the afternoon. Books you are not perhaps acquainted with, and people that I am sure you do not know, make up my occupations, and notwithstanding all the pleasure I hope for in Italy, I own I shall quit this place with some unwillingness. My health is very good, only about two months ago I found my blood thickening, and was forced to be bled. I have since taken some gentle physick once or twice, and am now well and in very good spirits.

The only book I have read lately that you can have any knowledge of, is the letters of Lady Mary Wortley Montague.[1] They have entertained me very much. What fire, what ease, what knowledge of Europe and of Asia ! Her account of the manners of the Turkish women is indeed different from any thing we have yet seen. One should have hardly suspected, that a Turkish husband with his four wives and twenty concubines, is very far from being absolute.

Will you be so good, Dear Madam, as to excuse the shortness of this letter. The post is *really* just going out and I have barely time to seal it. My love and duty to my father. I have just drawn a bill for fifty pounds at fifteen days after date.

I am, Dear Madam,
Most truly & affectionately yours,
E. GIBBON.

[1] Lady Mary died in 1761. A surreptitious edition, said to be edited by John Cleland, of her letters written during her travels in Europe, Asia, and Africa, was published in three volumes at London in 1763.

33.

To his Father.

Lausanne, April the 14th, 1764.
DEAR SIR,

The reason which has made me defer some time answering your last obliging letter was our waiting every post for Mr. Guise's last instructions. As he has never received them, and we have settled the time of our departure, I take the first opportunity of laying before you our plan of operations.

We propose moving from hence next Wednesday the 18th instant, and passing by Geneva and Mont Cenis to Turin, which we shall reach in about ten days. After some stay at that place, which I hope our old camp acquaintance Pitt[1] will make very agreable to us, we intend going by the Boromean Islands, Milan, Brescia, Verona, Vicenza, and Padua to Venice, which we must reach by the 30th of May to be present at the great ceremonies of Ascension day, where we shall have an opportunity of paying our court to the Duke of York.[2] I hope we shall have seen Venice in about a fortnight, after which we shall have nothing to prevent our setting out from thence, passing thro' Ferrara and Bologna and reaching Florence by the latter end of June. We intend from thence to retire to Sienne or some other quiet town, and pass about six weeks in the study of Italian. When we get back to Florence, that place with Leghorn, Pisa, Luca, &c., will furnish us ample matter for between two and three months till the latter end of October, when we propose going to Rome, pushing on directly to Naples and returning again to Rome the latter end of November. If we pass there about three months I shall be ready to come out of Italy the beginning of next March, and hope to bring back some improvement, as I had pretty well prepared myself in England, and as I hope I have not lost my time here. I think I know my fellow-traveller very well, and that knowledge convinces he is a very sensible good-natured prudent young man.

[1] George Pitt, first Lord Rivers (cr. 1776), served as Envoy at the Court of Turin from 1761 to 1768, in which latter year he was elected M.P. for Dorsetshire. He died in 1803, at the age of eighty-two.

[2] Edward Augustus, Duke of York, third child and second son of Frederick, Prince of Wales, born March 14, 1739, died September 17, 1767, at Monaco.

I wish, Dear Sir, I could have followed your Directions, but it was impossible for me to leave the town after paying all my bills without Drawing for £200, the remainder of which will barely carry me to Turin. I shall endeavour during my tour to live with the most exact œconomy and not to exceed the sum you have mentioned. I give you my word of honor that neither play nor women shall form any part of my expence, and I hope our being two will still contribute to diminish it. I am very sensible that it is often rather negligence than extravagance that runs away with my money, and I do assure that I will be as exact as I can. Consider, Dear Sir, that this is a sacrifice you make once in my life, and that a hundred pounds now are of more service to me than three times as much at any other time.

The passage of the mountains is very easy at present, and we have the advantage of going with a Sardinian officer who is very well acquainted with the country. As soon as I get to Turin I shall have the pleasure of writing to you. In the mean time I beg my compliments to the brothers, and my love and duty to Mrs. Gibbon, from whom I had a letter the other day.

I am, Dear Sir,

Most truly yours,

E. Gibbon.

34.

To his Father.

Turin, April 28th, 1764.

Dear Sir,

After a very tedious journey of nine days from Lausanne, I got safe to Turin the night before last. The roads thro' Savoy are very bad, but nothing could surpass the pleasantness of our passage over Mont Cenis. A very fine day, a most romantick variety of prospects, and a perfect consciousness that there could not be the smallest danger. I was carried over the mountain in a small chair by four men, who relieved each other during about five leagues. The uphill work was very hard, but upon the plain, &c., downhill, they went a kind of a trot which I can only compare to our double time. I am sure you will not blame me for having added a Guinea to the half crown at which the King has taxed this hard day's work.

Upon my arrival at Turin, I was much disapointed to find
Mr. Pitt was to set out for England as to-day. I saw him however yesterday, and nothing could be civiler than he was. He
talked very much of you and of Winchester Camp, and has recommended me to his Chargé d'Affaires a Mr. Dutems,[1] as well
as to the Count de Virry, a Minister of State, for whom likewise
Lord Mountstuart had given me a letter. We are (I believe)
to be presented at Court to-morrow. We shall see some company
and visit the King's palaces and manufactures, but I hardly
think we shall extend our stay here beyond the fortnight we
talked of at first. Every thing follows the example of the Court,
which from one of the most polite in Europe is become bigotted,
gloomy and covetous. Guise and I seem as yet very well satisfied
with each other. Such a society is desirable both as to entertainment and lessening the expence. As I mentioned in my last
letter that my draught at Lausanne would little more than send
me out of the town, you will not be surprised, Dear Sir, at my
having drawn for £100 here. As near as I can calculate at a
distance, I shall be obliged to take another Hundred at Venice,
two in Tuscany, and three at Rome and Naples as well as to get
out of Italy, which will make up all the 700 which you have
been so good as to mention, & which I am determined if
possible not to exceed, but to watch with as scrupulous an
attention over every expences as your goodness requires of me.
Thus, Dear Sir, you will in the two years and half I may be
abroad, have sacrificed about a thousand pounds extraordinary
to the most agreable part of my life ; a sacrifice I shall endeavour to repay by the behavior of my whole future life.

I propose writing next post to Sir Matthew Fetherston.[2]
Could not I make my peace for my Paris neglect, which is however
excusable by my care and attention to his commands in Italy ?

---

[1] Louis Dutens (1730–1812), chaplain to the Embassy at Turin in 1758,
had, in the absence of the Envoy (the Hon. Stuart Mackenzie), acted as
chargé d'affaires. He retained the post till the appointment of George Pitt
in 1762. In 1764 he was once more acting as *charge.* The Count de Viry
had been Sardinian Minister in London, where his services to Lord Bute
gained him from George III. a pension of £1000 a year, and a promise of
the post of minister for his son. Viry was at this time Foreign Secretary
to Charles Emanuel III.

[2] Sir M. Featherstonhaugh, Bart., F.R.S., M.P. for Portsmouth, died
March, 1774.

My love and duty attend Mrs. Gibbon and my best compliments the brothers. I shall not forget the Wax Candles. Shall I send you any Florence Wine ? I fancy we shall move towards the 10th to be at Venice some time before the 31st, and in Tuscany towards the end of the month. Our direction will be, *recommended to Mr. Schalkhauser and Hughell at Venice, and to Mr. Joseph Frescobaldi et fils Bankers at Florence.*

I am, Dear Sir,

Most truly yours,

E. GIBBON.

I was forced to draw at fifteen days sight; the Banker did not chuse to give me more and wanted to have had only eight.

35.

To J. B. Holroyd, Esq.,[1] *at Lausanne.*

Borromean Islands, May 16th, 1764.

DEAR LEGER,

Most certainly, I am a puppy for not having wrote to you sooner : it is equally certain that you are an ass if you expected it. *Hurry of running about, time taken up with seeing places, &c. &c., are excellent excuses ; but I fancy you will guess that my laziness and aversion to writing to my best friend are the real motive, and I am afraid you will have guessed right.

We are at this minute in a most magnificent palace, in the middle of a vast lake ; Ranging about suites of rooms without a soul to interrupt us, and secluded from the rest of the universe. We shall sit down in a moment to supper attended by all the Count's houshold. This is the fine side of the medal. Turn to the reverse. We are got here wet to the skin ; we have crawled about fine gardens which rain and fogs prevented our seeing ;

---

[1] At Lausanne, in 1764, Gibbon met Mr. Holroyd (afterwards Lord Sheffield). In his Journal for April 6, 1764, he says : "J'ai conçu une véritable amitié pour Holroyd. Il a beaucoup de raison et des sentimens d'honneur avec un cœur des mieux placé." The friendship then begun ripened into warm affection. "My obligations to the long and active friendship of Lord Sheffield," Gibbon says in the will by which he appoints his friend one of his executors, "I could never sufficiently repay." Of the warmth of his affection, and the nature of some of his obligations, the letters now published afford continual proof.

and if to-morrow does not hold up a little better, we shall be in some doubt whether we can say we have seen these famous islands. Guise says yes, and I say no. The Count is not here ; we have our supper from a paultry hedge alehouse, (excuse the bull,) and the Servants have offered us beds in the palace, pursuant to their master's directions.

I hardly think you will like Turin ; the Court is old & dull ; [1] and in that country every one follows the example of the court. The principal amusement seems to be driving about in Your Coach in the evening & bowing to the people you meet. If you go when the royal family is there, you have the additional pleasure of stopping to salute them every time they pass. I had that advantage fifteen times one afternoon. We were presented to a Lady who keeps a public assembly, and a very mournfull one it is. The few women that go to it are each taken up by their Cicisbeo ; and a poor Englishman, who can neither talk Pied-montese nor play at Faro, stands by himself, without one of their haughty nobility doing him the honor of speaking to him. You must not attribute this account to our not having staid long enough to form connections. It is a general complaint of our countrymen, except of Lord Berkely, who has been engaged for about two years in the service of a Lady, whose long nose is her most distinguishing fine feature.

The most sociable women I have met with are the King's daughters. I chatted for about a quarter of an hour with them, talked about Lausanne, and grew so very free and easy, that I drew my snuff-box,[2] rapped it, took snuff twice (a Crime never

[1] Charles Emanuel III., Duke of Savoy and second King of Sardinia, came to the throne on the abdication of his father in 1730. He died in 1773. "He is the most insignificant looking fellow I ever saw ; but he has so much good-nature, and such obliging manners, that one is soon reconciled to his appearance" (Scrope to George Selwyn, January 12, 1752).

[2] This was a characteristic habit of Gibbon's throughout life. In 1780 some verses were written by Richard Tickell, which purport to be addressed by Charles James Fox to his friend the Hon. John Townshend on his election to Parliament by the University of Cambridge. They contain the following lines :—

> " Soon as to Brookes's thence thy footsteps bend,
> What gratulations thy approach attend !
> See Gibbon rap his box : auspicious sign
> That classic compliment and wit combine."

Another description is given of Gibbon in " The Luminous Historian ; or,

known before in the presence-chamber,) & continued my discourse
in my usual attitude of my body bent forwards, and my fore
finger stretched out.   As it might however have been difficult
to keep up this acquaintance, I chiefly employ my time in seeing
places, which fully repaid me in pleasure the trouble of my
journey.   What entertained me the most, was the Museum and
the Citadel.   The first is under the care of a M. Bartoli, who
received us without any introduction, in the politest manner
in the world, and was of the greatest service to us, as I dare
say he will be to you.   The Citadel is a stupendous work ; &
when you have seen the subterraneous part of it, you will scarcely
think it possible such a place can ever be taken.   As it is
however a regular one, it does not pique my curiosity so much
as those irregular fortifications hewn out of the Alps, such as
Exiles, Fenestrelles, & the Brunette[1] would have done, could
we have spared the time necessary.*   The last of these places you
may see.

I mentioned you to M. Dutens, Chargé des Affaires de sa
Majesté Brittanique, in Pitt's absence.   He cannot send you
so unlimited a permission as you wanted, but if you will write
to him some days before you set out, specifying the time you
shall pass, & the names of the peoples to be inserted, he will
take care to have one sent to Suze.

*Our next stage from Turin has been Milan, where we were
mere Spectators, as it was not worth while to endeavour at
forming connection for so very few days.   I think you will be

Learning in Love," written by George Colman the Younger (*Eccentricities
for Edinburgh*, pp. 73, 74).

> " His person look'd as funnily obese
> As if a Pagod, growing large as Man,
> Had, rashly, waddl'd off its chimney-piece,
> To visit a Chinese upon a fan.
> Such his exterior ; curious 'twas to scan !
> And, oft, he rapt his snuff-box, cock'd his snout,
> And ere his polish'd periods he began,
> Bent forwards, stretching his fore-finger out,
> And talk'd in phrase as round as he was round about."

[1] Exilles commanding the valley of the Houlx, Fenestrelle holding the
Col de Fenestrelle, and La Brunette guarding the Pas de Suze, were
strongly fortified posts on the Italian side of the Alps.   The two latter forts
were destroyed in 1796 and 1798 respectively.

surprised at the great Church, but infinitely more so at the
regiment of Baden-Baden, which is in the Citadel. Such
steadiness, such alertness in the men, & such exactness in the
officers, as passed all my expectations. Next Friday I shall
see the Regiment reviewed by General Serbelloni. Perhaps I
may write a particular letter about it. From Milan we proceed
to Genoa, & from thence to Florence. You stare—But really
we find it so inconvenient to travel like mutes, and to lose
a number of curious things for want of being able to assist
our eyes with our tongues, that we: have resumed our original
plan, and leave Venice for next year. I think I should advise
you to do the same.*

Milan, May 18th, 1764.

*The next morning was not fair, but however we were able to
take a view of the islands, which, by the help of some imagination, we conclude to be a very delightfull though not an enchanted
place. I would certainly advise you to go there from Milan,
which you may very well perform in a day and half. Upon our
return, we found Lord Tilney [1] and some other English in their
way to Venice. We heard a melancholy piece of news from
them; Byng [2] died at Bologna a few days ago of a feaver. I am
sure you will all be very sorry to hear it.

We expect a volume of news from you in relation to Lausanne,
and in particular to the alliance of the Dutchess with the frogs.
Is it already concluded? How does the Bride look after her
great revolution? Pray embrace her and the adorable, if you can,
in both our names; and assure them, as well as all the spring, [3]
that we talk of them very often, but particularly of a Sunday;
and that we are so disconsolate, that we have neither of us commenced Cicisbeos as yet, whatever we may do at Florence. We
have drank the Dutchess's health, not forgetting the little woman [4]
on the top of Mont Cenis, in the middle of the Lago Maggiore,
&c. &c. I expect some account of the said little woman. Whether
she talks —— as much as usual and who is my successor? I

[1] John Child Tylney, second Lord Tylney, F.R.S., M.P. for Malmesbury.
[2] John Byng, youngest son of the Hon. George Byng, and grandson of
the first Viscount Torrington.
[3] *La Société du Printemps* was the name of the society of young ladies
at Lausanne, mentioned in the *Memoirs*.
[4] Madame Besson.

think Montagny had begun to supplant me before I went.* Salute all our friends in both our names. The Count, the Queen's own, Buch Tysen, The foot Guards & the Oxford stage (& Mr. George Hyde Clarke). I am sorry to hear from Grand, that the last was ill. I heard likewise that your military list was augmented by a Hanoverian : I dare say the canonading of *Amenebourg* has often been fought over. As to people of the town, embrace Grand, Pavillard, and the Mesery, make some Compliments to a great many more, and don't forget to kick Constant & Ditter-manches before you come away. *I expect your answer at Florence, and your person at Rome ; which the Lord* of his infinite mercy *grant. Amen.*

36.

To his Father.

Genoa, June the 4th, 1764.

DEAR SIR,

I dare say you will be surprised when you see the date of my letter, as according to my last from Turin, you must have imagined me at Venice. It was indeed our intention till we got as far as Milan, and saw the shoals of English that were pouring in from every side, and till we heard the same accounts from everybody of the crowds and dearness at Venice upon this occasion. Garrets hired as a great favor at four sequins a night, every thing else in proportion, and with regard to us, who could not have got there above two days before Ascension day, the greatest danger of lying in the street. A fortnight passed at Venice at this time would have occasioned a very considerable augmentation in my expences, greater I am afraid than would have suited you, and which I should have brought upon you merely for the sake of a ceremony, as I can take Venice in as convenient, and a much cheaper manner in coming home. I was happy enough to find Mr. Guise entirely of my opinion, & we both agreed to strike off to Genoa & from thence by the way of Leghorn into Tuscany. I can easily conceive how extravagant Venice would have been upon such an occasion, from what I have already experienced of the dearness of travelling in Italy. Upon the road the necessary expences of the posts, &c., are higher than in England, and with regard to the inns, the instant they discover you are an Englishman, they do not know what to ask. We are constantly obliged to reduce their demands to one half, and even then to pay them too much. At Pavie I remember they asked us about twelve shillings for our lodging two nights in a single room. We gave them about eight, which they took after about half an hour's wrangling.

This, Dear Sir, is the disagreable side of travelling. In every other respect my tour exceeds my most sanguine expectations, altho' I am not yet got to the most interesting part of Italy. Turin, Milan, and Genoa have afforded me very great entertainement, and very different scenes. You cannot expect, Dear Sir, an account of any one of them. The whole it would be impossible to give you, and I should hardly know what particulars to select. We had better reserve them till we meet at Beriton, where the history of my peregrinations may perhaps furnish out the amusement of some evening when there is no post. Indeed if negligence and conciseness can be ever excused in a Correspondent they ought to be in a traveller. The common excuse of having no time is almost verified. Your morning is taken up with running about to see places, your evenings are commonly engaged in company, and you are forced to employ the very few moments you have at home in setting down some account of the things you have seen.

But amongst all my avocations I cannot help mentioning Mr. & Mrs. Celesia, who have received us not only in the most polite but really in the most friendly manner. We have dined and supped several times with them ; once at their Country house which is still wilder than Beriton, and they have introduced us to the Doge and to several houses in the town. This afternoon we are going with them upon a party in the country. Mrs. Celesia seems to retain the warmest friendship for Mrs. Gibbon ; she is very sorry their correspondence has been dropt, and has some thoughts of renewing it herself. I likewise saw the other day Captain John Elliot,[1] who came in with his Frigate and sailed again in about a couple of hours for Minorca. He has been a great while beating about the Mediterranean.

Mr. Guise and I travel in great harmony and good humour.

---

[1] Captain J. Eliot, R.N., was connected through his sister-in-law, Mrs. Eliot of Port Eliot, (née Catherine Elliston), with Gibbon. He died unmarried, an admiral and governor of Newfoundland.

He is indeed a very worthy sensible man, and I hope I have
formed a friendship that will last as long as my life. He is very
far from being ignorant & will be more so every day, as he has a
very proper spirit of curiosity and enquiry. My inferior companion (my servant) is a very useful one in this country, and in
general a very good one. I never enjoyed a better state of
health, and hope I shall stand the heats of Florence pretty well.
I fancy I shall be obliged to draw again soon after my arrival
there, which will be in about ten days. I hope I need say nothing
of my sentiments which are always the same for Mrs. Gibbon. I
hope to write to her from Florence. My sincere compliments
wait upon the brothers.

I am, Dear Sir,

Most affectionately yours,

E. Gibbon.

37.

To his Stepmother.

Florence, June 20th, 1764.

Dear Madam,

Without any of those common apologies for not writing
which are generally made use of to fill up the first half page of a
letter, I shall tell you at once that I am got here safe and in
perfect health, tho' somewhat later than I intended. We proposed
going by sea from Genoa to Leghorn. We had taken a Felucca,
and were to have embarked the 7th, but a strong south-west wind
springing up the day before, made it impossible for any vessel to
stir out of the harbour, and kept us waiting six days a most disagreable state of anxiety and attendance. At last, seeing no
likelyhood of any alteration in the wind, we were forced to set out
by land, and to come round thro' Parma, Modena and Bologna.
As we stopt to see what was worthy our notice upon the road,
(excepting only Bologna, which will require a fortnight or three
weeks) we got here only last night, and are settled in an excellent
good *hôtel garni* kept by one Charles, an Englishman, whom the
Duke of Richmond is very well acquainted with as well as with
our footman Valentin (for we only take one between us), to whom
he has given an exceeding good character in writing.

Every step I take in Italy, I am more and more sensible of

the obligation I have to my father in allowing me to undertake the tour. Indeed, Dear Madam, this tour is one of the very few things that exceed the most sanguine and flattering hopes. I do not pretend to say that there are no disagreable things in it: bad roads, and indifferent inns, taking very often a good deal of trouble to see things which do not deserve it, and especially the continual converse one is obliged to have with the vilest part of mankind—innkeepers, post-masters and custom house officers, who impose upon you without any possibility of preventing it,—all these are far from being pleasing. But how amply is a traveller repaid for those little mortifications by the pleasure and knowledge he finds in almost every place. The actual beauties are always the very great singularity of the country, the different pieces of antiquity either dispersed or collected into cabinets, and the variety of master-pieces of sculpture and painting have already made me pass some of the most entertaining days I have yet known, and I have before me the pleasing reflexion that what I have yet seen is far inferior to what I shall find in this place as well as Rome and Naples. I flatter myself, that the works of the greatest artists, which I have continually before my eyes, have already begun to form my taste for the fine arts. I shall however endeavour not to become a Coxcomb, nor to take the knowledge of a few terms for real science. I shall perhaps bring back to England an unafected taste for those arts, I am afraid without the judgment of a connoisseur, and I hope without the ridiculous part of that character.

I have never lost sight of the undertaking I laid the foundations of at Lausanne, and I do not despair of being able one day to produce something by way of a Description of ancient Italy, which may be of some use to the publick, and of some credit to myself. At least I know that I have already collected a considerable stock of materials which is daily encreasing, and that from reading and travel I have made a number of observations which will enter, very properly enter, into such a work, and which will have at least the merit of novelty. You will excuse me, Dear Madam, from entering into particulars as to any part of what I have seen; the task would be endless, and I must employ in giving you a very imperfect account a time of which I want almost every instant. But as my memory is pretty good, and as I keep a very exact journal; the recollection of this part of my life may be no disagreable employment of some winter evenings at Beriton. I am going to take an Italian master, and shall endeavour to get as much out of him as I can during my stay here, which Mr. Guise and I seemed to have fixed at about two months.

We have several English here. Lord Exeter, whom we shall hardly see, as he sets out after dinner ; Mr. Ponsonby,[1] son to the Irish speaker, a very agreable young man whom we knew at Turin ; Mr. Littleton, son to Lord Littleton,[2] &c. Some more whom I have not yet seen. We make our first visit after dinner to Sir Horatio Mann,[3] who happens to be a distant relation of Mr. Guise. Indeed without that advantage his general behavior to the English assures of the politest reception and an introduction into the best company in town. From the universal character of Florence I expect to meet with a very agreable society. I hope we shall avoid the fate of Lord Fordwich[4] (whom I forgot to mention). The charms of a superannuated beauty have captivated him to such a degree as to make him totally forget his country, and to fix him at Florence these five or six years without the least prospect of his ever leaving it. The Duke of York is expected here to-night from Venice in his way to Leghorn, from whence he goes by sea to Marseilles and so to Paris. It is said he will finish his travels by a visit to his sister at Brunswick.[5] I suppose we must be all presented to him.

I was much disapointed to find no letters from England, and especially from my father ; as I had wrote to the banker at Venice to send all that might come to Florence. I hope none on either

---

[1] William Ponsonby (1744–1806), eldest son of Speaker Ponsonby, and first Lord Ponsonby.

[2] Thomas Lyttelton (1744–1779), son of the first Lord Lyttelton, afterwards known as "the wicked Lord Lyttelton," had engaged himself, while at Oxford, to a daughter of General Warburton. He was sent abroad, while the settlements were being arranged. The engagement was broken off in consequence of his bad reputation.

[3] Sir Horace Mann (1701–1786) was appointed Assistant Envoy at the Court of Florence in 1737. Three years later he became Envoy, and held the post till his death in 1786. From Florence he kept a close watch on the movements of Charles Stuart, and carried on his voluminous correspondence with Horace Walpole.

[4] George Nassau, Lord Fordwich (1738–1789), who succeeded his father in 1764 as third Earl Cowper, married in 1775 Miss Hannah Gore, and died at Florence in 1789.

[5] The Princess Augusta, eldest child of Frederick, Prince of Wales, born August 11, 1737, married the Duke of Brunswick.

side have miscarried. I wrote upon leaving Lausanne, as well as from Turin and Genoa. I shall be obliged to draw immediately for a hundred pounds; and as far as I can foresee my expences I hope I shall keep within my bounds. I am very sensible of the times I may have launched out a little too much, but I can safely say, that were I to perform the journey I have already I could not do it for a Guinea less. I have made some progress in the arts of œconomy and exactness, but those of the Italians are necessarily superior to mine. Will it be necessary, Dear Madam, to repeat any assurances of those sentimens which duty and inclination have an equal share in?

I am, Dear Madam,
Most truly yours,
E. GIBBON.

I shall not forget the wax candles. I shall send with them a small quantity of Florence wine.

38.

To his Father.

Rome, October the 9th, 1764.

DEAR SIR,

We set out from Florence last Saturday sevenight and are arrived here after a journey of about ten days. We came round by Lucca, Pisa, Leghorn and Sienna, and I think made a very agreable tour of it. I must acknowledge that I had the least pleasure in what my companion enjoyed I believe the most; the Opera of Lucca. That little republick, who could give usefull lessons of gouvernment to many states much more considerable, lays out a very large sum of money every autumn in entertaining an exceeding good Opera at the time that public entertainements are very dead in the other towns of Italy, and receives their money again with very good interest from the great affluence of strangers who resort to Lucca upon that occasion. Of the different tastes which a man may form or indulge in in Italy that of musick has hitherto been lost upon me, and I have always had the honesty never to pretend to any taste which I was in reality devoid of.

We past four days at Leghorn where I saw the Actons. They were so civil to me that I was much embarassed how to behave. The poor old Commodore is in a most melancholy situation. Last winter he had a most violent attack of the Apoplexy; whilst in that situation he was persuaded either from motives of interest or devotion to change his religion in which he had been till then very steady. The immediate consequence of which imprudent step was the total neglect of all his English friends, who from being very intimate with him have taken the unanimous resolution of not holding the smallest connection with him. I most sincerely pity him. At his time of life, to lose the only friends he had, (for he has never been able even to learn the language of the country) to be continually regretting England which he will never see again, and to find himself oppressed with every misfortune of age and infirmity, is a situation truly melancholy. He talked to me a great deal of you and of times which I had scarce any remembrance of, and I think from his manner and conversation that I never saw a more lively picture of an unhappy man. I thought it right to acquaint the English at Leghorn of my reasons for not neglecting him as they did, and they all seemed to approve of my behavior.

I am now, Dear Sir, at Rome. If it was difficult before to give you or Mrs. Gibbon any account of what I saw, it is impossible here. I have already found such a fund of entertainment for a mind somewhat prepared for it by an acquaintance with the Romans, that I am really almost in a dream. Whatever ideas books may have given us of the greatness of that people, their accounts of the most flourishing state of Rome fall infinitely short of the picture of its ruins. I am convinced there never never existed such a nation, and I hope for the happiness of mankind there never will again. I was this morning upon the top of Trajan's pillar. I shall not attempt a description of it. Only figure to yourself a column 140 feet high of the purest white marble, composed only of about 30 blocks and wrought into bas-reliefs with as much taste and delicacy as any chimney piece at Up-park.[1]

The sickness of Naples seems pretty well over. I shall not however yet venture to it. The concern you and Mrs. Gibbon express in her last letter, makes it my duty to avoid the appearance as well as the reality of danger. If I allow about three

[1] Near Stansted in Sussex, purchased in 1746 from the Earl of Tankerville by Sir Matthew Featherstonhaugh, M.P. for Portsmouth.

months to Rome, a month to Naples, and a fortnight or three
weeks to the road, &c., visiting again some of the most curious
things upon my return, I shall have but few idle moments, and yet
shall hardly be able to take my last leave of Rome before the end
of February. About six weeks may do for Bologna, Verona, &c.,
and Venice, and towards the middle or end of April I hope to
have finished a tour attended with the greatest pleasure, and I
flatter myself with some improvement. I shall then be ready,
Dear Sir, to obey your orders with regard to the time and manner
of my returning to England. The grand tour of Germany I do
not even think of, as I am sensible of the considerable and unavoidable expence it would be attended with. The route thro'
Bavaria to the Rhine and Low Countries, or that of the south of
France to the same parts, would have their several advantages and
might each employ about two months. However from the great
extent of country I must pass thro' so rapidly, they would not be
without an addition of expence. Believe me, Dear Sir, that is
a consideration I feel so often and so sensibly ; that rather than
any thing should disturb the pleasure of our meeting, I will come
down from Venice to Leghorn and embark for England. Satisfied
with the enjoyment of Italy and France, I will rather reflect upon
what I shall have seen than upon what I shall have lost. I wait,
Dear Sir, for your directions. I have asked for them rather soon,
both to unburthen my mind, and because we are neither of us
the most exact Correspondents. I have a hundred more things
to say. I would thank Mrs. Gibbon for the agreable news she sent
me in her last letter of your having entirely got over your late
indisposition, but my paper is out and I can only add that I am
and ever shall be,

Dear Sir,

Most sincerely yours,

E. GIBBON, JUNIOR. *May I add Major?*

39.

To his Father.

Rome, November the 10th, 1764.

DEAR SIR,

I received last Wednesday your letter of the 16th of
October, and could scarcely have thought that any one from you

could give me so much uneasiness as this has done. I have let slip one post in order to consider it with more attention, and I believe I must visit again every thing I have seen, or seemed to see, in the intermediate days. I must own, Dear Sir, that I am frightened both when I look back, and when I look forwards. A mortgage of £10,000 contracted about six years ago, £1200 taken out of Hervey's hands ; and now an urgent necessity of selling one of our very best estates ! Where must this end ? Believe me, Dear Sir, I am very far from meaning the smallest reproach. I am convinced that all these measures have been dictated by necessity, and that this necessity has been occasioned by the intricacy of affairs, the iniquity of men, and a variety of accidents over which prudence has no power. But this very conviction encreases my uneasiness. What may be one day my fate without half your knowledge of business, and deprived of all those ressources which you must have found in living so many years in the Country, and in managing and improving your estate ? With less œconomy and perhaps more wants, I may very easily find my way to a Gaol.

Notwithstanding all this, Dear Sir, I am very sensible of the unhappy difficulties of Otway's affair, and both duty and inclination would engage me to submit to every thing in order to extricate you from it. But for a sum which is not very considerable, will it be necessary to sell an Estate which I have heard you often speak of as the clearest and most valuable you are in possession of ? If it is absolutely necessary to sell something, would it not be better to endeavour to part with Putney ? I speak, Dear Sir, very much at random for want of knowing the respective values of the Estates, and what you are offered for Lenborough.[1] Indeed without some such knowledge I can scarcely say anything positive upon the subject ; more than that, if you still persist in that scheme, it would be very difficult for me to dispute any thing that you think expedient, or conducive to your own ease and happiness.

But in that case, Dear Sir, should you think the following

---

[1] The Manor and Mansion-house of Lenborough, in the county of Bucks, passed, by purchase from the families of Ingoldsby and Dormer, into the hands of Mr. John Rogers, of Buckingham, who, about the year 1730, sold them to the grandfather of Edward Gibbon. The "Mansion" was converted into a farmhouse for the tenant of the farm.

conditions unreasonable ?—1st. That upon the sale of the estate, after discharging the mortgage and deducting £1200 for Otway's affair, the residue of the money should be paid into a banker's hands and be lodged in the funds in our joint names. The interests should be solely yours, and we should have what we have so often desired, a sum of money ready for any emergency, and sufficient to execute any plan, either of bringing me into Parliament, or any thing else. Surely, Dear Sir, this scheme is preferable to purchasing more land. Have not we enough already ? The only thing that hurts me in this proposal is the air of distrust it seems to carry with it. Believe me, Dear Sir, when I say that I can as little doubt of your care and regard for me as of my own, and that if I take any precautions, they are such only, as I should think it equally prudent to take against myself. My other condition would be the same which I mentioned last year, that of changing my annuity into a rent charge upon the estate, and permitting me to convert that into another annuity which I apprehend would be at least double what I at present enjoy. I have often considered it coolly since that time, and a scheme which would make me easy and happy for life, appears to me much more eligible than any other which would make a small addition to my income at your expence. Marriage, and the consideration of posterity would be the only motives which could ever make me repent of such a step, and against these my circumstances, my constitution and a way of thinking grounded upon reasoning and strengthened by experience and habit, will I hope effectually secure me. My views will never extend beyond the happiness of your life, that of Mrs. Gibbon's and of my own. Let us mutually consult what may the most contribute towards that object without calculating what estate may at last remain *for the Elliots*.[1]

I hope you will excuse, Dear Sir, the warmth [with] which I have expressed myself on a subject so highly interesting to us both. I am sure I have not wrote a line that has not been dictated by those sentiments of respect, duty and gratitude upon which you

---

[1] The grandfather of Edward Gibbon died in 1736, leaving one son and two daughters. Catherine, the eldest of these two daughters, married Mr. Elliston, of South Weald, Essex, and her only child married, in 1756, Mr. (created in 1784 Lord) Eliot, of Port Eliot in Cornwall. Their three sons were Gibbon's nearest male relatives.

have so many claims, and which will always engage to place your
ease and happiness upon a level with my own. I shall wait your
order as to the time and manner of my coming home ; but I hope
you will not insist upon it's being before the month of June.

I am, Dear Sir,
Most sincerely and most affectionately yours,
E. G.

40.

To his Father.

Rome, December the 5th, 1764.

DEAR SIR,
This moment to my great surprize, Barazzi, the banker
of Rome, sent for me to shew me a letter he had just received
from the banker at Lausanne, who had given me my general
credit all over Italy, to recall that credit and to desire he would
give me no more money. This can be only owing to the last
draught from Florence having been protested, and as the banker
has probably sent the same advice to his other correspondents, my
character is ruined in every great town in Italy, and what makes
it more unfortunate is the draught I gave from hence about a
week ago for £100 more at twenty days' sight ; which will probably have the same fate. I feel my situation the more as I am
not conscious of having deserved it by distressing you with
extravagant draughts. After a mature deliberation you fixed
upon 700 pounds for my tour of Italy. I have always advised
you regularly before I drew, and I have never, Dear Sir, exceeded
my proportion of the sum. To what then am I to attribute this
unforeseen misfortune ? In your last letter you say nothing, and
yet you must have then received mine from Florence. Forgive
my warmth, Dear Sir, I scarce know what to think, write, or do.

I shall wait with the utmost impatience for an answer. Indeed I shall be very uneasy till it comes. Barazzi, who was very
civil upon the occasion, desires if you send me credit upon any
other banker (which will be absolutely necessary) that you would
apply to Andrew Drummond whom he corresponds with. Till
then it will be impossible for me to stir from Rome, or to live
with much pleasure in it, while I know there are people who may
very naturally suspect me of being a rogue or an adventurer.

Once more, Dear Sir, forgive a man who scarce knows what he writes, and believe me ever

Most sincerely yours,

E. G.

I beg, Dear Sir, a speedy answer.

41.

To his Father.

Rome, the 5th of December, 1764.

DEAR SIR,

Since I sent my letter, which is already sealed up in Barazzi's packet, I have considered that the new credit which it will be necessary to send me must be given by the London Banker upon the other towns I am to go to, as well as upon Rome; at least upon Naples, Bologna, Venice, and one or two principal places in France or Germany according as you intend I should come home. After so unfortunate an accident I can scarce hope Barazzi himself will give me any credit elsewhere; and I must be the more exact, as in several of those places I shall find the bankers prepossessed against me by the letter of the Lausanne banker which must have been circular. How can it have happened, Dear Sir, that a letter can have had the time to go from London to Florence, from Florence to Lausanne, and from Lausanne to Rome without my having had the smallest intimation of it from you?

I am, Dear Sir, once more

Most truly yours,

E. G.

42.

To his Stepmother.

Naples, January the 29th, 1765.

DEAR MADAM,

I am very sorry for the reason (it is really no excuse) which I have had for my late dilatoriness in writing. I have waited with great impatience for an answer to the letters I had wrote my father, have always hoped and imagined that I could scarce fail of receiving it the very next post, and living in that daily expectation have suffered several posts to elapse without writing

myself. Indeed I begin to fear that some letters must have miscarried. I hope however to hear from my father very soon, since
if I should return to Rome without having had any orders from
him as to the time and manner of my returning home, I should
find myself very much embarassed how to act.

We arrived here only last night, so that as yet I have seen
nothing ; not even the glorious prospect of the bay of Naples. A
thick foggy cloudy day (for such weather have we sometimes even
in this happy climate) hangs over it, and veils all its beauties.
The journey from Rome has satisfied at least one species of a
disagreable curiosity, that of being acquainted with the very worst
roads in the universe. You are sometimes sunk in sloughs and
sometimes racked and battered on the broken remains of the old
Appian way, and when after a tedious day you at last arrive at the
long desired inn, you soon wish for the moment of setting out
again. Governor Ellis[1] who is here, a man famous for attempting
the North West passage, and consequently acquainted with every
species of hardship, declares that he had rather circumnavigate the
Globe, than go from Rome to Naples. This single circumstance
may convince you, Dear Madam, how just are the common but
melancholy observations, of the wretched state of this fine country
and of the misery of its idle and oppressed inhabitants. They are
indeed painted in too lively colours to escape the notice of the
most inatentive traveller, and so shocking as to excite the pity of
the least feeling one. I will not repeat here, Dear Madam, my old
and lazy maxim of saying little because I have a great deal to say,
and of reserving every thing for your dressing Room. I assure
you without flattery, that I am very impatient to see it. I cannot say whether you will find me improved in any thing else, but
at least I think I am become a better Englishman, and that, without adopting the honest prejudices of a Hampshire farmer, I am
reconciled to my own country, that I see many of its advantages
better than I did, and that a more enlarged view has corrected
many errors of my præmature and partial observation.

We are at present in the midst of a most brilliant carnaval,

---

[1] Henry Ellis (1721–1806) wrote an account of an expedition in which he
served to discover the North-West passage. His *Voyage to Hudson's Bay, by
the Dobbs Galley and California in the years 1746 and 1747, for Discovering
a North-West Passage,* was published in 1748. He was afterwards appointed
successively Governor of Georgia and Nova Scotia.

and shall scarce be able to breath between balls, operas, Assemblies and dinners. I have not yet seen Mr. Hamilton our Minister,[1] but he is extremely liked by the English here, of whom most are our Roman or Florentine acquaintance. Our only Peer is Lord Berkely, with whom we are just going to dine. I imagine we shall be presented to the boy King next Sunday. It must be a most ridiculous farce of Majesty.

Will you be so good as to acquaint my father that I drew for £100 at twenty days' sight the morning I left Rome, and that not having time to write by that post I acquainted Mr. Darrel with it by a letter of four lines.

How superfluous is it, Dear Madam, to repeat my protestations of duty and affection to my father, of tenderness to yourself, or of real friendship, and my best wishes for your brothers.

E. G.

43.

To his Father.

Rome, the 19th of March, 1765.

DEAR SIR,

We are at last going to quit Rome, and altho' every reason for not writing much or often looks suspicious from an old offender like me, yet at present a laudable avarice of time makes me regret every moment I am not rambling about a place I am so soon to take my leave of.

I shall be obliged to draw (at as long a sight as I can) for two hundred pounds : not that I have run into any new expences I did not foresee before, but merely from a prudence which I think a proper one in the very nice situation into which the Florence affair has thrown me. I am sure I can have the money from Barazzi here, as Grand has renewed my credit upon him, but tho' I hope and believe he has done it equally upon the other Bankers, I am not at all sure of it, and might find myself exposed to the refusal of the banker at Venice, and without any acquaintance there who could vouch for my character and circumstances. As I hope to carry away a good £150 I am at least sure of getting to

---

[1] Mr. (afterwards Sir William) Hamilton (1730-1803) was appointed Envoy at the Court of Naples in 1764. In September, 1791, he married, as his second wife, Amy Lyon, who as Emma Hamilton became famous.

Genoa, where I have some previous knowledge of the banker, and where in case of any difficulty I could call on Celesia. I hope this precaution, which appeared to me in the light of a necessary one, will not be inconvenient to you. It shall make no alteration in the plan I laid down in my letters from Naples, and you may depend upon it, Dear Sir, that neither in point of time nor of money I will any ways exceed it.

I can scarce hope to receive any more letters from you, which reduces me to the necessity of chusing for myself. I shall however write to you, Dear Sir, from Bologna, Genoa, and one or two places in France to acquaint you with my motions till I have the pleasure before the end of June, of embracing you and Mrs. Gibbon at Beriton.

I am, Dear Sir,

Most truly yours,

E. G.

Lyons is the only place I can think of where you can direct to me to the post-house.

44.

To his Stepmother.

Venice, April the 22nd, 1765.

DEAR MADAM,

Your last letter which I received only at Bologna was a most pleasing renewal of a correspondence, which (somehow or another) had been a little interrupted, but which I shall always consider as both usefull and agreable to me, since I am sure of finding in all your letters the tenderness of a mother, the sincerity of a friend and the entertainement of a most knowing correspondent. I am indeed but too unworthy of such a commerce.

Of all the towns in Italy, I am the least satisfied with Venice ; objects which are only singular without being pleasing produce a momentary surprize which soon gives way to satiety and disgust. Old and in general ill built houses, ruined pictures, and stinking ditches dignified with the pompous denomination of canals, a fine bridge spoilt by two Rows of houses upon it, and a large square decorated with the worst Architecture I ever yet saw, and wonderfull only in a place where there is more land than water : such are the colours I should employ in my portrait of Venice ; a portrait certainly true in general, tho' perhaps you should attribute the very great darkness of the shades to my being out of humour with the place. Here are no English, and all communication with the natives of the place is strictly forbid. Our chief ressource is our Resident Mr. Murray,[1] an honest plain man, and a very good companion, who gives us most excellent dinners every other day.

I found here that my prudence in taking up a larger sum of money at Rome than I immediately wanted, was very far from being a vain precaution. I found this Banker a sour, suspicious old fellow, who began by vexing me very much in talking of my letters having been protested in presence of Guise, to whom I had never mentioned it. Indeed the Brute did it in so very abrupt a way that it seemed his chief design was to mortify me. Upon my mentioning that I believed the Lausanne banker had restored my credit, he began to make a number of difficulties, which I at last cut short by telling him that I neither wanted his money nor his company. It was very lucky I had it in my power to talk in that manner.

The part of your letter, Dear Madam, which related to my being at home in May made me a little uneasy. My father hinted something of that kind in a former letter. I am sorry that your's is wrote before the reception of my answer, as I should then know whether my father still expected my return so soon. It would be most highly inconvenient to me. I could indeed, going directly from hence, arrive in England by the end, and the end only, of May. But in order to do it, I must go the very straitest road, never stop, and give up a number of curious things which will scarce ever be within my reach again ! Cannot the meeting be put off till September ? Cannot Sir Thomas[2] protract his stay one month longer ? Will my missing one more meeting hurt the Battalion very sensibly ? I am forced to ask all these questions without being able to wait for their answers. I must here at once determine for myself and I am afraid of determining wrong. I could have wished, my father would have explained himself more clearly, whether he thought my return in May, a thing absolutely necessary and right, and am almost inclined to imagine

---

[1] John Murray, Resident at Venice, was appointed in November, 1765, ambassador at Constantinople. He died at Venice in August, 1775.

[2] Sir T. Worsley.

that he would have done so, if he had looked upon it in that light. I have still some hopes of receiving his answer to my letter from Naples, which I should immediately obey.

You may see, Dear Madam, in what a state of perplexity I am, and that I am not really yet determined what to say or what to do. However the prospect of my tour thro' the South of France (which will only delay my return about a month or six weeks) is so pleasing, and the means of obviating any inconveniences in the Battalion appear so easy, that I cannot help taking a resolution which I hope will not displease my father. I leave this place in a day or two and shall be at Turin about the beginning of May; from thence I shall proceed to Lyons, go down the Rhone to Avignon and wheel round by Provence and Languedoc to Bordeaux, where I shall easily find a ship bound for London. I have made this alteration, as it enlarges my tour, without making any difference either in time or expence. I shall only draw for another hundred, and my father may depend upon my being at Beriton by the end of June or the beginning of July; barring accidents of wind and weather. With what pleasure, Dear Madam, shall we meet. I assure you I have not forgot the Wax Candles. Venice is the place for them, but, as far as I can learn, tho' whiter they do not burn so well as ours. I cannot make out whether in point of price it is worth sending them.

I am, Dear Madam,

Most truly yours,

E. G.

45.

To his Father.

Lyons, May the 29th, 1765.

DEAR SIR,

After a pretty troublesome passage of Mount Cenis we are at last arrived here. I say at last, for it is at least a fortnight later than we expected, occasioned by several inevitable hinderances. Upon casting up as well as I could my accounts of time and money, I soon found how impossible it would be for me to execute my tour of the south of France within the limitations of both which I had proposed. I mean to execute it with any degree of pleasure or profit, to stay long enough in any place to be acquainted with the inhabitants, and not to hurt my health perhaps by travelling too quick in a very hot season and country. Perhaps, Dear Sir, if I had had time to have consulted you, you might have indulged me a little longer ; but it was an indulgence I was determined not to grant myself at the expence of the promise I had made you of being in England by the end of June or beginning of July. The only way I have of keeping my word is going from hence to England by the way of Paris, where I shall stay a few days. I have drawn from hence £100 at eight days' sight (which term was forced upon me). When I consider that my last draught from Rome was about the middle of March, I cannot think I have been extravagant in spending about £150 in ten weeks and a journey of above 700 miles. I own that when I consider I have only seen Paris and Italy in two years and a half, I am displeased with myself for having staid so long at Lausanne. Had I set out for Italy the autumn before, I might have passed last winter in the south of France, and yet been at home in the spring ; but it is easier to condemn than to repair past faults. Perhaps one day you may spare me, Dear Sir, some months to compleat what I have left unfinished at present—But my duty is now to set down contented at Beriton with you and Mrs. Gibbon, and I can assure you that never was duty more agreable to inclination.

At Suze at the very foot of the Alps I met Sir Thomas Worsley and family. We supped together and talked over national, provincial, and regimental affairs. He is just the same as he was ; only not so great a courtier. He seems much pleased with his intended scheme. I think it a very bad one. Naples has no advantage, but those of climate and situation ; and in point of expence and education for his children is the very last place in Italy I should have advised. Indeed I should have thought that the south of France would have suited him much better.

I shall write once more from Paris : till when, Dear Sir, believe me

Most sincerely yours,
EDWARD GIBBON.

46.

To J. B. Holroyd, Esq., at Berlin.

DEAR LEGER,

*Why I did not leave a letter for you at Marseilles ? For a very plain reason : Because I did not go to Marseilles. But, as you have most judiciously added, why did not I send one ? Humph ! I own that nonplusses me a little. However, hearken to my history. After revolving a variety of plans, and suiting them as well as possible to time and finances, Guise and I at last agreed to pass from Venice to Lyons, swim down the Rhosne, wheel round the South of France, and embark at Bourdeaux. Alas ! At Lyons I received letters which convinced me that I ought no longer to deprive my country of one of her greatest ornaments. Unwillingly I obeyed, left Guise to execute alone the remainder of our plan, passed about ten delicious days at Paris, and arrived in England about the end of June. Guise followed me about two months afterwards, as I was informed by an epistle from him, which, to his great astonishment, I immediately answered. You perceive there is still some virtue amongst men. *Exempli gratiâ*, your letter is dated Vienna, October 12th, 1765 ; it made its appearance at Beriton, Wednesday evening, October the 29th. I am at this present writing, sitting in my library, on Thursday morning, between the hours of twelve & one.

I have ventured to suppose you still at Berlin ; if not, I presume you take care that your letters should follow you. This ideal march to Berlin is the only one I can make at present. I am under command ; and were I to talk of a third sally as yet, I know some certain people who would think it just as ridiculous as the third sally of the Renowned Don Quixote. All I ever hoped for was, to be able to take the field once more, after lying quiet a couple of years. I must own that your executing your tour in so compleat a manner gives me a little selfish pain. If I make a summer's escape to Berlin, I cannot hope for the companion I flattered myself with. I am sorry however I have said so much ; but as it is difficult to increase your honour's proper notions of your own perfections, I will e'en let it stand. Indeed I owed you

something for Your account of the favourable reception my book [1]
has met with. I see there are people of taste at Vienna, and no
longer wonder at your liking it. Since the court is so agreeable,
a thorough reformation must have taken place. The stiffness of
the Austrian Etiquette, and the haughty magnificence of the Hun-
garian princes, must have given way to more civilized notions.
You have (no doubt) informed yourself of the forces and revenues
of the Empress. I think (however unfashionably) we always
esteemed her. Have You lost or improved that opinion? Princes,
like Pictures, to be admired, must be seen in their proper point of
view, which is often a pretty distant one. I am afraid you will
find it peculiarly so at Berlin.

I need not desire you to pay a most minute attention to the
Austrian and Prussian discipline. You have been bit by a mad
Serjeant as well as myself; and when we meet, we shall run over
with every particular which we can approve of, blame, or imitate.
Since my arrival, I have assumed the august character of Major,
received returns, issued orders, &c. &c. I do not intend you
shall have the honor of reviewing my troops next summer.
Three-fourths of the men will be recruits; and during my
pilgrimage, discipline seems to have been relaxed. I do not care
to expose the chosen seed to the prophane mockery of the un-
circumcised. But I summon you to fulfil another engagement.
Make me a visit next summer. You will find here a bad house,
a pleasant country in summer, some books, and very little *strange*
company. Such a plan of life for two or three months must, I
should imagine, suit a man who has been for as many years struck
from one end of Europe to the other like a tennis-ball. At least
I judge of you by myself. I always loved a quiet, studious, indolent life; but never enjoyed the charms of it so truly, as since
my return from an agreable but fatiguing course of motion and
hurry. However, I shall hear of your arrival, which can scarce
be so soon as January, 1766, and shall probably have the misfortune of meeting you in town soon after. We may then settle
any plans for the ensuing campaign.

En attendant, (admire me, this is the only scrap of foreign
lingo I have imported into this Epistle—if you had seen that of
Guise to me!) let me tell you a piece of Lausanne news. Nanette

---

[1] Gibbon's *Essai sur l'étude de la Littérature* was published in 1761. The
essay, translated into English, was published in 1764.

Grand is married to Lieutenant-colonel Prevôt, *a poor unfortunate half-pay officer*. Grand wrote to me ; and by the next post I congratulated both father and daughter. There is exactness for you. The Curchod (Madame Necker) I saw at Paris. She was very fond of me, and the husband particularly civil. Could they insult me more cruelly ? Ask me every evening to supper ; go to bed, and leave me alone with his wife—what an impertinent security ! It is making an old lover of mighty little consequence. She is as handsome as ever and much genteeler ; seems pleased with her fortune rather than proud of it. I was (perhaps indiscreetly enough) exalting Nanette de Illens's good luck and the fortune. " What fortune ? " said she, with an air of contempt—" not above 20,000 Livres a year." I smiled, and she caught herself immediately. " What airs I give myself in despising twenty thousand Livres a-year, who a year ago looked upon 800 as the summit of my wishes." [1]

I must end this tedious scrawl. Let me hear from you : I think I deserve it. Believe me, Dear Holroyd, I share in all your pleasures, and feel all your misfortunes. Poor Bolton ![2] I saw it in the newspaper. Is Ridley[3] with you ? I suspect not : but if he is, assure him I do not forget him tho' he does me. Adieu ; and believe me, most affectionately yours,[a]

E. GIBBON, JUN.

---

[1] Madame Necker, writing to Madame de Brentès, November 7, 1765, thus describes this visit of Gibbon to her married home : " Je ne sais, madame, si je vous ai dit, que j'ai vu Gibbon ; J'ai été sensible à ce plaisir au-delà de toute expression, non qu'il me reste aucun sentiment pour un homme qui je vois n'en mérite guère ; mais ma vanité féminine n'a jamais eu un triomphe plus complet et plus honnête. Il a resté deux semaines à Paris ; Je l'ai eu tous les jours chez moi ; il étoit devenu doux, souple, humble, décent jusqu'à la pudeur ; témoin perpétuel de la tendresse de mon mari, de son esprit et de son enjouement, admirateur zélé de l'opulence, il me fit remarquer pour la première fois celle qui m'entoure, ou du moins jusqu'alors elle n'avoit fait sur moi qu'une sensation désagréable " (*Lettres diverses recueillies en Suisse*, par le Comte Fédor Galovkin, pp. 265, 266 : Geneva, 1821).

[2] Theophilus Bolton, who was making the tour with Mr. Holroyd and Major Ridley, died of consumption at Genoa.

[3] Son of Sir Matthew Ridley, Bart., Major in the Welsh Fusiliers. He had served in Germany during the Seven Years' War, and was at this time Mr. Holroyd's travelling companion.

47.

To James Scott, Esq.

January the 14th, 1766.
At Miss Lake's, St. James's Place, an indifferent lodging.
2 Guineas a week. I fancy I shall not stay in it.

DEAR SIR,

I should have wrote to Beriton last post, or even (which I might have done) the post before. I am sorry at present to have so disagreable an excuse for the shortness of my present letter as a new attack in my shoulder, which has confined me to my lodgings yesterday and to-day. If I am not better to-morrow I will certainly have advice about it.

Mrs. Porten has not been well but has recovered. I have met Guise in town with his whole family, who have been exceedingly civil to me.—To-morrow (if I am able) I shall introduce d'Eyverdun[1] to Miss Comarque at the new play, to which she has obliged me to contribute a ticket. The number of separations encrease daily. They talk of Lords and Ladies Bolingbroke,[2] Warkworth,[3] Grosvenor,[4] Sr. James Lowther and Lady,[5] Mr. &

[1] M. Deyverdun had known Gibbon at Lausanne, and from 1766–69 was a frequent guest at Beriton. With his assistance Gibbon published the *Mémoires Littéraires de la Grande Bretagne pour l'an* 1767 (Londres : Chez T. Becket and P. A. de Hondt dans le Strand, 1767), which were discontinued in 1768, when Deyverdun, on his friend's recommendation, left England as tutor to the son of Sir T. Worsley, afterwards the Right Hon. Sir Richard Worsley. In 1783 Gibbon took up his abode with Deyverdun at the latter's house at Lausanne. Deyverdun died in July, 1789, leaving his house and land by will to Gibbon for his life.

[2] Lady Diana Spencer married in 1757 Frederick St. John, Lord Bolingbroke, the "Bully" who figures in George Selwyn's correspondence, from whom she was divorced, March 10, 1768. Two days later she married Topham Beauclerk, grandson of the first Duke of St. Albans, the friend of Dr. Johnson, and the collector of a magnificent library. During his long illness she nursed him, as Johnson, no friendly witness, admits, "with very great assiduity." He died in 1780. Lady Diana, whose skill as an artist is frequently alluded to by Walpole, died in 1808.

[3] Hugh, Lord Warkworth, eldest son of Sir Hugh Smithson, Bart., of Stanwick, who was created Duke of Northumberland in 1766, married July 2, 1764, Lady Anne Stuart, third daughter of the Earl of Bute. They were divorced in 1779. As Earl Percy he served in the American War at the battle of Lexington and elsewhere.

[4] See note to Letter 126.

[5] Sir James Lowther, Bart., first Earl of Lonsdale, married (1761) Lady Mary Stewart, eldest daughter of the Earl of Bute, and sister of Lady Warkworth.

Mrs. Onslow, &c. (would you believe it ?) Sr. M. & Lady F. Soon,
Dear Sir, I will write more at large, till when believe me,
Most truly yours,

E. G.

48.

To his Stepmother.

Miss Lake's in St. James's place, January the 18th, 1766.

DEAR MADAM,

I have the pleasure of assuring you that my Rheumatism (or what else you chuse to call it) has again sounded a
retreat & left me quite well. However I do still intend to consult a physician by way of precaution, & I think that Physician
shall be Heberden.[1] I have seen a number of servants, but
believe I shall pitch upon one who seems very clever without
having anything of the fine Gentleman, & whose demands surprize
me only by their reasonableness. I wrote to his last master at
Bath four or five days ago, & expect an answer with some impatience.—I believe I mentioned in my last that I was to introduce
d'Eyverdun to Miss C. at the play. They saw each other : the
Lady with some apparent pleasure ; the Gentleman with as little
horror as could be expected. I presented him, proposed a visit,
pressed for time & place ; & am by her own appointment to
carry him to pass the evening with her next Monday. The rest
must depend on himself. As to myself ; I hardly know myself
as yet, in this immense City ; & to speak honestly am not as
yet very highly entertained. I have had some invitations &
expect more, but I must acknowledge, I sometimes regret the
small parties where an acquaintance may pass the evening & sup
without form or invitation. I have however candor enough to
lay these defects rather upon the confined circle of my friends
than on the general manners of the Metropolis. Society (no

---

[1] Dr. William Heberden (1710–1801), one of the most famous physicians
of the century, and a distinguished scholar. He was called by Dr. Johnson
" Ultimus Romanorum " (a title which might be as justly applied to Sir
H. Halford), as being " the last of our learned physicians." He is hailed by
Cowper as " virtuous and faithful," perhaps because, as Dr. G. B. Hill
suggests, he bought and destroyed an unpublished manuscript by Dr.
Middleton on *The Inefficacy of Prayer.*

doubt) may be very agreable here, but the avenues to it are fortified with some care, and I wish I may be able to muster up that
modest assurance which is so necessary to force them. Several
more of my acquaintance Up park, Port Elliott, Hartley,[1] are
however come or coming to town & may serve to enliven it.
The public diversions are a great ressource, and the Cocoa Tree[2]
serves now and then to take off an idle hour. I am not even
without hopes of being enrolled in the School of Vice which,
notwithstanding the terrors of its name, is as agreable and I
believe as innocent a Club as any in this Metropolis. What I
want the most, is to be taken off the town and to get into private
keeping. You may guess I mean my old scheme of boarding in
a genteel family. You know I have talked of Toriano. I wish
it may succeed, but the very situation of the man which makes
it so agreable makes it likewise very difficult. Things must
be treated with a degree of delicacy. An acquaintance must be
formed, and I shall not think this winter ill-spent if it lays a good
foundation for next. In the mean time I am looking out for
something to stay my stomach. I have heard of a house near
Leicester fields which appears tolerable, and of another near Soho
whose very situation excludes it.

We wait for Tuesday Sevennight with impatience. Mr. Pitt
is in Town and spoke a great while last Tuesday. He is the
declared Advocate of the Colonies, but a very equivocal one of
the present ministry ; tho' great compliments passed between him
& Conway.[3] The debate yesterday (which lasted till nine in the

---

[1] Up Park, near Stansted in Sussex, the seat of Sir Matthew Feather-
stonhaugh, F.R.S., formerly M.P. for Morpeth, at this time M.P. for Ports-
mouth; Port Eliot, St. Germans, Cornwall, that of Gibbon's cousin, Mr.
Edward Eliot, M.P. for Liskeard, afterwards for Cornwall, created in 1784
Baron Eliot of St. Germans; and Hartley Manduit that of Sir Simeon
Stuart, M.P. for the county of Southampton.

[2] Under Lord Bute, the Ministerial Club, as it was at first called, used to
meet at the Cocoa Tree Tavern, in St. James's Street. In 1745 it had been
the great resort of the Jacobites. Gibbon describes a supper at the club
in his Journal for November, 1762. [*Memoirs of My Life and Writings—
Miscellaneous Works*, vol. i. p. 154 (second edition, 1814).] By the "School
of Vice" it is more than probable Gibbon meant White's Club, formed in
1736, at this time the great Tory gaming club. It contained within its
walls an Old and a Young Club, the Old being recruited from among the
members of the Young. Hence, perhaps, arose its name of the "School of
Vice."

[3] The Stamp Act, charging stamp duties on all legal documents executed

evening) was on printing the American papers. The friends to
secresy, thought it much better only to leave them upon the table
for the inspection and copies of about 500 people.—Almost all
the separations come to nothing except that of L. & Lady B. which
has taken place already.

I forgot upon the study table some maps which I want to
make up into an atlas. Will you be so good, Dear Madam, as to
collect all the French or Latin loose maps in the study and send
them to me by the first opportunity. Pray do not despise me so
far as to give me no commissions.

I am, Dear Madam,

Most truly your's and my father's,

E. GIBBON.

49.

To J. B. Holroyd, Esq.

Beriton, April 29th, 1767.

DEAR LEGER,

*I happened to-night to stumble upon a very odd piece
of intelligence in the St. James's Chronicle ; it relates to the
marriage of a certain Monsieur Olroy,[1] formerly Captain of Hussars.
I do not know how it came into my head that this Captain of
Hussars was not unknown to me, & that he might possibly be an
acquaintance of yours. If I am not mistaken in my conjecture,

in the Colonies, received the royal assent March 22, 1765, and came into
operation November 1, 1765. When Parliament reassembled on January 14,
1766, Pitt attacked the policy of the Act. General Conway, one of the
Secretaries of State, who replied to him, said that the sentiments which he
had expressed were substantially those of the ministers, and that, for his
own part, he would gladly resign his office if Pitt would take it. Grenville,
who followed, defended the Act, and it was in reply to him, on the same
evening, that Pitt delivered one of the most eloquent and famous of his
speeches. Ireland took a keen interest in the question, and the debate
happens to be fully reported by two Irish gentlemen, Sir Robert Dean and
Lord Charlemont; otherwise, like many others of the time, it might have
passed without record. In the same session, February 24 to March 17, two
resolutions were carried in both Houses, one declaring the right of Great
Britain to tax the Colonies, the other repealing the Stamp Act. Two Acts
of Parliament expressed these resolutions in legislative form.

[1] The name was so spelt in the newspapers. John Baker Holroyd
married in 1767 Miss Abigail Way, only daughter of Lewis Way, of Richmond,
Surrey.

pray give my compliments to him, & tell him from me, that I am
at least as well pleased that he is married as if I were so myself.
Assure him, however, that tho' as a Philosopher I may prefer
celibacy, yet as a Politician I think it highly proper that the
species should be propagated by the usual method ; assure him
even that I am convinced, that if celibacy is exposed to fewer
miseries, marriage can alone promise real happiness, since domes-
tick enjoyments are the source of every other good. May such
happiness, which is bestowed on few, be given to him ; the
transient blessings of beauties, and the more durable ones of
fortune, good sense, and an amiable disposition.

I can easily conceive, and as easily excuse you, if you have
thought mighty little this winter of your poor rusticated friend.
I have been confined ever since Christmas, and confined by a
succession of very melancholy occupations. I was scarce got to
Beriton, where I only proposed staying about a fortnight, when
a brother of Mrs. Gibbon's died unexpectedly, tho' after a very
long and painfull illness. We were scarce recovered from the
confusion which such an event must produce in a family, when
my father was taken dangerously ill, and with some intervalls has
continued so ever since. I can assure you, my dear Holroyd,
that the same event appears in a very different light when the
danger is serious & immediate ; or when, in the gayety of a
tavern dinner, we affect an insensibility that would do us no
great honor were it real. My father is now much better ; but I
have since been assailed by a severer stroke—the loss of a friend.
You remember, perhaps, an Officer of our Militia, whom I sometimes used to compare to yourself. Indeed the comparaison
would have done honor to any one. His feelings were tender
and noble, and he was always guided by them : his principles
were just and generous, and he acted up to them. I shall say
no more, and you will excuse my having said so much, of a man
you had not the least knowledge of ; but my mind is just now so
very full of him, that I cannot easily talk, or even think, of
any thing else. If I know you right, you will not be offended
at my weakness.

What rather adds to my uneasiness, is the necessity I am
under of joining our Militia the day after to-morrow. Tho' the
lively hurry of such a scene might contribute to divert my ideas,
Yet every circumstance of it, and the place itself, (which was

that of his residence,) will give me many a painful moment. I know nothing would better raise my spirits than a visit from you ; the request may appear unseasonable, but I think I have heard you speak of *an uncle* you had at Southampton. At all events, I hope you will snatch a moment to write to me, and give me some account of your present situation & future designs. As you are now fettered, I should expect you will not be such a *Hic et ubique*,[1] as you have been since your arrival in England. I stay at Southampton from the 1st to the 28th of May, & then propose making a short visit to town ; If you are any where in the neighbourood of it, you may depend upon seeing me. I hope then to concert measures for seeing a little more of you next winter than I have lately done, as I hope to take a pretty long spell in town. I suppose the Goat[2] has often fallen in your way : He has never once wrote to me, nor I to him : in the Country we want materials, and in London we want time. I ought to recollect, that you even want time to read my unmeaning scrawl. Believe, however, my dear Leger, that it is the sincere expression of a heart entirely yours.*

E. GIBBON.

50.

To his Stepmother.

Southampton,[3] May the 8th, 1767.
My birth-day. May I have many happy ones. Amen.

DEAR MADAM,

The post is really going out, at a most inconvenient hour, half after nine in the morning, and as usual I neglected writing the night before. All I can do now is to express the joy I received by your accounts of my father's improvement in point of health, and to return you some portion of joy, by telling you, that on Wednesday morning Mrs. Harrison was safely delivered

---

[1] The motto of the regiment of light dragoons, called Royal Foresters, in which Mr. Holroyd had been captain, and which was disbanded in 1763.

[2] A nickname for Mr. Guise.

[3] At Southampton Gibbon attended every spring the monthly exercise of the militia, of which, by the resignation of his father and the death of Sir T. Worsley (1768), he eventually became lieutenant-colonel commandant.

of a boy. Both mother and child are in the fairest way—The
bay horse is sold—the post chaise tempts one very much.

I am, Dear Madam,

Most truly yours,

THE MAJOR.

51.

To his Father.

Newport, I. of W., December the 1st, 1767.

DEAR SIR,

Here I am, and how much longer I may stay in this
little island, Lord knows. Jemmy Worsley is still at Guernsey
upon Election business. I have passed four or five days at
Stenbury with only Sir Thomas, his son, and Jemmy's sister,
rather quietly indeed than agreably. Last night we were
summoned to Newport quite unexpectedly, & this morning Sir
Thomas is gone to Newtown with three Lawyers in order to fix
the boundaries of some borough lands ; I expect him back to
dinner, as it is the monthly club of the island, & I fear will be
a drunken day. Upon the whole this is to me a very unpleasant
scene, but I am engaged in it & I can scarce tell how to get
away from it. The first step after the conveyances of my
borough land are finished, is to oblige the Mayor (Holmes
himself) to swear me in a burgess of Newtown ; for the constitution of that borough is of a very mixed nature. Man-
damus's for this purpose are every day expected from the King's
bench ; so that, should I leave the island *pendente lite*, I might be
recalled the next day. It is however some comfort that my
conscience will be less burthened than I expected. We were both
mistaken as to that terrible oath which regards only freeholds in
Counties.

As to our success or possibility of success you will excuse my
entering into particulars, especially upon paper & by the post.[1]

---

[1] Parliament was dissolved March 11, 1768, and the elections took place
in March. Gibbon seems to have assisted the Worsleys in the Isle of Wight
against the Castle interest and that of the Holmes family. In 1586, when
the Crown sought to create a parliamentary party in the House of Commons,
six members were returned to Parliament by the three boroughs of Newport,
Newtown, and Yarmouth, because in the Isle of Wight, through its military
captain and governor, the influence of the Crown was paramount. Gradually

In general we are sanguine, especially at Newtown.   Affairs are incomparably well managed by the advantage of having a great lawyer acting for himself.   He hurries things thro' the courts with a expedition that is rather uncommon in law proceedings. The enemy contrived however to insert into our friend's advertisement a most curious *quaere* which you have probably seen. The printer will ask pardon or be prosecuted.   Power as well as art is employed.   Yesterday we learnt that Captain Lee, who refused to promise his vote, was turned out of the government of Carisbroke Castle, (ten shillings a day) and the place given to Captain Holmet.   It seems to occasion a great outcry, and may perhaps do them more harm than good.

I am, Dear Sir,

Most truly your's and Mrs. Gibbon's,

E. G.

52.

To his Stepmother.

London, April the 18th, 1768.

DEAR MADAM,

The reason I have delayed (besides the usual one) was the real scarcity of news either of a publick or a private nature. As to myself I got safe to town, and have lived there in my usual manner; the Romans,[1] Boodle's,[2] the Theatre and some acquaintances whom you already know.   In all these places nothing new or interesting has occurred.   Ranelagh[3] is indeed opened.   I was

the leading families of the island acquired control over the three boroughs, and at this period they were disputed by the Worsley, Barrington, and Holmes families, the latter being descended from Sir Robert Holmes, who took New York from the Dutch, and "first bewitched our eyes with Guinea gold." At the election of 1768 the following members were elected for the respective boroughs:—Newport: Hans Sloane, Esq., and John Eames, Esq., one of the Masters in Chancery. Newtown: Sir J. Barrington, Bart., and Harcourt Powell, Esq. (re-elected). Yarmouth: Jervoise Clarke, Esq., and William Strode, Esq.

[1] A convivial club, meeting once a week, established by Gibbon and other travellers.

[2] Gibbon was a member of Boodle's Club, known as the *Savoir vivre*.

[3] Ranelagh Gardens, now part of Chelsea Hospital Gardens, stood on the site of a villa belonging to Lord Ranelagh, the Jones of Grammont's *Memoirs*. The Rotunda, an amphitheatre, with an orchestra in the centre, surrounded by "balconies full of little alehouses," was opened to the public May 24, 1742. The last entertainment given there was the installation ball

there last night for the first time. Notwithstanding the brilliancy
of the first moment, I must own I think it very soon grows
insipid to a by-stander, or by-walker if you like it better. I
acknowledge it indeed the most convenient place for courtships of
every kind. It is certainly the best market we have in England.
Lord Abingdon [1] is just going to make a pretty considerable
purchase; of Miss Warren, Mrs. Fitzroy's sister. The Lord wants
money, the Lady a title, so that as the bargain seems advantageous
to both parties we apprehend it will speedily be concluded.

I will not trouble you with election news, as it is both dull
and uncertain. I must however mention that I have seen
Serjeant Glynn, [2] who is encouraged by the Sollicitor General [3] to
pursue his petition, and who flatters himself that the Duke of
B. will lend his weight, and that the D. of G. will stand neuter.
He is strongly of opinion that Sir Thomas should be in town to
make interest, and *has intended for some time past* to write to the
Baronet who sleeps at Pilewell. The opponents (*without intending
anything*) have already canvassed most of the members. Indeed
there seems to be a general dislike to petitions (of which there
never was known so great a number), and I think most of the
returned members have a very good chance unless they are
attacked by formidable men. Such is the case of Preston [4]
fought by Lord Strange, and such I fear will be the case of
Yarmouth ; many people at least have a bad opinion both of our
cause and of our interest. [5] I do not think this can be called

of the Knights of the Bath in 1802. The gardens were closed in 1803. A
staple, fixed in one of the trees of the avenue, preserved, till a few years ago,
the traditions of the glories of Ranelagh when the gardens were lighted by
a thousand lamps.

[1] The Earl of Abingdon married, on June 7, 1768, the daughter of
Admiral Sir Peter Warren.

[2] Serjeant Glynn, well known as the advocate of Wilkes, was afterwards elected as second member for Middlesex at a by-election. He married
a daughter of Sir J. Oglander, of Nunwell, in the Isle of Wight, and had been
an unsuccessful candidate for one of the Isle of Wight constituencies at the
general election of 1768.

[3] John Dunning, afterwards Lord Ashburton.

[4] Sir Peter Leycester and Sir Frank Standish were found, November 29,
1768, not duly elected.

[5] The return for Yarmouth, I.W., was amended by order of the House of
Commons, dated January 19th, 1769, by erasing the names of Jervoise Clarke
and William Strode, and substituting those of George Lane Parker and
Thomas Lee Dummer.

carrying the three boroughs in the isle of Wight. Northampton
will be attacked and defended with great vigour and expence.[1]
That will be the second act of Lord H.'s Tragi-Comi-farce. As
Osborn & Rodney have exactly all the same votes, if Howe succeeds,
there must be a new election of a second member, and in that case
the two Noble Lords may probably quarrel about the man, which
may compleat the third act of the said farce. I shall say nothing
of Wilkes;[2] every man has his story and his opinion, which
mutually destroy each other. Wednesday will decide most of
these disputes, and you may depend on my immediately writing
some particulars of that great day. Lord B.'s tryal[3] is not yet
come out. I will take care to send it with _La Princesse de
Babylone_,[4] a new Romance of Voltaire which is a very agreable
absurd trifle. A propos, poor Voltaire is almost ruined. He had
intrusted most of his money to that expensive scoundrel the Duke
of Wirtenbergh,[5] who paid him a much greater interest for it than
anybody else would give. The Duke is ruined, the security worth

[1] On February 14, 1769, Sir George Osborne was found not duly elected,
and Thomas Howe was declared duly elected. The return of Sir George
Rodney was held to be valid. A note by Sir Denis le Marchant, appended
to Lord Orford's _Memoirs_, states that the expenses of the contest and petition
cost Lord Spencer £70,000.

[2] John Wilkes was expelled from the House of Commons in January,
1764, and outlawed in the following August. He returned to England in
February, 1768, and was at the bottom of the poll for the City (March 23).
He headed the poll for Middlesex, March 28, 1768. His outlawry was
reversed as technically illegal by the Court of King's Bench in the same
year; but his two convictions for republishing No. 45 of the _North Briton_,
and the _Essay on Woman_, were affirmed, and he was sentenced to two years'
imprisonment. He was expelled the House February 3, 1769; re-elected
February 16 and expelled February 27; re-elected March 16 and expelled
March 17. At the election on April 13 he polled 1147 votes to the 296 of
Colonel Luttrell; but the House resolved (April 15) that the election of
Wilkes was void, and Luttrell duly elected. He was discharged from his
imprisonment in 1770.

[3] Lord Baltimore was charged with decoying to his house a young
milliner named Sarah Woodcock, and with rape. On February 12, 1768, he
was committed for trial at the spring assizes at Kingston, and acquitted in
the following March.

[4] "Il y a," writes Madame du Deffand to Walpole, speaking of _La
Princesse de Babylone_ (April 3, 1768), "quelques traits plaisants, mais c'est
un mauvais ouvrage, et, contre son ordinaire, fort ennuyeux."

[5] During Gibbon's stay at Lausanne in 1763, the duke, brother of the
reigning duke, occupied a villa called La Chablière, a short distance from the
town.

nothing and the money vanished. Voltaire has dismissed several dependants who lived in his house, and even his niece Madam Denys, all with handsome presents ; and keeps only a man and three maids, with Père Adam an old Jesuit that plays at chess with him from morning to night. I am really sorry for the poor old man ; as he spent his fortune much better than he acquired it.

I hear Sir Simeon[1] is confined with the gout to Hartley. The reputation of his new Physician is quite ruined by it.

I am, Dear Madam,

Most truly your's & my father's,

E. Gibbon.

53.

To James Scott, Esq.[2]

Beriton, December the 20th, 1768.

Dear Sir,

Some particular and very urgent reasons, oblige me as well in my own name as in those of my father, and Mrs. Gibbon, to request your immediate presence at Beriton. Your own interest is deeply concerned, but what (I am convinced) will be a much more powerfull inducement, you will have an opportunity of adding a most essential obligation to those which your friendship has already conferred on our Family. As we have now a very pressing occasion for your advice and assistance, we shall flatter ourselves with the hopes of seeing you Friday evening.

I am, Dear Sir,

With the truest regard,

Your most sincere Friend and obedient humble Servant,

Edward Gibbon, Junior.

---

[1] Sir Simeon Stuart, Bart., M.P. for the county of Southampton, died in November, 1779.

[2] The bulk of the letters for the years 1768 and 1769 relate to the pecuniary affairs of the Gibbon family. Mr. Gibbon was the owner of estates at Maple Durham, in the parish of Beriton near Petersfield, at Lenborough in Buckinghamshire, and a house, garden, and lands at Putney. He had also inherited shares in the New River Company, and other investments. But he had for years lived beyond his income, and it was only to the wreck of this fortune that the historian succeeded in 1770.

54.

To his Father.

January the 2nd, 1769.

DEAR SIR,

We got safe to town. In my way I delivered the Lease to Fletcher with proper instructions. To-morrow we shall proceed on business with all possible dispatch. I have nothing to add more than that Wilkes is just chose against Bromidge, 285 to 69.[1] Such is the spirit of the times.

I am, Dear Sir,

Most truly yours,

E. G.

55.

To his Father.

January the 5th, 1769.

DEAR SIR,

Southouse (with whom Mr. Scott and myself passed three hours this morning) has examined the Putney Writings. I wish I could say he was satisfied with them. The former Deeds (while it was yet a Copyhold) he thinks of little or no consequence. The Deed of Enfranchisement is what he principally wants, nor is it sufficient that it may be enrolled in Chancery or in the Wimbledon Court Rolls. The Deed itself formerly in your possession is what he wants, for, says he, any purchaser would naturally be allarmed at it's not being to be found, and would immediately suspect that some incumbrance (perhaps for your life only) had been contracted on that security. I hope and sincerely believe that meer accident or neglect has deprived us of this important writing, but as it is so important, we must beg you would recollect all you can about it, and if possible give us some clue which may lead to a discovery of it.

There are later papers which he likewise calls for, an authenticated copy of my Grandfather's Will, your Marriage Settlement,

---

[1] On January 2, 1769, Wilkes was chosen alderman of the ward of Faringdon-Without against Bromwich, a paper-maker on Ludgate Hill.

both with my mother and with Mrs. Gibbon. He wants to be acquainted with the extent and nature of the fine and recovery passed by us ten years ago. The Counter Part of Gosling's Mortgage must be in your hands, and he thinks the sight of it *absolutely* necessary. In a word, unless everything is laid before him, we are only losing our time, and it is impossible to carry anything beyond meer speculation, not only with regard to any general Plan, but even in respect to the immediate money we may want. Whatever can be got either from Public officers or from the Goslings, &c., he will get, but he judges it both safer and cheaper that the materials should be laid before him, than that he should be forced to fish them out. He asked me questions about the Attornies employed in those several transactions, and wishes he could see any of their bills, which would inform him of what had been done. The several leases which actually subsist between you and any Tenants should be produced. In a word, he is of opinion that nothing can be done without the whole is probed to the bottom.

I must therefore desire that you would immediately send up every thing that can give any light into our affairs. As to Putney in particular, I must beg you would order Newney to deliver to my order the leases relating to that Estate. As soon as I have got some more materials I am again to see Southouse. I hope they will be speedily in Town, as an expensive Residence here is neither convenient nor at present agreable.—I have just received an answer from Boissier, who can make no offer as he is not acquainted with our terms, but declines an interview, and thinks it may suit other people better than himself.

I find the Chancery business cannot be got off, but it may be so easily delayed that there is no present apprehension from it. I hope to hear from you by the return of the post, and to receive *as soon as possible* every thing you can find. Mr. Scott is a most zealous friend, and on this as well as on every other occasion you shall ever find me most truly yours,

E. G.

56.

To his Father.

DEAR SIR,

Since my last we still go on, tho' indeed rather slowly. All that I can say is, that our slowness neither proceeds from our own negligence, nor even from the dilatoriness of Law, but merely from our having been destitute of the necessary Writings. Southouse has been very active, and has already seen Stephen Harvey, Gosling's Attorney and Mrs. Williamson. The two former (tho' he has a just idea of Harvey) promise the free use of all that is in their hands. The last has wrote to her brother & hopes the Deed may be recovered from him, notwithstanding he is so odd a man. Harvey believes he may have the Counterpart of the Mortgage. In a word, we are to meet again next Wednesday, when Southouse thinks we shall be in a condition to offer some security for the money we immediately want, as well as to trace the outlines of our general Deed of trust. As I find I cannot be a Party in it, I should wish to substitute my uncle Porten as Joint-Trustee with Mr. Scott.

We should be glad to receive as soon as Possible Mrs. Gibbon's marriage Articles ; In relation to which I shall not *forget* the conversation we had in the Study. It is my duty as well as my inclination to consider her in the light of a real Mother. 2. The Abstract of the Deeds in Gosling's hands ; Hervey, who thinks he has the counterpart of the Mortgage, is positive he delivered you this Abstract. 3. The Title, (whatever it is), by which we possess the Copper share, or at least some account of the Writings relative to it. To these particular enquiries I must add a general request of searching out any thing that may give us any new lights. You have (for instance) made some little purchases about Beriton, the title to which cannot be included in the general writings of the Manor, &c. For any thing of that kind the Cocoa Tree is a surer direction than my obscure lodgings (which are still those of Sir Thomas's), but I think it would be still better to send them at once to Mr. Southouse, Attorney at Law, Milk Street, Cheapside. I have already received and transmitted to him, the Putney Leases (Vane's signed). Yesterday I had a letter from John Harris, with some particulars of the Buckinghamshire Estate.

I find Southouse a true man of business ; civil but determined to know everything. He questioned me very plainly about my change of Religion, of re-conversion to which I gave him very satisfactory answers. Indeed he will know everything.

I think, Dear Sir, you must be easy after what he said of the Chancery affair. I asked with some anxiety how long it could be staved off. What does that signify ? answered he. We shall have the Money before it is wanted.

Depend on it, Dear Sir, we do not wish to flatter you with vain hopes (indeed to what end could they serve ?) and let this consideration dispell the Fantom which torments you and makes me so unhappy. Endeavour as far as lies in your power to reassume both a chearfull heart & and a chearfull countenance. They are indeed necessary to your health as well as to your Credit.

As for myself, I shall only say that as I cannot be happy, without your being so, I am willing to make every reasonable sacrifice to your tranquillity. The only restraints I shall wish to impose on you are such as will be conducive to our common Good. Perhaps it had been better for us all, had I insisted on them some years sooner.

> I am, Dear Sir,
> Most truly yours & Mrs. Gibbon's,
> E. G.

57.

To his Father.

DEAR SIR,

We had this morning a long conference with Southouse, who complains very much of the obscurity of our affairs, which is so great he cannot as yet form even a clear Idea of the difficulties which surround us. These difficulties however and the delays which they produce are chiefly owing to your neglecting either to keep or to send us the necessary writings.

Let me beg of you, Dear Sir, not to suffer any indolence or false delicacy to prevent your going to the bottom of your affairs. The time of temporary expedients is now passed. Nay, without a compleat knowledge of things, hardly anything can be done even at present, for as to borrowing any money on the Putney Estate,

Mr. S. thinks it not practicable till a clearer title is made out. He desires you would immediately send up the Writings of the Copper share ; as that is unencumbered it may form part of a basis for some temporary security. We will do every thing that can be done, but these obstacles are not to be so easily surmounted.

I am very unhappy at not being able to send you, *for the present*, a more favorable account, and am the more unhappy as I fear you will even magnify every difficulty, and really make things worse by the state of your own mind. Upon that head, Dear Sir, what can I say ! what have I to add on so melancholy a subject. Your health, your credit, Mrs. Gibbon's health and peace, (I feel for what she must have suffered) my own ease and fitness for any business, all depends on your resolution.

I am, Dear Sir,

Most truly yours,

E. G.

We have not yet got the Deed of Enfranchisement nor will even Mrs. W. discover her brother's habitation, but we hope to trace him out & prevail with him.

58.

To his Stepmother.

January the 21st, 1769.

DEAR MADAM,

Tho' I have nothing to add to my letter to my father, I cannot forbear writing a few lines to ask [how] you do yourself. I am too well acquainted with your sensibility not to have some fears. Send me some particular account of my poor father, his style makes me very unhappy : perhaps not the least so of the three ; for it is very irksome to wear a perpetuall mask of gaiety.

You will see, Dear Madam, how much we have laboured, and how little we have done. For God's sake, for all our sakes, press my father to recollect everything, to look out everything & to send us everything that he can. All our difficulties proceed from former carelessness.

I am, Dear Madam,

Most truly yours,

E. G.

59.

To his Stepmother.

London, January 31st, 1769.

DEAR MADAM,

I am glad to say that my father's fears from my silence these last two posts were without foundation, & am sorry to say that the hopes you conceived from it were not better founded. The truth really was that I wrote nothing because I had not anything to write. Yet we had not been idle. I have seen and talked to W., who answers the idea I had of him tho' not the character his sister gave of him. She represented him as a shy melancholy man, he is on the contrary a very sottish but dissipated man. On my applying for "G," he immediately produced an Alphabetical Index of Joe Taylor's papers—Nothing was there recorded under the name of Gibbon except some old things of my grandfather's relating to the Duc d'Autem privateer. He promised to make a further search & I am to call on him to-morrow, but I hope very little from him. I shall venture to talk of some gratuity, but in the mean time, we wish my father and yourself would recollect & search whatever can be found.

My father's last letter distressed me very much. He talks of my having doubts & suspicions. Whatever unguarded expressions may have dropped from me, I hope my past conduct & my present designs are far from deserving the reproach of doubts & suspicions. At the same time it is true, that tho' neither myself nor Mr. Scott nor even Mr. Southouse have any doubts, yet if we want to sell, or even to borrow money on the Putney Estate, any Purchaser will demand, 1st The Deed of Enfranchisement, & 2nd My Aunt Elliston's release for £2000 due to her, & charged by my grandfather on the said Putney Estate. It appears indeed by that will that of his eleven copper shares, six were left to my aunt Gibbon, five should therefore be still my father's property, and yet there appears only one & that sold to my father by Mrs. Elliot.

Mr. S. thinks it absolutely necessary that my father should come up next week to execute on that occasion, & at the same time his presence may be usefull to us in other respects : I hope in my next letter to be able to appoint the day for his coming up.

The Chancery Affair can easily be deferred till the clear title to Putney is made out, and if my father will not encrease our difficulties by his own fears we shall yet be happy.

I am, Dear Madam,

Most truly yours,

E. G.

60.

To his Father.

February 23rd, 1769.

Dear Sir,

I scarce thought that our present melancholy situation could receive any addition of uneasiness, but the displeasure your last letter expressed, convinced me that the meer blows of fortune are trifling when compared with the unexpected reproaches of those we love.

Since my arrival in Town Mr. Scott and myself have been constantly employed on the general plan which will, I flatter myself, give ease and security to us all. Mr. Southouse has almost finished the rough Draught of our Deed of Trust, the basis of all our solid hopes. The many delays which have occurred have never proceeded from our carelessness. So far from wishing to expose your name, I consulted S. on the practicability of omitting the particular Schedule, and a method has been agreed on—When that deed of Trust is finished, which will be, I hope, in a very short time, we shall desire your presence in town. I shall execute writings by which I make myself liable to near eight thousand pounds Debt. You will then be able to make use of Mr. Scott's money, & we shall find means to answer the Chancery Demands. As yet your credit is unhurt, and your own fears have been the only importunate Creditor. After this, Dear Sir, give me leave to ask whether your last expression that you are *still affectionately* was not somewhat severe.

I should be truly insensible if the steps you talk of taking in the Country did not *already* alarm me. They made me pass a very cruel night. The very obscurity of your language terrified me. What can those steps be? I must however say, that should you intend to procure an immediate supply, by any extraordinary methods, both Mr. Scott and myself must think ourselves disengaged from any promise, and our whole plan is entirely dissolved.

I have wrote, Dear Sir, from a full heart, for which I make no apology. It is by actions, not by words, that I shall ever seek to prove how truly I feel for yourself and poor Mrs. G., and how ardently I wish to make you, if possible, happy.

61.

To his Father.

London, March the 4th, 1769.

DEAR SIR,

The discovery of Williamson's papers, tho' in itself a most pleasing event, is however productive of some delay as well as trouble. Besides the Deed of Enfranchisement there are two very large boxes of writings, many no doubt very trifling, but some which certainly are, and others which possibly may be, of importance to us. Southouse will examine them with all possible diligence, but from the new matter which arises, he is obliged for a very few days to suspend the Deed of Trust, and during that time, as he has daily occasion to see me, he insists on my not leaving Town ; for which reason you must excuse me, Dear Sir, from accepting at present the interview which you desire, at Beriton.

Our plan is still the same as what seemed to be agreeable to your Wishes : To devote the Hampshire and Putney Estates to the payment of your debts, to convey the Copper and New River Shares to my use (on my giving up my present annuity of £300 p. annum) and to reserve the Buckinghamshire Estate for your support. Mr. Scott's £900 will be ready on the signing the Deeds, and we can *now* make out so good a title to Putney, that the disposal of it will be a matter of neither delay nor difficulty.

The only proposed alteration was that you should allow me to have the nominal possession of the Buckinghamshire Estate, subject to pay You the whole real profits of it in the form of an annuity to you, and the Estate itself chargeable with Mrs. Gibbon's jointure. The very harsh Reception this proposal has met with from you has given me the deepest concern, as I am conscious of the rectitude of my intentions & still persuaded of the propriety of

the measure. My motives could be only such as were both fair &
even kind. The nominal property of land could afford me no
pleasure, the *real management* of it must be attended with some
trouble. I am willing, nay desirous, to put it absolutely out of my
power to sell, mortgage, or alienate the smallest portion of it, and
wish to bind myself by the severest ties that the Law can invent,
to pay you regularly half yearly, a method which must be easy to
you and may sometimes be inconvenient to me—But I shall proceed no farther on a Subject which appears so disagreeable to you :
I hope indeed I have the less occasion to do it, as Mr. Scott's last
letter must have cleared up some passages of his first, which did
not strike you immediately in their true meaning.

I shall not, Dear Sir, swell this letter, with any vain protestations. I now see the fairest prospect of future ease and
tranquillity. During the course of this unfortunate transaction I
have endeavoured to have the approbation of my own conscience,
and of our real friends Mr. Porten and Mr. Scott. I flatter myself
that I shall one day obtain yours.

I am, Dear Sir,
Most truly yours and Mrs. G.'s,
E. GIBBON.

62.

To his Father.

Pall Mall, March the 22nd, 1769.

DEAR SIR,

It is impossible for me to express how much your last
letter surprized and grieved me ; as well from the particular
contents of it, as from the general strain of resentment &
dis-satisfaction which runs thro' the whole. To be accused of
neglect, of indifference, of unjust insinuations are reproaches,
which I can only bear because I am conscious of not having
deserved them. I wish to look forwards, & if at any time I
look back, it is only where such a retrospect, however unpleasant,
becomes necessary.

Our Deed of Trust has ever been considered by us all as the
Great Basis of our future conduct, & Mr. Porten, by our mutual
consent. We were to empower them to sell the Hampshire and
Bucks Estates, & to reconvey to us the Remainder (after
payment of Debts, &c.) on certain conditions, which have been

more than once explained. Such was the clear sense of this Deed, which I thought had been long since understood by us all. Indeed to put that sense into a Legal form was not in our power. Southouse is doing that, and it was thought as necessary as it is usual, that the Attorney's work should be revised by a Lawyer of some note, Mr. Pechell, a Master in Chancery and particular friend of Mr. Porten. To these four persons only, the two Trustees, one Attorney and one Council, has the affair been exposed.

With regard to my possessing the Buckinghamshire Estate in fee, irrevocably charged with your annuity and Mrs. G.'s jointure ; it was what, after the maturest consideration & the most disinterested advice, I cannot depart from. Should I ever be idiot enough to sell it whilst so heavily burdened, no such act could in the least affect your settled annuity or Mrs. G.'s jointure. I am however willing to give you my word of honor, that I will never sell or mortgage any part of it during your life ; and that I will immediately make a Will, by which (supposing I should die without children before you) I leave the Estate to you in fee simple. If any legal restraints can be devised, (other than such as make me for ever a meer life Tenant) I will consent to them with pleasure : I will do more, I will try to discover them.

So far, Dear Sir, from neglecting our immediate occasion for money, the Trustees are impowered to borrow whatever sums may be wanted before the Estates can be disposed of. But I must add that till the Deed is executed nothing can be done, and that you are therefore the Cause of the Delays with which you reproach us. I am the more sensible of a speedy dispatch as the Chancery affair cannot be put off much longer.

I am, Dear Sir,
Most truly yours,
E. GIBBON.

63.

To his Father.

London, March the 31st, 1769.

DEAR SIR,
According to your request I communicated your last proposals to our common friends. I must acknowledge that we all discovered many strong and almost insuperable difficulties in

it ; many of which related even to your own comfort and happiness, which will ever be a very principal consideration. But I
shall not at present trouble you with our objections ; as we
should not have time to execute this new scheme, however eligible
it might be ; at present every thing is nearly finished. The
Hampshire Deed is almost engrossed, the B[uckinghamshire] is
now before Council, and I can venture to assure you that in the
course of next week, I shall be able to write in order to fix the
positive day for your's and Mrs. G.'s coming up. Should we now
adopt your Proposal, every thing must begin again *de novo*, and
several weeks would elapse before we should be reinstated in our
present situation.

With regard to your last questions, I can now positively say
that neither household furniture nor stock are comprized in the
Deed, tho' we expect and depend on your word of honor, that the
latter, and such of the former as is not wanted, will be faithfully
applied by yourself to the same common purposes.

I believe I mentioned some time ago, that the particulars
of Debts will not be described in the Deed of Trust, but in
a private Schedule referred to therein. You will be so good,
Dear Sir, as to prepare and bring the materials of it with you.
The List you gave me at Beriton must already have suffered
some alterations, both as Debtor and Creditor. Besides Clarke's
Debt is as yet unknown.—Indeed it will be necessary that
previous to your coming up, you should send the Deeds of Copyhold (if any) and College Holding which we have not at present.
We should likewise be glad to hear your sentiments still further
with regard to Putney. The practice of Advertising is universal,
and it is in vain to think of secrecy.

I am, Dear Sir,

Most truly your's & Mrs. G.'s,

E. G.

64.

To his Father.

April 13th, 1769.

DEAR SIR,

Mr. Southouse whom I saw yesterday tells me, that I
may desire the favor of your company, with Mrs. G.'s, next
Thursday evening. He thinks that Friday and Saturday mornings

will suffice for our immediate business. As to the place, I should be glad to know whether you choose my lodgings or wish me to look out for any other place.—Should any thing (which I do not foresee) happen to defer your coming up, I shall take care to give you timely intelligence.—It is very difficult to say any thing positive as to money till we have finished writings, &c. However as to the C. affair, Mr. Scott will answer for it.

Mrs. G. distresses me every way.—I am truly concerned that it should be necessary for her to come up, at a time when I can easily conceive the state of her mind & spirits; but I am still more embarassed from her generous obstinacy. The sum of her Jointure is left in blank. Should she still object to the encrease of her Jointure, I must leave it as an engagement not of law, but of honor, of gratitude and of inclination.

You may depend on another letter by Sunday, till when

I am, Dear Sir,

Yours most truly,

E. G.

65.

To his Father.

April 18th, 1769.

DEAR SIR,

I waited till to-night before I took Lodgings, as I was not sure of your intentions. To-morrow morning I shall look out for one. I apprehend Suffolk Street or that neighbourhood will be at once private and convenient.—You will of course come in by Hyde Park Corner, and my servant shall attend at my lodgings at Mr. Taylor's, Grocer's, opposite to the Duke of Cumberland's, Pall Mall, to conduct you to your lodgings, where I shall immediately attend you. I should think that you had better not arrive till towards five o'clock, when Sir R. will be gone to dinner.

I am, Dear Sir,

Most truly yours,

E. G.

66.

To his Stepmother.

Thursday night, Cocoa Tree.

DEAR MADAM,

I was a good deal alarmed with your letter of yesterday, and as much pleased with that of to-day, which dispelled my uneasiness : before you receive this I flatter myself that my father will be quite recovered. I have seen Wentzel,[1] who very obligingly took my guinea to tell me that he could tell me nothing about my father's case without seeing him. On that head he was very cool and very fair ; a decay of the optic nerve, he said, was sometimes tho' seldom to be removed ; as to the opinions of our surgeons he treated them with infinite contempt.

I am glad that our Meeting was attended, that things may end with a good grace. Sir Simeon has been so dangerously ill with the gout, that I have not yet settled my resignation. Henry will attend next Tuesday.

I am, Dear Madam,

Most truly yours,

E. G.

67.

To his Father.

London, June the 1st, 1769.

DEAR SIR,

I am sorry that I cannot give you more pleasing accounts of our progress in the Putney affairs, but we find people very cool, and tho' many applications are made, yet nobody as yet has spoke seriously and to the point. We attribute this general slowness in a great measure to the vague description of an Estate seven miles from London, &c., and heartily wish you would allow us to particularize place, name, &c. Boissier has been over to S.'s at Wimbleton. It plainly appears that he wishes to buy, but to buy cheap, and that, notwithstanding his polite professions,

---

[1] The Baron de Wentzel was the most famous oculist of the day, and the discoverer of operations for cataract. He died in London in 1790.

he will do all in his power to keep off all other purchasers. Considering all these rubs, we could very much wish that you would set about giving us the particulars of the Hampshire Estates, that the summer may not steal away upon us, without any things being done.

I am much concerned to hear from Mrs. Gibbon that your Operation has not produced any good effects, tho' we could hardly expect any alteration in so short a time. As soon as we see a little more clearly into what can or cannot be done as to Putney, I propose coming down, as I wish to see you and Mrs. Gibbon, and I am sure London has now no charms for me.

I am, Dear Sir,

Most truly yours,

E. G.

We wish to know upon what terms your Putney Tenants who have no leases (Bateman, I think, & Stewart) hold their land and what they pay.

P.S.—If you think I can be of more service at Beriton than in London, I will attend you as soon as our Militia meeting is over, for till then I think I cannot decently be in Hampshire.

68.

To his Stepmother.

London, June 22nd, 1769.

DEAR MADAM,

Before I received your last letter I was displeased with myself for having been so long silent, and yet I should have been still more displeased if I had wrote, as I could say nothing that was agreable, nothing but what must lower my father's spirits as they every day do mine. Tho' we have had many enquiries about Putney, yet nothing like an offer has presented itself. We must therefore think of Beriton, and tho' I do not wish to complain, I must say that we are all surprized at my father's seeming indifference on that occasion. We feel for the situation both of his eyes & his spirits, but still we are surprized.—Things indeed draw so near a crisis that some resolution must be taken. Mr. Scott & Mr. Porten propose entering upon it next Week, and think my presence necessary. As soon as something is settled you may depend either on seeing me at Beriton, or at least on hearing every particular which can interest the common cause.

I am, Dear Madam,

Most truly yours & my father's,

E. G.

69.

To his Father.

Pall Mall, August the 17th, 1769.

DEAR SIR,

We have agreed with Mr. Wood for the £8500, the rents and profits till Michaelmas excepted. The writings are sent to his Lawyer's to-day, and as there is no difficulty in the title, we may look upon the affair as concluded. Our friends were clearly of opinion that the measure is prudent, and, every thing considered, I could not avoid being of the same opinion. But I shall say the less on that head as they propose writing themselves very soon. They wish me to remain here till Wood's Lawyer has signified his approbation. I hope to be with you Sunday, as I find myself in a far greater solitude in Town than at Beriton.

I am, Dear Sir,

Most truly yours,

E. G.

70.

To J. B. Holroyd, Esq.

Beriton, October 16th, 1769.

*MY DEAR HUSSAR,

I received your agreeable Missive about two days ago; and am glad to find that, after all your *Errors*, you are at last a settled man.[1] I do most sincerely regret that it is not in my power to obey your immediate summons. Some very particular business will not at present permit me to be long absent from Beriton. The same business will carry me to town, about the 6th of next Month, for some days. On my return, I do really hope and intend to storm your Castle before Christmas, as I

---

[1] In 1769 John Baker Holroyd purchased from Lord de la Warr the estate of Sheffield Place in Sussex.

presume you will hardly remove sooner. I should be glad to meet Cambridge ;[1] but the plain dish of friendship will satisfy me, without the seasoning of Attic Wit. Do you know any thing of Guise ? Have you no inclination to look at the Russians ?[2] We have a bed at your Service. Vale.

Present my sincere Respects to those who are dear to you ; Believe me, they are so to me.

Do I direct right to East Grinstead ? *

71.

To J. B. Holroyd, Esq.

Boodle's, Ten o'Clock, Thursday Evening.
[Dec. 1769.]

*DEAR HOLROYD,

My schemes with regard to you have been entirely disapointed. The business that called me to town was not ready before the 20th of last month, and the same business has kept me here till now. I have, however, a very strong inclination to eat a Christmas Mince-pye with you ; and let me tell you that inclination is no small Compliment. What are the trees and waters of Sheffield-place compared with the comfortable smoke, lazy dinners, and inflammatory Junius's, which we can every day enjoy in town ? You have seen the last Junius ?[3] He calls on

---

[1] Richard Cambridge (1717–1802) married in 1741 Miss Trenchard, and in 1751 settled at Twickenham in a villa which became the resort of many of the most distinguished men of the day. In 1751 he published the *Scribleriad*, a poem in six books, and from 1753 to 1756 wrote essays for the *World*. He was an intimate friend and old schoolfellow of Dr. Cooke, the father of Mrs. Way, sister-in-law to Mrs. Holroyd. Gibbon, accepting one of Mr. Cambridge's invitations to Twickenham, speaks of the Thames as an "amiable creature." On his way he was upset into the water, and obliged to return home. The ducking was, said Cambridge to Miss Burney, " God's revenge against conceit " (Madame d'Arblay, *Diary and Letters*, ii. 278).

[2] On October 2, 1769, the *Annual Register* notes that "part of the Russian fleet cast anchor at the mouth of the Humber. The whole fleet, consisting of twenty ships of the line, is to rendezvous at Spithead, where one or two straggling ships are already arrived. This fleet was separated in a storm, but has received no considerable damage."

[3] The letters signed "Junius" began to appear in the *Public Advertiser* on January 21, 1769: the last was published on January 21, 1772. The letter to which Gibbon alludes is that dated December 19, 1769, addressed

the distant Legions to march to the Capital, and free us from the
tyranny of the Prætorian Guards: I cannot answer for the
ghost of the '*Hic & ubiques*,' but the Hampshire Militia are determined to keep the peace for fear of a broken head.*—After all,
do I mean to make a visit next week ? Upon my soul I cannot
tell. I tell every body that I shall. I know that I cannot pass
the week with any man in the world, with whom the pleasure of
seeing each other, will be more sincere or more reciprocal. Yet
between you and [me] I do not believe that I shall be able to get
out of this town before you come into it. At all events I look
forwards with Great impatience to Bruton Street and the
Romans.

Believe me,
Most truly yours,
E. GIBBON.

72.

To J. B. Holroyd, Esq.

Pall-Mall, December 25th, 1769.

DEAR HOLROYD,

Some Dæmon, the enemy of friendship, seems to have
determined that We shall not meet at Sheffield-place. I was fully
resolved to make amends for my lazy scruples, and to dine with
you to-morrow ; when I received a letter this day from my
father, which irresistibly draws me to Beriton for about ten
days. The above-mentioned Dæmon, though he may defer my
projects, shall not however disapoint them. Since you intend
to pass the winter in retirement, it will be a far greater compliment to quit active, gay, political London, than the drowsy desert
London of the holydays. But I retract. What is both pleasing
& sincere, is above that prostituted word *compliment*. Believe
me, most sincerely yours.

A propos, I forgot the compliments of the season, &c. &c.

to the king. " The prætorian bands, enervated and debauched as they were,
had still strength enough to awe the Roman populace ; but when the distant
legions took the alarm, they marched to Rome and gave away the empire."
The point of the allusion is the case of Major-General Gansel (September 21,
1769), who, after being arrested for debt, was rescued by a sergeant and file
of musqueteers, acting under command of an officer of the Guards.

73.

To his Stepmother.

DEAR MADAM,

I only write two lines to tell you that Mrs. Elliot designs a visit to Beriton in her way to Cornwall. Perhaps she will be with you Tuesday, but I think Wednesday at farthest, and from my having really forgot it last night's post, my letter may perhaps be of no use. I am just come from an Excursion out of town with them. We are grown wonderfully intimate.

I am, Dear Madam,

Most truly yours,

E. G.

There can be no difficulty in using the Chaise ; as you must have paid the year beforehand.

74.

To his Stepmother.

Pall Mall, three o'clock.

DEAR MADAM,

I got to Godalming at half past nine, to Epsom (Lockwood was in town) at twelve and over Westminster Bridge at two, pretty good travelling ! I am perfectly well, very hungry and

Ever yours,

E. G.

75.

To his Stepmother.

Pall Mall, Saturday night.

DEAR MADAM,

The little Curate gave me the other day the pleasure of hearing you were perfectly well, I send two lines to return the same assurances with regard to myself. The Levite is now at Chatham, but will have his ears regaled next week, after Clarke and myself are returned from Holroyd's, whither we intend to run down to-morrow. In the midst of our amusements I shall consult the Oracle.—D'Eyverdun is not come back, nor has he replied a syllable to six letters of mine and Sir R.'s.[1] Lord Chesterfield, tired with waiting and fruitless enquiries, has sent his heir abroad under another Governor. I pity our friend, but fear he will not be able to justify himself either to his friends or to his own judgment. Jolliffe[2] has bought an excellent house in Little Argyle Street, very cheap. I had the honour of seeing in it *Madame la Mère*; vastly like one of the elderly ladies in Mackbeth. She was wonderfully gracious to me.

Adieu, Dear Madam,

E. G.

76.

To his Stepmother.

Pall Mall, Thursday evening.

DEAR MADAM,

I wrote last night with twenty people round me, and reperusing your letter this morning, I found I had only forgot to answer the most material part of it ; *the pews.* The thing itself is utterly indifferent to me, but as Sir Hugh has the Manor, I think the compliment is properly due to him, and I will write to him for that purpose to-morrow.

I am, Dear Madam,

Most truly yours,

E. G.

77.

To his Stepmother.

Pall Mall, February 17th, 1770.

DEAR MADAM,

Laziness and procrastination are poor excuses for silence ; yet such as they are I am too often forced to employ them. However at this time, I was partly satisfied by the frequent [accounts] I received from Beriton both by Pitman's journey &

---

[1] Gibbon and Sir Richard Worsley were endeavouring to obtain for M. Deyverdun a tutorship. He eventually went abroad with the young Stanhope, afterwards Lord Chesterfield.

[2] Probably Mr. Jolliffe, M.P. for Petersfield, and a country neighbour of Gibbon. He married, in November, 1769, the only daughter and heiress of Sir R. Hylton, Bart., of Hylton Castle, Durham.

the channel of Mr. Porten ; and I might perhaps have remained still longer in my Lethargy, had I not been rouzed by the unaccountable fate which your last letter has met with. Thro' some strange jumble between Mr. Porten's servant, the maid & Luke, it has dropt somewhere by the way. This *upon my honor* is the exact truth ; so that if there was any thing in it which requires a particular answer I must intreat you to repeat it.

Baron Wentzel is at last arrived, but says himself that he is at present overwhelmed with business. I submit it to my father and yourself, whether it may not be better to wait till he shall be somewhat more at leisure.

This great public scene is still as noisy & as nonsensical as ever. Particulars would be endless, & indeed the papers are now so daring that they almost forestall any private intelligence. Conjectures I leave to men more idle or more busy than myself. However the general opinion is that the next fortnight must decide the fate of the ministry.[1] If Lord North (whose spirit & abilities are certainly great) holds out till then, the minority will probably divide, desert, & run away.

A more agreable piece of private news relate to our old arrears, which we are in a fair way of recovering as the North already have. Abbot is in town and we are pushing the affair. This will amount to about £100 for myself, & near double for my father, and with this I close my Militia service. I have already conversed with Sir Simeon & propose resigning in a few days. However I will come to the meetings, if I am absolutely necessary, & should be glad to know the days.

I am, Dear Madam,

Your's & my father's,

E. G.

---

[1] On the 9th of January, 1770, the Earl of Chatham returned to public life, from which he had retired in October, 1768. His reappearance, and his attacks upon the Government, determined the Duke of Grafton, who had succeeded him as Prime Minister, to resign office. On January 28, Lord North, who was already Chancellor of the Exchequer, accepted the post of First Lord of the Treasury, which he held for eleven years.

78.

To his Stepmother.

Pall Mall, March the 20th, 1770.
Two o'clock in the afternoon.

DEAR MADAM,

You and my father know already that I have not obeyed your summons, but you do not know that it was impossible for me to obey it. Your letter was received at the Cocoa-tree yesterday afternoon, but was not sent to my lodgings till after I was gone out to dinner. I dined, went down to the House of Commons, staid out a very long debate, & was not in bed till four o'clock this morning. When I got up about twelve, I perceived your letter; but it was then much too late, since had I set out immediately I could not have reached Petersfield before ten o'clock at night. If this accident has prevented any meeting, I am really sorry for it, & will readily come any other day that it can be adjourned to. But I still flatter myself that my father found himself better than he expected.

The debate I mentioned was upon the Remonstrance :[1] it was carried, 284 against 127, that questioning the legal existence of Parliament is highly unwarrantable, tending to sedition and an abuse of the right of petitioning. To-day they go upon a most loyal address of lives & fortunes, after which a severe censure of the Mayor & Sherifs is expected ; but as the nature of that Censure has not transpired, so the consequences of it cannot be foreseen.

I am, Dear Madam,
Most truly yours,
E. GIBBON.

[1] On March 14 the Lord Mayor (Beckford) presented to the King at St. James's "an Address, Remonstrance, and Petition of the Lord Mayor, aldermen, and livery of the city of London," praying for the dissolution of Parliament as not representing the people, and for the removal of "evil ministers." On March 15 a motion was carried by 271 to 108 for a copy of the Remonstrance to be laid on the table of the House. On March 19 it was resolved by 284 to 127 that the Remonstrance tended to disturb the peace of the kingdom. Beckford died June 21, 1770.

79.

To his Stepmother.

Pall Mall, April 19th, 1770.
A good voyage to the Nabob.

DEAR MADAM,

Pitman was a monkey to alarm you about me. I was indeed troubled last week with something not unlike my old complaint, a difficulty of breathing and a soreness upon the breast and stomach. As it was attended with a good deal of pain and feaverish heat, I sent for Dr. Turton, a young but very sensible Physician, (Mr. Eliott employs him likewise) & who I believe has every requisite except those of gravity & a tye-Wig. He set me up very soon, but I have since had a return, & upon the whole he thinks it is growing into something of an intermittent feaver : if that should prove to be the case, he intends throwing in the bark : In the mean time I live low & keep a good deal at home. I hope my father's complaints will be of no more consequence than mine.

Believe me, Dear Madam,
Most truly yours,
E. G.

80.

To his Stepmother.

Pall Mall, June the 26th.

DEAR MADAM,

Your Wastecoat is most universally admired, and I shall be much obliged to you for another exactly the same. I hope to pay my respects to Mr. and Mrs. Gould (to whom I beg my compliments) some time next week, but cannot yet fix the day. In the meantime I am in wonderfull haste, just going to Vauxhall. [1]

Dear Madam,
Ever Yours,
E. G.

[1] The Spring Gardens at Vauxhall (properly Fulke's Hall, the manor of Fulke de Breauté) were formed in the reign of Charles II. From 1732 onwards, under the management of Jonathan Tyers, the music, vocal and instrumental, and the masquerades, or *Ridottos al fresco*, attracted the fashionable world of London. The gardens were closed in 1859. The name of their enterprising manager is preserved in Tyers Street.

81.

To James Scott, Esq.

Beriton, July the 3rd, 1770.

DEAR SIR,

We are very happy to find by your last letter, that your health and spirits are in so very good a state. I sincerely wish, that it were in my power to return you as favourable an account of my poor father, but indeed I apprehend him to be in a very bad way. Within these ten days or fortnight he has been much worse than before. Dr. Cuthbert was sent for last night from Portsmouth and has just left us. He is convinced that my father's disorder must end in a dropsy, and fears that his liver is affected. He neither eats nor sleeps, and is indeed very ill. You may judge that Mrs. Gibbon & myself are very far from being easy or happy.

Such an account, Dear Sir, promises you but little amusement at Beriton, yet it is in such times that the company of a real friend is the most acceptable. Yours would be most truly so to us all, and particularly to myself. There are other subjects, which it is as cruel to press, as inconvenient to neglect. I can hardly venture to say that your presence would produce any effect, but I am too well assured, that without your presence nothing can be done.

I am, Dear Sir,

Most truly yours,

E. G.

82.

To J. B. Holroyd, Esq.

Beriton, August the 9th, 1770.

DEAR HOLROYD,

I am much obliged to you for persisting to court a friend who has the appearance of neglecting you. But when you are told the reason of it, you will rather pity than blame me. It is my poor father's illness that confines me here, and cannot permit me to stir till the affair is decided : a confirmed Dropsy and Asthma which have either produced or been caused by a general decay of the constitution allows us no hope of his recovery.

You may easily suppose that I am in a very improper frame of mind for the easy flow of a familiar epistle. I shall therefore only speak to business. The men I spoke of are the two Smiths, the father who lives at Havant, and the son who lives at Wickham in this county. Both, especially the son, are famous for surveying and valuing *Timber* (the surveying land is a separate branch, and quite out of their way). My father has always had reason to be satisfied with their skill and honesty. Their price for surveying is a guinea a day, or so much in the pound (I don't know exactly what) if they sell the timber. I will make any further enquiries you desire, and in the meantime, wish you would sometimes raise my spirits by a friendly salutation.

I am, Dear H.,

Most truly yours,

E. G.

83.

To James Scott, Esq.

Beriton, November the 6th, 1770.

DEAR SIR,

You, who have passed the summer with us, and a melancholy one it has been, are more sensible than any one else can possibly be, how difficult it is to give any account of my poor father. If I had wrote last week, I should have said that he was better than when you left Beriton, not indeed as to strength, but in regard to spirits, appetite, and sleep, the last of which was indeed procured him by a very gentle opiate of Mrs. Gibbon's. Now, on the contrary, I think him much worse. His breath is very bad, he is greatly swelled, and this morning had a fainting fit, which alarmed us exceedingly.

I am very much obliged to you and Mr. Porten for obtaining this delay from the G[osling]s, and hope the interest will be paid as it ought. Should my father be a Little better, I shall try to steal up to London next week, and the more so, as I am very desirous of seeing Mr. Porten.

May health and amusement attend you at Bath. If any thing

should happen that could be either *agreable* or *necessary* for you
to know, you may depend on hearing from me.

I am, Dear Sir,

Most sincerely yours,

E. G.

84.

To James Scott, Esq.

Beriton, November the 13th, 1770.

DEAR SIR,

Yesterday evening, about six o'clock, it pleased God to
take my poor father out of the World.   My situation and that of
poor Mrs. Gibbon will excuse my saying any more on the melancholy occasion, than that I am and ever shall be,

Dear Sir,

Most truly yours,

E. GIBBON.

85.

To J. B. Holroyd, Esq.

Beriton, November 18th, 1770.

DEAR HOLROYD,

The melancholy and long expected event of my father's
death happened last Monday the 12th instant.   The expectation
itself through the course of a very painful illness had in some
measure prepared me for it.   Yet notwithstanding these just
motives of consolation it has been a very severe shock.   The
multitude of affairs I find myself so suddenly involved in, will
not allow me to say when I can hope to wait on you, or indeed
what portion of the Winter I shall be able to spend in town.   I
must however go there next week on particular business.   I
should think myself very lucky, if, during my stay (which will be
about ten days) anything should call you to London.   I shall be
in my old Lodgings opposite to the Duke of Cumberland's, Pall
Mall.

Believe me, my dear Holroyd,

Most sincerely yours,

E. GIBBON.

86.

To his Stepmother.

Pall Mall, November 26th, 1770.
DEAR MADAM,

I hope that Mrs. Porten's Commission was executed to your satisfaction; I had mentioned to her the sending down the things ready made, but was told what I apprehended before, that without a measure it was not possible—Mrs. Williams,[1] as I understand from Mr. Scott, is ready to wait on you whenever you please, but till I know something more of Miss Massey, I have not made any offer of bringing the other down, nor do I well see how it will be possible for me to hear any thing from Essex in time, as I still propose being in Hampshire next Monday. I wish, my Dear Madam, that I may meet you in an easier state of mind, and that the justest regrets may by degrees receive relief from the power of reason and from that of time.

> Believe me, Dear Madam,
>   Most truly yours,
>   E. GIBBON.

I have had a letter from Northamptonshire, a very odd one.

87.

To his Stepmother.

Pall Mall, November 27th, 1770.
DEAR MADAM,

I went this morning with Mr. Porten to Doctor's Commons to take out letters of administration, a formality, as I found, indispensably necessary. There I was told, that before I could properly administer, a proxy, in the enclosed form, must be signed by you, in the presence of two Witnesses. If you will be so good as to return it by Thursday's post, the business will be entirely finished Saturday Morning.

I am sorry to find by a letter from Mr. Bayley, that you have not yet left your own room. Let me intreat you, Dear Madam,

---

[1] Arabella Mallet, a daughter of David Mallet's second wife, married Captain Williams, of the royal engineers. The second Mrs. Mallet was Lucy, daughter of Lewis Elstob, steward to the Earl of Carlisle.

to allow your friends to see you, and not to refuse the reliefs of
air and change of place. As to myself they have so good an
effect on *my* health, that were I to consult a Physician, I should
be at a loss what bodily complaint to alledge.

I am, Dear Madam,

Most truly yours,

E. G.

88.

To his Stepmother.

Pall Mall, December the 1st, 1770.

DEAR MADAM,

I was very happy to hear from Mr. Bayley to-day, that
you was returned to Beriton, & that after a first shock, which I
dread for myself, your reason began to prevail over what must
ever be lamented, but which cannot be recalled. You are, I am
sure, my Dear Madam, so well convinced of my sentiments, and
I am so conscious myself of the weakness of reflection and
argument, that I shall say no more on the subject.

Finding that there were no hopes of Miss Massey, I called on
Mr. Scott this morning, and have, I believe, engaged Mrs.
Williams for the middle of next week. This morning I was at
Doctors' Commons, all was perfectly right, and what was added
proved quite superfluous. Some things that could not be finished,
as well as a little uncertainty about the time Mrs. Williams can
be ready, will defer my departure till about Wednesday or
Thursday. There are many reasons why I wish to return to
Beriton, as soon as I can.

I am, dear Madam,

Most truly yours,

E. GIBBON.

89.

To James Scott, Esq.

Pall Mall, December the 4th, 1770.

DEAR SIR,

I have now been about ten days in town. The scene
of Beriton was too melancholy to support, and with respect to
health as well as to spirits I found a change of scene and air

absolutely requisite. Mrs. Gibbon went for a few days to Bayley's, who, both husband and wife, have behaved in the most friendly manner on the occasion. To-morrow I propose returning to Beriton, and shall carry with me Mrs. Williams, a daughter of Poet Mallet, whose lively company will I hope contribute to divert poor Mrs. Gibbon during the gloom of the Winter.

With regard to business, you are sensible, Dear Sir, that it is not yet in my power to say much about it. The most pressing part I have attended to, and the interest to Goslings will be entirely paid by next Saturday. The next month which I shall spend at Beriton will afford me time and opportunity for looking into the state of it, the profits and expences of the farm, the value of the Estate, and the probable encrease of it in respect to timber; I hope to return to town with such materials as may enable me rationally to decide which of the Estates it will be most prudent to part with. At present I incline (and it seems to be very much Mr. Porten's sentiment) towards keeping and letting Beriton. As soon as a resolution is taken, not a moment should be lost in the execution. I shall always hope, Dear Sir, for the continuance of your advice and friendship, and beg that you would believe me,

Most sincerely yours,
E. GIBBON.

90.

To his Stepmother.

Pall Mall, December the 4th, 1770.

DEAR MADAM,

I write only two lines just to say that I hope to dine with you Thursday in company with Mrs. Williams : but as the time still depends on that Lady, whose notes to Mrs. Scott are far from sufficiently clear, I still look upon it as somewhat uncertain, whether I may not be kept here a day or two longer. In the mean time, believe me, my Dearest Madam, with every wish that friendship, duty or gratitude can suggest,

Most truly yours,
E. GIBBON.

91.

To his Stepmother.

Pall Mall, December 5th, 1770.

DEAR MADAM,

Mrs. Williams who has just left me came to me in order to say that it was impossible for her to be ready before Saturday. I could not refuse her so short a delay. Every thing is now settled, and I cannot foresee any thing that can prevent our dining at Beriton next Sunday. The disapointment really vexed me : both because I think my presence at Beriton proper and even necessary, and because I am impatient to see you again,

Believe me, Dear Madam,

Most truly yours,

E. GIBBON.

92.

To his Aunt, Miss Hester Gibbon.

December, 1770.

DEAR MADAM,

In the midst of the justest affliction nothing could afford me a greater consolation than your kind letter : as it convinced me that the nearest relation of my poor father shared my grief, and still interested herself in my future Welfare. Some immediate business which called me to town prevented my answering it directly, nor indeed did I find myself able to enter so soon into the melancholy detail which you are desirous of hearing.

The first affliction with which my father was visited, was a gradual decay of sight, which at last terminated in an almost total blindness. With his sight he lost almost every pleasure of life, as he could no longer enjoy the country nor attend to the business of the farm, in which for many years his chief amusement and occupation had consisted. Tho' he bore this severe stroke with surprizing fortitude and resignation, yet the effect it had on his health and spirits began to alarm us very much, when last spring we were still more terrified by the symptoms of an approaching dropsy : a shortness of breath, swelling of the legs and body and the loss of rest, strength and appetite. The Physician who attended him encreased our apprehensions by confessing his own difficulties, as he was well assured that Mr. G.'s constitution could not support the usual methods external or internal, which might otherwise be proper for his disorder. In the month of August however a favourable Revolution seemed to happen. Dr. Addington,[1] whom a friend in London consulted, advised the use of broom ashes. They immediately produced a very great evacuation of Water, reduced my father's legs and body to their natural size, and for a while gave us very great room to hope, tho' our hopes were at the same time mixed with so many fears as prevented us from writing to any of our friends at a distance. My father himself kept us from taking such a step, by insisting that Mrs. Eliott should not be acquainted with his situation, for fear her tenderness should bring her to Beriton and expose him to an interview to which his strength and spirits were not equal. At length, Dear Madam, after several turns in his disorder, which all gave him a temporary relief, without in the least restoring his strength, my poor father was on Tuesday the 6th of last month taken with a fainting fit. They returned several times during the week with more or less violence, but during the intervals between them he was perfectly easy and composed. The fatal one of Monday the 12th began about Noon and lasted near six hours, tho' we have every reason to think that he suffered very little in the last struggle. Nature was entirely exhausted and his disorder, whatever appearances it might assume, was a total decay of the constitution.

Long before the melancholy event my father was sensible of his approaching end, and prepared himself for it with the truest resignation ; besides his private prayers he was attended by the Clergyman of the Parish, from whom he received the Communion, who testified the highest satisfaction in his edifying behaviour. But my father's best preparation was the comfort of a well-spent life. He was followed to the grave by the tears of a whole country which for many years had experienced his goodness and charity.

[1] Anthony Addington (1713–1790), father of the Prime Minister, was originally a physician at Reading. In London he became Chatham's doctor, and was in 1788, after his retirement from practice, consulted on the condition of George III., whose early recovery he alone predicted.

There is one circumstance indeed which I would conceal even from you, were it possible to conceal it from the World. Economy was not amongst my father's Virtues. The expences of the more early part of his life, the miscarriage of several promising schemes, and a general want of order and exactness involved him in such difficulties as constrained him to dispose of Putney, and to contract a mortgage so very considerable that it cannot be paid unless by the sale of our Buckinghamshire Estate. The only share I have ever taken in these transactions has been by my sensibility to my father's wants and my compliance with his inclinations, a conduct which has cost me very dear, but which I cannot repent. It is a satisfaction to reflect that I have fulfilled, perhaps exceeded my filial duties, and it is still in my power with the remains of our fortunes to lead an agreable and rational life. I am sensible that as no Estate will answer the demands of vice and folly, so a very moderate Income will supply the real wants of Nature and Reason.

I have now, Dear Madam, gone thro' the heads of what I apprehended to be most interesting to you. Should there be any other points, about which you wish for farther information, I shall esteem myself happy in giving you all the satisfaction in my power, as well as in embracing every opportunity of convincing you, with how much truth and regard

I am, Dear Madam,

Your affectionate Nephew and faithfull humble Servant,

E. GIBBON.

93.

To his Stepmother.

Pall Mall, January the 15th, 1771.

DEAR MADAM,

Since I have been in town I have done a good deal of business ; you easily guess the subjects, and as particulars will be long, I shall refer them to the time of my return to Beriton, which I hope and trust will be the latter end of next week. Let me only say that agreeable to your opinion I am getting the writings out of Southouse's hands.

I flatter myself, Dear Madam, that your health and spirits gain ground every day, and that Mrs. Williams's lively oddities

begin to entertain you. I beg you would present my respects to
her. She will soon perceive that her tooth-powder was not forgot.
Her Sister's play[1] was received last Saturday with great and
deserved applause. I tryed to see Cotti Sunday morning to
rejoice with him.

I am, dear Madam,

Most truly yours,

E. G.

94.

To his Stepmother.

DEAR MADAM,

Nothing was ever more judicious than your advice of
getting my writings out of the Old Fox's den. The difficulty he
gives me shews the necessity of it. I have not yet been able
either to get a word or a line from him; and Mr. Porten, whose
time is more taken up than ever, strongly dissuades me from
leaving town till they are in my power. Pray give my compliments to Mrs. Williams, and try to convince her that business
not pleasure, Writings not Ridottos[2] detain me here. One
comfort for her is, that the Manor Court was fixed for the 6th
of February, and that I suppose it will be necessary for me to be

---

[1] Madame Celesia's play of *Almida*, acted at Drury Lane.

[2] The *Ridotto al fresco* was introduced at Vauxhall in 1732. The word
is said to be derived from the Latin *reductus*, and to mean "music reduced
to a full score." It came to mean an entertainment of music and dancing,
and was used as a synonym for masquerades. Bramston, in *The Man of
Taste*, speaks of the way in which the use of a foreign word sanctioned
things which in plain English would have seemed objectionable—

> "In Lent, if masquerades displease the town,
> Call 'em ridottos, and they still go down."

The word survived in the *Redoutensaal* of Vienna and the *Redoutentänze* of
famous composers. Other authorities derive the use of the word from the
sense in which it is employed by Dante, *i.e.* a "shelter," or "place of refuge."
Hence it came to mean a "place of convivial meeting." In Udino's Italian-
French-German Dictionary (Frankfurt, 1674) the German equivalent is
given as *Spielhaus*. The transition from this to "ball-room" is not difficult.
Byron in *Beppo* correctly defines the popular meanings of the word—

> "They went to the Ridotto—'tis a hall
> Where people dance and sup, and dance again;
> Its proper name, perhaps, were a masked ball,
> But that's of no importance to my strain."

on the spot, two or three days at least before that most unpleasant meeting.

I should be much obliged to you, if you would send me by Saturday's Machine, the papers of Lenborough. I think it would be right to send up Lord Halifax's bill in order to have it accepted.

I am, Dear Madam,

Most truly yours,

E. G.

My compliments to the Calf.

95.

To his Stepmother.

January the 29th, 1771.

DEAR MADAM,

At all events you may depend on seeing me next Sunday. I hope sooner, but I fear that it will be difficult to assure it. In the meantime I hope you will assure Mrs. Williams that business not pleasure keeps me in this wicked town.

I have received Lord Halifax's Draught.

I am, dear Madam,

Most truly yours,

E. G.

96.

To his Stepmother.

Saturday night, half an hour past nine, '71.

DEAR MADAM,

Till this moment, it was my firm intention to set out to-morrow morning at seven o'clock. An unforeseen business has just arisen which will put off my journey till Wednesday. Messieurs Scott and Porten who are both with me desire their compliments. Thursday night I returned from Bucks, well, much tired, but *hugely* pleased with my Expedition.

I am, dear Madam,

Ever yours,

E. G.

97.

To his Stepmother.

Pall Mall, February the 2nd, 1771.
Dear Madam,

I have advanced with some care and some success in gaining an Idea of the Bucks Estate. The Tenants are at Will, and from a comparison with my rents with the neighbouring ones, particularly Lord Verney,[1] there is great probability that my Estate is very much underlet. My friend Holroyd, who is a most invaluable Counsellor, is strongly of that opinion.

I am at a loss what to say about Mrs. Lee's letter, as I do not well understand what you mean by her mistake, but if the account is fair and can be conveniently paid from the farm money, I think it would be right to satisfy her. However a short delay can make but little difference.

I am sorry to hear that William has the gout. My best wishes to him, respects to Mrs. Williams & compliments to the Calf.

> I am, dear Madam,
> Most truly yours,
> E. G.

98.

To James Scott, Esq.

Pall Mall, February 4th, 1771.
Dear Sir,

After passing the Christmas at Beriton, I returned to town about three Weeks ago. The friendly part you have taken in my affairs, would render me inexcusable, if I omitted to acquaint you with what has been done, as well as to consult you in relation to what ought to be done.

With regard to the Goslings I have paid them a full year's interest to last November. Seven hundred and forty-seven Pounds is a severe pull, and I told Clive in a jocose manner but with great truth, that if he was tired of being my Landlord, I was most heartily so of being his tenant.

---

[1] Ralph Verney, Viscount Fermanagh, and second Earl Verney in the Peerage of Ireland, formerly M.P. for Carmarthen, was at this time M.P. for Buckinghamshire. At his death, in 1791, the title became extinct.

In my last I expressed an inclination of parting with Lenborough rather than with Beriton, but in these complicated affairs,
so many opposite reasons combat each other that I now incline
to execute, if possible, the original plan. We always knew the
Bucks to be a most desirable Estate, but I am now convinced
that it is a very improvable one. My Lands are let at twenty-
three per acre, those of Lord Verney in the same parish and
intermixed with mine let for nine & twenty. See the difference.
$23\frac{1}{2}$, 29; £636, £785. And this account I had too from
John Harris, who seems frightened out of his Wits, for fear I
should raise the rents ; which it is always in my power to do, as
the Tenants are only at will, and without any leases. But I
shall soon know things more exactly, as a very trusty and able
man is sent down to value the Estate.

The Hampshire Estate on the other hand receives a great
drawback from the Woods and Manour ; the former produce no
interest, nor can I afford to wait the slowness of their growth ;
the latter, tho' extremely valuable to a Sportsman and Country
Gentleman, would be to me only a source of vexation, expence,
lawsuits, quarrels, &c. &c. &c.

In order then to proceed in that line, it was necessary to get
all those Writings, which old Southouse has kept these two years
without any receipt, that we might examine whether we had a
good saleable title. The old Gentleman has shewn a reluctance
in the restoring them which was very far from pleasing. The
best and perhaps the true motive is his carelessness of business,
and frequent stay in the Country, but even that was a sufficient
reason for taking my business out of his hands. I am strongly
recommended by Mr. Porten and other friends to employ Mr.
Newton, a man of character and ability, who has great experience
in the branch of buying and selling Estates. I shall not take
that or any other step of consequence without your praevious
approbation, and in case you have not any person in view I
should directly employ Newton. Southouse refuses to deliver up
the Copy of our Deed of trust, which was designed for the
trustees, without your order. Would it be disagreable to you, to
send us a line by the return of the post, directing him to deliver
up the Deed to your brother Trustee ?

As soon as I have put this business in train I shall return for
some time to Beriton, to compleat the surveys and other things

begun there. I say nothing of Mrs. G., as I presume you correspond with her.

I am, Dear Sir, with every wish for your health and amusement,

Most truly yours,

E. G.

99.

To his Stepmother.

Pall Mall, February 12th, 1771.

Dear Madam,

If the weather with you is only half as uncomfortable as it is in town, Beriton must indeed be a most dismal place. We are cut in two with the cold, and buried in the deepest snow that ever I saw in London. This circumstance makes my presence with you the less necessary, as it would not be possible for Brick-nall or any body else to do anything in the surveying way. As soon as I see a possibility I shall write to him to undertake it, and shall beg Hugonin to assist him with his directions. The Woods (an account of which he has given me) amount to £3500. It was about what I expected. I had a letter from Hugonin, to whom I excused me not attending the Court. He desires to become my tenant for a field. I am ignorant of circumstances, but *think* he would not ask anything improper.

The business of settling the Beriton title, with the Lawyer here, seems to be now the most urgent affair. I hope, but cannot promise, that by the end of next week it may be sufficiently advanced to allow me to come down. I most truly pity poor Mrs. W., and should think that if Beriton is so insupportable to her, she might come up by herself in the Machine. I hope her spirits, your health and Patton's gout are all better.

Will you be so good as to order Tregus up to town with the horse. He must bring him to Wisdom's Livery Stable, Park Lane, Hyde Park Corner, who is prepared to receive him.

I am, dear Madam,

Most truly yours,

E. G.

100.

To his Stepmother.

Pall Mall, February 25th, 1771.

DEAR MADAM,

Things advance so very slowly, that I propose to run down to Beriton for a fortnight, and shall certainly be with you Wednesday. It is therefore unnecessary to say any more at present, than that I beg you would not wait dinner for me, as it is very uncertain whether I shall arrive before Evening.

I am, Dear Madam,
Most truly yours,
E. G.

101.

To his Stepmother.

Grosvenor Street, Tuesday evening.

DEAR MADAM,

I write a very few lines with a very bad pen at a very late hour, to say that my cold is a great deal better, that I hope you will get some company at Beriton, were it even Miss Higgons, that I hope William has got the better of his gout, and that we are all in confusion with the Idea of sending a Lord Mayor to the Tower. I hope Bricknall is returned and that he goes on with vigour.

I am, Dear Madam,
Most truly yours,
E. G.

102.

To his Stepmother.

Boodle's, March 29th, 1771.

DEAR MADAM,

I have let slip some posts without writing, and I can hardly say why I have done so. Nothing of business has occurred ; I am sure you are well convinced how much I interest myself in your health, your amusements, how much I wish you had some company at Beriton. Why cannot you get the Roberts from the Isle of Wight?

As to my own cold it has at length been tired of keeping me company. The news of the town are great. You know that two wild beasts have been sent to the Menagerie in the Tower,[1] but such beasts are hardly worth speaking of.—Trcgus of course goes on breaking in the colt, and I hope with regard to that and everything else at Beriton you will be so good as to issue your orders, and to believe me

Most truly yours,
E. GIBBON.

103.

To his Stepmother.

Pall Mall, April 13th, 1771.

DEAR MADAM,

I am much obliged to you for the Certificate, but it came too late to be of any service to my poor Chaise. Whilst I was in the country, a regular process in the Exchequer (a matter of form) was commenced, and the date of the payment in the Country was too late. Mr. G. Scott whom I consulted read me a lecture on the heinous sin of cheating Government, and the business ended in my paying the tax with all its arrears, sixteen pounds.

Mrs. Denton's invitation gives me great pleasure, as I am persuaded that Bath, if you can settle there in a manner agreeable to yourself, will be a very proper and a very convenient place. I must add, though I hope there is no occasion to say it, that nothing in my power shall be wanting to make it so.

Are all the poor sheep at Havant dead of the rot? We are frightened in town with the apprehensions of famine, and it is said there is no probability of a tolerable harvest. Wheat in that

---

[1] On March 14, 1771, the House of Commons ordered that the printer of the *London Evening Post* be taken into the custody of the sergeant-at-arms. He was arrested by the messenger of the House under the Speaker's warrant; but was discharged from custody, and the messenger committed, by the city magistrates. For this breach of privilege Alderman Richard Oliver, M.P. for the City, was committed to the Tower by order of the House of Commons, March 25, 1771. The Lord Mayor, Brass Crosby, was committed on March 27.

melancholy prospect must be rising, and I should think—but I have no sort of business to think—and am sure you will give your order with a much more enlightened zeal for our Interest than I could possibly do myself.

Mrs. Eliot is in town, I dined with them last Sunday. They say, as usual, every thing that *is proper* on every occasion. The next day (Monday) I dined with Sir Matthew [Featherstonhaugh], and last night I passed in a gay varied scene called a Masquerade at Soho.[1] There will be another next week, at the Haymarket, and yet *we* have had no Earthquake.

> I am, dear Madam,
> Most truly yours,
> E. G.

104.

To his Stepmother.

Pall Mall, April 27th, 1771.

Dear Madam,

It is very near eleven o'clock, and you know that I am a very dry Writer. I only wish to tell you that I am well, and that I hope you are so.

How do you like Sir John Dalrymple?[2] I hope Bricknall is not idle, and should think it high time for him to have done.

> I am, dear Madam,
> Most truly yours,
> E. G.

105.

To his Stepmother.

Pall Mall, May the 4th, 1771.

Dear Madam,

I am rather vexed than disappointed at the delays of the formal Mr. Bricknall. All men of business are like him when

---

[1] The Soho masquerades were given at Carlisle House by Mrs. Theresa Cornelys, whom Walpole calls "the Heidegger of the age." It was here that, the year before, the Duke of Gloucester appeared as Edward IV. with Lady Waldegrave as Elizabeth Woodville.

[2] Sir John Dalrymple published in 1771 the two first volumes of his *Memoirs of Great Britain and Ireland.* His style was parodied by Dr. Johnson, who said, "Nothing can be poorer than his mode of writing; it is the mere bouncing of a schoolboy!"

they know you cannot easily get out of their hands. Mr. Newton in town, tho' far preferable to old Southouse, is full of delays and avocations. I press him as much as I can to get through the Writings, and hope you will be so good as to do the same both in your own name and in mine with the aforesaid Bricknall.

You know that the country merely in itself has no charms for me, and I do not see *that as yet* my presence can be of any use. I therefore propose staying here the remainder of the month; towards the middle of it I shall see my friend Holroyd, who is obliged upon some particular business to make the tour of Ireland, Scotland and Yorkshire,[1] but who will certainly be at Beriton, as the active little man writes me word, by the end of June. By that time I hope we may persuade Mr. Scott to make us a visit, which may in many respects be of use. In the mean time I am only concerned at the solitary life you lead there, and though nobody that I know possesses more resources against the complaint of Ennui, yet I could wish you had more living company than Sir John Dalrymple. Surely Mrs. or at least Miss Roberts could come over. In the mean time I have sent you Robertson's book,[2] in which I think you will find much entertainment and information.

Mrs. Eliott, with whom I dined yesterday, told me she had just wrote to you. I suppose she acquainted you with the doubtful tho' pleasing suspense they are in since Colonel Nugent's death.[3] We are *amazing* friends, and I am actually employed in fishing out intelligence for them, by the means of my connections with Lord Berkeley.

> I am, with best *Wishes* to William,
> Dear Madam,
> Most truly yours,
> E. G.

[1] Mr. Holroyd owned property in Ireland, and at Greave Hall, near Ferrybridge, in Yorkshire.

[2] William Robertson (1721–1793) published in 1758 his *History of Scotland during the Reigns of Queen Mary and James VI.*, and in 1769 his *History of the Reign of the Emperor Charles the Fifth.*

[3] Lieutenant-Colonel Nugent, of the 1st Foot Guards, son to Viscount Clare, and groom of the bedchamber to the king, died at Bath, April 26, 1771. The Eliots were connected with Lord Clare through the Craggs family.

106.

To his Stepmother.

May the 13th, 1771.

DEAR MADAM,

I believe I must write to that old fellow Mr. Bricknall who cannot measure the Estate, *pour trois raisons ;* however in time he must finish it, and we are so far engaged with him, that there is no retreating. As to the Wheat, I think that there can be *no doubt* about selling at the present advanced price, but in that and every thing else I beg you would use your own judgment, and that you would be convinced how much I think myself obliged to you for using it. With regard to the Servants I could not avoid giving Richard a Livery, and think that the other servants ought to have theirs, at least of the slightest kind.

I am, dear Madam,

Most truly yours,

E. G.

107.

To his Stepmother.

Pall Mall, June the 1st, 1771.

DEAR MADAM,

I have deferred writing to you for some posts, in expectation of hearing of Mrs. Eliott's visit, who I find from Mr. E—— was still with you on Tuesday. The hour of eleven (the common excuse) only allows me time to say that I am well, and propose being at Beriton in eight or ten days.

I hope the eternal Bricknall is not idle, and must intreat you to quicken him. If Mrs. E. is still with you, I beg you would present my love and compliments. I am this instant come from a very agreeable dinner in Spring Gardens.

I am, dear Madam,

Most truly yours,

E. G.

108.

To his Stepmother.

June 11th, 1771.

DEAR MADAM,

I know you will excuse short letters, and that you are persuaded that the *expression* of my love and regard are very unnecessary. It was my intention to have been at Beriton next Sunday, but the Scotch affair of Mr. Lockwood & myself has just intervened. The final Deeds I have sent to King's Cliffe this post, nor can I leave town till Mrs. Eliott has returned them from Cornwall. I hope that before Sunday Sevennight, I may have the pleasure of assuring you how truly

I am, your

E. G.

109.

To his Stepmother.

Pall Mall, Saturday Evening, June 22nd, 1771.

DEAR MADAM,

Mrs. Hester Gibbon makes some very unmeaning difficulties about signing the Scotch Papers. I hope notwithstanding that Mr. Lockwood will be able to clear these up to her, and that it will be in my power, as it really is in my inclination, to dine at Beriton next Thursday. Unless you have any objection to it, I propose inviting Mr. Scott, as his company may be agreeable, and his advice of use to us.

I am, dear Madam,

Most truly yours,

E. G.

Your Commissions shall be taken care of.

110.

To his Stepmother.

Pall Mall, June 25th, 1771.

DEAR MADAM,

I only write two lines to desire that you would not be surprized if you do not see me Thursday. I have neglected so

many little things that I fear they will require another day.
Friday you may depend on seeing or hearing from me. I hope
the former, as I am extremely desirous of being at Beriton.
Most truly yours,
E. G.

111.

To his Stepmother.

Sheffield Place, August the 2nd, 1771.

DEAR MADAM,

I got here Tuesday Evening, and find great satisfaction
in a pleasant place, and a friend's Company. According to the
present plan, we, family and all go to Brighthelmstone next
Sunday. From thence Holroyd and myself shall set off and
arrive at Beriton, Wednesday, or more probably Thursday.
Should anything *on his side* occasion any further delay, I will
apprize you of it by Wednesday's post.

I hope Mr. Scott is arrived in good health and good spirits.
Present him with my best Compliments and every proper Apology,
for my running away at the very time when we expected his
Company.

I am, Dear Madam,
Most truly yours,
E. GIBBON.

112.

To J. B. Holroyd, Esq.

August 18th, 1771.

DEAR HOLROYD,

I am glad you are returned. I detest your races. I
abhor your assizes. Supposing therefore that all will be ended,
and you at Sheffield place again by Saturday the 27th instant, I
propose being with you, the Wednesday or Thursday following,
with a design of passing a few days in your chateau, and from
thence, bringing you away in triumph to my cottage. Till when
we bid you heartily farewell.

GIBBON.

113.

To his Stepmother.

1771.

DEAR MADAM,

I am much obliged to your friendship, for the advice you have given me with regard to my future conduct, and shall always pay the most sincere deference to it. Both prudence and inclination will engage me to get rid of the farm as soon as such a complicated piece of business can be transacted. With respect to my expences they shall always be proportioned to my income, and I am already preparing to discharge a cook, a groom, and other unnecessary Servants. There is one part of your letter which has given me, Dear Madam, very great uneasiness. You say that you have heard from undoubted authority that my own imprudences had so much embarrassed me, as to oblige me to make a concession which otherwise I might not have done. Were I conscious of these imprudencies, I should fairly acknowledge them, and endeavour by future behaviour to make some amends for past follies. But an innocent person has a right to speak a very different language. I know my own innocence, and without any vain protestations of it, I will at once come to such facts as must either establish it, or else expose me not only as a prodigal, but as a man devoid of honour and veracity. I therefore solemnly affirm the truth of the following facts.

1. When I returned from Switzerland about twelve years and a half ago, my father told me his affairs were a good deal embarrassed, and desired that I would joyn in cutting off the entail and in raising £10,000. I was then a raw lad of one and twenty, unacquainted with law or business, and desirous of obliging my father. He then gave me three hundred a year, a moderate allowance to which his eldest son would have had a natural claim, had no such transaction intervened.

2. Upon and within that allowance, I have constantly lived, except during two years and a half that I was abroad the second time. Whilst I was abroad I spent about seven hundred a year, a sum which, with the unavoidable expences of travelling, barely supports the appearance of an English gentleman.

3. I have never on any occasion received from my father any pecuniary inducements to consent to any step whatsoever, except

once, four hundred pounds, near £100 of which were arrears of my allowances, and about the same sum I returned to my father when he wanted it very much.

4. I have never lost at play a hundred pounds at any one time ; perhaps not in the course of my life. Play I neither love nor understand.

5. I have never taken up any money for myself, in any way whatever.

6. Neither at my father's death nor at any other period have I ever had any other debts than common tradesmen's bills, which are paid from one year to another, and even those to a very trifling amount.

I have tried to answer a general charge, as far as a general charge can be answered. But for our mutual satisfaction, let me intreat you, Dear Madam, to communicate that part of my letter to the persons from whom you received your intelligence. Desire that without sparing me they would contradict *by facts* any of those which I have advanced, or that they would mention any which I have suppressed. If they are unable to do this, your candour must allow that they were either weakly deceived, or wicked Deceivers. As I neither know nor wish to know who they are, Charity induces me to believe the former rather than to suspect the latter.

I think, Dear Madam, you will excuse my warmth. I should deserve the imputation could I submit to it with patience. As long as you credit it, you must view me in the light of a specious Hypocrite, who meanly cloaked his own extravagancies under his father's imprudence, and who ascribed to filial piety what had been the consequence of folly and necessity. As long as you credit it, I must be deprived of the esteem of a person, whose good opinion and friendship it will ever be my wish and study to deserve.

114.

To his Stepmother.

10 minutes after Eleven, Saturday Night, 1771.

DEAR MADAM,

I have only time to tell you (being this moment come home) that I have received Arnold's draught, that I go into

Bucks, Tuesday, shall return here Thursday, for Holroyd is in a violent hurry, and hope to be at Beriton Sunday. Should there happen any alteration I will write. *Mes compliments à la vache Espagnole, et le White Calf.*

I am,

Ever yours,

E. G.

115.

To J. B. Holroyd, Esq.

October 6, 1771.

*DEAR HOLROYD,

I set down to answer your Epistle, after taking a very pleasant ride.—*A Ride! and upon what?*—Upon a horse.— " *You lye!* "—I don't. I have got a droll little Poney, and intend to renew the long-forgotten practice of Equitation, as it was known in the World before the 2nd of June of the year of our Lord one thousand seven hundred and sixty-three. As I used to reason against riding, so I can now argue for it ; and indeed the principal use I know in human reason is, when called. upon, to furnish arguments for what we have an inclination to do.*

I am obliged to you, for looking me out this Lancashire Man, who may assuredly be of use, and no less so for your intercession with Gosling or Clive. If he and his Partner will condescend to receive my Tribute, I am in no violent hurry to dispose of the Place, which under Mrs. Gibbon's management is certainly no losing Game. She thanks you for your Papers, and has delivered the *Roster* to Mr. Luff, who, though it is new, likes it hugely.

*What do you mean by presuming to affirm, that I am of no use here ? Farmer Gibbon of no use ! *Last week* I sold all my Hops, and I believe well, at nine Guineas a hundred, to a very responsible Man. Some people think I might have got more at Weyhill Fair, but that would have been an additional expence, and a great uncertainty. Our quantity has disapointed us very much ; but I think, that besides hops for the house, there will not be less than 500*l.* ;—no contemptible Sum of thirteen small Acres, and two of them planted last year only. *This week* I let a little Farm in Petersfield by auction, and propose raising it from 25*l.* to 35*l.* pr. annum : and Farmer Gibbon of no use !

To be serious; I have but one reason for resisting your invitation and my own wishes; that is, Mrs. Gibbon I left nearly alone all last Winter, and shall do the same this. She submits very chearfully to that state of solitude; but, on sounding her, I am convinced that she would think it unkind were I to leave her at present. I know you so well, that I am sure you will acquiesce in this reason; and let me make my next Visit to Sheffield-Place from town, which I think may be a little before Christmas. I should like to hear something of the precise time, duration, and extent of your intended tour into Bucks. Adieu.*

116.

To J. B. Holroyd, Esq.

Beriton, October 25th, 1771.

DEAR HOLROYD,

To shew that I am not an ungratefull Wretch, I wrote immediately to Damer,¹ and to shew that I am a very careless one, I directed the letter to another person, whose Epistle went to Damer. Lord Milton's heir was ordered to send me without delay a brown Ratteen Frock, and the Taylor was desired to use his interest with his cousin the Duke of Dorset. The mistake has been rectified, but I have not yet had an answer. Is your Bucks Scheme settled, do you start and where do I meet you? I will attend you either in London, at Winslow, or at Denham,² where under your protection, I believe I might trespass for one night on Mr. Way. From thence, " Teucro duce et auspice Teucro," I will

¹ The Hon. John Damer, eldest son of Lord Milton, afterwards created Earl of Dorchester. His mother was Lady Caroline Sackville, daughter of the first Duke of Dorset, and sister of the then existing Duke; married, in 1742, to Joseph Damer, Lord Milton.
² Denham, Bucks, built in 1667 by Sir Roger Hill, came to Lewis Way through his marriage with Abigail Locke, Sir Roger's granddaughter. Lewis Way, who died January 24, 1771, left by his first wife one son, Benjamin, who succeeded to Denham, and one daughter, Abigail, wife of J. B. Holroyd. By his second wife he left another son, Gregory Lewis Way, the translator of *Fabliaux; or, Tales abridged from French Manuscripts of the Twelfth and Thirteenth Centuries*" (edited by George Ellis, and published in two volumes in 1796–1800), who is more than once mentioned in these letters. Denham Place was the "pastoral retreat" of Sir Humphrey Davy.

try to find out my little dairy. My Hops are well sold, with
judgement, and that Judgement my own, for even Mrs. G. wanted
me to keep them for Wayhill Fair, where they were a mere drug.
The little farm, I told you of, I have raised from £25 to £38 pr.
annum, but *Plâit au ciel*, that I had neither Farm, nor Tenants,
they suit not my humour. *I have wrote on the wrong side of the
paper.*

Your four-footed friend is not thought to have attained years
of strength and discretion, however if you are impatient he shall
be forthcoming. A two-legged friend of yours I breakfasted
with this morning at Up-park,—Lascelles ; he seems civilized.
We abused you, your place, Wife, children, &c. &c., pretty much.
Adieu.

E. G.

Pray write to me as soon as I wish, but much sooner than
I deserve.

117.

To J. B. Holroyd, Esq.

Beriton, Nov. 18, 1771.

*MOST RESPECTABLE SOUTH SAXON,

It would ill become me to reproach a dilatory correspondent.

"Quis tulerit Gracchos de seditione querentes ? " Especially
when that Correspondent had given me hopes of undertaking a
very troublesome Expedition for my sole advantage, and indeed
great would be the advantage. Yet thus much I may say, that I
am obliged very soon to go to town upon other business, which, in
that hope, I have hitherto deferred. If by next Sunday I have
no answer, or if I hear that your Journey to Denham is put off
sine die, or to a long Day, I shall on Monday morning set off for
London, and wait your future Will with *Faith, Hope, and Charity.*
Adieu.

I have had no answer from J. D., but will see him if in
Town.*

118.

To his Stepmother.

Sheffield Place, January the 8th, 1772.

DEAR MADAM,

I am safe housed at Sheffield Place where I arrived last Monday, and find it a very hospitable shelter against the snow which covers the Country. Here I shall stay till at least Sunday seven-night, and hope to receive the Map and Greyhound by the hands of Tregus. Aubrey has refused in a manner (though very polite) as shews plainly that the Puppy only sought to gratify his own Vanity. The Oracle is now writing a proper letter for the young Goose. Should anything immediately result from it, you may depend on the earliest intelligence.

I am, dear Madam,

Ever yours,

E. G.

119.

To his Stepmother.

Sheffield Place, January 14th, 1772.

DEAR MADAM,

What a villain that B[ricknall] is. Pray leave neither him nor his assistant one moment's peace or quietness till we get the Plan. If you can get it, as I think you must within ten or twelve days. It will be best to send Tregus over with it, and Miss Holroyd, for so long will I wait here in the expectation of it. The Oracle is very impatient to see it. He proposes to be in town himself by the beginning of next month. We shall then give our attention to the transaction with the G[oslings], which will be neither so simple nor so easy as we once flattered ourselves. The magnanimous Spirit of my Governor keeps me however from desponding.

I am, Dear Madam,

Ever yours,

E. G.

120.

To his Stepmother.

Sheffield Place, January 20th, 1772.

DEAR MADAM,

I know not what to say or do about that Anabaptist as Holroyd calls him. You will, I am sure, persecute him with all the zeal of an Inquisitor, and if he should be in town after I get there (which will be next Sunday), pray send me his direction that I may flog him myself. Holroyd, who will be soon in town likewise, wants to see a State. of what I rent of others, and what is rented of me, with the term in each of them. If it would not give you too much trouble, you might (I should think) make it out, with Luff's assistance.

I have got Mr. Barton's account; the balance to Lady-Day amounts to £82 14s. 10d., which you will please to pay him if you have the money. I am sorry to hear from him, though not from yourself, that you are confined with a cold, I hope not a serious one. My cold is only in my hands, pen and Ink, which are all frozen. Do you hear anything of Petersfield House?

I am, Dear Madam,

Sincerely yours,

E. G.

121.

To his Stepmother.

Pall Mall, February the 4th, 1772.

DEAR MADAM,

What a fool, what a great fool, what an egregious fool he is! I called upon him yesterday morning in Palace Yard, and as a particular favourite was admitted into a bed-chamber up two pair of stairs to breakfast with him and Madame. N.B. that Madame is incognito, sees no company, has no cloaths, but seems however better satisfied with the air of Westminster than with the solitude of Petersfield. The conversation turned partly on the Hampshire Election,[1] and I unwarily said things without any

---

[1] Lord Henley, M.P. for the county of Southampton, succeeded his father as second and last Earl of Northington in January, 1772. At the election to fill this vacancy Sir Henry Paulet St. John was elected.

meaning, which made him stare, and for which, had I then received your letter, I deserved to have had my bones broken.

Very astonishing indeed these Denmark affairs.[1] We are just as much in the dark about them in London, as you can be at Beriton. It seems that the King, whether from nature or any *officious* helps of medicine, is totally incapable of Government. The Physician and the Queen ruled him entirely, and had led him into measures which had disgusted the old Ministry, the Nobility and at last the Army. The Mal-contents linked themselves with the Queen Dowager and her son, and the weak Monarch is now in their hands. Mothers-in-law are very dreadful animals, and he stands a very poor chance indeed. His wife is sent to a castle, and it seems to be the General opinion, that if an Order of —— Ladies were to be founded, she would be the Sovereign of it. Do you not think that our wise K—— might have suffered his Mama[2] to dye in peace without knowing it ? They now reckon her life by hours.

I will immediately send you the new Play[3] which is not much

[1] Caroline Matilda, posthumous child of Frederick, Prince of Wales, was born in July, 1751. She married in October, 1766, Christian VII., King of Denmark. Before her departure from England, her portrait was painted by Sir Joshua Reynolds, who complained that she was so constantly in tears that he could do justice neither to her nor to himself. The marriage proved unhappy. Her husband appears to have been a low brute, whose excesses impaired whatever mind he originally possessed. The queen, on her side, was guilty, at the least, of imprudences which were used against her by her enemies. During his travels, the king had made a favourite of a young physician named Struensee, who practically became Prime Minister, and, with his friend Brandt, governed Denmark. The Queen Dowager, Juliana Maria, stepmother of the king, placed herself, with her son Frederick, at the head of the malcontents. In January, 1772, Struensee and Brandt were arrested, and, after a protracted inquiry, executed in the following April. The queen was imprisoned at the Castle of Cronenbourg. From this prison she was released by the intervention of her brother, George III., and passed the few remaining years of her life at Zell, in Hanover, where her great-grandmother, Sophia Dorothea, had died in captivity. There she died in 1775, at the age of twenty-four.

[2] The Princess Dowager (1719-1772), youngest daughter of Frederick II., Duke of Saxe Gotha, widow of Frederick, Prince of Wales, mother of George III. and the Queen Caroline of Denmark, died at Carlton House on February 8, 1772.

[3] Either Joseph Cradock's adaptation of Voltaire's play *Les Scythes*, acted at Covent Garden under the title of *Zobeïde*, with a prologue by Goldsmith, or Cumberland's *Fashionable Lover*, as acted at Drury Lane. Both plays were published early in 1772.

liked. There is nothing else. The Spanish Romance[1] does not come out till next month. I am totally a stranger to Mrs. Williams and her misfortunes. You warded off the blow by talking of your journey to Bath ; but I hope you will seriously and speedily think of it, as I am convinced that your health as well as spirits would find the greatest benefit from such an excursion.—Business is at a stand till Holroyd comes to town, which will be in a few days. I hope that soon after his arrival I shall be able to write something to the purpose.

I am, dear Madam,

Most truly yours,

E. G.

122.

To J. B. Holroyd, Esq.

London, 1772.

*Dear Holroyd,

The sudden Change from the sobriety of Sheffield-Place to the Irregularities of this Town, and to the Wicked Company of Wilbraham,[2] Clarke,[3] Damer, &c. having deranged me a good deal, I am forced to employ one of my secretaries to acquaint you of a Piece of News I know nothing about myself. It is certain, some extraordinary Intelligence is arrived this Morning from Denmark, & as certain that the Levee was suddenly prevented by it. The Particulars of that Intelligence are variously & obscurely told. It is said, that the king had rais'd a little Physician to the Rank of Minister & Ganymede : such a mad Administration had disgusted all the Nobility, that the Fleet and army had rose, and shut up the King in his Palace. *La Reine se trouve mêlée la dedans*, & it is reported that she is confined, but whether in Consequence of the Insurrection, or of some amorous amusements of her own, does not seem to be agreed. Such is the rough Draft of an Affair that nobody yet understands. *Embrassez de ma Part Madame, et le reste de la chère Famille.*

Gibbon.

et plus Bas—Wilbraham, Sec.*

---

[1] *The History of the Famous Preacher, Friar Gerund de Campazas, otherwise Gerund Zotes.* London, 1772. 2 vols., 8vo.

[2] George Wilbraham, of Delamere Lodge, Cheshire.

[3] Godfrey Bagnal Clarke, M.P. for Derbyshire, who had made the tour of Italy at the same time as Gibbon.

123.

To his Stepmother.

Saturday Evening, near eleven, '72.

DEAR MADAM,

I did not intend to have troubled you till Monday or Tuesday, but I have this moment found a note from Mrs. P. requesting some game, to answer a hare, on Wednesday. At this season I know of no game but a Turkey. Holroyd is in town, as active but not so effectual as I could wish. He is pleased with Bricknall's *four* plans, but wishes that he would sketch out the outlines of them, on a single piece of paper, that their relative situation may be seen at one view. Adieu, Dear Madam, and believe me,

Ever yours,

E. G.

124.

To J. B. Holroyd, Esq.

Boodle's, 10 o'clock, Monday night, Feb. 3rd, 1772.

*I love, honour, and respect every member of Sheffield-place ; even my great enemy Datch,[1] to whom you will please to convey my sincere wishes, that no *simpleton* may wait on him at dinner, that his wise Papa may not show him any pictures, and that his much wiser Mamma may chain him hand and foot, in direct contradiction to Magna Charta and the Bill of Rights.

It is difficult to write news—because there are none. Parliament is perfectly quiet ; and I think that Barré,[2] who is just now playing at Whist in the Room, will not have exercise of the lungs, except, perhaps, on a Message much talked of, and soon expected, to recommend it to the wisdom of the H. of C. to provide

---

[1] The name by which Mr. Holroyd's son called himself.

[2] Colonel Isaac Barré (1726-1802), succeeded Lord Fitzmaurice as M.P. for Chipping Wycombe in 1761. He afterwards sat for Calne. He had served under Wolfe at Quebec, and appears in West's famous picture of the death of Wolfe. At the battle he lost his left eye, and in his picture by Sir Joshua Reynolds the right side of his face is turned towards the spectator. He was a prominent opponent of Lord North, and held office under the first Pitt, and subsequently in the Rockingham and Shelburne administrations.

a proper future remedy against the improper marriages of the younger branches of the royal family.[1] The noise of Luttrell[2] is subsided, but there was some foundation for it. The Colonel's expenses in his bold enterprise were yet unpaid by government. The Hero threatened, assumed the Patriot, received a sop, and again sunk into the Courtier. As to Denmark, it seems now that the king, who was totally unfit for government, has only passed from the hands of his Queen Wife to those of his Queen Mother-in-Law. The former is said to have indulged a very *vague* taste in her Amours. She would not be admitted into the Pantheon,[3]

[1] The Duke of Cumberland married, in October, 1771, Mrs. Horton, a daughter of Simon Luttrell, Lord Irnham (afterwards Earl of Carhampton), "a young widow of twenty-four, with the most amorous eyes in the world, and eyelashes a yard long." The Duke of Gloucester, a few months later, avowed his clandestine marriage with Maria, an illegitimate daughter of Sir Edward Walpole, and widow of the second Earl of Waldegrave. The Royal Marriage Bill was brought in, in consequence of these marriages, on February 20, 1772, and became law in the following March.

[2] Colonel Luttrell (1743–1821), brother of the Duchess of Cumberland, had been declared by the House to be elected for Middlesex against Wilkes in April, 1769, although the latter polled 1143 votes to Colonel Luttrell's 296. He was made adjutant-general of the land forces in Ireland; but in 1772, being discontented with the post, threatened to resign his seat for Middlesex, and so renew the struggle with Wilkes. The circumstances in which the appointment was made are noticed by Junius (August 22, 1770).

[3] Walpole, writing in May, 1770, speaks of "a winter-Ranelagh erecting in Oxford Road at the expense of sixty thousand pounds." "Imagine Balbec in all its glory!" he writes, when it was approaching completion in April, 1771. The Pantheon, built by Wyatt, was opened on January 27, 1772, "to a crowded company of between fifteen hundred and two thousand people. In point of consequence, the company were an olio of all sorts; peers, peeresses, honourables, and right honourables, jew brokers, demireps, lottery insurers, and quack doctors" (*Annual Register*). It was destroyed by fire on January 16, 1792.

Gentlemen and ladies could only subscribe to the Pantheon on the recommendation of a peeress, in order to prevent, as the proprietors announce in the *Gazetteer* (December 17, 1771), "such persons only from obtaining subscriptions whose appearance might not only be improper but subversive of that elegance and propriety which they wish on every occasion to preserve." On the other hand, once admitted to be subscribers, they could introduce friends of any or no character. The struggle between the two factions was decided by the efforts of a number of gentlemen, headed by Mr. William Hanger, who, with drawn swords, succeeded in forcing an entrance for Mrs. Baddeley. Possibly Gibbon meant, instead of repeating "Gentlemen Proprietors," to mark the contrast by writing "Gentlemen Subscribers" in the second sentence. The dispute is alluded to in a poem from whence the *Gentlemen Proprietors* exclude all beauty, unless unspotted and immaculate (tautology, by the by). The *Gentlemen Proprietors*, on the other hand, are friends and patrons of the Leopard Beauties. Advertising challenges have passed between the two Great Factions, and a bloody battle is expected Wednesday Night. *A propos*, the Pantheon, in point of Ennui and Magnificence, is the wonder of the XVIIIth Century and the British Empire. Adieu.*

125.

To J. B. Holroyd, Esq.

Boodle's, Saturday night, Feb. 8, 1772.

*Though it is very late and the bell tells me that I have not above ten minutes left, I employ them with pleasure in congratulating you on the late Victory of our Dear Mamma the Church of England.[1] She had last Thursday 71 rebellious sons, who pretended to set aside her will on account of insanity : but

published in 1772, called *The Pantheon Rupture; or, A Dispute between Elegance and Reason.* In their dialogue Elegance says—

"I glory to keep on a *virtuous course,*
 And hate the very name of a *divorce;*
 Besides the *Managers* admit none in,
 That e'er were known to have committed sin ;—
 The needy dame, who makes of love a trade,
 These *Realms of Virtue* must not dare invade ;
 The company's selected from a class
 Too chaste to suffer *demireps* to pass.

REASON.

But, *Elegance,* before more time you waste,
 Inform me, pray, are all those Ladies chaste ?

ELEGANCE.

Chaste! surely yes.—The Managers admit
 None but chaste Ladies, in their virtuous set;
 Besides, if any one a slip hath made,
 A *Title* hides it with oblivion's shade."

[1] Parliament met January 21, 1772. On February 6, Sir W. Meredith presented a petition from the "Feathers Tavern Association," signed by two hundred and fifty clergymen, lawyers, and physicians, praying that their professions might be relieved from the necessity of subscription to the XXXIX. Articles. The House decided, by 217 to 71, not to receive the petition.

217 Worthy Champions, headed by Lord North, *Burke*, Hans Stanley, Charles Fox, Godfrey Clarke, &c., though they allowed the thirty-nine clauses of her Testament were absurd and unreasonable, supported the validity of it with infinite humour. By the by, C. F. prepared himself for that holy war, by passing twenty-two hours in the pious exercise of Hazard ; his devotions cost him only about £500 per hour—in all £11,000. Gaby lost £5000. This is from the best authority. I hear, too, but will not warrant it, that Will Hanger,[1] by way of paying his court to L. C., has lost this winter £12,000. How I long to be ruined !

There are two county contests, Sir Thomas Egerton and Colonel Townley in Lancashire,[2] after the county had for some time gone a-begging. In Salop, Sir Watkin, supported by Lord Gower, happened by a punctilio to disoblige Lord Craven, who told us last night, that he had not quite £9000 a-year in that county, and who has set up Pigot against him. You may suppose we all wish for God Almighty[3] against that Black Devil.

I am sorry your journey is deferred. No news from Fleet Street. What shall I do ? Compliments to Datch. As he is now in Durance, great minds forgive their enemies, and I hope he may be released by this time.——Coming, sir. Adieu.

You see the P[rincess] of W[ales] is gone. Hans Stanley says, it is believed the Empress Queen[4] has taken the same journey.*

126.

To J. B. Holroyd, Esq.

London, Feb. 13, 1772.

DEAR H.,

The principal object of my writing to-night is to acquaint you, that the old Anabaptist has escaped Damnation by sending in his papers, &c., on the 10th Instant, the destined

---

[1] Afterwards the third Lord Coleraine.

[2] Lord Archibald Hamilton, M.P. for Lancashire, accepted the stewardship of the Manor of East Hendred, January, 1772. Sir T. Egerton was elected in his place.

[3] An allusion to the Welsh opinion that Sir Watkin Williams Wynn was as great a person. On the death of Sir John Astley, M.P. for Shropshire, Sir Watkin was elected.

[4] Maria Theresa did not die till November, 1780.

day of judgement. *They arrived safe in town last night, and will be in your hands in their intact virgin State in a day or two. Consider them at leisure, if that word is known in the Rural life. Unite, divide, but above all *raise*. Bring them to London with you : I wait your orders ; nor shall I, for fear of tumbling, take a single step till your arrival, which, on many accounts, I hope will not be long deferred.* No news from Fleet Street ! What is their surveyor about ?

Clouds still hover over the Horizon of Denmark. The public circumstances of the Revolution are related, and, I understand, very exactly, in the foreign Papers. The secret springs of it still remain unknown. The town, indeed, seems at present quite tired of the subject. The Princess's death,[1] her Character, and what she left, engross the Conversation. She died without a will ; and as her savings were generally disposed of in Charity, the small remains of her personal fortune will make a trifling object when divided among her Children. Her favourite, the P[rincess] of B[runswick] [2] very properly insisted on the K.'s immediately sealing up all the papers, to secure her from the Idle reports which would be so readily swallowed by the great English Monster. The business of L. and Lady Grosvenor[3] is finally compromised, by the arbitration of the Chancellor[4] and Lord Cambden. He gives her £1200 a year separate maintenance, and £1500 to set out with ; but, as her Ladyship is now a new face, her Husband, who has already bestowed on the public seventy young Beauties, has conceived a violent but hopeless passion for his chaste Moiety. Her brother Vernon told me, that he has now in his hands a counter-affidavit of Countess Denhoff, in which she declares that she received a sum of money to swear the former, the contents of which are totally false. Such infamous conduct may blast her, but can never acquit the other ; any more than another allegation of her friends, which must be only whispered to Mrs.

---

[1] *i.e.* The Princess of Wales.

[2] Her eldest child, Augusta (1737–1813), married, in 1764, the Duke of Brunswick-Wolfenbüttel.

[3] Henrietta Vernon, married to Lord Grosvenor in July, 1764, was seduced by the Duke of Cumberland. Lord Grosvenor brought an action against the duke for criminal conversation, July 5, 1770, and recovered damages in the sum of £10,000. Lady Grosvenor, who was separated, not divorced, married, in 1802, General Porter, M.P. for Stockbridge.

[4] Lord Apsley.

H[orton], viz. that though the D[uke] of C[umberland] possessed the inclination, he wanted the power to injure *any* husband. Poor Mrs. H. ! Yet why do I say poor ?—*Lord Chesterfield is dying.[1] County Oppositions subside.* Adieu. *Je me recommande.* Entirely yours.

127.

To his Stepmother.

Pall Mall, Feb. 17th, 1772.

DEAR MADAM,

I would tell you that I have been somewhat out of order ; a foulness or fullness, call it as you please, in my stomach which occasioned an ache as well there as in my head, and indeed a general languor all over me. Turton, whom I called to my assistance, despising the solemn nonsense of the faculty, has given me Pills with some James's Powder in them, & I think the enemy has, or at least is sounding a retreat ; he has been marching off all this morning in very *loose* order.

Bricknall is gone down to Holroyd in the same condition as I received him. I expect that great man in town in a few days, and hope that his active Genius will hasten and facilitate everything. You are so good as to say, dear Madam, that you had no objection to your Annuity being transferred from Bucks to Hants.

I propose sending you the draught of a Deed to that effect, which you will please to return with any observations that may occur to you. When do you go to Bath ?

Ever yours,
E. G.

128.

To J. B. Holroyd, Esq.

Feb. 21, 1772.

DEAR H.,

An exact man should acknowledge the receipt of Letters, Papers, &c. How do I know for instance whether my Hampshire Acres, the long expected fruits of my Anabaptist's Labours, may not be sunk, irrecoverably sunk in the Sussex Dirt ? *However,

---

[1] Lord Chesterfield died March 24, 1773.

notwithstanding my indignation, I will employ five minutes in telling you two or three recent pieces of News.

1. Charles Fox is commenced Patriot, and is already attempting to pronounce the words *Country*, *Liberty*, *Corruption*, &c. ; with what success, time will discover. Yesterday he resigned the Admiralty.[1] The most probable account seems to be, that he could not prevail on Ministry to join with him in his intended repeal of the Marriage Act (a favourite measure of his father, who opposed it from its origin,) and that Charles very judiciously thought Lord Holland's friendship imported him more than Lord North's.

2. Yesterday the Marriage Message came to both Houses of Parliament. You will see the words of it in the Papers ; and, thanks to the submissive piety of this Session, it is hoped that the Princes of the next Generation will not find it so easy as their Uncles have done to expose themselves and to burthen the Public.

3. To-day the House of C. was employed in a very odd way. Tommy Townshend[2] moved, that the Sermon of Dr. Knowell, who preached before the House on the 30th of January (*id est*, before the Speaker and four Members,) should be burnt by the Common Hangman, as containing arbitrary, Tory, High-flown doctrines. The House was nearly agreeing to the Motion, till they recollected that they had already thanked the Preacher for his excellent discourse, and ordered it to be printed. Knowell's Bookseller is much obliged to the Right Honourable Tommy Townshend.

When do you come to Town ? I want Money, and am tired of sticking to the Earth by so many Roots.* No news from Fleet Street. *Embrassez de ma part la Sainte famille.* Adieu.

Ever yours,

E. G.

[1] Fox only retired from the Government on the Royal Marriage question. In January, 1773, he resumed office as one of the Lords of the Treasury.

[2] Afterwards Lord Sydney. Dr. Nowell's sermon, which, it was alleged, inculcated passive obedience, was preached January 30, 1772, at St. Margaret's, Westminster. The vote of thanks was voted January 31, and the sermon printed by desire of the House. On February 21 it was moved that, for the future, the thanks of the House should not be voted till the sermon was printed and delivered. The motion here attributed to Townshend was an expression of his opinion, given in the course of the debate. Lord North evaded the motion by moving the order of the day. On February 25 a motion was proposed and carried to expunge the entry of the vote of thanks.

129.

To his Stepmother.

Pall Mall, February the 22nd, 1772.

DEAR MADAM,

I write by return of the Post, as you desire it, but have not anything to say. Mr. Bayley, whom by this time you have probably seen, saw me the day before yesterday, well, *perfectly well*, and sucked me quite dry as to news.

I am, Dear Madam,

Ever yours,

E. G.

130.

To his Stepmother.

March 5th, 1772.

DEAR MADAM,

I know you are so good as to be satisfied with my short notes, which, from hurry and laziness, I defer to the moment the post is going out. I am perfectly well and have entirely thrown off all remains of my late disorder. Holroyd will be in town in a very few days, and I hope will furnish me with materials for a more ample Letter. I now write from Atwood's, a new Club into which I have been chose, and am now thouroughly established. It is unnecessary to add how much I am,

Dear Madam,

Ever yours,

E. G.

131.

To his Stepmother.

Pall Mall, March 21st, 1772.

DEAR MADAM,

I admit the justice of your kind reproaches, and without attempting any idle excuses, I will endeavour to prove my repentance by my amendment. We are now (Holroyd and myself) very busy, but with much less success than I could wish. Though it has been mathematically demonstrated to the Goose, that at twenty-two, he would make near 3 pr. cent. of his money, the Goose, for such he most truly is, after a long shuffling dilatory suspense, without being able to find out his own foolish mind, has this morning told me that he must at least for the present decline it. We immediately proceed to an Advertisement, and the Oracle has made the value of the thing so clear even to me that I am almost as sanguine as himself. We are soon to have a Conference about Beriton. He thinks the map you have sent will be of use, and prevent his losing his Way, when he goes down with me about Easter, as he will certainly do. As from Bricknall's slowness it was impossible to let the Farms at Lady Day, they can only be let at Michaelmas : and we, however reluctantly, go through another and last Harvest. I am doubly anxious that it should be the last, not only to have my own affairs in a smaller compass and clearer order, but likewise to release you, dear Madam, from a melancholy situation, which your affection for me has persuaded you to undertake.

* Sir Richard Worsley[1] is just come home. I am sorry to see many alterations, and little improvement. From an honest wild English buck, he is grown a *philosopher*. Lord Petersfield displeases every body by the affectation of consequence : the young baronet disgusts no less by the affectation of wisdom. He speaks in short sentences, quotes Montaigne, seldom smiles, never laughs, drinks only water, professes to command his passions, and intends to marry in five months. The two lords, his uncle as well as Jemmy, attempt to show him that such behaviour, even were it reasonable, does not suit this country. He remains incorrigible, and is every day losing ground in the good opinion of the public, which at his first arrival ran strongly in his favour. Deyverdun

---

[1] Sir R. Worsley succeeded to the baronetcy on the death, in 1768, of Sir Thomas Worsley. He was M.P. for Newport, Isle of Wight, 1774-84, and for Newtown, Isle of Wight, 1790-1802. He was sworn a privy councillor, and made Governor of the Island in January, 1780. He was also Comptroller of the Royal Household. He published his *History of the Isle of Wight* in 1781. In 1782, on the accession to office of the Rockingham administration, he was deprived of the Governorship of the Island in favour of the Duke of Bolton. As Diplomatic Resident at Venice, he made the collections and sketches which are reproduced in the *Museum Worsleyanum* (2 vols., 1794-1803). He died in 1805. His only son predeceased him. His estates passed, through his only sister, Henrietta Frances (married to John Bridgman-Simpson, Esq), to her only child, Henrietta, who married the Earl of Yarborough.

is probably on his journey towards England, but is not yet come.*

The attention of the Public is much engaged about the Marriage Bill. The Princes of the Blood will lose their natural rights, and a most odious law will be forced upon Parliament. I do not remember ever to have seen so general a concurrence of all ranks, parties, and professions of men. Administration themselves are the reluctant executioners, but the King will be obeyed, and the bill is universally considered as his, reduced into legal or rather illegal form by Ld. Mansfield and the Chancellor. By the bye, the Duke of Manchester told me the other day that since the bill Lady Waldegrave has authorized all her friends to declare that she *is* married. The Duke and Duchess of C[umberland] are in town, but live in princely solitude. He drives her about the streets in a Phaeton, and they have sometimes concerts to which none but the Luttrel family are admitted.

I am, Dear Madam,

Ever yours,

E. G.

132.

To his Stepmother.

Pall Mall, April 8th, 1772.

DEAR MADAM,

According to the indulgent conditions you have been so good as to allow me, I only write to say that I am perfectly well, and that I hope to be at Beriton towards the end of next week. The day is still in suspense from some arrangements which do not entirely depend on myself, and which have occasioned my missing a post or two. I believe that I shall be able to fix it by Saturday or Tuesday at furthest.

I am, dear Madam,

Ever yours,

E. G.

133.

To his Stepmother.

Pall Mall, April 15th, 1772.

DEAR MADAM,

It was not in my power to write last Saturday night, as my friend Clarke, on whom my motions partly depended, had not yet settled his plan of operations. I can now say that I hope to dine with you on Thursday. The aforesaid Clarke (who I think will please you) will make us a visit next week : I shall return with him to Aldershot near Farnham, and from thence to town. So near a prospect of seeing you naturally stops my pen. The bill I received, and suppose it useless to send down a draught, as I shall follow the post in a very few hours.

I am, Dear Madam,

Most truly yours,

E. G.

134.

To J. B. Holroyd, Esq.[1]

Beriton, April 21st, 1772.

Dear H.,

I am just arrived, as well as yourself, at my Dii Penates, but with very different intention. You will ever remain a Bigot to those Rustic Deities ; I propose to abjure them soon, and to reconcile myself to the Catholic Church of London. The inhabitants of this evil Country are frightened and have frightened me about advertising for proposals. *It has never been done, ergo it will never do, &c.* There is a Man near Chichester who has made offers, will only take the whole, buy all the stock. It is even *said*, that he does not seem astonished at 18 or even 20 Shillings for the Low Hill Ground, and every one is convinced that his purse is adequate to his proposals. Suppose I was to write him a polite Epistle—his character—first offer—willing to listen to his proposals, for taking Miss Nancy Beriton into private keeping, before I throw her upon the town. Decide.

Mrs. G. is well, and salutes you ; but is not a little mortified

---

[1] This letter affords a curious, though extreme, instance of Lord Sheffield's editorial methods. The letter numbered XXXII. in Lord Sheffield's edition of "Letters to and from Edward Gibbon, Esq." (1814), is dated October 13, 1772. It begins with the first four lines of this letter, which was written on April 21, 1772. The next nine lines are taken from the commencement of the letter written on October 3, 1772. The five following lines consist of the letter written on November 3, 1772. The next four lines are taken from the letter dated October 30, 1772. The two following lines are from the letter written on October 15, 1772. Thus what purports to be a real letter in itself, proves to be a patchwork composed from five letters extending over a period of six months.

at not seeing you. She is doubtfull of herself and of Luff, and wished you to examine into the *Present* State of Europe. I foresee I must look you over some day or other. In the mean time, I embrace Madame (*autant qu'il m'est permis*) Datch, the Capering Lady, and the rest of your family, Bipede and Quadrupede. I expect Clarke to-morrow, and shall be in town the middle of next week.

I am, yours sincerely,

E. G.

135.

To his Stepmother.

Pall Mall, April 29th, 1772.

DEAR MADAM,

To-day one o'clock, I arrived in Town from Aldershot, perfectly well ; and now as ever,

Most sincerely yours,

E. G.

136.

To his Stepmother.

Pall Mall, May the 5th, 1772.

DEAR MADAM,

I excuse the cheat and consent to the money being employed as you mention. I hope I shall not be obliged to take my revenge before I go into the Country. When I have said that, after three very pleasant days at Aldershot, I am returned with caution to my usual way of life in town, I have no private news to add, except that the Masquerade was dull and magnificent. I had the sole care of Mrs. I. above two hours ; a Parisian husband ! As to public news I believe you may depend on the L. of D[enmark]'s divorce, that Fregates[1] are going for her, and that she will reside at Zell. My compliments to Mr. Bayly. Clarke returns him a thousand thanks and wishes to feast his

---

[1] May 27, 1772.—"This afternoon three ships belonging to his Britannic Majesty cast anchor in the road of Elsineur. They are to convoy her Danish Majesty to Stade in her way to Zell" (*Annual Register*).

cars in St. James's Street. Sir—The bell is going by—I have just done. Why do I always write at eleven o'clock at night?

I am, dear Madam,

Ever yours,
E. G.

I have wrote to Chatfield.

137.

To J. B. Holroyd, Esq.

Pall Mall, May 26, 1772.

Dear H.,

The reason, or if You like it better the pretence of my long silence, was the waiting for an answer from my farmer, to whom I had wrote in consequence of your permission. It came two or three days ago. He thanks me for my offer, but has made a purchase in Sussex, and my farm no longer suits him. This is surely the Season for letting it. Shall I advertise? in which case an advertisement must be thought of? or would it be better to impower Hugonin (whose honesty I can trust as much, and whose knowledge far more than my own) to treat in conjunction with Mrs. Gibbon, with any *Good* Men, who may offer? *I wish you lived nearer, or even that you could pass a week at Beriton. When shall you be at Richmond, or would there be any *use* in my going down to Sheffield for a day or two? In thee alone I put my trust, and without thee I should be perplexed, discouraged, and frightened; for not a single fish has yet bit at the Lenbourough bait.

I dined the other day with Mr. Way [1] at Boodle's. He told me, that he was just going down to Sheffield. As he has probably unladen all the politics, and Mrs. Way all the scandal of the town, I shall for *the present only* satisfy myself with the needfull; among which I shall always reckon my sincere compliments to Madame, and my profound respects for Mr. Datch.

I am, dear H.,

Truly Yours,
E. G.

---

[1] Probably Mr. Benjamin Way, the brother of Lady Sheffield. His wife was a daughter of Dr. Cooke, Provost of King's College, Cambridge.

It is confidently asserted that the Emperor and K. of P. are to run for very deep stakes over the Polish Course.[1] If the news is true, I back Austria against the aged Horse, provided little Laudohn rides the match. *N.B.*—Crossing and jostling allowed.*

138.

To his Stepmother.

June the 10th, 1772.

DEAR MADAM,

Two reasons (assisted, as you will, by a laziness of nature) have kept me silent for several posts. The one of a pleasant, the other of a disagreeable kind.

1. Deyverdun is at length arrived, and has explained fully to my satisfaction the reasons of his whole conduct, tho' they are such as it is not permitted me to reveal. Lord Chesterfield was not in the least offended at having been obliged to wait, and my friend with young Stanhope sets out for the University of Leipsic about the middle of next week. As I have so short a period to enjoy his Company between two such intervals of separation, I am obliged to give up every other engagement, and to sacrifice every other business in order to snatch the hours which he is able to give me. He begs his most gratefull compliments to you, and laments that his time will not allow him to present them himself.

2. The other reason was an inflammation in my Eyes, which is now perfectly removed, but which I had most richly deserved by going from a melting Garrick's to cool myself at Vauxhall.

The Oracle is astonished at the general neglect of the World about Lenborough. He commands me, if they do not come in sooner, to raise the rents myself at Michaelmas. In the meanwhile he is not in a hurry about the farm, thinks that both

---

[1] In Poland, desultory hostilities had been carried on for several years between the Roman Catholics, favoured by France, and the Dissidents (*i.e.* those embracing any other form of Christian faith), supported by Russia. Taking advantage of the anarchy which King Stanislaus Poniatowski was powerless to control, Frederick the Great, the Empress Catherine, and the Emperor Joseph II. proposed to occupy those provinces which were respectively most contiguous to their own dominions. The result was the partition of Poland, August, 1772. Field-Marshal Laudohn (1716-1790) is said to have been of Scottish origin. During the Seven Years' War he had proved himself, at the head of the Austrian forces, a formidable antagonist to Frederick the Great.

transactions should move together, and is sure that I do not lose by it. I am not disinclined to follow his advice, and my only objection is on your account. I am exceedingly glad to hear the Goulds are preparing to visit us. I say *us*, for I hope to meet them on or before the last day of this month. I shall likewise write to Holt. Pray how does the Corn—and the *Hops* look?— I called on Sir John Miller this morning and found him laid up with the small-pox. Sir Matthew is breaking up very fast.

I am, Dear Madam,

Ever yours,

E. G.

139.

To James Scott, Esq.

Pall Mall, Cocoa Tree, June the 16th, 1772.

DEAR SIR,

I have not troubled you during the Winter, as I had frequent opportunities of hearing of your health, and as I well knew that neither of us were extremely fond of writing. But it is now time to put you in mind that the season is approaching when Beriton is the most tolerable. The Colonel and Mrs. Gould will make us a visit, and I flatter myself that our last Summer there will not be the least agreable. I propose being down the first of next month, and, unless it was inconvenient to you, have a particular reason for wishing to meet you there. The Clarkes (as you may well suppose) are impatient, and will expect to hear from me as soon as I get down: but as your company and assistance will be of the greatest use, I must make a praevious visit into Sussex, and spend some days with Holroyd, till you can conveniently come. I must therefore beg the favour of a line.—My fair Prospects about Lenborough are very much darkened by many unforeseen accidents. However all will come round again. D'Eyverdun begs to be remembered to you. He has spent only a fortnight in England, and sets out again to-morrow night with Mr. Stanhope.

I am, Dear Sir,

Most sincerely yours,

E. GIBBON.

140.

To his Stepmother.

Pall Mall, July 2nd, 1772.

DEAR MADAM,

You will excuse a Laconic Epistle when I tell you, that I hold fast the lively hope of dining with you, as well as with Colonel and Mrs. Gould (to whom I beg my respects) next Monday. Should the Bans be forbid by any lawfull cause or impediment, I will write a line Saturday night.

I am, Dear Madam,

Ever yours,

E. G.

141.

To Mrs. Holroyd, Sen.

Beriton, near Petersfield, Hampshire, July the 17th, 1772.

MADAM,

*There is not any event which could have affected me with greater surprise and deeper concern, than the news in last night's paper, of the death of our poor little amiable friend Master Holroyd,[1] whom I loved, not only for his Parents' sake, but for his own.   Should the news be true (for even yet I indulge some faint hopes,) what must be the distress of our friends at Sheffield !   I so truly sympathize with them, that I know not how to write to Holroyd ; but must beg to be informed of the state of the family by a line from you.   I have some Company and business here, but would gladly quit them, had I the least reason to think that my presence at Sheffield would afford the least comfort or satisfaction to the man in the world whom I love and esteem the most.

I am, Madam,

Your most obedient humble Servant,

E. GIBBON.*

---

[1] John William Holroyd, at that time the only son of Mr. Holroyd.

142.

To J. B. Holroyd, Esq.

Beriton, July the 30th, 1772.

MY DEAR HOLROYD,

It was my intention to set out for Sheffield as soon as I received your affecting Letter, and I hoped to have been with you as to-day ; but walking very carelessly yesterday morning, I fell down, and put out a small bone in my ancle. I am now under the Surgeon's hands, but think, and most earnestly hope, that this little accident will not delay my journey longer than the middle of next week. I share, and wish I could alleviate, your feelings. I beg to be remembered to Mrs. Holroyd.

I am, My Dear Holroyd,

Most truly yours,

E. GIBBON.

143.

To James Scott, Esq.

Beriton, August the 2nd, 1772.

DEAR SIR,

Though I have been near three weeks in the country, I have still been prevented from writing to you by the want of anything to say, as well as by the fear of hurrying you away from a place so conducive to your health. But the C.'s have been silent, and my other affairs are so unfortunately at a stand, I am not sorry to protract that unpleasant one. I am going next Wednesday into Sussex to condole with my friend Holroyd on the loss of his only son. But you will find in the mean time Mrs. G. and a sincere welcome at Beriton. Should your friendship oblige you to go to town (which I think cannot be suddenly) I will attend you there, and endeavour to make the Journey as little inconvenient to you as I possibly can.

I am, Dear Sir,

Most truly yours,

E. G.

144.

To his Stepmother.

Sheffield Place, August the 7th, 1772.

DEAR MADAM,

I found a good deal of Company at Up-Park, Harry[1] and Tutor, Franklin and Wife, Batten and son ; Sir James and Lady Peachy came to drink Tea, and I should have passed a very pleasant day, had it not been for the spectacle of poor Sir Matthew, who is visibly and *litterally* dying. *I set out at six yesterday morning, got to Brighthelmstone about two—a very thin season, everybody gone to Spa. In the evening I reached this place. My friend appears, as he ever will, in a light truly respectable ; concealing the most exquisite sufferings under the show of Composure and even chearfulness, and attempting though with little success to confirm the weaker mind of his Partner.* I apprehend (tho' with much uncertainty) that my stay will not exceed a fortnight. Adieu, Dear Madam, remember me to Mr. Scott and the Baylys who (I hope) are with you, and believe me,

Ever yours,

E. G.

145.

To his Stepmother.

Sheffield, August 21st, 1772.

DEAR MADAM,

I thought by this time to have been leaving this place, but I find my friend who is still very low, expresses so much uneasiness at the Idea of my quitting him, that I cannot refuse him the remainder of the month. *If Mr. Scott, as I suppose, is at Buriton, he has himself too high a sense of Friendship not to excuse my neglecting him. Once I had some hopes of engaging Mr. and Mrs. H. to make an excursion to Portsmouth, Isle of Wight, Southampton, &c. : in which case they would have spent

---

[1] Eldest son of Sir Matthew Featherstonhaugh, and his successor in the baronetcy.

a day or two at Beriton.* At present there is a possibility though
no great likelyhood of such a scheme being put in execution.

I am, Dear Madam,

Ever yours,

E. G.

146.

To his Stepmother.

Sheffield Place, August 25th, 1772.

DEAR MADAM,

*A sudden resolution was taken last night in favour of
the Tour mentioned in my last. We set out, Mr. and Mrs. H.,
a Mr. Faukier and myself, next Thursday, and shall dine at
Beriton the following day, and stay there most probably three or
four days. A Farmhouse without either Cook or Housekeeper
will afford but indifferent entertainment, but we must *exert* and
they must *excuse*.* Our Tour will last about a fortnight, after
which my friend presses me to return with him, and in his present
situation, I shall be at a loss how to refuse him.

I am, Dear Madam,

Ever yours,

E. G.

147.

To J. B. Holroyd, Esq.

Beriton, September the 25th, 1772.

Blessings on the man (his name is now buried in oblivion) who
first invented the loud trumpet of Advertisements. Blessings on
those two great men, the intrepid Holroyd and the prudent
Hugonin, without whose charitable aid the wretched Gibbon
must for ever have grovelled in the mire of Beriton.

We much depended, as you may remember, on the Rumsey
Farmer and the Distiller. But—*omne quod humanum instabile.*
The latter never replied to the letter which I sent him, the
former missed the appointed Wednesday and threw me into an
agony of despair, which was soon changed into joy on the
discovery that I had escaped a very indifferent Tenant. Many

candidates succeeded, a letter from Norfolk, and farmers of
various appearance and from different places. Luff (I believe he
used no foul play) always chose to show the farm, and then conducted them to Hugonin, who debated the matter with them over
a bowl of Punch and then acquainted me with the result. It
would be tedious and at present of little use to expatiate on the
objections, difficulties, &c. At last a Farmer named Winton
from Shoreham who knows you (by the bye, all the farmers abuse
you, a high compliment!) made his appearance : the father is a
man of substance, 200 a year of his owne, the son a brisk active
fellow about thirty, both of unexceptionable character, and
throughout the whole transaction uncommonly fair and candid.
They take all my stock at an appraisement, sheep excepted (they
don't like the sort), and allow me a year for repairs, about which
they gladly take Hugonin for Umpire, and have not indeed
demanded any one unreasonable thing. I have given at their
request a thirty years' lease, and immediately signed a legal article.
Monday sennight the stock will be appraised by one on each side.

In a word, all is settled and (though I have given up something of the proposed rent) I should think it one of the most
agreeable days of my life, were it not embittered by the uneasiness
I feel on Mrs. G.'s account. She refused to yield an iota of her
pretensions, and even to allow the Tenant any Rick Yard, or a
way from the Lawn into his farm-yard. She was repeatedly told
that every farmer did and ever would reject the farm on such
terms. At length she gave Hugonin authority to say that she
had given up all thoughts of the place : but her temper both then
and since has been very different from what I could wish it. She
is angry if she is not constantly consulted, and yet takes up
everything with such absolute quickness, that we all dread to
consult her. She is at present I fear equally offended with me,
with Hugonin and Mr. Scott. Nothing shall however abate my
regard for her, and as soon as I can discover whether she will fix
on Bath or some country place, she may command every service
within my power. All this *sub sigillo amicitiæ.*

I am summoned to dress. The Jolliffes dine here. Adieu.
Every kind wish to Mrs. H.

148.

To J. B. Holroyd, Esq.

Beriton, 3rd October, 1772.

I am so happy, so exquisitely happy, at feeling so many Mountains taken off my shoulders, that I can brave your indignation, and even the three-forked lightning of Jupiter himself. My reasons for taking so unwarrantable a step (approved of by Hugonin) were no unmanly despondency (though it daily became more Apparent how much the farm would suffer, both in reality and in reputation, by another year's management), but the following grounds. 1. The being secure against repairs for so long a term, and 2. The giving the Tenant a durable interest to use my land like his own. The Revolutions of this country may take various turns within that period; nor do I recollect that, although you fixed on 21 years, you so strongly disapproved of a longer term. However the Mischief is done; and I can only wish that, at or about Michaelmas in the year of our Lord God one Thousand seven hundred and ninety-three, you convince me that Gib-ben knows no more of country business than Maria, which by that time most probably will be very true. The rent after deducting Ponds, Yards, &c. (which every tenant objected to) is very little short of the grand desideratum twenty and ten, a price which fills the country round with terror and amazement. The Tenant is confessedly rich, and in this whole transaction about Covenants, repairs &c., has shewn himself the reverse of *eminently troublesome.* The father may perhaps be slovenly, the son who is properly my Tenant is (in H.'s opinion) a very active, clever, sensible fellow.

But to turn from the past to the future. *My Bucks Tenants* have all consented (though 'tis very " *heard* ") to pay Church and Poor, but before they sign the paper, they wish to wait on me, either here or in London, and Harris hints to me their intended request, " That they may have the cutting of the Hedges for wood for their own use, but not to sell any; and to cut such hedges as I think proper, and so much in the year; to be done in a husband-like manner, and to do all their own repairs, thatching and everything." On consulting Hugonin, I found that what they ask is allowed in this part of the country, so that I am almost enclined by sending them a gracious permission to secure their signature and prevent the deputation of the Savages. However I wait for orders. It is of more consequence to consider what further steps may be taken with regard to the disposal of Lenborough ; for as I now see land, I am very impatient to get ashore. Suppose *you made Gosling* acquainted with all difficulties being smoothed and made him a final offer for—the Mortgage *and £5000* shall we say ? It is surely worth it. If he refuses We have no resource but the hazardous one of a Auction. Think of it : and of the steps to be taken, and whether in the last case we may not *divide* with success.

Mrs. G. is now cheerfull and I hope satisfied : but I fancy *will hardly accept* of your obliging invitation this year. To-morrow we appraise the stock. The *week after I carry my* Hops to Weyhill. On my return we shall find much to do in settling the plan of selling my corn during the winter, selecting the choicest furniture and preparing for *an auction of the rest*. She is then desirous of going to look about her at Bath, where I shall attend her, and on my return shall be impatient to examine London in quest of a comfortable habitation. We shall probably meet when you are on your Surrey (I suppose Richmond) scheme, and you will find me a sure resource in the bleak season when you can get nobody else. Adieu.

149.

To J. B. Holroyd, Esq.

Beriton, 15th October, 1772.

Dear H.,

I am most seriously uneasy with regard to what you say of Mrs. H., her health, her spirits and her thinness. I wish she may receive benefit from Dr. Pepys's prescription, but am of opinion that change of air and amusements would prove the best Physician. Recollect the service our little tour was to her, consider that the evenings are growing long and Sheffield Place affords no variety of objects or company. *You know she loves Bath*, which is now in season, and I should think that place would fill up the gloomy vacuity between this time and Christmas. *If among a crowd of acquaintances one friend can afford you any comfort, I am quite at your service there.*

You know as much as I do of Lord Verney's tythe.   Harris
has not answered that part of my letter; probably he had not
seen his Lordship.   I write to him by this post to enquire into
that matter, & to order him absolutely *to lett the Underwood*, and,
if he can, to prevail on the Tenants to pay something more for
the liberty of cutting the hedges.   Whatever is done about the
sale must be *done quickly*, and on that account I fear not so well.
The Goslings are impatient.   I know not how to ask them for
another year, and to take up so large a sum for one Year only
would be attended with much difficulty and expence.   They wish,
if I cannot speedily dispose of Bucks, I would pay off part by the
sale of the New River share, for which I know they have a
hankering.   It is a most delicious bit of Property, and I should
be sorry to part with it for such a price as one commonly gets
by a forced sale.   If they would give me a *rotund* sum for both,
it might perhaps tempt.   I wish to hear from you soon.   Everything is hastening to a dissolution.   Winton has taken my stock
(*all* the horses), but the appraisement came short of what I
expected (not quite £1000).   I believe many of the things, live
and dead, were old.   Last Monday I went with Mr. Scott to
Weyhill fair, and sold my hops pretty well.   The sheep are
moving off very fast.   My Corn, a noble stock, will be threshed
out and sold *sous les Yeux de* Mr. Luff.   The household furniture
will be sold by auction after my departure, but I reserve a great
deal (most assuredly the three pictures) for my house in Town.
Hugonin undertakes the repairs, so that I see nothing which can
prevent my quitting this damned place in about a fortnight or
three Weeks.   As soon as I have deposited Mrs. G. at Bath, I
shall be quite my own Master.   Adieu.

E. G.

150.

To J. B. Holroyd, Esq.

Beriton, 21st of October, 1772.

To quit a subject now become a matter of curiosity, I shall
only say that in this country the Hampshire Gentleman is supposed to have lett his farm exceedingly high, and that on every
side he hears compliments from the Gentlemen and clamours

from the Farmers. He did not *sneakingly conceal, &c.* The
Tenant pays for the seeds, the Fallows were given him, from the
opinion of Hugonin, &c., who agreed that they were very ill
made. But now, hark forward.

The Gosling's impatience will I fear hurry us very unpleasantly.
Their proposal of *the New River* share would not suit in any
respect. It brings in at least £260 pr. annum, yearly encreasing,
and must, I should think, as freehold be worth thirty years'
purchase ; call it £8000. The average (for it varies prodigiously)
of *the Copper share* is under £100. I cannot think it would sell
for more than £1500. When that was done, instead of a surplus
of Money, I should find myself possessed of two Landed Estates,
with at least £7000 mortgage on one of them, and for a time
totally disabled from buying a house or forming any plans of life,
for a great deal of the farm stock must go towards paying a
variety of middling debts of my most careless Father, which it
was unnecessary to trouble you with. So that scheme will never
answer. I tell my Fleet Street friends that if it will be very
inconvenient to them to allow me another year, or even to stay
the Winter, I must endeavour to get their Mortgage transferred
for a twelfmonth to some other Person, which cannot be done
without trouble and expence. In either case we must act with
vigour. I am so far from chusing to *sell under* 30 *years' purchase* (a bare £20,000 without Manor, &c.) that I think *that
a very sorry price : They are still at old Rents. Why cannot we
try an auction of the whole* before we divide ? *I wish to see you,
and think Denham* a good place of Rendez-vous : But before I
can get from hence, carry Mrs. G. to Bath, and traverse to Bucks,
it will grow *towards the* 10*th of November.* Will that do ? To
another man, I should talk nonsense about trouble, obligation,
gratitude, &c. &c. To you, I only say, If I can't meet you at
Denham, *take R. Way with you,* carve Lenborough and let the
Deed itself serve you for a reward. I have had another letter
from Harris : not a word *about Lord V.* But he speaks of *Mr.
Monkeith,* a rich man who liked the Estate, and objected only to
the Poor's tax. I desired he would give him my direction at the
Cocoa Tree, and inform that that objection was removed. Adieu.
You do not say a word about Mrs. H. I hope she is better.

E. G.

151.

To J. B. Holroyd, Esq.

Beriton, October 30th, 1772.

DEAR H.,

The steps you are taking seem perfectly right and promise success. I have not heard anything from Monkeith as yet, but have received a letter from Mr. Scott in town that Clive would send a purchaser (I know nothing more) to talk with my lawyer Newton. The more irons in the fire the better. Partly for business and principally to breath, for I am almost suffocated, I propose running up to town (you shall have a line from thence) Sunday and down here again Thursday.

I was in hopes by this time to have been in motion. Our preparations have been thrown a full fortnight back by the illness and death of Mrs. G.'s brother, that poor invalid whom you saw at Beriton. It can hardly be called a loss, as his life would only have been a burthen to himself and others ; yet a few moments must be given to Nature, and a few days to decency. By the best calculations it must be at least the 20th instead of the tenth before I can meet you in Bucks. However, if your days are counted and you judge my presence necessary, all other business must yield to that most important one. Adieu. Excuse a double letter, I did not perceive I was writing on a half sheet. *Sincerely glad to hear Mrs. H. is better. Still I think Bath would suit her. She, and you too I fear, rather want the Physic of the mind than of the body. Tell me something about yourself.* Once more—Adieu.

Cocoa Tree, Tuesday, Eleven o'Clock, Nov. 3rd, 1772.

I see pleasure but not use in a Congress, therefore decline it. I know nothing as yet of a purchaser, and can only give you full and unlimited powers. If you think it necessary, let me know when you sell ; but, however, do as you please. Where am I to write to you next ; you are acquainted with our Route. Adieu.

152.

To J. B. Holroyd, Esq.

Beriton, 15th November, 1772.
Dear H.,

As the day draws near and my cares diminish, I think my hurry encreases—expect only four lines—Way's terms I leave to you, his own appear *smart* to me.—An indifferent plan I have found and will bring with me, but without a measurement.— If Way is employed, some deference must I think be paid to his opinion about the time of sale. The delay is short and the difference he talks of immense; else I am tired of being a Landlord at 2¾ and as Tenant at 4½ per cent. I told you of my letter to Fleet Street several weeks ago, refusing the Copper share, and requesting, if *necessary*, another year. I have had no answer: silence I suppose gives consent. If you are in town you might call. I go from this place for ever, next Thursday. Mrs. G. will hover about Up-Park and Maple Durham about a fourteen days longer, till the servants she takes to Bath are recovered from Inoculation. She insists on my not going with her, as it is so much later than we first imagined. I go to town directly to look for a House. Another business, but that is a pleasant one.

E. G.

Harris does not like to have anything to say to Lord V[erney]. Once (he says) my father attempted to take the Tythe in kind: it amounted, *toute dépense faite*, only to £8. Can you account for it?

153.

To his Stepmother.

Newman Street, Thursday Night, '72.
Dear Madam,

I got safe to town about four o'clock, and now write from Mrs. P.'s fire-side, who desires her best compliments to you. Farther particulars by Saturday night's post, though I much fear the Houses will not do. By that time I hope you will be removed from the ruins of Beriton. Has Mr. Barton got his pony? The saddle met with an accident the other day, but Poynter has orders to repair and deliver it to the Rector; he will easily find

out his books. I found a note from Jolliffe, who wants to see me
to-morrow morning ; but I have something else to do.

I am, dear Madam,

Most truly yours,

E. G.

Your ticket by this time is bought. If you have the £20,000,
I shall charge brokerage.

154.

To his Stepmother.

November 21st, 1772.

DEAR MADAM,

Had I not promised you some account of my proceedings
by to-night's post, I should have deferred it till Tuesday, for
though I have seen much I have done little or nothing. Houses
rise to my enquiry every moment, but where is a perfect house or
perfect man to be found ? Lady Rous's is one of the most pleasing (Bentinck Street),[1] but I neither like the offices nor two pair
of stairs. Mrs. Bernard's worthy Tenant (Sir Everard) declares
that he will neither suffer any one to see his house nor quit it
till the last extremity of the law. The Lord of Petersfield,[2] to
whom I am indebted for three blank Visets, has sent me word of
a house in Argyle Street which I am to see Monday, as well as
another strongly recommended by a Lady in Mrs. Porten's street
(Newman Street). My wise friends check my impatience : my
foolish ones, whom on this occasion I think wiser, encourage it ;
however I will do nothing rash.—Henry means to go down to
Beriton next week ; he has left some things there which he fears
will be swept away in the general inundation. Wherever you are,
dear Madam, whether at the proud Up-park or the humble Maple
Durham, I beg my best Compliments to the natives, and the
earliest intelligence of your intended motions, which I much fear
it will be out of my power to attend without losing sight of my
enchanted palaces.

I am, Dear Madam,

Most truly yours,

E. G.

[1] Sir John Rous, M.P. for Suffolk, died October 31, 1771, and from his
widow Gibbon took 7 Bentinck Street, where he lived till September, 1783.

[2] William Jolliffe, M.P. for Petersfield, Commissioner of Trade and
Plantations.

155.

To his Stepmother.

Pall Mall, Dec. 2nd, 1772.

DEAR MADAM,

It pleased my Lord Godolphin to speak by a letter directed to Beriton a few days since, which he hopes you had. Since the receipt of your last, he paused, as not knowing whether he should direct to the top or bottom of the hill.

The stops I have met with about my houses would require pages instead of lines, but I believe in the end I shall settle in Bentinck Street. I am at this moment in such hot pursuit of it that I fear it will be out of my power to attend you to Bath, without running risks to which I am sure you would be sorry to expose me. I wish you may find Bath easier or be yourself less difficult than I have been in London. I hope the best of the sale, but am sensible that it must in a great measure be left to the Chapter of Accidents. I will write to Sir Hugh about the business of Patrick's, which falls in luckily enough. Your ticket I have enclosed, two days ago it was undrawn. May it be the rival of 345! Adieu! dear Madam. Give my compliments to Mr. & Mrs. Bayley, and if I do not hear from you sooner, let me hear a good account of your Bath journey; till I receive it I shall not easily satisfy myself for not having attended you there.

Yours sincerely,

E. G.

You have received two letters from me since my arrival, both from Mrs. Porten's. If you have not had the last, I suspect her servant and want to enquire into it.

156.

To J. B. Holroyd, Esq.

Pall Mall, Dec. 11th, 1772.

DEAR H.,

*By this time, I suppose you returned to the Elysian fields of Sheffield. The Country (I do not mean any particular reflections on Sussex) must be vastly pleasant at this time of the Year! For my own part, the punishment of my sins has at length

overtaken me. On Thursday, the third of December, in the
present year of our Lord, one Thousand seven hundred and
seventy-two, between the hours of one and two in the Afternoon,
as I was crossing St. James's Church Yard, I stumbled, and *again
sprained my foot;* but, alas ! after two days' pain and Confinement,
a horrid monster, *ycleped the Gout,* made me a short Visit ; and
though he has now taken his leave, I am full of apprehensions
that he may have liked my company well enough to call again.

The Parliament, after a few soft murmurs, is gone to sleep, to
wake again after Christmas,[1] safely folded in Lord North's [2] arms.
The town is gone into the Country, and I propose *visiting
Sheffield* about Sunday se'nnight, if by that time I can get my
household preparations (I have as good as taken Lady Rous's lease
in Bentinck-Street) in any forwardness. Shall I *angle for Batt?*
No news stirring, except the Dutchess of G[loucester]'s pregnancy
certainly declared.[3] Way called on me the other day, and has
taken my plan with him to consider it ; he still wishes to defer to
Spring ; talks of bad roads, &c. and is very absolute. I remon-
strated, *but want to know whether I am to submit.* Before I go
out of town *I must call to settle with* the Gosling. I am afraid of
some peremptory declaration, though I flatter myself they would
not materially injure me by a precipitated sale. *Adieu. *Clarke,*
who is writing near me, begs to be remembered. The savage
is going to hunt Foxes in Northamptonshire, Oxfordshire,
Gloucestershire, &c. Yours sincerely.*

157.

To J. B. Holroyd, Esq.

Tuesday Evening, 15th December, 1772.
DEAR H.,

My letter which crossed yours has already apologized
for my silence and inactivity. Yesterday morning, however, I

---

[1] Parliament adjourned from December 23, 1772, to January 22, 1773.

[2] An allusion to Lord North's habit of sleeping in the House of Commons.
He slumbered, as Gibbon says in his Autobiography, between the Attorney-
General (Thurlow) and the Solicitor-General (Wedderburn), who roused him
when it was necessary that he should speak. On one occasion a member of
the Opposition exclaimed, in reproach of his somnolence, " Even now the
noble lord is slumbering over the ruin of his country ! " " I wish to Heaven,"
muttered Lord North, slowly opening his eyes, " that I was ! "

[3] Her daughter, Sophia Matilda (1773-1844), was born May 29, 1773.

went to see a house for you in Duke Street to be lett for any term or in any manner. The pro and con are dispatched in a few words—Vile street, good quarter—An excellent house, spacious and convenient, but a little old-fashioned—The price ten Guineas a week.—Colonel Amherst had been already applied to by somebody else, but will neither lett nor leave his furniture.

I enquired about a house ready furnished in Hill Street, 400 Guineas a year for not less than three years certain. I shall pursue my enquiries, now I am getting stronger, but I think for your sake as well as my own I shall defer my Visitation four or five days.

I have not slept about my house in Bentinck Street, for, as I have accepted Lady Rous's lease, I call it my own. Ireland the Upholder visited it with me this morning, and, to omitt other particulars, talked of Book-cases, quite agrees in the proscription of Mahogany. The paper of the Room will be a fine shag flock paper, light blue with a gold border, the Book-cases painted white, ornamented with a light frize: neither Doric nor Dentulated (that was yours) Adamic. The Dog was to have sent me drawings to-night to enclose to you, but has disapointed me. I am afraid I can hardly wait for them. I am called to supper. Adieu.

158.

To J. B. Holroyd, Esq.

London, December, 1772.

DEAR H.,

I was indeed alarmed, both at the cause of your apprehensions and at your temper of mind—so much alarmed that I knew not what to say, and therefore said nothing. I have this moment (on my return from the play) received your comfortable epistle, and rejoyce with you and Mrs. Holroyd.—I have nothing new to tell you concerning houses, only that the Courtier promised to send you particulars of a desirable one in Saville Row. Were I worthy to advise I would recommend to you to take up with a common lodging house (of those there are plenty) at so much a week ; the first fortnight will shew you numbers of more desirable ones. Adieu.

E. G.

159.

To J. B. Holroyd, Esq.

Saturday Night, 19th December, 1772.

DEAR H.,

I am sorry at not hearing from you to-night, because I apprehended that if our poor little friend had been perfectly recovered you would have been impatient to have told me so. Mrs. Clive has had your note and I suppose has separated in consequence : but I don't myself think the house will do,—the street ! You may have coach-house and stables in the neighbourhood, but the man (who is impatient for a positive answer) cannot keep the house (as to the commencement of rent) longer than the 10th of January. I tried this morning a house in Henrietta Street, Cavendish Square—lett the day before—I have just heard of another in Dover Street, a charming situation, not less than six months certain, seven Guineas a week. I will see it Monday morning. Several things about my house and another unexpected affair will not allow me dine at S. P. before Thursday, when you may positively expect me. I called at Payne's the other day, he has secured such of your members as remained. The next time I call I will mention Lord B. Adieu.

160.

To his Stepmother.

Pall Mall, December 21st, 1772.

DEAR MADAM,

I should be very uneasy at your prolonged silence, especially at this critical juncture, if I had not heard from Mr. Scott that you are arrived at Bath safe, though not perfectly well. I hope, as indeed I have hoped for several posts past, that a letter is now on the road to tell me that you have got the better of your fatigues and indisposition, that you begin to relish the new scene, and that you have seen a house to your mind. For me, I have at last pitched on Lady Rouse's house in Bentinck Street, which I have only taken till I find whether the place, situation,

&c., will suit me. My upholsterer is hard at work, and whilst he is employed, I shall set out next Thursday for Holroyd's, stay about a fortnight, send up for my books and *young* Housekeeper about the middle of next month, and get into my new Habitation towards the end of it; in which last article I possibly flatter myself too lightly. I think I shall be comfortable, and when I have shaken off the load of Lenborough dirt, not unhappy, which in this life is saying a great deal. In the meantime I have absolutely settled with Clark and Rout, and got a discharge for £900 less than I at first expected. I am rather vain of my conduct of that intricate business. Adieu, Dear Madam, Mrs. Porten begs her love and Compliments to you. I desire you would present mine (though love is rather too strong) to Mrs. Gould.

I am, most truly yours,
E. GIBBON.

The Jolliffes have advanced and I have retreated almost by equal steps.

161.

To his Stepmother.

Pall Mall, December 22nd, 1772.

DEAR MADAM,

I have nothing about myself to add to my letter of last night, except to answer your obliging anxiety about my Gout, which Mr. Scott took the trouble of mentioning to you. A sprain in the same foot as last year brought on a kind of inflammation which was suspected to be that dignified disorder; but I much doubt the fact, and be it as it may, the whole was over in four or five days, and I am now strong and well.

You know, dear Madam, how many various calls I have upon me, but yours will always stand the first, and will be answered whenever it is most convenient to you.

I am, Dear Madam,
Most sincerely yours,
E. GIBBON.

162.

To his Stepmother.

Pall Mall, December 31st, 1772.

DEAR MADAM,

I am called upon to perform a melancholy office, and to acquaint you with what I am sure you will esteem a loss, whatever accession of fortune you may derive from it.

Last Sunday sevennight I dined with our friend Mr. Scott at Mrs. Porten's, and thought him remarkably well and in spirits. On Thursday I went down into Sussex, and the bad foggy weather we had in town prevented my calling upon him in the mean time. He was however already very much out of order, with a bad cold apparently and a general weakness; his Apothecary however thought him in no danger, till Dr. Fothergill, who was sent for, apprehended there was a great deal, though he would not suffer the people of the House to acquaint him with it. They, on the Monday 28th instant, thought it incumbent on them to inform Mr. Oliver, the only friend of his they knew, of his dangerous situation. Mr. Oliver, on the receipt of their very pressing letter, immediately dispatched a Post Office Express to Mr. Gibbon of Petersfield, and the Express (returned by the care of Mr. Bayley and Griffiths of the Cocoa Tree) reached me last night very late at Sheffield Place. I came up to Town this morning, but was too late. Your kinsman and my friend had already terminated a blameless and happy life by a very easy death about three o'clock Tuesday afternoon. There was so little appearance of a visible illness that Dr. Fothergill could only call it a sudden but general decay of Nature.

After consulting with Sir Stanier Porten [1] we both judged it would be right to take no steps with regard to his Effects till you could be informed of what had happened. We went to his Lodgings this afternoon, and in the presence of the Landlord, the Apothecary and Mr. Newton's Clerk, we examined every probable place in search of a Will but found none. All the papers that seemed of any moment we locked up in a trunk and put our Seal upon it. The principal one is a bond of £1980 from me to Mr. Scott only a few days ago to pay off the Clarkes. I heartily wish

[1] See note to Letter 204.

that you may be my Creditor. I suppose it will be necessary and proper for you immediately to examine Mr. Scott's Lodgings at Bath, which I think was more his regular residence than London. If no Will should be found anywhere, you are his natural heir, nor do I understand that it will be necessary for you to come to town to administer unless you chuse it.

As I do not see that I can be of any immediate use to you, I propose returning to Sheffield to-morrow for about ten or twelve days more, but if I am wanted sooner, shall be ready at an hour's warning either to attend you in London or to execute any of your directions. Sir Stanier, who sincerely laments our old friend, proposes to undertake what requires the most immediate care, but it will be necessary for him to know whether, in case of a Will, Mr. Scott has left any orders concerning his funeral, or whether you would chuse to give any particular ones yourself. If the matter is left to him, we had agreed that it should be in the Parish Church plain, decent and private. Tuesday next is the last day, and it would, I should think, be better to send your letter to Sir Stanier by a Post Office Express under cover to the Earl of Rochefort, Cleveland Row, which franks the Express.

The nature of the subject and the length of this letter prevents me from adding any more than that I most sincerely wish you every happiness of the next and of many succeeding years.

I am, Dear Madam,
Most truly yours,
E. GIBBON.

163.

To J. B. Holroyd, Esq.

Pall Mall, January 16th, 1773.

DEAR H.,

Mrs. G. fastened upon me as soon as I got to town, and was in some measure the cause of some of the blessings you might possibly honour me with when Yesterday's post arrived at Sheffield. Mrs. G. succeeds without a Will to Mr. Scott, and though she certainly finds a sum of money, yet I believe it turns out very short of her expectations. She means to return to Bath, but you will still I fancy find her here.

I have not as yet got you either footman or stables. The

latter seems almost impossible.   In at least twenty yards, my man Henry has received the *same* answer ; that it is not worth their while to let them for less than a year : so that I fear you will be reduced to a livery stable.   In consequence of the Advertisement I had five or six Candidates at my *Lever*, but none tolerable.   We shall see enough.   Goose or Couse (what do you call him ?) waited on me yesterday morning ; but although the Sultan referred us to his Vizier, he had not signified to him that the House was agreed for.   I assured him it was ; he believed me, and on the morning after your landing will wait on you with the Inventory and a short paper.   The maid, a most usefull Servant as he says, is apprized of your coming and expects your servants.   So much for business, and indeed so much for everything, for I have kept so close to Mrs. G. that I don't know a syllable of news.—If the Fosters are still with you salute them.   Tell Mr. Harry that Mrs. G. has not the honour of being acquainted with any Monkey whatsoever.   Mrs. H.'s watch is in the hands of Trajan, some relation I presume of the Emperor.

> Tandis que tristement sur ce globe qui balance,
> J'appercois à pas lents la mort qui s'avance ;
> Le Francois emporté par do legers desirs,
> Ne voit sur ce cadran qu'un circle de plaisirs.

Mrs. H. when in town will, I fancy, be of the Frenchman's way of thinking.   *Ainsi soit il.*   Adieu—Yorkshire arrived in town very gratefull and not entirely dislocated.

164.

To his Stepmother.

Bentinck St., February 11th, 1773.

DEAR MADAM,

Though I cannot applaud your punctuality in giving me one line the first night of your arrival, yet a very excellent Cheese had already informed me that you had reached Marlborough, and were not unmindful of me.   I still waited from post to post till I could date my thanks from my own house in Bentinck St.   After some expence of temper occasioned by the cursed delays of upholsterers, I am got into the delightfull mansion and already enjoy the long wished comforts of it.   May you soon be settled as much to your satisfaction at Bath as I am in London. Sir Matthew is expected here to-morrow, but I hear nothing of Eliotts; I suppose they will come up for the winter about the beginning of May. I am so unfashionable as not to have fought a duel yet. I suppose all the Nation admire Lord B.'s behaviour.[1] I will give you one instance of his—call it what you please. L. T.'s pistol was raised, when he called out, "One moment, my Lord—Mr. Dillon, I have undertaken a commission from the French Embassador—to get him some Irish poplins—should I fall, be so good as to execute it. Your Lordship may now fire." L. B. is certainly quite out of danger, but the cure will be long and painfull.

I am, Dear Madam,

Ever yours,

E. G.

165.

To his Stepmother.

February the 27th, 1773.

DEAR MADAM,

After having been silent longer perhaps than I ought to have been, suffering post after post to slide away with a firm resolution to write the very next (and what is one day's difference ?), I am now as usual driven to the sound of the bell and the verge of eleven. Will you for once accept as a letter the information that I am perfectly well, and that I only wish you as happily settled in a house at Bath as I am in London ? Holroyd admires Brook Street, but not the side where his father lives.[2] The opposite side has a fine prospect from the back rooms.

---

[1] The duel in question was fought between Lord Bellamont and Lord Townshend. The cause, according to the *London Evening Post*, was the offence taken by Lord Bellamont at the abrupt refusal of Lord Townshend, then Viceroy of Ireland, to see him at Dublin. As soon as Lord Townshend arrived in England, Lord Bellamont sent him a message that he would be glad if the affair could be "settled *à la militaire*." The duel took place February 2nd, in the Mary-le-bone Fields, when Lord Bellamont received a shot near the groin, and then fired his pistol in the air. Lord Ligonier was Lord Townshend's second, and Mr. Dillon acted for Lord Bellamont.

[2] Isaac Holroyd, who, by his wife, Dorothy Baker, was the father of John Baker Holroyd, lived at Bath, where he died in May, 1778. With him lived his only surviving daughter, Sarah Martha Holroyd, who died unmarried,

Adieu ! Dear Madam, and either in long or short letters, believe me,

Ever yours,

E. G.

166.

To his Stepmother.

London, March 25th, 1773.

Dear Madam,

You are clearly in the right. If seldom, long letters : if short ones, often. 'Tis perfectly equitable, but now to my old reasons there is a new one added,—this abominable fine weather which will not allow me a quiet hour at home, without being liable to the reproaches of my friends and of my own conscience. It is the more provoking as it drives me not out of a stinking Apothecary's, but from my own new clean comfortable dear house, which I like better every week I pass in it. I now live, which I never did before, and if it would but rain, should enjoy that unity of study and society, in which I have always placed my prospect of happiness. Though I do not find my expences rise higher than I calculated that they would, I have not yet practised much of that Economy with which the voice of Fame has complimented me : but at least I keep (in general) better hours than I ever yet could bring about in London.

With regard to the Cornish journey. I will fairly lay before you the state of my mind. As we are often tempted to sacrifice propriety to inclination, I am afraid that I should have deferred it another summer in favour of Derbyshire. Your company has fixed me, but I thought when you was in town we had settled it for the autumn. If you wish to be early in your visit, I will calculate that the Autumn begins with August, and will then attend you at Bath, or if you chuse to go *still* earlier, I will bring you back ; for I fancy my stay at Port Eliott will hardly be so long as yours. I hear nothing of the Lord of it, but I know that the *copper* Lockwood impatiently expect him in town.

some years later, at Bath. She translated, says Miss Burney, from the French version a German work, in four thick volumes—Sturm's *Religious Meditations and Observations for every Day in the Year.* Both Mr. and Miss Holroyd are frequently mentioned in the letters.

Holroyd, who begs to be remembered to you, has got a new scheme of regulating the Tythe-laws, holds meetings, writes declarations and employs his great soul and his little body entirely on the business. Mrs. Porten is, I much fear, in a very bad way : her old complaint, but the fits more violent and more frequent. We shall not possess her long.

This morning, the fact is certain, an Address was delivered to Lord B[ellamont] from the Grand Jury of the County of Dublin, thanking him for his proper and spirited behaviour. Incomparable Hibernians ! A Judicial Body appointed to maintain and execute the Laws publicly applaud a man for having broke them.

> I am, Dear Madam,
> Ever yours,
> E. G.

167.

To his Stepmother.

Bentinck Street, May the 5th, 1773.

DEAR MADAM,

Your kind letter and just reproaches, instead of making me do immediately what I had resolved to do every post-night for a fortnight before, put off my letters two or three days longer. The Snail of Love-lane, I saw this morning, and he tells me that he had sent you a satisfactory explanation of his conduct ; if it appears otherwise to you, and that his delays are still inconvenient to you, I beg that you would draw upon me, and hope you are persuaded that, as I have two hundred pounds in Fleet Street, you are welcome to one of them.

With Holroyd's assistance, who is determined to extricate me out of all my troubles, the sale of Lenborough by auction at Buckingham is fixed for the 24th of this month. He goes down with me, and the Estate has been carefully divided into four lots, rising successively in value above each other, so that, if any parts should remain upon my hands a while longer, they will be the best. These precautions are requisite in the present scarcity of money, which gives me little hopes of selling the whole together, and even the sanguine Holroyd is apprehensive that I shall be obliged to buy it in again and provide for the mortgage by some other measures, at least of the procrastinating kind.

Were it not for these worldly cares, I should be a very happy
man. I never formed any great schemes of avarice, ambition or
vanity: and all the notions I ever formed of a London life in my
own house, and surrounded by my books, with a due mixture of
study and society, are fully realised. I have seen the Eliotts
several times, and think he and I take to one another very well
this year. They both express great pleasure at the thoughts of
seeing us in Cornwall. I shall be glad to know whether the time
I mentioned will suit. I am obliged to you for your invitation to
Bath, and am lost in admiration at the size of your house, which
enables you to spare a bed-chamber and drawing-room; tho' after
all, I can offer you the same apartment in my little Palace, which
is absolutely the best house in London. The Waste-coats are
sincerely pretty, without gratitude or compliment. The Madeira
I have got from Oliver; it is incomparable, but saddled with nine
or ten pounds due for cellarage ever since Mr. Scott's arrival in
England. Where was the Rum, for Oliver knows nothing about
it? Apropos the Beriton pictures; should you think it worth
while to frame and put them up at Bath? They will not suit my
rooms and will be soon spoilt in a Lumber-room. If you do not
chuse them, I believe I shall let them take their choice at
Christie's, though I find by a very good painter's opinion that we
much over-rated their value. My compliments to the Goulds, &c.
Poor Mrs. Porten has long and frequent attacks, but her spirits
are still good.

I am, Dear Madam,

Ever yours,

E. G.

168.

To J. B. Holroyd, Esq.

Boodle's, May 11th, 1773.

DEAR H.,

I hope you got safe to S. P.; that the most amiable
Ram, and the less admirable Bull, are both in health and spirits;
that Maria remembers me; and that Mrs. H. is quietly metamor-
phosed from a Lady of the town (an awkward expression) into
a country Gentlewoman. We dined to-day at the Romans, seven,
who all talked of you—Lord A. was very happy to meet *Holroyd*,

and enquired whether *Wilbraham* was gone into Sussex. Is your plan settled? when do you come? and are you resolved to take a bed in Bentinck Street? You will disapoint me extremely if you do not, for it is a point of ambition I have set my heart upon.

*I am full of worldly cares, anxious about the great 24th, plagued with the public Advertiser, and distressed by the most dismall dispatches from Hugonin. Mrs. Lee claims a million of repairs which will cost a million of money.

The House of Commons sat late last night. Burgoyne made some spirited motions "that the Territorial acquisitions in India belonged to the State" (that was the word); "that grants to the servants of the Company (such as jaghires) were illegal; and that there could be no true repentance without restitution." [1]

---

[1] The charges against Lord Clive, the famine in Bengal (1770), and the financial embarrassments of the East India Company, had for many months attracted public attention. In April, 1772, a Select Committee of the House of Commons was appointed to investigate the Company's affairs. During the recess (June 10 to November 26) the directors applied to Lord North for a loan of £1,500,000. On November 26 Parliament met, being specially summoned to discuss the state of India, and Lord North proposed and carried a motion for a Secret Committee of Inquiry. Four months later (March 9, 1773), Lord North proposed to lend to the Company £1,400,000, on condition that its dividends were restricted, and its surplus revenues appropriated to the liquidation of the debt. On these conditions, the Company was to enjoy possession of the territorial acquisitions till 1779, when its exclusive charter expired.

On May 3, the General Court of Proprietors of East India Stock petitioned Parliament against arbitrary interference with their territorial rights. The petition was ordered to lie on the table, and Lord North introduced the outlines of his scheme for the reconstitution of the Company. The chief changes were the appointment by the Crown of a governor-general and the establishment at Calcutta of a Supreme Court of Judicature. These changes and the provisions for the loans were embodied in two Bills, which received the royal assent on June 21 and July 1 respectively (13 Geo. III. cc. 63 & 64).

On May 10, whilst Lord North's proposals were under discussion, General Burgoyne moved three resolutions: (1) That all acquisitions made by military force or by treaty with foreign powers do of right belong to the State; (2) that to appropriate such acquisitions to private use is illegal; (3) that such acquisitions have been appropriated by private persons.

The first two resolutions, which virtually transferred to the Crown the territorial acquisitions made by the Company in India, were carried that night without a division. The third, which was practically an indictment of Lord Clive, was rejected on May 21.

John Burgoyne (1722-1792) married Lady Charlotte Stanley in 1743, and through Lord Derby's influence was now M.P. for Preston. He was made a

Wedderbourne[1] defended the Nabobs with great eloquence but little argument. The motions were carried without a division ; and the hounds go out again next Friday. They are in high spirits ; but the more sagacious ones have no idea they shall kill. Lord North spoke for the enquiry, but faintly and reluctantly. Lady C. is said to be in town at her mother's, and a separation is unavoidable ; but there is nothing certain. Adieu.*

Sincerely yours,

E. G.

169.

To his Stepmother.

London, May the 27th, 1773.

DEAR MADAM,

I find that I am not the only lazy being in the Universe, and my friends without any diminution of regard can leave me at least *three weeks* without a line, and totally at a loss what to answer when I am questioned whether they are got into their new house, &c. However, as you will be in suspence about the 24th instant, I must for once break an old rule and tell you that Holroyd accompanied me to Buckingham in his way to Ireland. The auction was very cold, as all auctions are at present, and the highest sum that was bid was £19,000 by an Agent of Lord Temple. By the advice of H., my faithfull friend and Minister, I was immoveably fixed at £20,000, which, *all things considered,* is not amiss. The Agent had gone to the utmost of his instructions, but I have very good reasons to believe, that either from him or some other person I shall get the money very soon. Till that event happens I shall not be easy.

The Snail of Aldermanbury has promised to send you down

major-general in 1772. His motion on the East India Company was his chief political achievement, his surrender at Saratoga (October 17, 1777) the most striking episode in his military career, and his comedy, *The Heiress* (1786), his chief literary success.

[1] Alexander Wedderburn (1733–1805), Solicitor-General (January 22, 1771), succeeded Edward Thurlow (Lord Chancellor, 1778) as Attorney-General, became Lord Chief Justice of the Common Pleas and Lord Loughborough in June, 1780, was Lord Chancellor from 1793 to 1801, created Earl of Roslyn in 1801, and died in 1805.

the Deed transferring from Bucks. to Hampshire.   I hope it will
be satisfactory to you.

I am, dear Madam,

Ever yours,

E. G.

170.

To J. B. Holroyd, Esq.

June 12th, 1773.

DEAR H.,

*Lenborough is no more.—Lrd. Temple acted like a
Jew, and I dare say now repents of it.   In his room Way found
me a better man, a rich brutish honest horse Dealer, who has
got a great fortune by serving the cavalry.   On Thursday he saw
Lenborough, on Friday came to town with R. W., and this morning at nine o'clock we struck at £20,000, after a very hard battle,
in which he squeezed from me a promise of throwing him back
a hundred for trouble, &c.   As times go I am not dissatisfied ;
the worst of it is the time of payment, which I could not prevail
on him to fix sooner than November, though he gave me hopes
of getting it somewhat earlier.   Gosling must wait till then.
R[ichard] W[ay] and the new Lord of Lenborough (by name
Lovegrove) dined with me ; and though we did not speak the
same language, yet by the help of signs, such as that of putting
about the bottle, the natives seemed well satisfied.

The whole world is going down to Portsmouth,[1] where they
will enjoy the pleasure of smoke, noise, heat, bad lodgings, and
expensive reckonings.   For my own part, I have firmly resisted
importunity, declined parties, and mean to pass the busy week in
the soft retirement of my *bocage de* Bentinck Street.

Yesterday the East India Company positively refused the
Loan,—a noble resolution, could they get money anywhere else.[2]

---

[1] The king left Kew on Tuesday, June 22, 1773, and reached Portsmouth
between ten and eleven the same morning, in order to review the fleet
at Spithead, consisting of twenty ships of the line, two frigates, and
three sloops.   He returned to Kew on Saturday, June 26.   "A very great
number of yachts, and other sailing vessels and boats, many of them full
of nobility and gentry," followed the royal yacht *Augusta*, and "an incredible
multitude of people" lined the shores.

[2] On June 11, 1773, the Court of Proprietors of East India Stock determined
to reject the loan and conditions offered by the Government ; but on June 19
the East India Loan Bill was read a third time in the Lower House.
Parliament was prorogued from July 1, 1773, to January 13, 1774.   Sujah
Dowlah was the Nawab of Oude (see note to Letter 192).

They are violent, and it was moved, and the motion heard with
some degree of approbation, that they should instantly abandon
India to Lord North, Sujah Dowlah, or the Devil, if he chose to
take it.*

My respectfull salutations wait on Madame. If with the
handkerchiefs she was to bring me over some Irish linnen for
shirts, it would be an action worthy of her humanity.   Adieu.

E. G.

171.

To his Stepmother.

London, June 15th, 1773.

DEAR MADAM,

          At length the Buckinghamshire transaction is at an
end.   Lord T., after tormenting himself or me to very little
purpose, absolutely refused to give more than £19,000, but a Mr.
Lovegrove, an Oxfordshire man, who has made his own fortune,
applied to Mr. Richard Way, viewed the Estate, and after a long
altercation agreed with me at £20,000, and an excellent purchase
he has made, though the weight of interest, the importunity of
the Goslings and the scarcity of money oblige me to be satisfied
with what I have been able to get for it.   By Michaelmas I shall
be a clear, though a poor man ; since, when I have discharged the
Mortgage and cancelled the bond which I gave Mr. Scott for the
Clarke's money, very little indeed that I can call my own will
remain of that noble estate.   My only comfort, and a very cold
one, is that, though these incumbrances must be paid at my
expence, they were not contracted by my imprudence.   But to
leave these melancholy reflections on a subject which is now
irretrievable.

          Newton will I believe send you down the Deed engrossed
in a day or two.   The confidence, Dear Madam, which you express
in me, pleases without surprizing me, and I hope the business will
be settled to your satisfaction.   Apropos you forget your half-
year, which now at least you must allow to be due.   Do you chuse
to draw upon me, or shall I send you the money in Bank Notes ?

          By what I can collect at Spring Gardens, Mrs. E. will go into
Cornwall in a few days, but will not pass through Bath in her
way.   Eliott stays something longer, but, as well as I can judge,
the beginning of August will suit them perfectly well.   I therefore

still persist in my design of attending you about that time, and
am impatient to see both your new house and its owner.   I
wish you could see how comfortable I am established in mine.

I am, Dear Madam,

Ever yours,

E. G.

172.

To his Stepmother.

Bentinck Street, July 13th, 1773.

DEAR MADAM,

You will excuse my silence when I tell you I have a
friend with me, who takes up the greatest part of my last Friday
se'nnight.   Mr. d'Eyverdun most agreeably surprized me by
walking into my library.   His young Lord Chesterfield has come
over for a few weeks, and as he went down almost immediately
with Lovel Stanhope to the Duke of Chandos, my friend has
established himself in my house during the too short period of his
visit.   You may easily suppose how much I think he embellishes
my little habitation.   I carry him about, we converse, read and
write, and are together almost every hour in the day without the
least constraint on either side.   The town is growing empty and
what is commonly called dull, but with such a companion and my
books you will believe me when I say that I do not regret the
pleasures of the winter.   Even the latter would be sufficient, and
were it not to see you, the charms of Cornwall would scarcely
induce me to leave London in one of the hottest summers that we
have felt for a great while.

The Eliott family is moving away by different detachments.
Mrs. Eliott and William, Miss and Edward have already reached
Cornwall, but it is impossible to discover when the Lord of St.
Germains means to follow them.   I have sounded him, and by his
dark equivocal hints can only learn that he is certainly not upon
the point of his departure.   His slowness will I fear retard our
intended visit and derange my subsequent operations.   He will
surely not be in Cornwall till the beginning of next month, and
the decent time we must give him to settle himself will soon
carry us to the end of it.   I will send the earliest intelligence I
can obtain of his motions, for I know by experience that a state
of suspense even in trifles is painfull.

You will receive, dear Madam, by the Bath coach a representation which is said to be very like a person whom I believe is not indifferent to you. Whatever you may think of his face, be persuaded that his heart is sincerely your own. Adieu. d'Eyverdun desires his compliments and respects to you. If he should go to Bath, which is not impossible, his first visit would be to Charles Street.

173.

To his Stepmother.

Bentinck Street, July 31st, 1773.

DEAR MADAM,

You know how glad I am to catch at a pretence for not writing ; my present one is the uselessness of it when we are so soon to meet ; and as your friend John Buncle[1] says, we can talk the value of a good octavo volume in the course of a morning. I still however hang on the good pleasure of the Lord of Boroughs, but he now seems to hint that another week will wind up his stay in town ; if so, a fortnight will do my business, and I shall hope to be at Bath about the 15th of next month. I am much obliged to you for your kind offer of coming down immediately, and should with pleasure accept of it, were I not detained here by some things that I wish to finish, and for which my Library is absolutely requisite ; laugh at the bookworm if you please, but excuse the nature of the animal. As to poor d'Eyverdun he is not his own master, or you would most assuredly see him. He is now at York with his Lord ; but I hope to catch a sight of him before I leave London, and he England. The Eliots testify a strong inclination to see us in Cornwall, a passionate one indeed. I hope we shall like one another, but I could wish Mrs. Bonnefoy[2] were of the party. We are huge friends. Adieu.

Dear Madam,

Ever yours,

E. G.

[1] Thomas Amory, into whom, says Hazlitt, "the soul of Rabelais passed," published (1756-66) *The Life of John Buncle, Esq.*—a curious book, which is in part autobiographical.

[2] Miss Anne Eliot, sister to Mr. Eliot, of Port Eliot, married Captain Hugh Bonfoy, R.N. Two portraits of her by Sir Joshua Reynolds are in existence—one painted in 1746, the other in 1751.

174.

To J. B. Holroyd, Esq., at Edinburgh.

Bentinck Street, Aug. 7th, 1773.

DEAR H.,

I beg ten thousand pardons for not being dead, as I certainly ought to be. But such is my abject nature, that I had rather live in Bentinck Street, attainted and convicted of the sin of laziness, than enjoy your applause either at old Nick's or even in the Elysian fields. After all, could you expect that I should honor with my correspondance a wild Barbarian of the bogs of Erin ? Had the Natives intercepted my letter, the terrors occasioned by such unknown Magic characters might have been fatal to you. But now you have escaped the fury of their Hospitality, and are arrived amongst a Cee-vi-leezed Nation, I may venture to renew my intercourse.

You tell me of a long list of Dukes, Lairds, and Chieftains of Renown to whom you are recommended ; were I with you, I should prefer one David to them all. When you are at Edinburgh, I hope you will not fail to visit the Stye of that fattest of Epicurus's Hogs,[1] and inform yourself whether there remains no hope of its recovering the use of its right paw. There is another animal of *great*, though not perhaps of *equal*, and certainly not of *similar* merit, one Robertson ;[2] has he almost created the new World ? Many other men you have undoubtedly seen, in the country where you are at present, who must have commanded your esteem. But when you return, if you are not very honest, you will possess great advantages over me in any dispute concerning Caledonian merit.

[1] David Hume, who was now living at Edinburgh, was, from 1763 to 1766, Secretary to the Embassy at Paris under the Earl of Hertford. The description is quoted from Mason's satire (published in 1773), *An Heroic Epistle to Sir William Chambers on his Book of Gardening*—

> "David, who there supinely deigns to lie,
> The fattest hog in Epicurus' sty,
> Though drunk with Gallic wine and Gallic praise,
> David shall bless Old England's halcyon days."

[2] William Robertson, the historian (1721-1793), whose *History of Scotland* (1758) and *History of Charles the Fifth* (1769) had already appeared, was now engaged on his *History of America* (1777).

Boodle's and Atwood's are now no more. The last stragglers, and Clarke in the rear of all, are moved away to their several castles ; and I now enjoy, in the midst of London, a delicious solitude. My Library, Kensington Gardens, and a few parties with new acquaintance who are chained to London, (among whom I reckon Goldsmith and Sir Joshua Reynolds,[1]) fill up my time, and the monster *Ennui* preserves a very respectfull distance. By the bye, your friends Batt, Sir John [Russel], and Lascelles, dined with me one day before they set off ; for I sometimes give the prettiest little dinners in the world. But all this happiness draws near its conclusion. About the 16th of this month Mr. Eliot carries me away, and after picking up Mrs. G. at Bath, sets me down at Port Eliot. There I shall certainly remain six weeks, or, in other words, to the end of September. My future motions, whether to London, Derbyshire, or a longer stay in Cornwall, (pray is not "motion for stay" rather in the Hibernian style ?) will depend on the life of Port Eliot, the time of the meeting of Parliament, and perhaps the impatience of Mr. Lovegrove, Lord of Lenborough.

One of my pleasures in town I forgot to mention, the un-expected visit of d'Eyverdun, who accompanies his young Lord (very young indeed !) on a two months' tour to England. He took the opportunity of the Earl's going down to the Duke of Chandos's, to spend a fortnight (nor do I recollect in my life a more pleasant one) in Bentinck Street. They are now gone together into Yorkshire, and I think it doubtfull whether I shall see him again before his return to Leipsic. It is a melancholy reflection that while one is plagued with acquaintance at the corner of every street, real friends should be separated from each other by unsurmountable bars, and obliged to catch at a few transient moments of interview. I desire that you and My Lady (whom I most respectfully greet) would take your share of that very new and acute observation ; not so large a share, indeed, as my Swiss friend, since Nature and fortune give *us* more frequent opportunities of being together. You cannot expect News from a Desert, and such is London at present. The papers give you the full harvest of public intelligence ; and I imagine

---

[1] After the death of Goldsmith in 1774, Gibbon seems to have succeeded to his place as Sir Joshua's companion to places of amusement, masquerades, and ridottos (*Life and Times of Sir Joshua Reynolds*, vol. ii. p. 273).

that the eloquent Nymphs of Twickenham[1] communicate all the transactions of the polite, the amorous, and the marrying World. The great Pantomime of Portsmouth was universally admired ; and I am angry at my own laziness in neglecting an excellent opportunity of seeing it. Foote has given us the 'Bankrupt,'[2] a serious and sentimental piece, with very severe strictures on the licence of scandal in attacking private Characters. *Quis tulerit Gracchos de seditione loquentes?*[3] Adieu. Forgive and Epistolize me. I shall not believe you sincere in the former, unless you make Bentinck Street your Inn. I fear I shall be gone ; but Mrs. Ford[4] and the Parrot will be proud to receive you and My Lady after your long peregrinations, from which I expect great improvements. Has she got the Brogue upon the tip of her tongue ?*

175.

To his Stepmother.

Bentinck Street, August 7th, 1773.

Dear Madam,

I just write two lines to say that Mr. Eliot proposes staying another week, and then escorting you down to Cornwall. My motions are uncertain since they still depend on those of another, but, if no alteration happens in his plan, I think you may expect to see us both at Bath, Monday the 16th. Charming hot weather ! I am just going to dine alone. Afterwards I shall walk till dark in *my* Gardens at Kensington, and shall then return to a frugal supper and early bed in Bentinck Street. I

---

[1] The family of Richard Owen Cambridge.

[2] Samuel Foote's *Bankrupt* was produced at the Haymarket in July, 1773, Foote himself taking the part of Sir Robert Riscounter. The play was published in 1776, with a dedication to the Marquis of Granby. It contains a vigorous attack on the licence of the press and of the " impudent, rascally Printer." " The tyranny exercised by that fellow," says Sir Robert, "is more despotic and galling than the most absolute monarch's in Asia. . . . I wonder every man is not afraid to peep into a paper, as it is more than probable that he may meet with a paragraph that will make him unhappy for the rest of his life."

[3] Gibbon quotes incorrectly from Juvenal (*Sat.* 2, l. 24)—

" Quis tulerit Gracchos de seditione querentes? "

[4] Gibbon's housekeeper.

lead the true life of a Philosopher, which consists in doing what I really like, without any regard to the world or to fashion.

I am, Dear Madam,
Ever yours,
E. G.

Mr. Barton breakfasted with me yesterday. He seems to think us both very well lodged.

176.

To his Stepmother.

Newman Street, August 13th, 1773.

DEAR MADAM,

Mr. Eliot dined with [me] to-day, and the time of our departure is positively settled (he desired one day more for particular business) to Tuesday next. I mentioned your fears to him, but he like a hero laughs at them all, and indeed I should have laughed at him if he had not. We mean to accept your kind offer of the two beds, and then to continue our march as soon as may suit with your conveniency. I think we shall reach Bath Tuesday evening, but as heat, accidents, &c., may stop us, we hope you will neither expect nor make any preparation for us. In the mean time your commissions shall not be neglected; though the choice of a present for the *youth* perplexes me. I think of a pocket-book which will give him the air of a man of letters and Business. Mrs. Porten, who sets out to-morrow morning for Margate on a party of pleasure, with the spirits of five and twenty, desires her compliments to you.

I am, Dear Madam,
Ever yours,
E. G.

177.

To J. B. Holroyd, Esq.

Port Eliot, Sept. 10th, 1773.

DEAR H.,

By this time you have surely finished your Tour, touched at Edinburgh, where you found a Letter, which you have not answered, and are now contemplating the beauties of the Weald of Sussex. I shall demand a long and particular account of your peregrinations, but will excuse it till we meet ; and for the present, expect only a short memorandum of your health and situation, together with that of my much-honoured friend Mrs. Abigail Holroyd. A word, too, if you please, concerning Father and Sister ; to the latter I enclose a receipt from Mrs. G., who is now with me at Port Eliot.

Blind as you accuse me of being to the beauties of Nature, I am wonderfully pleased with this country. Of her three dull notes, *Ground*, *Plants*, and *Water*, Cornwall possesses the first and last in very high perfection. Think of a hundred solitary streams peacefully gliding between amazing Clifs on one side and rich meadows on the other, gradually swelling by the aid of the Tide into noble rivers, successively losing themselves in each other, and all at length terminating in the Harbour of Plymouth, whose broad expanse is irregularly *dotted* with two-and-forty Line of battle Ships. In *Plants*, indeed, we are deficient ; and though all the Gentlemen now attend to Posterity, the country will for a long time be very naked. We have spent several days agreeably enough in little parties ; but in general our time rolls away in an equal kind of insipidity. Our civil Landlord possesses neither a pack of hounds, nor a stable of running horses, nor a large farm, nor a good library. The last only would interest me ; but it is singular that a Man of fortune, who chuses to pass nine months of the year in the country, should have none of them.* One possession he has indeed most truly desirable ; but I much fear that the Danae of St. Germains has no particular inclination for me, and that the interested Strumpet will yield only to a Golden Shower.[1] My situation is the more perplexing as I cannot with any degree of delicacy make the first advance. A propos, do you still think of starting for the Town ... [illegible] will be very serviceable on the occasion.

*According to our present design, Mrs. G. and myself shall return to Bath about the beginning of next month. I shall probably make but a short stay with her, and defer my Derbyshire Journey till another year. Sufficient for the summer is the evil thereof, of one distant country Excursion. Natural inclination, the prosecution of my great Work, and the conclusion of my

[1] Alluding to negotiations between Mr. Eliot and himself for a seat in Parliament.

Lenborough business, plead strongly in favour of London. However, I desire, and one always finds time for what one really desires, to visit Sheffield Place before the end of October, should it only be for a few days. I know several houses where I am invited to think myself at home, but I know no other where I seem inclined to accept of the invitation. I forgot to tell you, that I have declined the publication of Lord C[hesterfield]'s letters.[1] The public will see them, and upon the whole, I think with pleasure ; but the whole family were strongly bent against it ; and especially on d'Eyverdun's account, I deemed it more prudent to avoid making them my personal enemies.

Yours,
E. G.*

Pray did you use the house in Bentinck Street ?

178.

To his Stepmother.

Bentinck Street, October the 20th, 1773.

DEAR MADAM,

I am neither dead nor lost, as you might naturally suppose. My visit to Sir William [2] produced another to the Bishop of Landaf [3] in Oxfordshire. We proceeded by slow journeying, arrived safe in town Sunday evening, and yesterday I left my little friend in the hands of his Aunts. I ought to have given you a line sooner—but procrastination—— Next Sunday I go into Sussex. Adieu, and believe me,

Dear Madam,
Ever yours,
E. G.

---

[1] Lord Chesterfield's letters to his son, Philip Stanhope, were sold by that son's widow, Mrs. Eugenia Stanhope, and published in 1774, "from the originals in her possession." M. Deyverdun was at this time tutor to the young Lord Chesterfield [1755-1815], a distant kinsman of the deceased Earl. According to Walpole, an injunction was applied for to prevent the publication of the letters. Terms were, however, arranged by which the publication was permitted, on condition that the family expunged certain passages, and regained possession of such copies as had been made of the unpublished *Portraits*, or *Characters* (Walpole to Mason, April 7, 1774).

[2] Probably Sir William Guise.

[3] Shute Barrington, afterwards Bishop of Durham.

179.

To J. B. Holroyd, Esq.

Dec. 4th, 1773.

*We have conquered ; Winton was amazed at the tempest just ready to burst over his head. He does not desire to go to law, wishes to live in peace, has no complaints to make, hopes for a little indulgence. *Hugonin is now in the attitude* of St. Michael trampling upon Satan ; he holds him down, till Andrews has prepared *a little chain of Adamant* to bind the foul fiend. In return, receive my congratulation on your Irish Victory.[1] Batt told me yesterday, as from good authority, that administration designed a second attempt this session ; but to-day I have it from much better, that they always discouraged it and that it was *totally an Iernian scheme.* You remark that I saw Batt. He passed two hours with me ; a pleasant man ! He and Sir John [Russel] dine with me *some day next week: you will have both their portraits ; the originals are engaged.* Walton *is perfectly dry;* both the copies will be done from the first pictures ; in both they are unquestionably the best, and my Lady has more spirit and sense than in the second. Ah ! my Lady, my Lady, what rumours have you diffused in the regions of Bath relating *to Sappho*[2] and your Slave. Adieu. I am called to cut in for the next Rubber. Town is empty, dirty and comfortable. Newton is at his Villa : I *hope my Cabinet afforded a refined tête-à-tête to the* congenial souls.

E. G.

180.

To his Stepmother.

Bentinck Street, December 7th, 1773.

DEAR MADAM,

I break a long silence to write a little more than three lines. Though I cannot call it a silence, since we were regularly

---

[1] A tax had been proposed in the Irish Parliament of two shillings in the pound on the estates of absentee landlords. The motion was lost by 122 to 102.

[2] Mrs. Holroyd, through her sister-in-law, Miss Holroyd, who lived at Bath, had apparently hinted to Mrs. Gibbon at a possible attachment between Edward Gibbon and Miss Fuller, niece to Mr. Rose Fuller, of Rosehill, Sussex, M.P. for Rye.

informed once a week, of the most essential points ; each other's
healths, and amusements. Of my amusements indeed the Sheffield
newspaper (like most other newspapers) reported more than it
could easily prove. The intelligence you received of fair eyes,
bleeding hearts, and an approaching daughter-in-law, is all very
agreeable Romance. A pair of very tolerable eyes, I must confess,
made their appearance at Sheffield, and what is more extraordinary
were accompanied by good sense and good humour, without one
grain of affectation. Yet, still I am *indifferent*, and she is *poor* ;
remove those two little obstacles : and Miss H.'s intelligence
might have some foundation. I came only four or five days ago
from Sussex : the pleasing consciousness of being of some use
and comfort to my friend, who is greatly mended, kept me there
much longer than I intended. I am now pursuing the conclusion
of Lenborough ; some entertaining delays of the law have driven
us a little beyond the appointed time, but I flatter myself we
shall finish either before or immediately after the Holydays.

Mrs. Porten is young again. I mentioned Pitman to Sir Stanier,
but wished I could have been more particular as to his pretensions
and the *precise object* of his present ambition. I should be glad
to be of service to him, especially as you interest yourself on his
account ; but am not even acquainted with the Johnsons, Governor
Duprey, or any people of weight in that line. Besides, one ought
to have favours to grant to have a right to ask any.—Caplin
packed up your books. The old trunk, he says, was unequal to
the weight and journey. However, it is still in Covent Garden.

I am, Dear Madam,
Most truly yours,
E. Gibbon.

181.

To J. B. Holroyd, Esq.

Bentinck Street, Dec. 16th, 1773.

Do not be in such a passion. I think I use you very tolerably,
nor did I ever set up for the Supplement to the Cambridge Mail.[1]
By the bye, you have had a full account from that region of the
visit, the picture and the conspiracy, which entirely failed through

---

[1] The Cambridges, the " eloquent Nymphs of Twickenham."

my blundering management. The surprize was, notwithstanding that disapointment, very fine indeed, and moved me exceedingly. Our day at Twickenham passed off very easily, though two o'clock is a strange hour for dinner; but it suits our Father and consequently must be right. I am glad you was pleased with Sheffield. The designed visit from thence will be I suppose after your excursion. As to my being present at it, fate and circumstances must determine. I neither fly to or from a Baron and Baronne; with regard to these it is probable I shall like them the better for being inclined to like me.

*To the vulgar eye of an Idle man London is empty; but I find many pleasant companions both dead and alive. Two or three days ago I dined at Atwood's with a very select party. Lord G. Germaine[1] was of it, and we communed for a long time. —You know L. Holland is paying Charles's debts. They amount to £140,000. At a meeting of the Creditors, his Agent declared that after deducting £6000 a year settled on Ste.,[2] and a decent provision for his old age, the residue of his wealth amounted to no more than £90,000. The creditors stared till Mr. Powell, a creature, declared that he owed everything to the noble Lord, that *he happened* to have £5000 in long annuities, and begged he might be permitted to supply the deficiency. How generous! Yet there are people who say the money only stood in his name. —"My brother Ste.'s son is a second Messiah," said Charles the other day. How so? "Because born for the destruction of the Jews." *

My compliments to Mr. Walton, best wishes to Lascelles, duty to My Lady, and love to the Maria and to Sappho[3] if she is with you.—What! nothing for fear of tales being told out of school. Adieu. As to business Lenborough moves slowly,

---

[1] Lord George Sackville, son of Lionel, Duke of Dorset, assumed, in 1770, the name of Germain on succeeding to the Northamptonshire estates of his aunt, Lady Betty Germain (died December 16, 1769), second wife of Sir John Germain, Bart., whose first wife, Lady Mary Mordaunt, brought him the property. Lord George was dismissed from the army for his conduct at the battle of Minden (August 1, 1759). He was at this time M.P. for East Grinstead. He became Secretary of State for the Colonies in Lord North's administration, was created Lord Sackville in 1782, and died in 1785.

[2] The Hon. Stephen Fox, eldest son of Lord Holland, succeeded his father, July, 1774. He died December 26, 1774.

[3] Miss Fuller.

either from temper or design Matthews starts difficulties that will certainly carry us beyond the Holydays—Winton grows pert again, and Hugonin mollifies. I have just wrote him a stinging letter, and insist on a written allowance of time. The House is clear by the Lease. I may carry it away.

E. G.

182.

To J. B. Holroyd, Esq.

Bentinck Street, Thursday Morning, 23rd December, 1773.

The enclosed requires an immediate answer, as my business both in respect to Mrs. Lee and Winton seems brought to a crisis. Answer therefore yourself, and in my name send instructions, and if you can, comfort to Hugonin. Whether you decide (as to the Sporting Farmer) for severity or leniency, Hugonin will be desired by to-night's post to comply implicitly with your mandate. —Adieu, I hear you do not go to Denham till to-morrow, and that there was some design to carry my Lady to the School of Wives [1]—proper enough! A wife is taught by that play how to support and reclaim an irregular Husband. Pray what was the meaning of your being in town, but not in Bentinck Street, yesterday morning? *Pray* be more exact in your return. Again Adieu. Write to Francis Hugonin, Esq., Nursted, Petersfield, Hants, as soon as you can.

183.

To his Stepmother.

Bentinck Street, Dec. 25th, 1773.

DEAR MADAM,
         I am in a very awkward situation, detained in town (not that I dislike my prison) by the weekly and almost daily expectation of finishing Bucks, which is still delayed by the cold slow-paced forms of the Law; and at the same time desirous of

---

[1] *The School of Wives*, a comedy by Hugh Kelly (1739–1777), was produced at Drury Lane on December 11, 1773. Walpole speaks of it as "exceedingly applauded," though "Charles Fox says" it "is execrable."

running down for four or five days to Sheffield Place, on a sort of appointment with Lord and especially with Lady Pelham:[1] in this polite age, married women of Fashion, and not your Miss Sappho Fullers are the object of the Man of the World.

Whenever you please to draw for £100 on Messrs. Gosling and Clive, Fleet Street, they have order to honour, which for the future I should think would be the easiest and properest way. At your conveniency you will be so kind as to enclose a receipt in a letter. Mrs. P. joins with me in the honest old compliments of the season. She is a little out of order to-day! I hope very little. If I knew where Pitman's mother-in-law lived I would call upon her.

Adieu ! Dear Madam,

Believe me most truly yours,

E. G.

184.

To J. B. Holroyd, Esq.

January, 1774.

Way's letter trifling—He says nothing to the great point of the Modus. I have wrote to him to-night to call for his Evidence, which I should have for some day next week, when I am to meet my Horse-Jockey. Matthews is unaccountable. He declines coming up with his client ; more shuffling, I fear.

*I have a letter from Hugo, a *dreadful* one I believe, but it has lain four days unperused in my drawer. Let me turn it over to you.

Foster is playing at what he calls Whist ; his partner swearing inwardly. He would write to you to-night, but he thinks he had rather write *next* post ; he will think so a good while. Every thing public, still as death. Our Committee of the Catch Club[2] has done more business this morning than all those of the house

---

[1] Thomas, Lord Pelham of Stanmer (afterwards first Earl of Chichester), was at this time surveyor-general of the Customs of London. He married Miss Anne Frankland, granddaughter of Sir Thomas Frankland, Bart.

[2] "The Noblemen and Gentlemen's Catch Club" was founded in 1761, to encourage the composition and performance of catches and glees. Members were elected by ballot. It met every Tuesday from February to June at the Thatched House Tavern. The club still flourishes. Gibbon speaks as if he were a member; but his name does not occur in the lists of the club.

of Commons since their meeting. Roberts does not Petition.¹ This
from the best authority, and perhaps totally false. Hare is married
to Sir Abraham Hume's daughter.² You see how hard pressed I
am for news. Besides, at any time, I had rather talk an hour,
than write a page. Therefore adieu. I am glad to hear of your
speedy removal. Remember Bentinck Street.*

185.

To J. B. Holroyd, Esq.

January 29th, 1774.

On recollection it appeared superfluous to send you Hugo's
letter. It was wrote before he received yours. Winton bullies,
Mrs. Lee scolds, but I am fearless. Clarke³ promises me Franks
from day to day, and prevented me from applying to any body else.
I heard from R. Way; his declaration of my not warranting the
Modus quite sufficient: it is sent to Lovegrove, whose only
objection it appeared to be. He and his Lawyer decline a personal
interview, and talk of what they should have done four months
ago, laying the abstract of the Title before Mr. Duane. Patience
is a virtue.

*I am now getting acquainted with authors, Managers, &c.
good company to know, but not to live with. Yesterday I
dined at the Breetish Coffee-house,⁴ with *Garrick,*⁵ *Coleman,*⁶

¹ By the death of Sir R. Ladbroke a vacancy occurred in the representation of the City. The candidates were the Lord Mayor (Bull) and Roberts.
The result of the poll, by which the Lord Mayor was elected, was declared
on December 4, 1773. A scrutiny was demanded on behalf of Roberts, but
it was abandoned.

² James Hare, the politician and wit ("the Hare and many friends"), was
M.P. (1772–74) for Stockbridge, and (1781–1801) for Knaresborough. He
married (January 21, 1774) Miss Hannah Hume, sister of Sir Abraham
Hume, Bart., F.R.S., the famous collector of minerals and pictures, and one
of the founders of the Geological Society.

³ Godfrey Clarke, M.P. for Derbyshire.

⁴ The British Coffee-house, in Cockspur Street, was a favourite resort of
Scotchmen. The Duke of Bedford, soliciting the votes of the sixteen Scottish
peers in 1750, is said to have enclosed all the letters under one cover, and
addressed it to the British Coffee-house.

⁵ Garrick and Colman were managers of the two rival theatres, Covent
Garden and Drury Lane.

⁶ George Colman (1732–1794) was at this time a formidable rival to
Garrick. His five-act comedy, *The Man of Business*, was produced at Covent

Goldsmith,[1] *Macpherson,*[2] *John Hume,*[3] &c. I am this moment come from Coleman's Man of Business. We dined at the Shakespeare, and went in a body to support it ; between friends, though we got a Verdict for our Client, his Cause was but a bad one. It is a very confused Miscellany of several Plays and Tales ; sets out brilliantly enough, but as we advance the Plot grows thicker, the Wit thinner, till the lucky fall of the Curtain preserves us from total Chaos.

Bentinck Street has visited Welbeck Street. Sappho is very happy that she has left Lewes : on Sheffield-place she squints with regret and gratitude. Mamma consulted me about buying Coals ; we can't get any round ones. Quintus is gone to head the Civil War. Of Mrs. Frances I have nothing to say. I have got *my intelligence for insuring,* and will immediately get the preservative against fire. Foster has sent me *eight-and-twenty pair of Paris silk stockings,* with an intimation that My lady wished for half-a-dozen. They are much at her service ; but if she will look into David Hume's Essay on National Characters, she will see that I durst not offer them to a Queen of Spain. *Sachez qu'une Reine d'Espagne n'a point de jambes.*[4] Adieu.*

Garden in January, 1774. It is, as Gibbon describes it, made up from Terence and other writers; "so full of modern lore," writes H. Walpole, "of rencounters, and I know not what, that I scarce comprehended a syllable."

[1] Goldsmith (1728-1774), whose play, *She Stoops to Conquer,* had been produced at Covent Garden under Colman's management (January, 1773), died April 4, 1774, scarcely more than two months after this dinner. Gibbon signed the Round Robin, drawn up at Sir Joshua Reynolds's by Burke, asking Dr. Johnson to write Goldsmith's epitaph in English instead of Latin.

[2] Probably James Macpherson (1736-1796), whose *Fragments of Ancient Poetry collected in the Highlands* were published in 1760. At this time he was settled in London, where he was engaged in historical literature, a translation of the *Iliad,* and political writing on behalf of the Government.

[3] John Home (1722-1808), the author of *Douglas* (1756), had helped to bring Macpherson's Ossianic poems before the public. His *Douglas* was played at Covent Garden (1757); his *Agis* (1758) and *Siege of Aquileia* (1760) were given at Drury Lane.

[4] Gibbon refers not to the essay on *National Characters,* but to that on *Polygamy and Divorces.* Hume quotes a story from Madame d'Aunoy's *Mémoires de la Cour d'Espagne.* "When the mother of the late King of Spain was on her road towards Madrid, she passed through a little town in Spain famous for its manufactory of gloves and stockings. The magistrates of the place thought they could not better express their joy for the reception

186.

To J. B. Holroyd, Esq.

February 7th, 1774.

Quarrelled with you ! aye sure, and if she had beat you it would have been perfectly agreeable to the rule of Right, and the fitness of things. A space of time *not less* than four natural days, each day consisting of twenty-four hours, My Lady is to pass in Bentinck Street, only making some occasional excursions to various parts of the Cities of London and Westminster. Garrick I believe acts Hamlet to-morrow night, and will probably repeat it once or twice within a fortnight : I am not sure whether I might not muster up interest enough to determine it for one Night rather than another. As to you, I much want your presence. I fear Lovegrove will not turn out much better than Winton. In spite of R. Way's positive Evidence, he insists that I had warranted the *Vicarial Tythes*. Adieu. Gib sends his Love to Maria. I will enquire about *Capability*.[1] Give me intelligence of your motions.

187.

To his Stepmother.

Bentinck Street, February 16th, 1774.

DEAR MADAM,

The indolence of Bath and the hurry of London are alike enemies to very exact correspondencies, and I much fear that both of us will sometimes experience their baleful influence. I am prepared to give and receive a *reasonable measure* of Toleration, in

of their new queen, than by presenting her with a sample of those commodities for which alone their town was remarkable. The *major domo*, who conducted the princess, received the gloves very graciously; but, when the stockings were presented, he flung them away with great indignation, and severely reprimanded the magistrates for this egregious piece of indecency. *Know*, says he, *that a queen of Spain has no legs*. The young queen, who at that time understood the language but imperfectly, and had often been frightened with stories of Spanish jealousy, imagined that they were to cut off her legs. Upon which she fell a-crying, and begged them to conduct her back to Germany, for that she could never endure the operation; and it was with some difficulty they could appease her" (Hume's *Philosophical Works*, ed. 1854, vol. iii. p. 205).

[1] Probably a reference to Lancelot Brown (1715–1783), the landscape gardener, known as " Capability Brown."

the full conviction that the most sincere friendships have the least occasion for the regular repetition of such outward demonstrations.

Besides this general apology for my delay, I have another on this occasion. The Musical Counsellor whose opinion you desired was absent on a visit to Lord Craven. He is now returned, and thus he says, " If the Lady in question, and who wishes to perfect a fine voice, has no other object than her own amusement, Parsons [1] will do very well: but if she considers Music as a profession, Bach [2] is infinitely preferable, both as a much more finished Master, and, as having the principal direction of the Queen's concert," and that chance indeed I should think a much properer one, than poor Sir Stanier. The Under Ministers of the King's business are seldom those of Her Majesty's amusements.

I have received a letter from Mrs. Dawkes, but very little to the purpose, and containing neither facts nor dates. I have called on her, but did not find her.

Holroyd and Madame come to my house next week. I shall be glad to see them on many accounts, and particularly him on my Bucks business. Delays and difficulties are started in which I begin to suspect there may be something more than the mere procrastination of the Law.—I dined with Mrs. P. to-day. She looks forward to Easter as the Jews to their Messiah. I flatter myself that her hopes will be better founded.

I am, Dear Madam,

Ever yours,

E. G.

188.

To J. B. Holroyd, Esq.

February, 1774.

*Did you get down safe and early ? Is My Lady in good spirits and humour ? You do not deserve that she should be, for hurrying

---

[1] William Parsons (1746-1817) was appointed Master of the King's Band of Music in 1786, was knighted in 1795, became instructor in music to the princesses in 1796, and acted as a stipendiary police magistrate at Great Marlborough Street.

[2] Johann Christian Bach (1735-1782) was organist at Milan Cathedral, 1754-59. He married an Italian prima donna, and came to London, where he held the appointment of Director of Public Concerts.

her away. Does Maria coquet with Messieurs Divedown ?[1] Adieu.
Bentinck Street looks very dismal. You may suppose that nothing
very important can have occurred since you left Town ; But I will
send you some account of America[2] after Monday, though indeed
my anxiety about an old Manor takes away much of my attention
from a New Continent. The mildness of Clarke is rouzed into
military Fury ; but he is an old Tory, and you are a Native
of the Bog. I alone am an Englishman, a Philosopher, and a
Whig.*

189.

To J. B. Holroyd, Esq.

*Heads of a Convention between Mr. Newton and Mr. Gibbon in
Love Lane, March the 11th, 1774.*

Agreed—

1. That a proposal of Arbitration such as was wished for should
be accepted when offered.

2. That Mr. Way, to whom it was made, is the proper channel
through which it should be answered.

3. That Mr. Palmer, a man of very fair character, assisted by
two gentlemen of the Law, are very proper Arbitrators.

4. That from Parole and written evidence, they should determine whether the small tythes were warranted, and in case they
were, what abatement should be made to the purchaser for a
doubtfull or imperfect Title to them.

5. As it may be apprehended that Lovegrove, if their Decision
was unfavourable to him, might direct his quibbles to some of
the many other inexhaustible resources of the Law, it is submitted
to Mr. H., whether the whole business, with regard to the general
title, great tythes, time and obligation to compleating the purchase, had not better be left to the final award of three Gentlemen
of character, than litigated for half a Century in Chancery.

---

[1] The Rev. Dr. Dive Downes.

[2] Two recent events had brought American affairs into prominence.
The news of the attack upon the tea-ships in Boston Harbour (December 16,
1773) had just reached England, and the Privy Council had voted the
Petition of the House of Assembly of Massachusetts for the recall of
Governor Hutchinson and Lieutenant-Governor Oliver to be " groundless,
vexatious, and scandalous."

6. As such an Arbitration will demand several important preliminaries, that an early meeting should be proposed to Messieurs Lovegrove and Matthews, where they may confer with Messieurs Newton, Gibbon, and perhaps Holroyd.

7. That the letter, a copy of which is enclosed, should be written by next Tuesday's post to Mr. Way if approved of. *Judge and Alter.*

190.

To J. B. Holroyd, Esq.

Boodle's, Wednesday Evening, March 16th, 1774.

Your Epistle of Sunday was not received till Monday night 12 o'Clock, Consequently your Commissions ceased of Course.

*I was this morning with Newton. He was positive that the attempt to settle the preliminaries of Arbitration by Letters, would lead us on till the middle of the Summer, and that a Meeting was the only practicable Measure. I acquiesced, and we blended his Epistle and yours into one, which goes by this post. If you can contrive to suit to it your Oxford journey, your presence at the Meeting would be received as the descent of a Guardian Angel.

Very little that is satisfactory has transpired of America. On Monday Lord N[orth] moved for leave to bring in a Bill to remove the Customs and Courts of Justice from Boston to New Salem ; a step so detrimental to the former town, as must soon reduce it to your own terms ; and yet of so mild an appearance, that it was agreed to, without a division, and almost without a debate.[1] Something more is, however, intended, and a Committee is appointed to inquire into the general state of America. But administration keep their Secret as well as that of Free Masonry, and, as Coxe profanely suggests, for the same reason.

---

[1] The Boston Port Bill was brought in by Lord North on March 14, 1774, and received the royal assent on the 31st. It was followed on March 28 by the Bill for regulating the government of Massachusetts Bay. A third Bill was introduced (April 15) for "the impartial administration of justice;" it provided for the transfer of persons accused of being concerned in the late riots for trial in England. All three Bills were passed during the session. Governor Hutchinson was superseded by General Gage, who was sent out with four regiments.

Don't you remember that in our Pantheon Walks we admired the *modest beauty* of Mrs. Horneck ?[1] *Eh bien!* alas ! she is * * *. You ask me with whom ? with Scawen, of the Guards ; both the Storers, Hodges, a Steward of Lady Albemarle's, her first love, and half the town besides. A Meeting of Horneck's friends assembled about a Week ago, to consult of the best method of acquainting him with his frontal honours. Edmund Burke was named as the Orator, and communicated the transaction in a most Eloquent speech.

N.B.—The same Lady, who, at public dinners, appeared to have the most delicate Appetite, was accustomed, in her own Apartment, to feast on pork steaks and sausages, and to swill Porter till she was dead drunk. Horneck is abused by the Albemarle family, has been bullied by Storer, and can prove himself a Cornuto, to the satisfaction of every one but a Court of Justice. O Rare Matrimony ! *

191.

To J. B. Holroyd, Esq.

March 29th, 1774.

Lenborough.—Last Sunday morning I saw R. Way in Bentinck Street. He had seen Lovegrove both in country and in Town, but it seems very difficult to make any thing of him. Way pressed him to call upon me or Newton to settle the preliminaries of the Arbitration. He replied, that without Matthews he could do nothing. Matthews on the other hand, when Newton wrote to him, said, that he could be of no use in town till the conveyances were ready for signing. Such damned shuffling. Way promised to call on Palmer, who in general has accepted the office of Arbitrator, and get him to write to Lovegrove to convince him of the necessity of settling things previously as to the object of the Arbitration, and penalty of the parties. On his return into the country he will see Lovegrove and Matthews,

---

[1] Mrs. Horneck, wife of Captain Charles Horneck, Goldsmith's " Captain-in-Lace " (" Verses in Reply to an Invitation to Dinner at Dr. Baker's : " *Works*, ed. Cunningham, vol. i. p. 110), was one of the most abandoned women of the time. She eloped with her husband's brother-officer, Captain Scawen, who had in the previous year fought a celebrated duel with " Fighting Fitzgerald."

and assure them how strongly I *appeared* resolved for chancery, if I found any farther delay or difficulty. Would it were over !

Beriton.—Mrs. Lee, on receiving Andrews's letter, wrote to him to desire he would send it up to me (as it seemed written without my knowledge), and to press that I would disclose my real intention about repairs, maintaining that according to Law, Honor and my former declarations, I am obliged to fulfil them, hinting however, that if I can settle the business with Winton, Mrs. Lee desires to hear no more about it. On that ground I can direct a most excellent letter to Hugonin, which may tame the monster without making it desperate.

*America.—Had I wrote Saturday night, as I once intended, Fire and Sword, Oaths of Allegiance and high treason tryed in England, in consequence of the refusal, would have formed my letter. Lrd. North, however, opened a most lenient prescription last night ; and the utmost attempts towards a new settlement seemed to be no more than investing the Governor with a greater share of executive power, nomination of civil officers, (Judges, however, for life,) and some regulations of Juries. The Boston Port bill passed the Lords last night ; some lively conversation, but no division.

Bentinck-street.—Rose Fuller the Great was against the Boston port Bill, and against his niece's going to Boodle's masquerade. He was laughed at in the first instance, but succeeded in the second. Sappho and Fanny very indifferent (as Mama says) about going. They seem of a different opinion.* This morning d'Eyverdun arrived : When you consider him, morning walks, dinners, Evenings, the general idleness of town, and my peculiar employment, you must not swear, if I am not very punctual. Adieu. Duty to My Lady, and love to Maria. I hope the *latter is quite well ;* for Miss Huff insinuated somewhat to the contrary.

192.

To J. B. Holroyd, Esq.

April 2nd, 1774.

DEAR H.,

*You owe me a letter ; so this extra goes only to acquaint you with a misfortune that has just happened to poor Clarke, and which he really considers as such, the loss of a very excellent father. The blow was sudden ; a thin little Man, as abstemious as a hermit, was destroyed by a stroke of Apoplexy in his Coach, as he was going out to dinner. He appeared perfectly well, and only two days before had very good-naturedly dined with us at a Tavern, a thing he had not done for many years before. I am the only person that Clarke wishes to see, except his own family ; and I pass a great part of the day. A line from you would be kindly received.

Great news, you see, from India.[1] Tanjore—four hundred thousand pounds to the Company ; Sujah Dowlah—600,000.* Tygor Roch[2] is certainly got off from the Cape to Mauritius in a French ship. Adieu.

[1] In 1773, the East India Company at Madras and the Nabob of the Carnatic were allies; the Rajah of Tanjore, though nominally an ally, was known to be in correspondence with Hyder Ali and the Mahrattas. The Company agreed for a sum of money to reduce the Rajah and transfer his dominions to the Nabob. The bargain was fulfilled, and the news, transmitted to the Board of Directors, reached London, March 26, 1774. In October, 1773, Sujah Dowlah, Nawab of Oude, offered Warren Hastings a large sum of money if the Company would conquer and transfer to him the Rohilla country, north of his dominions and east of the Ganges. At the same time the provinces of Corah and Allahabad were sold to Sujah Dowlah by the Company.

[2] Captain David Roche sailed with his wife on board the *Vansittart*, East Indiaman, in May, 1773, in order to take up an appointment in the Company's service at Bombay. On the voyage he quarrelled with Lieutenant James Ferguson, whom he killed at the Cape in September, 1773. It was alleged that Roche had treacherously assassinated his antagonist; but, on his trial at Cape Town, it was proved that Ferguson was the assailant, and that Roche had killed him in self-defence. Strong feeling was aroused about the affair, because Roche was wrongly identified with a notorious duellist of the day. The governor of the Cape obtained a passage for Roche in a French frigate to Mauritius, whence he reached Bombay. On arrival there, he was arrested and sent home to England. Examined before the Privy Council on July 10, 1775, he was committed to Newgate. A special commission was issued (August 5) to try him, and at the Old Bailey, on December 11, 1775, he was again acquitted of the charge of murder. (See *A Plain and Circumstantial Account of the Transactions between Captain Roche and Lieut. Ferguson*, etc. London, 1775.)

193.

To his Stepmother.

London, April 2nd, 1774.

DEAR MADAM,

My Bucks affair is not settled, and I much fear that it will occasion me more trouble than I at first expected. Mr. Lovegrove's difficulty—not to call it by a harsher name—turns on a point of fact not of law, and is so very unreasonable that he must be condemned either in the more eligible way of arbitration (which I hope will be settled) or in the Court of Chancery, should I be reduced to the sad necessity of calling it to my aid. The uneasy suspense that it has kept and will keep me in for some time, defers my intended visit to Bath, and disappoints Mrs. Porten, as well as myself, of a pleasure which we had assured ourselves of enjoying.

I am at present engaging in two other tasks of a very different nature, the receiving one friend and the comforting another. d'Eyverdun arrived in Bentinck Street last Tuesday, and will I believe go abroad again in about a month with Lord Middleton.[1] I dined with him to-day at Tommy Townshend's,[2] his pupil's guardian. It's an unworthy office for him ; but Lord M. appears a very tame bear, and if we can fix a quiet annuity, he may after this Tour enjoy ease and independence for the rest of his life. Upon recollection this paragraph must seem very unintelligible to you, as I do not believe that I mentioned to you, his having been forced to quit Lord C[hesterfield], by the little peer's strange behaviour, the uncertainty that he could be of any use to him or to himself, &c.

---

[1] Lord Midleton was the son of the third Lord Midleton and his wife, Albinia, eldest daughter of the Hon. Thomas Townshend.

[2] Thomas Townshend (1733-1800), son of the Hon. Thomas Townshend and grandson of the second Viscount Townshend, was the "Tommy Townsend" of Goldsmith's *Retaliation*, in which he describes Edmund Burke as—

   "Though fraught with all learning, yet straining his throat,
   To persuade Tommy Townsend to lend him a vote."

He was M.P. for Whitchurch in four successive Parliaments, and held a series of important or lucrative offices. He was created Baron Sydney in 1783, and Viscount Sydney in 1789.

My other occupation, which claims at present the far greater
part of my time, is attending my poor friend Clarke, who has just
lost a very excellent father by a very sudden and terrible stroke.
The old gentleman, who was perfectly well, died of a stroke of
apoplexy in his coach as he was going out to dinner. Clarke feels
it severely, and as he seems pleased with my company, I seldom
leave him, except when he goes to his sister.

Is not Mr. Eliot at Bath ? How does he do at present ? Is
Mrs. E. with him ? Do they think of coming to town ? Be so
good as to say everything proper in my name, and

Believe me, Dear Madam,
Most truly yours,
E. G.

194.

To J. B. Holroyd, Esq.

April 13th, 1774.

DEAR H.,

*At length I am a little more at liberty. Clarke went
out of town this morning. Instead of going directly into Derbyshire, where he would have been overwhelmed with visits, &c. he
has taken his Sister, brother, and aunts, to a little Villa near
Farnham, in which he has the happiness of having no neighbourhood. If my esteem and friendship for Godfrey had been capable
of any addition, it would have been very much encreased by the
manner in which he felt and lamented his father's death.* Incredible as it sounds to the generality of sons, and as it ought to
sound to most fathers, he considered the old Gentleman as a
friend. *He is now in very different circumstances than before ;
instead of an easy and ample allowance, he has taken possession
of a great Estate, with low rents and high incumbrances. I hope
the one may make amends for the other : under your conduct I
am sure they would, and I have freely offered him your assistance,
in case he should wish to apply for it.

In the mean time I must not forget my own affairs, which
seem to be covered with inextricable perplexity. R. Way, as I
mentioned about a Century ago, promised to see Lovegrove and
his Attorney, and to oil the wheels of the Arbitration. As yet
I have not heard from him. I have some thoughts of writing

myself to the Jockey, stating the various steps of the affair, and offering him, with polite firmness, the *immediate* choice of Chancery or Arbitration.

For the time, however, I forget all these difficulties, in the present enjoyment of Deyverdun's Company; and I glory in thinking, that, although my house is small, it is just of a sufficient size to hold my real friends, male and *female*; among the latter My Lady holds the very first place.*

Apropos of My Lady, Harry Hobart the other day gave me a *very pleasing hint*, which he received from his wife. If there is any foundation for it, I sincerely congratulate you.

We are all quiet.—American business is suspended, and almost forgot. The other day we had a brisk report of a Spanish War.[1] It was said they had taken one of the Leeward Islands. It since turns out that we are the Invaders, but the invasion is trifling. Batt and Sir John not returned. Are you alone? I have received another dozen of handkerchiefs, and you, by this time, have got your books and silver spoons, which Caplin has sent by the coach. Adieu.

Bien obligé non (at present) for your invitation. I wish My Lady and you would come up to our Masquerade the 3rd of May.[2] The finest thing ever seen. We sup in a transparent temple that costs £450.*

195.

To J. B. Holroyd, Esq.

April 21st, 1774.

DEAR H.,

*I begin to flag, and though you already reproach me as a bad Correspondent, I much fear that I shall every week become a more hardened Sinner. Besides the occasional obstructions of *Clarke and Deyverdun*, I must entreat you to consider, with your usual candour, 1. The aversion to Epistolary Conversation, which it has pleased the Demon to implant in my nature. 2. That I

---

[1] This probably refers to an attempt on the part of the English to collect sugar duties at the island of Toracola (Crabb Island) near Porto Rico, and the reply of the governor of Porto Rico that the island belonged to Spain. In the *Morning Chronicle* for April 12, 1774, it was reported "that the Spaniards had bombarded the town of Kingston in Jamaica."

[2] The masquerade was given at the Pantheon, by Boodle's Club.

am a very fine Gentleman, a Subscriber to the Masquerade, where you and My Lady ought to come, and am now writing at Boodle's, in a fine Velvet Coat, with ruffles of My Lady's chusing, &c.[1] 3. That the aforesaid fine Gentleman is likewise a Historian ; and, in truth, when I am writing a page, I not only think it a sufficient reason of delay, but even consider myself as writing to you, and that much more to the purpose than if I were sending you the tittle tattle of the town, of which indeed there is none stirring. With regard to America, the Minister seems moderate, and the House obedient.

Ilugonin's last letter, by some very *unaccountable accident*, had never reached me ; so that yours, in every instance, amazed me. I immediately wrote him groans and approbation. Winton, however, gives me very little uneasiness. I see that he is a bully, and that I have a stick. But the cursed business of Lenborough, in the midst of Study, Dissipation, and friendship, at times almost distracts me.* R. Way seems to have done nothing with the Jockey, (who indeed is as strange as Winton himself, singular luck enough I have had) nor have I yet ventured to cross the Rubicon by writing to him. *I wish your journey here* and into Oxfordshire was to take *place soon*, and yet I hardly know what

---

[1] Gibbon was always careful, if not elaborate, in his dress. George Colman the younger, in his *Random Records* (1830), vol. i. pp. 121, 122, describes his meeting as a boy with Gibbon and Johnson :—

"On the day I first sat down with Johnson, in his rusty brown, and his black worsteads, Gibbon was placed opposite to me in a suit of flower'd velvet, with a bag and sword." The "costume," he adds in a note, "was not extraordinary at this time, (a little overcharged, perhaps, if his *person* be considered,) when almost every gentleman came to dinner in full dress." "Each," he continues, "had his measured phraseology; and Johnson's famous parallel, between Dryden and Pope, might be loosely parodied, in reference to himself and Gibbon. Johnson's style was grand, and Gibbon's elegant; the stateliness of the former was sometimes pedantick, and the polish of the latter was occasionally finical. Johnson march'd to kettle-drums and trumpets; Gibbon moved to flutes and hautboys; Johnson hew'd passages through the Alps, while Gibbon levell'd walks through parks and gardens. Maul'd as I had been by Johnson, Gibbon pour'd balm upon my bruises, by condescending, once or twice, in the course of the evening, to talk with me ; the great historian was light and playful, suiting his matter to the capacity of the boy ;—but it was done more *suá* (sic); still his mannerism prevail'd ;—still he tapp'd his snuff-box,—still he smirk'd, and smiled ; and rounded his periods with the same air of good-breeding, as if he were conversing with men.—His mouth, mellifluous as Plato's, was a round hole, nearly in the centre of his visage."

you could do for me. *I am surely in a worse condition than before I sold the Estate, and what distresses me is, that *His ego nec metas rerum, nec tempora pono.*

Both Deyverdun and Clarke wish to be remembered to you. The former, who has more taste for the Country than ——,[1] could wish to visit you, but he sets out in a few days for the Continent *with Lord M[iddleton]*.* Your letter for the latter was immediately mentioned and very kindly received. He is now at Aldershot with his family, and on this *occasion only* I write to him almost every post, as I am this moment preparing to do. Therefore Adieu.

E. G.

196.

To his Stepmother.

Bentinck Street, April 23rd, 1774.

DEAR MADAM,

When I already began to chide my own laziness, a little gentleman from Bath brought me a very elegant proof of your kind attention to me. The little man himself I could not see, as I happened to be abroad twice when he called upon me; but I had the pleasure of hearing through him that Mr. Eliot was quite or almost recovered. I beg you would assure him and Mrs. Eliot how much I rejoice in the news.

Clarke has now been at his house near Farnham some days. Next week he is obliged to visit town on some business, and expresses a violent intention of carrying me down with him. The pleasure of being of service to an afflicted friend, may make even the country agreeable. In that case I should leave Deyverdun in possession of Bentinck Street, though I should grumble at giving up any part of his short stay.

I have likewise seen another heir, younger and much more cheerful than Clarke, though extremely decent, I mean Sir Harry Fetherstone.[2] At present everything carries the appearance of sobriety and economy. The Baronet, instead of flying to Paris

---

[1] Word erased.

[2] Appearances proved deceitful. Amy Lyon, afterwards Emma Hamilton, became the mistress of Sir H. Featherstonhaugh at Up-Park in 1780, and was discarded by him just before the birth of her second child.

and Rome, returns to his college at Oxford, and even the house
at Whitehall is to be left. Lady Fetherstone talked to me a great
deal about you. Do you correspond with her?

Our attention is now very much taken up with a very grand
Masquerade, which Boodle's is going to give at the Pantheon.
We have a great deal of money and consequently of taste. Flying
bridges, transparent temples and eighteen thousand lamps in the
Dome are the general subject of conversation. For my own part
I subscribe, but am very indifferent about it. A few friends and
a great many books may entertain me, but I think fifteen hundred
people the worst company in the world.

I am still in very perplexing suspence about Bucks.

Adieu, Dear Madam,

Most truly yours,

E. GIBBON.

197.

To J. B. Holroyd, Esq.

May 4th, 1774.

DEAR H.,

Most sincerely do I condole with you on the effects of
Fanaticism. That furious principle which has sometimes over-
turned Nations has in this instance indeed been contented with
unsettling the reason of a Cook : but the domestic Calamity must
have been attended with very unpleasant circumstances, and I
shall think it a very happy Catastrophe when the poor Wretch is
safely and quietly lodged in Bedlam.

198.

To J. B. Holroyd, Esq.

May 4th, 1774.

*Last night was the Triumph of Boodle's. Our Masquerade
cost two thousand Guineas ; a sum that might have fertilized a
Province, (I speak in your own style,) vanished in a few hours,
but not without leaving behind it the fame of the most splendid
and elegant Fête that was perhaps ever given in a seat of the
Arts and Opulence. It would be as difficult to describe the magnificence of the Scene, as it would be easy to record the humour
of the night. The one was above, the other below, all relation.

I left the Pantheon about five this morning, rose at ten, took a good Walk, and returned home to a more rational entertainment of Batt, Sir John [Russel], and Lascelles, who dined with me. They have left me this moment; and were I to enumerate the things said of Sheffield, it would form a much longer letter than I have any inclination to write. Let it suffice, that Sir John means to pass in Sussex the interval of the two terms. Every thing, in a word, goes on very pleasantly, except the terrestrial business of Lenborough. Last Saturday se'nnight I wrote to Richard, to press him to see Lovegrove, and urge the Arbitration. He has not *condescended* to answer me. All is a dead Calm, sometimes more fatal than a storm. For God's sake send me Advice. I seem to be in a much worse situation than before I agreed with him.*

Adieu. My Lady's and Maria's healths were drank unanimously to-day. Deyverdun sets off for Lausanne in about ten or twelve days with Lord Middleton, Tommy Townshend's Nephew.

199.

To his Stepmother.

Boodle's, May 24th, 1774.

DEAR MADAM,

Instead of censuring my indolence (though you might as usual do it with very just reason), listen to a tale of wonders.

On Sunday last, when my servant came to the place where I had dined, with the carriage, he told me that Mrs. Gibbon was come to town, had sent to Bentinck Street and wished to see me that evening. It appeared somewhat singular that you should have run up to town without giving me any notice, and somewhat unkind that you should not have made Bentinck Street your Inn. —But, *guess my surprize when a further enquiry discovered to me that it was not Mrs. Gibbon of Bath, but Mrs. Gibbon of Northamptonshire. I immediately went to Surrey Street where she lodged, but though it was no more than half an hour after nine, the Saint had finished her evening devotions and was already retired to rest. Yesterday morning (by appointment) I breakfasted with her at eight o'clock, dined with her to-day at two in Newman Street, and am just returned from setting down. She is in truth a very great curiosity, her dress and figure exceed everything we had at the Masquerade. Her language and ideas belong to the last century. However, in point of religion she was rational, that is to say silent. I do not believe that she asked a single question or said the least thing concerning it. To me she behaved with great cordiality, and in her way expressed a great regard.* In a light of interest, however, her regard is of little consequence to me ; if I may judge from her appearance her life is a better one than mine. Please to communicate a proper part of this intelligence to our Cornish friends. She expressed the utmost disappointment at not finding Mrs. Eliot and her children in town. I am sorry to hear that we have less chance than ever of seeing them since Hams, Cheeses and my little friend John [1] are gone down to Bath.

My knowledge of Mr. Eliot's disinclination to writing has prevented me from giving him the trouble of an answer. My despair of equalling the elegant raillery of the Goddess has kept me silent on that quarter likewise. Lazyness you will say never wants an excuse.

As the Summer advances (and sorry I am to say that it advances much faster than my Bucks business), I now fear that Mrs. P. and myself must defer our Bath journey to the latter season of the Year. There would however be a way which would bring us together much sooner. You have been long and impatiently expected at Sheffield Place, where I propose to pass at least the month of July. From Charles Street to Bentinck Street it is a pleasant drive ; from Bentinck Street to Sheffield Place little more than a morning walk. Mrs. P. tells me that she has just wrote to you. She ought to go to a Masquerade once a year. Did you think her such a girl ?

I am, Dear Madam,

Most truly yours,

E. G.

200.

To J. B. Holroyd, Esq.

Boodle's, May 24th, 1774.

*I wrote three folio pages to you this morning, and yet you complain. Have reason, and have mercy ; consider all the excellent reasons for silence which I gave you in one of my last, and

---

[1] The second son of Mr. Eliot, of Port Eliot.

expect my arrival in Sussex, when I shall talk more in a quarter of an hour than I could write in a day. A propos of that arrival ; never pretend to allure me, by painting in odious colours the dust of London. I love the dust, and whenever I move into the Wold,[1] it is to visit you and My lady, and not your Trees. About this day month I mean to give you a *visitation*. I leave it to Guise, Clarke, and the other light Horse, to prance down for a day or two. They all talk of mounting, but will not fix the day. Sir John [Russel], whom I salute, has brought you, I suppose, all the news of Versailles.[2] Let me only add, that the Mesdames, by attending their father, have both got the small-pox. Your Attorney has your Case. I congratulate you. I can make nothing of Lovegrove, or his Lawyer. You will swear at the shortness of this letter.—Swear.*

201.

To J. B. Holroyd, Esq.

Bentinck Street, June 4th, 1774.

I hope you, Templar, Doves, &c., got down safe. Compliments to Maria and My Lady.—I passed this morning, three horrid hours at Searle's Coffee House.[3] I was a Hero, La Brute not exceedingly clever, and M. more candid than I had yet seen him. We almost parted once in the mutual defiance. At last they consented that on Monday and Tuesday, the two Attornies should examine the Deeds at Gosling's, compare them with the Abstract and lay the whole before Duane : and likewise that they should search Offices about my title to the great Tythes *without prejudice* to the General Warranty which was agreed to by letter. If we coalesce at all, *Arbitration* ; if not, *Chancery*. The latter I fear, and I must own that I fear it in every respect. Adieu.

E. G.

---

[1] The Weald of Sussex [S.].

[2] Louis XV. died May 10, 1774, of small-pox. " Two of the King's daughters," writes Walpole (May 15, 1774), " though they never had the small-pox, attended him." Both the princesses caught the disease, but recovered. Louis XVI. and his two brothers were vaccinated, and the successful results did much to establish the practice on the Continent.

[3] Since the days of the *Spectator*, the Grecian, Squire's, and Serle's Coffee-house had been the resort of lawyers.

202.

To J. B. Holroyd, Esq.

Saturday Evening, 11th June, 1774.

The enclosed came to-day—The business of the search is finished, and will I fancy be laid before Duane. The Omens are a *little* more favourable ; when I see farther I write. I will not affront either you or myself by thanking you for your offers— Embrace My Lady,—Clarke who is in town for 48 hours salutes ; he talks of taking Sheffield in his way to his Kentish Estate—the time not determined. The *Fete Champetre*[1] would fill volumes : by all accounts dull ones. Adieu.

203.

To J. B. Holroyd, Esq.

25th June, 1774.

I am alive.

You know how much rather I would send my person than Epistle to Sheffield. Therefore you will, I flatter myself, for-give my silence when I tell you that on Monday the 4th of July I shall certainly dine at the aforesaid place. Clarke will cross the country from Aldershot nearly about the same time. My Lenborough business is almost at a stand, as I shall then tell you more particularly. It is indeed a damned affair.

Salute My Lady and Maria.

204.

To his Stepmother.

Bentinck Street, June 29th, 1774.

DEAR MADAM,

*Do you remember that there exists in the World one Edward Gibbon, a Housekeeper in Bentinck Street ? If the standard of writing and of affection was the same, I am sure he would ill deserve it. I do not wish to discover how many days

---

[1] The *fête* was given by Lord Stanley at The Oaks, near Epsom, in Surrey, on June 9, to celebrate his approaching marriage with Lady Betty Hamilton, June 23, 1774. The *fête* was the subject of Burgoyne's *Maid of the Oaks*, played at Covent Garden in November, 1774.

(I am afraid I ought to use another word) have elapsed since the
date of my last, or even of your last letter ; and yet such is the
sluggish nature of the beast, that I am afraid nothing but
the arrival of Mrs. Bonfoy, and the expectation of Mr. Eliot, could
have rouzed me from my Lethargy. The Lady gave me great
satisfaction, by her general account of your health and spirits, but
communicated some uneasiness, by the mention of a little encounter,
in the style of one of Don Quixote's, but which proved, I hope, as
trifling as you at first imagined it. For my own part, I am well
in mind and body, busy with my Books, (which may perhaps
produce something next year, either to tire or amuse the World,)
and every day more satisfied with my present mode of life, which
I always believed was calculated to make me happy. My only
remaining uneasiness is Lenborough, which is not terminated.
By Holroyd's advice, I rather try what may be obtained by
a little more patience, than rush at once into the horrors of
Chancery.

But let us talk of something else.* You remember surely Mrs.
Hobson (Miss Comarque). She is just returned to England under
a different name. She is now Madame la Baronne de Bavois. Her
second husband is an old Swiss Officer about seventy, a man of
family, but with as little money as character, who most probably
married her for a fortune which he now begins to discover was
spent to his hands. They talk of leaving England very soon, and
fixing themselves in some cheap Provincial town in the South of
France. The Baronne is more ridiculous, and will I fear be more
miserable than ever. Mrs. Porten, out of regard to the laws of
Hospitality, gave them a dinner last Sunday, & insists on my
doing the same to-day, and her brother Sunday next. She grows
younger every day, but Sir Stanier much older. *You remember, I
think in Newman Street, a good agreeable Woman, Miss Wybolt.
The under Secretary[1] is seriously in love with her, and seriously

---

[1] In the list of marriages for 1774 appears the following :—" Dec. 8,
1774. Sir Stanier Porten, Knt., to Miss Mary Wibault of Titchfield St."
(Ann. Register). Sir Stanier Porten, Gibbon's uncle, was in 1760 made
Consul-General at Madrid. In 1772 he was knighted in order to qualify
him to act as proxy to Sir George (afterwards Lord) Macartney, K.B. In
May, 1774, he was an Under Secretary of State, and was appointed Keeper
and Registrar of His Majesty's papers and records for the business of State
at Whitehall. He became a Commissioner of the Customs, and died at
Kensington Palace, June 7, 1789.

uneasy that his precarious situation precludes him from happiness. We shall soon see which will get the better, Love or reason. I bet three to two on love.*

I cannot find your last letter (a sad memento); did not you ask me with whom Deyverdun was gone abroad? with young Lord Middleton. Lady Fetherston (as they are to return next spring) is mad to get him, but I should fancy Sir Harry must be consulted—I hear confusedly of strange Revolutions in the Gould family.

Next week I go to Sheffield place. Holroyd, who passes a few days with me, was sincerely concerned to hear that you had no thoughts of the Journey this summer. His Father, I find, has had a violent attack.

I am, Dear Madam,

Most truly yours,

E. G.

The Goslings will obey your commands, whenever you please to signify them.

205.

To J. B. Holroyd, Esq.

Bentinck Street, August 6th, 1774.

With regard to your influencing the Jury, I am convinced that B. is in the right. Out of twelve Jurymen, I suppose six to be incapable of understanding the question, three afraid of giving offence, and two more who will not take the trouble of thinking. Remains one who has sense, courage and application. Ergo B. is in the right. But as he has *no right* on this occasion to be in the right, and as you were *not Foreman*, I am totally against *your committing* yourself with such a fellow, giving him anything under your hand or *permitting him to publish your letters.* If *it be really true* that you were mistaken as to the date of the Defamation, you have gone further than perhaps you might have done in the article of damages, but as I still think you committed no injustice, I cannot see that the Jury, much less any individual of it, owe him any reparation. Considering the profession of the two men, very high damages were surely required for the accusation of so scandalous a crime, which was certainly groundless since it was *afterwards* disproved in a Court of Justice. What you supposed to be the case (and by the bye I would in a polite letter ask the question of the Judge) was no more than an aggravation, and an aggravation too of a public rather than a private nature, consequently relating rather to punishment than to damages.—Upon the whole I disapprove of your corresponding with B., who seems capable of any rascally trick. Nothing that he can publish will affect your character, especially in an affair where it is well known that you had neither interest nor passion to mislead you. However if you think differently, or find yourself too far engaged with him, your letter is proper and guarded.

You make me very uneasy by a part of your last; pray send me a speedy, and if you can a favorable account of Dr. H[eberden]'s visit.—She has been so well a great while.— Clarke is now in the Country,—Aldershot. I heard from him yesterday. His health there has been various, and is not I fear quite settled. I break off to get into my chaise for Twickenham. People may talk of the town's being empty in September, my only complaint is the thickness of my engagements. I have not by many degrees been so diligent as I intended. I have conversed with Cadell,[1] and find him ready and even willing. He proposes next March (if I am prepared) and 750 Copies. *Deliberabimus.* The snails of the Law are copying the Tythe deed, and we shall soon see the effect of it. Hugonin's letter I have not yet read, it is only a week since it was received, no hurry. I believe I must goad Gilbert in his enquiries, in case you cannot do it without giving room to surmises.

E. G.

---

[1] Thomas Cadell was born in 1742, in Wine Street, Bristol. He was apprentice, partner, and ultimately (1767) successor, to Andrew Millar, the bookseller and publisher of the Strand, one of "the Gentlemen Partners" who published Johnson's *Dictionary*. In conjunction with Strahan, Cadell brought out the works of Johnson, Robertson, Blackstone, Henry, and other writers. He was printer to the Royal Academy from 1778 to 1793. He died in 1802.

206.

To J. B. Holroyd, Esq.

Bond Street, Wednesday Evening, 10th August, 1774.

DEAR H.,

Though I can assure you that the first stage from S. P. was heavy and awkward, yet I am very glad that I came to Town. Sir Edmond's intelligence was but too well founded, and poor Clarke is here in a very unpleasant way. His Aunts and Sister are come up on purpose. He is attended by Dr. Thomas and the family Apothecary who has known his Constitution from a child ; yet both are at a loss, his spirits, stomach and head are all violently affected : the disorder seems of an intermittent nature. I now write from his lodgings. I had seen him in the morning (for last night he could not see me) and left him taking a medicine ; he threw it up with a large quantity of black bile, and has been in bed (but not easy) since two o'clock. Adieu. Embrace My Lady and Maria for me. May the great Saturday be *correct*. I shall write soon. Send me some account of the progress of Architecture.

207.

To J. B. Holroyd, Esq.

12th August, 1774.

DEAR H.,

I write two lines to acquaint you *that Clarke* is much better than he was ; all doors have been set open for the retreat of the unwelcome guest, and in a great measure he has taken the hint. Spirits have rose with health, and he desires to be remembered to S. P.—Wilkes is dangerously ill, we shall lose much amusement. The Victory of the Russians is real but not decisive.[1] If you have an Irish *Cream-cheese* to spare, Bentinck

---

[1] The Russian forces under Peter Alexandrovich Romanzow (1725-1796) drove back the Turks and surrounded their camp at Shumla, sixty miles south of Silistria, and one of the keys of Constantinople. Peace was, in consequence of these successes, signed July 21, 1774, between Russia and Turkey at Kainardji, by which Azof was ceded to Russia and the freedom of the Black Sea established.

Street is ready to receive it. Success to the *august morrow*. It will be over ere you receive this. Adieu.

I shall remember your frank, but the paper is not in my pocket, nor the name in my memory.

208.

To J. B. Holroyd, Esq.

Bond Street, Tuesday morning, eleven o'clock, August, 1774.

DEAR H.,

Since my last we have had an alarm, a very terrible one indeed. On Sunday Clarke was better than I had yet seen him, and said that he felt himself getting well apace. He slept several hours in the night, but about five o'clock the Monday morning, he was seized with a fit so very violent that it totally deprived him of his speech and almost of his senses ; a blister and plaister to his feet were immediately applied, and Turton was called in to consult with Dr. Thomas his ordinary Physician.

They both judged him in the most imminent danger, and particularly were alarmed by a numbness (which he complained of as soon as he could speak), and which was the same symptom as had proved the forerunner of his father's apoplexy. He recovered however from his fit, and even from the immediate consequences of it sooner than could have been expected, was perfectly sensible last night, and this morning appears even cheaiful and easy. But his Physicians still think him in danger of a Relapse, and to his friends the prospect is still shocking. You will easily forgive me for not writing on any other subject. Adieu.

209.

To J. B. Holroyd, Esq.

August the 20th, 1774.

I begin with what I am sure will interest you the most, notwithstanding your own schemes, I mean the state of Clarke's health. It is surprisingly well, as likewise his spirits, both far better than by his own account they have been for many months.

The recovery is indeed perfect ; may it be lasting. But his Doctors have still their fears.

Now to your designs, I have turned them on every side and will give you my opinion as distinctly as so very slight a knowledge of your county will permit.

1. I cannot yet think you ripe for a county member.[1] Five years are very little to remove the obvious objection of a *novus homo*, and of all objections it is perhaps the most formidable, as it rouzes the foolish pride and envy of all the animals—bears, hogs, asses and Rhinoceroses who have slept in the country for some generations. To these only (who by the courtesy of England are called Gentlemen) are you as yet known, and by these you will never be liked. Seven more years of an active life will spread your fame among the great body of Freeholders at large, and to them you may one day offer yourself on the most honourable footing, that of a candidate whose real services to the County have deserved and will repay the favor which he then solicits. You must recollect, too, some very good reason you gave me yourself, why the attempt might be more convenient and the success more desirable seven years hence than at present.

2. Consider that you are rising in rebellion against an establishment which, however feeble, always fights with very great advantages. When a vacancy happens—either by death or resignation, any Gentleman who thinks himself qualified has a natural right to offer his services, and as he may succeed without envy, so he may retreat without shame. Your *prise d'armes* must hurt you, I think, if you were not victorious. *People grumble;* Englishmen love to grumble, and are satisfied with having done it. You see many obstacles. Goodwood[2] reluctant, Ld. Ash.[3] hostile, the green plumb[4] probably interested, and a large previous

---

[1] Mr. Holroyd proposed to stand for the county of Sussex. He apparently hoped that he might represent the eastern half, and relied on the influence of the Duke of Dorset at Buckhurst. But the Richmond influence carried both east and west, and Mr. Holroyd withdrew his candidature. The members returned were Sir Thomas S. Wilson and Lord George H. Lennox.

[2] The Duke of Richmond.

[3] Probably Lord Ashburnham, of Ashburnham Place, near Battle in Sussex.

[4] Probably William Hall, second Viscount Gage, who married Elizabeth Gideon, sister of Sir Sampson Gideon, afterwards Baron Eardley of Spalding, and is said to have introduced the greengage into Sussex. See Letter 210.

subscription backed by strong interest. As to the multitude, you cannot conceive the effect of the magic sounds, *disturbing the peace of the County*.

3. To all this you oppose 'hur own if hur can catch hur.' But I should much distrust the strength of your desired Ally.[1] Unpleasant recollections, a stately and supposed proud behaviour, a solitary life, since he never troubles himself with County meetings, must, I should apprehend, very greatly diminish his popularity, and conceal those abilities which you so justly value, but which few of your country boors are qualified to understand or esteem. Is the mere Dorset[2] interest a *commanding one ?*

4. You say that you are not apprehensive at Lewes of a horrid silence or hiss. Perhaps not. But should you be so easily satisfied ? Who do you design should propose you at the nomination meeting ? for much depends on that, not only as to the hopes of success, but even the dignity and propriety of the declaration. The person to move and the person to second it (for both are necessary) should be distinguished in the County, either by character or property ; Minden[3] would certainly do very well. You will tell me that your connection is not sufficiently formed to request such a favour. But is not that a proof that things are yet unripe ?

5. If you proceed, which upon the whole, I strongly dissuade, I would (in case of a favourable answer from Minden) immediately epistolize or rather visit Goodwood. I would declare my intention of taking the *sense* (if any can be found) of the General meeting, requesting that if it should prove favourable to Lord G. L[ennox] and myself, we might previously agree to advertise and act together. A refusal would permit you to retreat with honour, consent would enable you to advance with vigour and confidence, and even the proposal would place you on the *much desired footing* of a future Candidate. After all, for God's sake remember the expence, and do not trust your fortune and your passions to the danger of a Contest.

Duane after a very long delay has at last given his opinion

[1] Lord George Germain.

[2] John Frederick, third Duke of Dorset, who succeeded his uncle in 1769, was appointed Ambassador at Paris in 1783. He died in 1799.

[3] Probably refers to Lord George Germain, who was M.P. for East Grinstead, and possessed estates in Sussex. See note to Letter 181.

concerning the tythes, and the opinion is favourable. He thinks the title, *clear, safe, and even compellable*, but directs that the original grants of James the first's time should be searched for in the proper office and copied. This will be attended with some expence, but it cannot be avoided. Newton, whom I saw to-day, writes by this post to Matthews and sends him the opinion. So that in a short time we may I think either come to an amicable conclusion, or meet them in arms on *firm ground*. I hear nothing of the insurance. Cream cheese will be welcome.—To my Lady and the monstrous Maria, *salut*.

210.

To J. B. Holroyd, Esq.

Saturday evening.

I am in a violent hurry—Clarke is extremely well—I have sent you the Deputation. The old Lady expects to hear from me *soon*. I wish your Geographer was arrived, and that Gilbert had discovered the Tythe owners. *By your submission to the voice of reason, you eased me of a heavy load of anxiety. I did not like your enterprize.* 'Who is the green plumb?' Why the brother-in-law of Sampson to be sure.[1] As to papers, I will shew you I can keep them safe till we meet. *What think you of the Turks and Russians? Romanzow is a great Man. He wrote an account of his amazing success to Mouskin Pouskin[2] here, and declared his intention of retiring as soon as he had conducted the army home; desiring that Pouskin would send him the best plan he could procure of an English Gentleman's farm. In his answer, Pouskin promised to get it; but added, that at the same time he should send the Empress *a plan of Blenheim*, a handsome Compliment, I think. My Lady and Maria, as usual.* Where is my Cheese?

211.

To J. B. Holroyd, Esq.

Bentinck Street, Sept. 10th, 1774.

*Since Heberden is returned, I think the road lyes plain before you; I mean the Turnpike road. The only party which in good

---

[1] See note to Letter 209.
[2] The Russian Ambassador in London.

sense can be embraced is, without delay, to bring My Lady to
B[entinck] S[treet], where you may inhabit two or three nights,
and have any advice (Turton, Heberden, &c.) which the town
may afford, in a case that most assuredly ought not to be trifled
with.   Do this as you value our good opinion.   The Cantabs[1] are
strongly in the same sentiments.   There can be no apprehension
of late hours, &c. as none of Mrs. II.'s raking acquaintance are in
town.*   As to Burtenshaw's Manifesto, I can form no judgement
of an imperfect fragment, except that it appears to me very
artful.   The case relative to you I have reconsidered, but find no
reason to alter my opinion.

1st.   An answer on your side cannot be necessary, since he had
no right to single you out.

2dly.   It cannot be expedient, since a fellow of so much passion
and cunning will surely in the end either provoke you or entangle
you in an unworthy contest.   If however you have given him
hopes of an answer, I would positively declare to him that it should
be the last, and that no consideration should tempt me to a reply.

You give me no account of the Works.   When do you inhabit
the library ?   *Turn over—great things await you.*

*It is surely infinite condescension for a Senator to bestow his
attention on the affairs of a Juryman.   A Senator ?   Yes, sir, at
last *Quod nemo promittere Divum auderet, volvenda dies en ! attulit
ultro.*   About ten days ago Eliot spent an hour with me, talked
sensibly of his will, and his children, and requested that I would
be Executor to the one and Guardian to the other.   I consented
to accept an office which indeed I consider as an essential duty of
social life.   We parted.   *Yesterday morning, about half an hour
after seven, as I was destroying an army of Barbarians, I heard a
double rap at the door, and my Cornish friend was soon introduced.   After some idle conversation he told me, that if I was
desirous of being in Parliament, he had an *independent* seat very
much at my service.*   You may suppose my answer, but my
satisfaction was a little damped when he added that the expence
of the election would amount to about £2400, & that he thought
it reasonable that we should share it between us.   I paused, and,
recovering myself, hinted something of Parental extravagance,
and filial narrowness of circumstances and want of ready money,
and that I must beg a short delay to consider whether I could

---

[1] Probably the Cambridges of Twickenham.

with prudence accept of his intended favour, on which I set the highest value. His answer was obliging, that he should be very much mortified if a few hundred pounds should prevent it, and that he had been afraid to offend me by offering it on less equal terms. His behaviour gave me courage to propose an expedient, which was instantly accepted with cordiality and eagerness, that when his second son John (who is now thirteen) came of age I would restore to him my proportion of the money.

I am not disposed to build Castles in Spain, but I think my conduct prudent. Before that time my own honest industry or the deaths of old Ladies *may* make me a richer man : or else I can offer (some years hence) a fair and liberal bargain, that I will settle Beriton on John, in case I have no children, with the proviso that on the birth of a child, I shall pay him the money with legal interest. The agreement will be easy for me, and advantageous to them. *This is a fine prospect opening upon me, and if next spring I should take my seat, and publish my book, it will be a very memorable Era in my life. I am ignorant whether my Borough will be Leskeard [1] or St. Germains. You despise Boroughs, and fly at nobler game. Adieu.*

212.

To J. B. Holroyd, Esq.

Bentinck Street, Sept. 14th, 1774.

You must not suppose that I mean to keep up with you *this Prussian firing* of four times in a minute, a letter every other day. I shall now hold my tongue for some time. Burtenshaw's end I like better than his beginning. Your expedient is excellent, honourable and safe : therefore execute it without delay, and think no more about the whole business. I receive your congratulations ; as to consequences, your scheme has the most apparent, mine the most real generosity, but there is not any hurry for either.—*Clarke* is returned, very indifferent the first day, but now perfectly well, at least for the present. Wilbraham is likewise come up to make some preparations and to buy a little gold chain (vulgo a ring) for his squirrel. Both salute you.—The World may now be in flames when it pleases, provided the Sun

---

[1] Gibbon was M.P. for Liskeard.

fire office be safe ; your Man was with me this morning ; a very compleat puppy !—Not a word of *My Lady !* is she quite lively and sleepy ? Nor a word about the *Journey to town ;* there never was a more rational proposal, indeed there never was. From My Lady *I pass to the cheese.* It was divine in every respect but immortality. I fear the season is too far advanced for another— Enquire.

213.

To his Stepmother.

Bentinck Street, Sept. 17th, 1774.

DEAR MADAM,

Without reproaching you for your silence (which would indeed be the height of assurance) give me leave to inform you of a piece of news, with regard to which I am sure you will share my very agreeable feelings. Mr. Eliot has in the most liberal manner assured me a seat in Parliament, an event which changes the colour of my whole future life. After such intelligence I could add nothing but what would be flat and insipid.

I am, Dear Madam,
Most truly yours,
E. GIBBON.

214.

To J. B. Holroyd, Esq.

24th Sept., 1774.

As the matter admitted of no delay, and the paper was anonymous, it went by this morning's coach. Otherwise I am a great friend to County meetings & resolutions to abide by their sense. They form a happy medium between the Juntas of Grandees in town, and the Mob-archy of the rout of freeholders, and preserve *the peace of the County* without sacrificing its independence. Moreover, I do not comprehend your plot—— You are totally in the wrong in not coming to town. Does the Bath journey hold ? Mrs. G. grows impatient, but it will most wonderfully delay the fall of the Roman Empire. I gave your holy paper, and reasonable request to Caplin. He graciously promised to consider of it. Clarke is infinitely better, town very lively.

Dine next Tuesday at Atwood's with Duke of Portland, &c. Smythe is sensible, for he agrees with me, and I hope September 24th, 1774, has tranquillized you.

215.

To his Stepmother.

Bentinck Street, Oct. 4th, 1774.

Dear Madam,

Last Friday I went down to Sheffield Place at the particular request of Mr. H., to advise with him about a Parliamentary scheme of his own, but which proved impracticable. We then were talking only of next Spring, but the next day I received from Clarke the unexpected intelligence.[1] The Sunday I wrote to Mr. Eliot directing my letter into Cornwall, where I supposed him long since arrived, and I now wait impatiently for an answer. As to my journey, it has now become impossible ; the election will be over before I can get there. Indeed, as I can have no interest there but his assistance, his presence is alone necessary or useful. However, in my letter I offered *to fly*. If you will answer for Mr. Eliot's intentions I will answer for his power. His disturbance could arise only from his indolent temper, the surprize and perhaps some little concern about Grampound which does not relate to me. As he is in firm possession, the suddenness of the occasion is at all events more favourable to him than to any concealed or secret enemies. Therefore, I do indeed consider myself as secure. Before his offer, I could contentedly have borne my exclusion, but I could not now support the disappointment, and were it to happen, I would instantly and for ever leave this kingdom. A few days will now determine my fate, and you may depend on the first intelligence of it.

I am, Dear Madam,

Ever yours,

E. Gibbon.

[1] Parliament was dissolved on September 30, "six months before its natural death. . . . The chief motive is supposed to be the ugly state of North America, and the effects that a cross winter might have on the next elections" (Walpole to Mann, October 6, 1774). The result of the elections was, on the whole, favourable to Lord North.

216.

To J. B. Holroyd, Esq.

7th October, 1774.

I do not find that Harcourt has advertised in *any* of the Papers, and begin to doubt whether he will stand. Yet I wish you would curb your impatience, and adopt my slow and cautious plan. Your *visit to Goodwood* I cannot thoroughly like, nor do I think that a seat, were it obtainable *on those terms*, would be any very distinguished honour. As for us, we are all in a hurry with London, Westminster, &c. : but I could not write particulars without copying sheets of lyes from the Papers.—Clarke[1] is pretty well *at present.* He does not go into Derbyshire, and expects, like me, but with more Philosophy, the news of his success. Deyverdun is arrived to-day with his friend Lord M., who I believe is *satisfied* with his travels. He is with me, and I have nothing more to say. I gave My Lady a little sermon about her un-wellness, which I hope she will profit by and consent to seek for some advice.

217.

To J. B. Holroyd, Esq.

October the 10th, 1774.

Since you have broke loose, my cold counsels must be changed into warm wishes, and, as far as my nothingness can extend, into warm actions. Yet my outset may appear careless and dilatory in not writing to you or to the others on Saturday night. Your damned coach kept the parcel all the evening, and it was not delivered to me till yesterday morning, therefore it was impossible to write sooner than to-day. It is very few borderers that Sir Hugh can collect, but I am sure he will do his utmost. I had a proper opportunity of writing to Lady Fetherstone, which I thought was still better than to Lascelles. I have wrote to L. likewise. I am sorry that you have started, but since you have done the deed, I wish you had done it sooner. *Sir Thomas*[2] *has now*

---

[1] Lord G. Cavendish and Godfrey Bagnal Clarke were elected members for Derbyshire.

[2] Sir Thomas Spencer Wilson, with Lord G. H. Lennox, was returned for Sussex.

the advantage of time and the show of a nomination. I shall be impatient to hear of your success with the Grandees. The few Elections already over have been conducted (thanks to the Grenvillian Act[1]) with a sobriety, a chastity and a parsimony unexampled in this venal country. My devoirs to My Lady, and the Cantabs ; assure the latter that I much regret my running away from them. After Wednesday I shall hourly expect some Cornish news. Adieu.

Surely M. d'Harcourt uses both the County and his friends very ill in not taking the least notice of either. Do not they grumble ? I congratulate you on the prospect of dining with your old acquaintance at the Mansion House.[2]

218.

To J. B. Holroyd, Esq.

October 13th, 1774.

I received this day your two Epistles, the one per post, the other per coach. Your first was perfectly clear, and convinced of what you repeat in the second, that an honourable retreat is your only resource. Yet even that is difficult. What can you say ? that you decline for the peace of the County ? You advertised against a declared Candidate. Personal respect for Sir T[homas] W[ilson]? Do you owe him any compliment ? Besides you cannot approve of him without betraying the honour of the East. It is much easier to advance than to retire, because you never can give the true reason of a retreat. Suppose you only say—To the Gentlemen, &c. " The Encouragement I have received from my " numerous friends deserves and claims my warmest acknowledge- " ments, but the powerful interest already formed in the *Western* "*part of the County* and in the neighbourhood of the place of

---

[1] On March 7, 1770, a Bill for regulating the proceedings of the House of Commons on controverted elections was introduced, and became law in April, 1770. It was subsequently known as the Grenville Act, from its chief supporter, George Grenville. The decision of controverted elections was under the Act transferred from the committee of the whole House to a select committee specially chosen for each case. Originally passed for five years, it was made perpetual in 1774.

[2] John Wilkes was elected Lord Mayor, October 8, 1774.

"Election induces me to spare them the trouble of so long
" and probably so useless a journey.

I am, &c.,
J. B. HOLROYD."

It is nonsense, but I see no better nonsense you have to write.
I wish you had never begun it. Remember my old slow plan. It
is now more likely to succeed than ever.

I am now in constant expectation of hearing from Cornwall.
Adieu. Duane has thoroughly opposed my great tythes.

E. G.

219.

To J. B. Holroyd, Esq.

October the 14th, 1774.

I am sure you have generosity enough to hear with pleasure
the news which I have just received, that I am elected Member of
Parliament for Liskeard.

E. G.

Franks do not take place till the 20th.

220.

To his Stepmother.

Bentinck Street, October 15th, 1774.

DEAR MADAM,

I fancy Mrs. Eliot has already conveyed to you the
pleasing intelligence which I received to-day, that I am elected
Member for Liskeard.

I am,
Ever yours,
E. G.

The right of franking does not commence till the 20th.

221.

To J. B. Holroyd, Esq.

Boodle's, October the 22nd, 1774.

By this time I suppose your Election over, and would bet two
to one that Sir James[1] has carried it,—a lucky circumstance for

---

[1] Sir James Peachy, Bart., was bottom of the poll for Sussex.

you ; he will fill the place, and some years hence, when you have shaken off the *novus homo*, you may assert the liberty of the East.— You are now quiet, and I want to hear about the Bath scheme. Amusement, Piety, *Health* all recommend it ; and I think that with the opening of next month you and My Lady should find yourselves in Bentinck Street, stay two or three days for consultations, purchases, &c., and then set out for Bath, which will allow me a clear fortnight there before I am summoned to town. I want a speedy answer about your plan.

Duane's opinion has been sent, but with very little effect. Lovegrove is at Bristol, I believe dying—Matthews shuffles as usual. I have directed a very clear, peremptory Epistle—Hugonin was much disposed for you, and even Sir Harry, if I may trust a letter from his Mama. Adieu. I do not like My Lady, and think that on her account you should come up directly.

Shall I order the Papers to be directed to me at S. P. ?

222.

To his Stepmother.

Bentinck Street, October the 29th, 1774.

DEAR MADAM,

 You know I am never fond of long letters, and the less so when I have the near prospect of seeing you very soon. About the middle of the week after next, that is, about the 8th or 9th of November, Mrs. Porten and myself propose getting into my chaise, and, lying one night on the road, to arrive the second day in New Charles Street. My aunt is well *at present* and in vast spirits on the occasion. As my time is now circumscribed I should have set out sooner, were I not detained by some circumstances relative to the Holroyds. They have left me this morning after a short stay of only two nights in town. You will not alarm the family at Bath, but *I really think her very far from well.*

   I am, Dear Madam,
     Most truly yours,
       E. GIBBON.

223.

To J. B. Holroyd, Esq.

Bond Street, November 3rd, 1774.

Though I have nothing to say, I must write two lines to say what you know already, how truly I sympathise with you. I hope at last Mrs. H. will hear with patience of Bath, and of the cold Bath. I am sure the latter (for air, exercise, and gentle amusement) would be of infinite service to her. My time as you see is so strictly defined, that I cannot wait longer than Thursday next. Deyverdun goes with us, and Clarke, who is advised to try the waters, will possibly follow us. Both desire to be named to you. My compliments to the Lady Cambridges; and many thanks to my fair Guest in particular. Next Monday I visit Twickenham.

O rare Sir Thomas Wilson! Adieu.

E. G.

224.

To his Stepmother.

Bentinck Street, Nov. 5th, 1774.

Dear Madam,

Next Wednesday Mrs. P. and myself start from town, and hope to enjoy the pleasure of drinking Tea in Charles Street on Thursday. Deyverdun, who is returned to England with Lord Middleton, means to be of the party: that is to say he will get into the machine, when we mount the chaise, and will keep company with us in the journey. We mean to live with you and upon you, but as Mrs. P. is large and your house is small, I should think, if you procured us two bed-chambers and a dining-room in the neighbourhood of Charles Street, *we should have more room to swing a cat.* However, I submit every arrangement to your wise Counsels, and am,

Dear Madam, ever yours,

E. G.

225.

To J. B. Holroyd, Esq.

Spinham lands, Nov. 9th, 1774.

I am not a little uneasy in not hearing either Monday or Tuesday from S. P. Is Mrs. H. worse either in health or spirits? Has she tryed the Cold bath, or does she at least hear the sound of it with less reluctance? I am still of opinion that Bath in every respect would be the best place for her *to make some stay in*, and if my intreaties or authority could have any weight, I would wish you to give them their full force. I am now (Mrs. Porten and Deyverdun are with me) above half-way on my journey. As your father is infirm and sister a female, shall I secure you a Lodging, &c.? By this time I suppose Sir Thomas is Knight of Sussex. *Cedat fortunæ Ratio.* Adieu.

My Compliments to the Ladies Cambridge. I have used their Parent like a Dog; but it was unavoidable.

226.

To J. B. Holroyd, Esq.

Bath, Nov. 13th, 1774.

I arrived at Bath, Thursday night, and saw the Pater and Sorella [1] the next morning : the former in my opinion surprizingly well. They gave me very satisfactory information as to health and designs. If you really arrive the eighteenth, we shall have one week together in this enchanted spot, where the Goddess of Pleasure is supposed, by the vulgar, to hold her Court. You may possibly see Guise, but I fear Clarke will not be prevailed on to leave Town. I have most strongly pressed him, and I think you will call on him in your passage, wherein I suppose of course you will lodge in Bentinck Street. I conclude : my coffee-house materials are most vile, and I hope this will not find you at Sheffield. My fellow travellers, Aunt and Deyverdun, are well, and Mrs. G. has almost choaked us with kindness and good things. Adieu.

E. G.

[1] *I.e.* Mr. Isaac Holroyd and Miss Sarah Holroyd.

227.

To J. B. Holroyd, Esq.

Nov. 29th, 1774.

All safe and well. I am just returned from the Cock-pit. The K.'s speech vigorous with regard to America.[1] Our address a loyal Echo.

I have talked with Barré about Tremlet, he is an intimate friend both of the Colonel and of Dunning, and they think him equal to all his Bath Atchievments.—Lord Clive[2] *certainly* cut the jugular vein with a pen knife—it is called a feaver frenzy. To-morrow we are sworn in, and the amiable virtues of Sir Fletcher[3] will most assuredly procure him a Unanimity. I hope Bath still agrees with My Lady. I wish I could send you a favourable account of poor Clarke, but he is really very bad; his looks more shocking than ever, neither strength, rest nor appetite. Dr. Addington, his Physician, *hopes* his liver is not touched, but thinks him in one of the worst habits of body he ever saw,—his complaint bilious and obstructions of the bowels; dreads an inflammation. It is a melancholy subject.

Adieu. See Mrs. G.

228.

To his Stepmother.

Boodle's, Nov. 29th, 1774.

DEAR MADAM,

Our journey was successful and agreeable. Mrs. P. arrived in town perfectly well, and, I believe, writes to you by this post. This morning I took my seat, and found it in every respect an easy one. Poor Clarke is extremely ill, and I fear there is very great if not immediate danger. His present physician is Dr. Addington, with whom I am very much pleased. As to Bath, it would be impossible to transport him.

I am, Dear Madam,

Most truly yours,

E. GIBBON.

---

[1] The new Parliament met November 29, 1774.
[2] Lord Clive died November 22, 1774.
[3] Sir Fletcher Norton was re-elected speaker, November 29, 1774.

229.

To J. B. Holroyd, Esq.

Bentinck Street, December 2nd, 1774.

I wish I could speak more favourably of poor Clarke, but I much fear that there is very little hope. It is in vain to enquire whether his complaint is bilious, that is a very *soft* word ; but his situation is as bad as you can conceive. Dr. Addington (whose skill is I believe equal to his humanity), as well as his very sensible Apothecary, seems only undetermined between the fear of a *short* fit or a *long* palsy. His Constitution is broke up. He has been persuaded to think of a settlement which may save a noble Estate from the hands of an idiot Brother, and Skipwith and myself are to be Trustees ; painful and ungrateful office, yet there is not a moment to be lost.

*I send you inclosed a dismal letter from Hugonin. Return it without delay, with observations. A Manifesto has been sent to Lovegrove, which must, I think, produce immediate peace or war. Adieu. We shall have a warm day on the Address next Monday. A number of young Members ! Whitshed,[1] *a dry Man*, assured me, that he heard one of them ask, whether the King always sat in that Chair, pointing to the Speaker's.* I embrace My Lady. Deyverdun thanks and salutes.

E. G.

Sackville Street complained yesterday of silence.

230.

To J. B. Holroyd, Esq.

December, 1774.

Poor Clarke is too melancholy a subject to dwell much upon. Had I wrote last night I should have said that symptoms appeared rather more favourable, but I must now have contradicted myself. I fear there remains but little hope. If I have any really good news to send you I will not lose a moment. Otherwise permit me to be silent on that unpleasant head.

[1] James Whitshed, M.P. for Cirencester.

Monday last was our first engagement. You have seen the
Address,[1] Lord John Cavendish's amendment, and the numbers—
264 to 73. Burke was a water-mill of words and images ; Barré
an Actor equal to Garrick ; Wedderbourne artful and able. Lord
G. Germaine, though An Anti-American, remained silent ; Hartley,[2]
Sir William Maine[3] and some other new Members lost their
maidenheads with very little credit. Once or twice I was a little
lewd, but am now well pleased that I resisted the premature
temptation. I divided with the Majority. Your Lewes friend
Sir Thomas[4] (to the general surprize) with the minority.

As to private affairs, It is a strange pair of brutes that I am
engaged with. I send your letters as instructions to Hugonin.
As to Lovegrove we expect his *Ultimatum*. The Bishop of
Landaff gives a very bad character of Matthews.

Last Tuesday I dined at Lethiuellier's[5] with Maudit,[6] Lascelles,
and Sir Thomas Millar. Next Tuesday they dine in Bentinck
Street, with the addition of Batt.[7] From some circumstances
it appears that my romantic attack on Lord A. might have
succeeded. Adieu.

Embrace my Lady. The treaty between moles and paper is
far advanced.

---

[1] The Address was carried on December 5, 1774. An amendment, claiming
the fullest information on American affairs, was moved in the Lower House
by Lord John Cavendish.

[2] David Hartley, M.P. for Kingston-upon-Hull.

[3] Sir W. Maine, Bart., of Gatton Park, Surrey, M.P. for Canterbury.

[4] Sir Thomas Miller, Bart., of Chichester, M.P. for Lewes.

[5] Benjamin Lethieullier, at this time M.P. for Andover, whom Gibbon
met at Up Park in 1762, was brother to Lady Featherstonhaugh, and a
relation of Smart Lethieullier, the antiquary.

[6] Israel Mauduit, pamphleteer and woollen-draper, best known for his
Considerations on the Present German War (1760), was agent for Massachu-
setts Bay. It was on his application that Wedderburn was heard before the
Privy Council, in answer to the petition for the recall of Hutchinson and
Oliver.

[7] "Lawyer Batt," whose name often occurs in these letters, was John
Thomas Batt, of Newhall near Salisbury, successively a Master in Chancery,
and a Commissioner for the auditing of the Public Accounts. He was a
"prime favourite" of Miss Burney, and a friend of Walpole, Lord Malms-
bury, and Sir J. Reynolds.

231.

To Mrs. Holroyd.

Bentinck Street, Dec. 17th, 1774.

DEAR MADAM,

With regard to my silence, poor Clarke is too good and too melancholy an excuse. I know not what to say about him; he is reduced to nothing, and his disorder is attended with every bad symptom. Yet his Physicians—Addington and Thomas—are on the whole less desponding than they were some days ago.

Surely no affair was ever put into better hands than mine has been. Your skill and friendship I am not surprized at, but Mrs. Porten is a most excellent procuress, and The Lady Mother has given as proper an answer as could be expected. There is only one part of it which distresses me, *Religion*. It operates doubly, as a present obstacle and a future inconvenience. Your evasion was very able, but will not prudence as well as honour require us being more explicit in the *suite?* Ought I to give them room to think that I should patiently conform to family prayers and Bishop Hooper's Sermons? I would not marry an Empress on those conditions. I abhor a Devotee, though a friend both to decency and toleration. However, my interests are under your care, and if you think that no more need be said on *the awkward* subject, I shall acquiesce.

After all, what occasion is there to enquire into my profession of faith? It is surely much more to the purpose for them to ask how I have already acted in life, whether as a good son, a good friend, whether I game, drink, &c. You know I never practised the one, and in spite of my old *Dorsetshire* character, I have left off the other. You once mentioned Miss F. I give you my honour, that I have not either with her or any other woman, any connection that could alarm a wife. With regard to fortune Mrs. P. speaks in a very liberal manner; but above all things, I think it should not be *magnified*. If it should be necessary to hint at incumbrances, your delicacy I am sure could place them in such a light as might raise the character of the living without injuring the memory of the dead. You see how serious I am in this business. If the general idea should not startle Miss, the next consultation would be how, and where the Lover may throw himself at her feet, contemplate her charms, and *study her character.* After that we may proceed to other more minute enquiries and arrangements.

Mrs. Porten knows she was *blind.* Her brother is married. —How go on your Civil Wars ? Next week Foote and Coleman will be with you. Adieu.

Dear Madam,
Most truly yours,
BENEDICT GIBBON.

Excuse me to Holroyd for a post or two.

232.

To J. B. Holroyd, Esq.

Bentinck Street, December 20th, 1774.

Hear, but be silent especially to Mrs. G.—*The Gout* has attacked my left foot, and that Imperious Mistress, if I presumed without her permission to dispose of myself—— However, she seems inclined to pardon and to leave me. In that case poor Clarke is my next difficulty ; without a hope of recovery he may linger longer, than some days ago I thought was possible. Should I find myself at liberty, I have *engaged* myself to visit the Widow the first week in January ; ten days from that date will lead me to the meeting of Parliament, an awful meeting indeed ! You will *receive with this the resolutions of the American Congress.*[1] I shall certainly be in town (if your impatience soon drives you from Bath) *to house you and My Lady in your passage.* Deyverdun is not averse to go to S. P. when I go to Up-park.

E. G.

233.

To J. B. Holroyd, Esq.

Dec. 24th, 1774.

I do not upon the whole like your Sackville Street plan. At least I should not like it, were it not for an unlucky guest I have

---

[1] Delegates from eleven Colonies met at Philadelphia, September 5, 1774, and constituted themselves a Congress. A Declaration of Rights was drawn up, in which it was shown that recent Acts of Parliament had infringed those rights. Resolutions were passed to suspend all imports from, or exports to, Great Britain and Ireland and their dependencies, till American grievances were redressed. An association was formed to carry out these resolutions, and on October 26 Congress dissolved.

got in the house. I do not mean my Gout, for that is on the wing, but a bad kind of small-pox which has attacked one of my Virgins in the Garret.

I am deep in America with Maudit, passed four hours with him yesterday, and I shall dine and spend the day tête-à-tête with him next Monday. He squeaks out a great deal of sense and knowledge, though after all I mean to think, perhaps to speak, for myself. I likewise (at his house) conversed with Governor Hutchinson,[1] with whom I mean to get acquainted.

Tremlett I will try to see in May, but his book is not worth the 18 pence he gave for it. I mean barring the good Spanish. That Spanish is in truth the original, composed by one Miguel de Luna in the sixteenth century, as a pretended translation from an imaginary Arabic Manuscript of General Tarikh.[2] The History is a Romance mixed up with gross improbabilities and anachronisms. Adieu. Young Cooke[3] of Turin dined with me to-day. I thought it a civility to Denham, though I believe only half the house will thank me for it. He is a *very* fine Gentleman. Adieu. I salute My Lady. Do you salute *Madame ma Mère*, Sunday morning, tell her that I am sorry for her Rheumatism, have taken care of the Lees, and will epistolize her Monday or Tuesday.

À propos—I thought of the Arabic MS., but had almost forgot

---

[1] Thomas Hutchinson, Governor of Massachusetts, and Andrew Oliver, Lieutenant-Governor, had corresponded with a private friend in England, Thomas Whately, formerly secretary to George Grenville. Their letters were purloined and placed in the hands of Franklin, who sent copies to the House of Assembly of Massachusetts. The House petitioned for their recall in consequence of the language they had used in these letters. The petition was dismissed by the Privy Council. Hutchinson, however, returned home early in 1774. He had already published (1764-68) two volumes of his *History of the Colony of Massachusetts*. He died in 1780, at the age of seventy-eight. The third volume of his history was published from his manuscripts in 1828.

[2] The work in question is *La verdadera Hystoria del rey Don Rodrigo: compuesta por Abuleacim Tarif Abentarique*. Nuevamente traduzida de la lengua Arabiga por M. de L[una]. In two parts. Granada, 1592-1600, 8vo. It was really written by Miguel de Luna, and, as Gibbon points out, the Arabic MS. is imaginary. The book was translated into English as *The Life of Almanzor*, translated into Spanish by M. de Luna. London, 1693. 8vo.

[3] Probably a nephew of Mr. Benjamin Way, of Denham, Mrs. Holroyd's brother, who married Miss Elizabeth Cooke.

to tell you that Gilbert of Lewes was with me this morning. He has discovered the owner of the Tythes, an Attorney—Mr. Charles Down of Hythe, where he is at present, but who lives in town.

I fear to put the Saint to any expence, and remembered what you said of negotiating in person. Therefore agreed that when Gilbert comes to London next month, we would see Down together; in the interim—silence. But if you think not a moment should be lost, I can by a line despatch Gilbert to Hythe.

Again—Adieu.

234.

To his Stepmother.

Bentinck Street, Dec. 28th, 1774.

Dear Madam,

My poor friend died last Monday, and has left me—together with Mr. Skipwith—his Executors and Trustees, a very painful and perhaps thankless office. You will easily suppose that the shock, however expected, and the hurry of melancholy business, have swallowed up the remembrance of any lesser disappointment, and indeed engross all my thoughts. The Holroyds dine with me to-morrow.—You will be so kind as to excuse the Christmas draught for a week or ten days at farthest.

I am, Dear Madam,
Most truly yours,
E. G.

235.

To J. B. Holroyd, Esq.

B. S., Thursday Evening, January 5th, 1775.

Winton has *submitted*,
His whole rent is remitted.

But what is to become of you and My Lady? are you both swallowed up in the Sussex roads? Deyverdun desires to be remembered. A letter of business from his Lord M[iddleton], which he daily expects, still detains him in town. Give him a line

about your motions and *tell him when* you may be ready to receive
him. I say to him, rather than to me, because I lie Saturday night
at Twickenham and dine on Sunday with the Widow. The 17th
(Tuesday se'nnight) I shall be in Bentinck Street again, as our
Parliamentary Campaign opens on Thursday. Adieu. I write
with severall people in the room, and am called away to a Chess
party. Will *Maria excuse* my silence ? but she should early be
taught that men retreat, when young Ladies advance.

I have had two very long days with Skipwith on poor Clarke's
affairs ; they are indeed in a very distressed condition, and reckoning the brother and sister's fortunes, £100,000 will hardly clear
them, but the means are large, my colleague indefatigable, and it
is the only office of friendship now left in my power. I could only
wish that our authority was less circumscribed.

On re-reading Sir Hugh's letter, which I had not yet done, I
find that after Winton's brother arrived they went to Petersfield,
consulted with another Lawyer, and when they had *shamefully and
scandalously* abused Andrews, paid the money and gave up everything, Straw demand, &c. They think no more of law, but will
pay their rent quarterly into my own hands only. Cannot I refuse
it (it will be disagreeable), and oblige them to pay it on the *spot to
any person* I shall empower ?

236.

To his Stepmother.

Bentinck Street, January 7th, 1775.

DEAR MADAM,

After the loss of my poor friend, I begin to be a little
relieved from the load of business and anxiety which his confidence has devolved upon me in conjunction with Mr. Skipwith,
and with assistance the affairs of poor Clarke will soon be brought
into a regular method, which in time may enable us to discharge
our trust and to deliver a very noble Estate from a very heavy
incumbrance of debt. I now propose to spend the ten days that
remain before the meeting of Parliament,[1] at Up-park. The
change of air will not I fancy do me any harm either in mind or
body ; I mention the latter, as I find Sir Stanier betrayed me.

---

[1] Parliament met January 19, 1775.

The Gout has now asserted his rights in an unquestionable manner, but on this occasion he has exercised them in a very gentle manner, and I can say with truth, that I find myself rather benefitted than injured by his transient visit. I hope you may be able to send me as good an account of the Rheumatism.

The Willow Garland you sent me has not much disconcerted my Philosophy, and indeed the sanctity of the Lady, had a little prepared me for, and reconciled me to, the disappointment. I am only sorry that the ill-success of a negociation conducted with so much ability and of so promising an appearance should have given you a disgust for the honourable profession of Ambassadress. On the contrary, I should hope that in the well-furnished market we might, either now or hereafter, find the opportunity of retrieving our first miscarriage.

Sir Stanier and Lady Porten exhibit a very pretty picture of conjugal fondness and felicity, and yet they have been married very near three weeks.

I have now, dear Madam, sent you the Christmas Draught, and hope the short delay has not been attended with the least inconveniency to you. It was occasioned by the obstinacy of Winton, who obliged me to distress for rent. Hugonin obeyed very spirited orders with skill and alacrity, and the well-timed chastisement has rendered the Brute perfectly tame and submissive. His character indeed is of much less consequence to me than his substance, which is of a very responsible nature. Excuse me for dwelling a moment on so trifling and disagreeable a subject.

I am, Dear Madam,

Most truly yours,

E. GIBBON.

I set out about twelve o'clock, take a dinner and bed with the Cambridges and dine to-morrow at Up-park.

237.

To J. B. Holroyd, Esq.

18th January, 1775.

I received at Up-park your *long expected rescript*. Yesterday I returned to town. Our party was numerous. Lady F. proposed

to have her brothers,[1] Sir Thomas and Lady Miller, &c. But so
uncertain are human affairs that accidents disapointed her. In
their room we had the fox-hunting friends of Sir Harry. Lord
Egremont, who is civil and sensible; General Pitt with his wife,
a determined Sportsman (I mean Sportswoman) who hunted all
the morning and slept all the evening. On my return I slept
with Hugonin. He was lamentable, as you may suppose, about
Winton's repairs, &c. Yet I am satisfied Winton is cowed, and
my Repairs which were represented as a most dreadful account
leave Hug. in debt to me. They are all furious against Jolliffe,
and Lutterel endeavours to prove that the Lord of Buriton is the
real Lord of the Manor of Petersfield. I think I am obliged to
him. Will you have some matches? they may entertain My Lady
whom I salute.

Lord Beauchamp [2]—Lady F. Wyndham.
Mr. T. Conway—Lady Holland [3] (when brought to bed).

I did hear two more, but I fear confusion and mistake.
When do you come to town? Hugonin intends to meet you.
Wednesday Evening. Such a fog as I never saw in London.

238.

To J. B. Holroyd, Esq.

Boodle's, Jan. 31st, 1775.

*Sometimes people do not write because they are too idle, and
sometimes because they are too busy. The former was usually
my case, but at present it is the latter. The fate of Europe and
America seems fully sufficient to take up the time of one Man;
and especially of a Man who gives up a great deal of time for the
purpose of public and private information. I think I have sucked
Mauduit and Hutcheson very dry; and if my confidence was

---

[1] Sir M. Featherstonhaugh married, in 1746, Sarah Lethieullier, who died
in 1788. One of her brothers was Benjamin Lethieullier, M.P. for Andover.
See note to Letter 230.

[2] Lord Beauchamp, at this time a widower, married, in May 22, 1776, as
his second wife, Lady Isabella Shepheard, eldest daughter of the last Lord
Irvine.

[3] Lady Mary Fitzpatrick, daughter of the first Earl of Upper Ossory,
married, in 1766, Stephen Fox, second Lord Holland. She died October 6,
1778, without marrying a second time.

equal to my eloquence, and my eloquence to my knowledge, perhaps I might make no very intolerable Speaker. At all events,
I fancy I shall try to expose myself.

Semper ego auditor tantùm? nunquamne reponam?

For my own part, I am more and more convinced that we have
both the right and the power on our side, and that, though the
effort may be accompanied with some melancholy circumstances,
we are now arrived at the decisive moment of persevering, or of
losing for ever both our Trade and Empire. We expect next
Thursday or Friday to be a very great day. Hitherto we have
been chiefly employed in reading papers, and rejecting petitions.
Petitions were brought from London, Bristol, Norwich, &c., &c.,
framed by party, and designed to delay. By the aid of some
parliamentary quirks, they have been all referred to a separate
inactive committee, which Burke calls a Committee of Oblivion,
and are now considered as dead in law. I could write you fifty
little House of Commons stories, but from their number and
nature they suit better a conference than a letter. Our general
divisions are about 250 to 80 or 90.*

Gilbert was with me this morning. He has been with the
Tythe Owner, whom Martin knows very well. The former seems
inclined to sell but by auction. I wish you would send for Gilbert
and settle something with him. I must soon write to Mrs. G.
What must I say? When do you fix the rent of Newhaven?
Remember Lady Day approaches: and we must say something
definitive to Martin. Caplin knows not any proper servant, but
will be so kind as to enquire, for his friend Mr. H. What
wages, &c., do you give? Adieu. I embrace My Lady.

E. G.

230.

To his Stepmother.

London, Jan. 31st, 1775.

DEAR MADAM,

*An idle Man has no time, and a busy Man very little.
As yet the House of Commons turns out very well to me, and
though it should never prove of any real benefit to me, I find it at
least a very agreeable Coffee-house. We are plunging every day
deeper into the great business of America; and I have hitherto

been a zealous, though silent, friend to the Cause of Government, which, *in this instance*, I think the Cause of England. I passed about ten days, as I designed, at Up-park, but was a little disappointed in my party. Instead of the Brothers I found Lord Egremont and fourscore fox-hounds. Sir Henry is very civil and good-humoured. But from the unavoidable temper of youth I fear he will cost many a tear to Lady F. She consults everybody, but has neither authority nor plan. In my return I called on the Bayleys and lay at Nursted.

The Troubles of Buriton are perfectly composed, and the Insurgents reduced to a state, though not a temper, of submission. You may suppose I heard a great deal of Petersfield. Lutterel means to convict your friend of Bribery, to transport him for using a second time old stamps, and to prove that Petersfield is still a part of the Manor of Buriton. I remain an impartial Spectator.* I like the Epigram much. Don't you apprehend that the Eliots [are] at Bath? Their Cornish friends talk of it. If I should run down at Easter, would you secure me a Wife? It is surely a good Market. Adieu, Dear Madam.

I am ever yours,
E. G.

240.

To J. B. Holroyd, Esq.

Wednesday Evening (February 8th, 1775).

*I am not damned, according to your charitable wishes, because I have not acted; there was such an inundation of speakers, young Speakers in every sense of the word, both on Thursday in the Grand Committee, and Monday on the report to the house, that neither Lord George Germaine nor myself could find room for a single word. The principal men both days were Fox and Wedderburne, on the opposite sides; the latter displayed his usual talents. The former taking the vast compass of the question before us, discovered powers for regular debate, which neither his friends hoped, nor his Enemies dreaded. We voted an address (304 to 105), of lives and fortunes, declaring Massachusets Bay in a state of rebellion. More troops, but I fear not enough, go to America, to make an army of 10,000 men at Boston; three Generals, Howe, Burgoyne, and Clinton. In a few days we stop

the ports of New England.¹ I cannot write Volumes : but I am
more and more convinced, that with firmness all may go well ; yet
I sometimes doubt Lord N[orth]. I am now writing with Ladies
(Sir S. Porten and his Bride), and two card tables, in the Library.
As to my silence, judge of my situation by last Monday. I am on
the Grenvillian Committee of Downton.² We always sit from ten
to three and a half ; after which, that day, I went into the House,
and sat till three in the morning.* I will shew your letter to
Caplin as well for Porter as footman. I do not understand your
new scheme. *Your drawing-room will never do !* Write soon
about Gilbert.

E. G.

I will write soon again.

241.

To J. B. Holroyd, Esq.

Wednesday Eve, 15th February, 1775.

A letter to-day from Mrs. G.: she has heard of the Tythes-
man being found, wishes to buy by private Contract, fears the
price, distrusts Gil[bert] ; and wishes to hear from you through me.
I shall use your hints to-morrow. I have found you a Servant—
George Barton, a Native of Cheshire. Sir Harbord,³ whom he last
lived with, gives him (to me) a very good character ; he is a middle-
aged, sober, well-looking man, loves the country, takes care of
horses, and likes your terms so well that, if you chuse it by
return of post, he will attend you. The post this instant rings,
d'Eyverdun exists. Next week I think the fishery Bill. There
is some reason to think (Barré told me just now) that the New
York Assembly has dissented from the Congress.⁴ Adieu.

¹ Lord North proposed (February 10) a Bill restricting the trade of
America with Great Britain, Ireland, and the West Indies, and excluding
the colonists from the Newfoundland fisheries.

² The two members returned for Downton, Thomas Dummer and Thomas
Duncombe, were declared not duly elected, and Sir Philip Hales and John
Cooper declared duly elected.

³ Sir Harbord Harbord, afterwards Lord Suffield, M.P. for Norwich.

⁴ Efforts were made by Lord North to secure the loyalty of the province
of New York, which at first repudiated the non-importation agreement of
Congress, refused to print letters of the committee of correspondence
appointed to carry out that policy, and declined to choose delegates to the
second Congress which was to be held in May, 1775. Patriotic feeling,
however, prevailed, and New York decided in April, 1775, to fall into line
with the other colonies.

242.

To J. B. Holroyd, Esq.

Saturday Evening, February 25th, 1775.

Enclosed I send you Aunt's power of Attorney. It is not legal, owing I suppose to her ignorance of forms, but *still it expresses her sentiments*, and will, I think, relative to her, authorize you to take any measures that may be expedient for the general good, and they must be taken without delay. I think if we *could get a tolerable lease* of the Tythes for a good term of years, it would be a stop-gap in our favour till at better leisure we could purchase them.

*We go on with regard to America, if we can be said to go on; for on last Monday a conciliatory Motion of allowing the Colonies to tax themselves was introduced by Lord North, in the midst of lives and fortunes, War and famine.[1] We went into the House in Confusion, every moment expecting that the Bedfords would fly into Rebellion against those measures. Lord North rose six times to appease the storm; all in vain; till at length Sir Gilbert [Elliot] declared for Administration, and the Troops all rallied under their proper standards. On Wednesday we had the Middlesex Election.[2] I was a Patriot; sat by the Lord Mayor,[3] who spoke well, and with temper, but before the end of the debate fell fast asleep. I am still a Mute; it is more tremendous than I imagined; the great speakers fill me with despair, the bad ones with terror.

[1] On February 1, 1775, Lord Chatham, in the House of Lords, brought in a Bill for settling the troubles in America, by which it was enacted, *inter alia*, that no tax should be imposed on the colonists by the British Parliament without the consent of their own representative assembly. The Bill was rejected; but it probably influenced Lord North, who, on February 20, brought forward, in the Lower House, his conciliatory scheme. This was a resolution proposing that, if the colonists should make a satisfactory provision for the defence and government of the province, the right of taxing them should be suspended. Sir G. Elliot represented the Bedford party in the House of Commons.

[2] On February 22 Wilkes proposed a motion rescinding every step which the late Parliament had taken with reference to the Middlesex election. Gibbon voted for the motion against the Government. The motion was lost by 239 to 171.

[3] Wilkes.

When do you move? My Lady answered like a woman of sense, spirit, and good nature. "Neither she nor I could bear it." She was right, and the Dutchess of Braganza[1] would have made the same answer.* How do you like your footman? Sir H. only parted with him because the Man wanted to set up his Trade in his own Country. Adieu.

243.

To J. B. Holroyd, Esq.

Tuesday Evening, February 28th, 1775.

The Bell rings—— I like the intended Journey of Sunday. For sundry reasons think you had better auspicate by Twickenham, and reserve Bentinck Street, for the *bonne bouche* week. Still dumb: but see, hear, laugh sometimes, am oftener serious, but upon the whole very well amused. Adieu.

244.

To his Stepmother.

March the 30th, 1775.

Dear Madam,

*I hardly know how to take up the pen. I talked in my last pen of two or three posts, and I am almost ashamed to calculate how many have elapsed. I will endeavour for the future to be less scandalous. Only believe that my heart is

---

[1] Robert Jephson's successful tragedy *Braganza* was played at Drury Lane in February, 1775, Mrs. Yates taking the part of Louisa, Duchess of Braganza. Gibbon is probably referring to this play in comparing Mrs. Holroyd to the spirited Duchess. The answer of "My Lady" is in keeping with the character of the Duchess as depicted in the play—

> " I have a woman's form, a woman's fears,
> I shrink from pain and start at dissolution.
> .   .   .   .
> Yet summoned as we are, your honour pledged,
> Your own just rights engaged, your country's fate,
> .   .   .   .   Still would I on,
> Still urge, exhort, confirm thy constancy,
> And, though we perished in the bold attempt,
> With my last breath I'd bless the glorious cause,
> And think it happiness to die so nobly."

innocent of the lazyness of my hand. I do not mean to have
recourse to the stale and absurd excuse of business, though I
have really had a very considerable hurry of new Parliamentary
business : one day, for instance, of seventeen hours, from ten in
the morning till between three and four the next morning. It is,
upon the whole, an agreeable improvement in my life, and forms
just the mixture of business, of study, and of society, which I
always imagined I should, and now find I do, like. Whether
the House of Commons may ever prove of benefit to myself or
Country is another question. As yet I have been mute. In the
course of our American affairs, I have sometimes had a wish
to speak, but though I felt tolerably prepared as to the matter,
I dreaded exposing myself in the manner, and remained in my
seat safe, but inglorious. Upon the whole (though I still believe
I shall try), I doubt whether Nature, not that in some instances
I am ungrateful, has given me the talents of an Orator, and I
feel that I come into Parliament much too late to exert them.*

The H.'s have passed a fortnight with me and went away
yesterday. I regret them much. We often thought and talked
of you, and the more so, as we stumbled on your friend Mrs.
Ashby. She is an agreable Woman, though we cannot think her
either handsome, or proper for your daughter-in-law. *Do you
hear of Port Eliot coming to Bath ? and, above all, do you hear
of Charles Street[1] coming to Bentinck Street, in its way to Essex,
&c. Adieu.

Dear Madam,

I am most truly yours,

E. GIBBON.*

245.

To J. B. Holroyd, Esq.

Saturday Night, 8th April, 1775.   Atwood's as usual.

A Letter from Aunt. She supposes me too much taken up
with Public business to write. And yet, alas ! throughout that
public business I have remained silent, and notwithstanding
all my efforts chained down to my place by some invisible—
unknown invisible power. Now America and almost Parliament
are at an end. I have *resumed my History* with vigour and

---

[1] Mrs. Gibbon's residence at Bath.

adjourned Politicks to next Winter. Deyverdun will render account of his own Commissions. Lord Stamford and Booth Gray *hunt* Brown for your service. He is difficult to catch. I embrace My Lady and Maria. *She* (I mean My Lady) is good and grateful. Adieu.

Lovegrove still shuffles : I know not what to do.

246.

To his Stepmother.

April 11th, 1775.

DEAR MADAM,

    I am sorry to hear of your rheumatism, but the return of Spring is much in your favour. I wish you would follow Mrs. Porten's method, who is never out of order above four and twenty hours at a time, and is still, take her upon the whole, one of the youngest women I know about town. I am glad to find that Mr. Eliot is coming to Bath ; he will be in town, I suppose, some days after the end of the Sessions. His friends continually ask me about him, and when his name is drawn upon a Ballot it is a standing joke in the House of Commons. It will certainly not be in my power to attend him and to visit you as I could have wished during the very short period of our Holidays. I never yet found myself more taken up with business : one part of it, though indeed the most trifling, you will not, I believe, be displeased at, *a presentation at Court next week*. I likewise have an engagement to meet Lord North at dinner, which will probably be followed by another at his own House (but this between ourselves). Besides all this, the melancholy duty which I am discharging to poor Clarke makes it impossible for me to move for some time, as my Colleague—Skipwith—takes the country business and leaves me that of town, which is much more perplexing and tedious than I expected. So you see, dear Madam, that you must return my visit, and I hope you will seriously think of it. Deyverdun kisses your hands, and will soon send you something in verse or prose.

I am, dear Madam,

Most truly yours,

E. G.

Be so good as to give me a line on Mr. E.'s arrival, with some idea of his intended motions, that I may epistolize him.

247.

To his Stepmother.

House of Commons, May the 2nd, 1775.

Dear Madam,

I accept the Pomeranian Lady with gratitude and pleasure, and shall be impatient to form an acquaintance with her. My presentations passed graciously, and I am glad that I can now walk about the Rooms on a footing with other people. Sir S. P. had no concern in the business which was transacted by the Lord of the Bed-chamber in one place, and the Chamberlain on the other. *My dinner at Twickenham was attended with less ceremony and more amusement. If they turned out Lord N. to-morrow, they would still leave him one of the best Companions in the Kingdom. By this time I suppose the Eliots with you. I am sure you will say every thing kind and proper on the occasion. I am glad to hear of the approbation of my Constituents for my vote on the Middlesex Election ; on the subject of America, I have been something more of a Courtier. You know, I suppose, that Holroyd is just stept over to Ireland for a fortnight. He passed three days with me on his way.*

Adieu, Dear Madam. You have had but a disagreable Winter, I think, in point of health. A Journey to town, Essex, &c., would do you a great deal of good.

Ever yours,

E. G.

218.

To J. B. Holroyd, Esq.

15th May, 1775.

Since your departure a considerable event has happened with regard to Deyverdun, which disconcerts many of our schemes. Sir Abraham Hume[1] has proposed to him to go abroad with his younger brother for four years. Our friend was undetermined especially as the first year or eighteen months were to be passed in the uncomfortable University of Gottingen. But as he was

---

[1] See note to Letter 184.

offered in a very handsome way a Life annuity of £100 per annum which will secure him a Philosophic independence free from the odious necessity of riding post with young cubs, reason has compelled him to accept and me to acquiesce. He sets out soon, though he still hopes to see you. A fortune that would enable a Man to give him an Equivalent on less unpleasant terms would just now be a very desirable thing.

Returned this moment from an American debate. A Remonstrance and Representation from the Assembly of New York, presented and feebly introduced by Burke, but most forcibly supported by Fox.[1] They disapprove of the violence of their neighbours, acknowledge the necessity of some dependence on Parliament with regard to Commercial restraints and express some affection and moderation ; but they claim internal taxation, state many grievances and formally object to the declaratory Act. On the last ground it was impossible to receive it. Division 186 to 67. The House tired and languid. In this season and on America, the Archangel Gabriel would not be heard. On Thursday an attempt to repeal the Quebec bill,[2] and then to the right about, and for myself, having supported the British, I must destroy the Roman Empire.

Are we not very popular in the Bog? Is your business done, and when do you *superas condere ad auras?* I frequently hear from the Heroine of Brighthelmstone, and in the brevity of my Rescripts treat her with the dignity of a Sultan. Adieu.

No news from Lovegrove. The affair begins to make me seriously unhappy.

249.

To his Stepmother.

London, May 16th, 1775.

DEAR MADAM,

To-day Deyverdun, myself, and another gentleman dined at home. After drinking coffee in the Library, we went down stairs again, and as we entered the Parlour, our ears were saluted with a very harmonious barking, and our eyes gratified by the

---

[1] May 15, 1775.

[2] May 18, 1775. This Act, passed in the spring of 1774, sanctioned the free exercise of the Roman Catholic religion in Canada.

sight of one of the prettiest animals I ever saw. Her figure and coat are perfect, her manners genteel and lively, and her teeth (as a pair of ruffles have already experienced) most remarkably sharp. She is not the least fatigued with her voyage, and compleatly at home in Bentinck Street. I call her *Bath*. Gibbon would be ambiguous and Dorothea disrespectful. However it may still be changed. A thousand thanks, and if the E.'s are arrived, many compliments.

I am, dear Madam,

Ever yours,

E. G.

250.

To J. B. Holroyd, Esq.

May 30th, 1775.

You will probably see in the Papers, the Boston Gazette Extraordinary. I shall therefore mention a few circumstances which I have from Governor Hutchinson.

That Gazette is the only account arrived. As soon as the business was over the Provincial Congress dispatched a vessel with the news for the good people of England. The vessel was taken up to sail instantly at a considerable loss and expence, as she went without any lading but her ballast. No other letters were allowed to be put on board, nor did the crew know their destination till they were on the Banks of Newfoundland. The Master is a man of character and moderation, and from his mouth the following particulars have been drawn. *Fides sit penes auctorem.*

It cannot fairly be called a defeat of the King's troops; since they marched to Concord, destroyed or brought away the stores, and then returned back.[1] They were so much fatigued with their day's work (they had marched above thirty miles) that they encamped in the evening at some distance from

---

[1] On April 18, 1775, General Gage despatched several hundred British troops from Boston to destroy some military stores collected at Concord. On the 19th they reached Concord; but, on the return, they were attacked by the Colonial Minute-men, and were only saved from annihilation by the detachment which Gage had sent to their support at Lexington. The battle was immediately followed by the investment of Boston by the American militia.

Boston without being attacked in the night. It can hardly be called an engagement, there never was any large body of Provincials. Our troops during the march and retreat were chiefly harrassed by flying parties from behind the stone walls along the road and by many shots from the windows as they passed through the villages. It was then they were guilty of setting fire to some of those hostile houses. Ensign Gould had been sent with only twelve men to repair a wooden bridge for the retreat ; he was attacked by the Saints with a minister at their head, who killed two men and took the Ensign with the others prisoners. The next day the Country rose. When the Master came away he says that Boston was invested by a camp of about fifteen hundred tents. They have canon. Their General is a Colonel Ward, a member of the late Council, and who served with credit in the last War. His outposts are advanced so near the town, that they can talk to those of General Gage.

This looks serious, and is indeed so. But the Governor[1] observed to me that the month of May is the time for sowing Indian corn, the great sustenance of the Province, and that unless the Insurgents are determined to hasten a famine, they must have returned to their own habitations: especially as the restraining act (they had already heard of it) cuts off all foreign supply, which indeed generally become necessary to the Province before Winter. Adieu.

251.

To J. B. Holroyd, Esq.

Bentinck Street, June 3rd, 1775.

The American news becomes every hour more problematical. Darby, the master of the Ship, has not condescended to show to any one the original of the Salem Gazette. He has refused to come to Lord Dartmouth, and what is still more extraordinary, though he says he left his ship at Southampton, a person of consequence sent down there by Government has not been able to learn the least news about it. Yet on the other hand a ship from New York is certainly arrived at Bristol with the report that a Skirmish at Boston was talked of. No news from Gage. What

---

[1] *I.e.* Hutchinson.

am I to do about Handkerchiefs ?   I thought the letter you sent
me for Downs was an order for them.   He sent them to me
without my application, and they are already marked and used.
On the other hand Mrs. B[enjamin] W[ay] is outrageous.   It is
all your fault and must be cleared up by you.   I think I see
some hopes about Lovegrove, though too faint as yet to be worth
any detail.   I rejoyce in My Lady's health.   What is the name
of her friend the Dutchess's Captain ?   Deyverdun is on the wing.
I wish you would make and send me a cheese.   I must eat two
before I think of Sheffield.   Bath, who desires his compliments,
promises himself a very pleasant summer there.

E. G.

252.

To his Stepmother.

London, June 7th, 1775.

DEAR MADAM,

The post after I received your last letter, I wrote to
Eliot to know whether he had any intention of coming to town
from Bath, but his Lazyness has not yet condescended to answer
me.   With the frankness that our friendship permits and requires,
I will fairly tell you the state of the case.   If he does not visit
London, decency and perhaps gratitude call upon me to meet him
at Bath ; but if he relieves me from that necessity, the Autumn
will be a much more convenient time for me to make my
appearance in Charles Street.   The season is more agreable, and I
am just at present engaged in a great Historical Work, no less
than a History of the Decline and fall of the Roman Empire,
with the first Volume of which I may very possibly oppress the
public next winter.   It would require some pages to give a more
particular idea of it : but I shall only say in general that the
subject is curious, and never yet treated as it deserves, and that
during some years it has been in my thoughts and even under my
pen.   Should the attempt fail, it must be by the fault of the
execution.   Adieu, Dear Madam ; all Compliments, where they are
due, and believe me,

Most truly yours,

E. G.

253.

To J. B. Holroyd, Esq.

June, 1775.

Though Darby's vessel cannot be found, it is pretty clear he is no impostor. He arrived in his boat at Southampton, and probably left his ship in some creek of the Isle of Wight. He has now left town, and is gone, it is said, on a trading voyage to purchase Ammunition in France and Spain. Do you not admire the lenity of Government? This day news came that a Ship arrived at Liverpool from Rhode Island. She sailed the 20th, the day after the Skirmish, and has brought a general confirmation of it. There was a report this evening of the arrival of the Sukey[1] from Gage, but it certainly is not true, and you know as much of the matter as Lord North.

254.

To J. B. Holroyd, Esq.

London, June the 17th, 1775.

I have not courage to write about America. We talk familiarly of Civil War, Dissolutions of Parliament, Impeachments and Lord Chatham. The boldest tremble, the most vigorous talk of peace. And yet no more than sixty-five rank and file have been killed. Governor H[utchinson] assures me that Gage has plenty of provisions fresh and salted, flour, fish, vegetables, &c. : *hopes* he is not in danger of being forced——

What can I know of the Tythes? Gilbert has done nothing. I acquainted Mrs. G. with it in a very polite Epistle, which she has answered by a very polite silence.

After calling twice on Sir Richard Sutton, I sent to know when I could have the honour, &c. He was gone for the summer that very morning.—My Lady has received Sevigné,[2] that is

---

[1] The sloop sent by General Gage from Boston.

[2] A new edition of Madame de Sévigné's letters appeared at Paris in 1775—*Recueil des lettres de Madame la Marquise de Sévigné à Madame la Marquise de Grignan sa fille.*

one of the new volumes; instead of the other, a different book
(I fancy Danville's *Geographie Ancienne*) was sent; as it may
be of more use to me than to her, the error should be mutually
rectified. Deyverdun goes next week. Yesterday I gave a dinner
on his account to the Humes, Sir Charles Thompson and Sir
Richard Worsley. He is going to marry the youngest Miss
Fleming :[1] love and £80,000.—This day I sent almost a *Charte
blanche* to Lovegrove (do not be frightened) offering to warrant
according to Duane's directions or wishing to know what he
should expect as a compensation. The letter was settled between
Newton and me, and if it does no good, will do no harm.
Adieu.

E. G.

255.

To J. B. Holroyd, Esq.

29th June, 1775.

America is too great a subject—Tythes are best in your
hands—Nothing satisfactory from Lovegrove, to whom I have
offered Warranty secundum. Duane, Arbitration or a treaty
about some compensation—Now Lord Stamford and his brother
are out of town. *I know not how to get at Brown.* The Roman
Empire will derange Sheffield ; *the Press is just set to work*, and I
shall be very busy the whole *summer in correcting* and composing.
Deyverdun wrote to me from Calais ; he will not be fixed till his
arrival at Gottingen. He has left me somewhat dull and
melancholy. My respects to my Lady, Mama and the *sweet
Maria.* Adieu. Batt dined with me yesterday, Thursday
evening. You mistook me when I talked of his visiting Sheffield.
It was not Lawyer Batt *but Dog Bath*, who sends you his compliments, and proposes to himself great amusement in Sussex.
What does Foster (Mac) in England ? He speaks of the Bog
with great modesty.

---

[1] Sir R. Worsley married, September 20, 1775, Miss Seymour Dorothy
Fleming, daughter and coheiress of Sir John Fleming, Bart., of Rydal,
Westmoreland, and Brompton Park, Middlesex.

256.

To his Stepmother.

July the 3rd, 1775.

DEAR MADAM,

I wish you would believe, what is really the case, that before I received your letter I intended to have written this very post. It is true that I had the same intention for many posts before, and that the glorious spirit of procrastination always told me that the next would do just as well: I do not mean as to your franks, for those I must confess I had absolutely and irrecoverably forgotten. *Deyverdun had left me just before your letter arrived, which I shall soon have an opportunity of conveying to him. Though, I flatter myself, he broke from me with some degree of uneasiness, the engagement could not be declined. At the end of the four years he has an annuity of £100 for Life, and may, for the remainder of his days, enjoy a decent independence in that Country, which a Philosopher would perhaps prefer to the rest of Europe. For my own part, after the hurry of the town and of Parliament, I am now retired to my Villa in Bentinck Street, which I begin to find a very pleasing Solitude, at least as well as if it were two hundred miles from London; because when I am tired of the Roman Empire, I can laugh away the Evening at Foote's Theatre, which I could not do in Hampshire or Cornwall.* You know I am not a writer of news, but I cannot forbear telling you that the Dutchess of Bedford made regular proposals of marriage to the young Earl Cholmondely, and was as regularly refused. Poor as he was (he replied to Mr. Fitzpatrick the Embassador) he was not quite poor enough to accept them.

I am, Dear Madam,

Most truly Yours,

E. GIBBON.

257.

To Mrs. Holroyd.

Boodle's, Thursday Evening, 13th July, 1775.

The parsimony of your spouse, who rather chuses to build Gateways than to buy books, has hitherto *deprived you of Hume.*

Having just got the best Edition, I have sent you a good one. By this time you have probably *received Sevigné*. Enclosed Mr. H. will *find Aunt's letter*. I have not read it, as I never read more business than is absolutely necessary. You will please to inform him that a letter on his plan has been sent to Lovegrove. *I write no news*, 1st because there are none authentic, and 2dly because you will see dear MacFoster to-morrow.

How does sweet Maria? You have both used me ill in sending me no intelligence about her. I shall soon write again to the Baron and inform him of the reasons *which may delay my* Journey. Those that would hasten it you will know.

Your slave,

E. G.

258.

To J. B. Holroyd, Esq.

July 20th, 1775.

Do you believe that my inclination leads me to S. P. ? If you do not, you are a D— fool to give yourself the trouble of asking me. If you do, you may as well believe that I am giving you reasons and not pretences. I am just now in the most busy moment of my life, nor is it so small a work as you may imagine to destroy a great Empire. I do not merely mean correcting the sheets from the press : that might certainly be performed at S. P., as both Printer, Strahan,[1] and Author, an odd circumstance, are Senators. But from a natural impatience, as you well know, I have begun to *print the head before the tail* was quite finished ; some parts must be composed, and, as I proceed in the reviewing, so many emendations and alterations occur, which require the neighbourhood of my Library, that in any other region of the Earth, I should find myself every day at a full stop. As well as I can see before me, I think that I may give you September : *but I promise nothing*. As soon as I find it within my power, I shall order my chaise. Therefore be silent and resigned.

[1] William Strahan (1715–1785), Printer to His Majesty, was at this time M.P. for Malmesbury. At the election of 1780 he was returned for Wootton Bassett; but did not seek re-election after the dissolution in 1784. He purchased in 1770 from Mr. Eyre a share in the King's Patent as a printer. His character is sketched in Nichols' *Literary Anecdotes of the Eighteenth Century*, vol. iii. pp. 390–397.

General Frazer,[1] *with whom* I dined to-day at *the British*, talks
of visiting you next month. *Do you remember my Aunt whom
you invited, and who is much disposed to accompany me?* I was
thinking that your mother's illness might render that *less convenient. If it does you may give her a civil Epistle.* You recollect
de Salis ; he is in town, and asked after you.—As to public affairs,
we are in hourly expectation of a battle, and flying reports arrive
but do not prevail. They are certainly premature. What do
you think of £1700 a year for 31 years on poor Ireland to gain
Flood, and to pay some of the C. F's debts without making a
friend of him, but only to buy his place at an extravagant price?[2]
My domestic affairs seem calm ; the Wintons are quiet, and the
other brute has graciously accepted the Arbitration of Palmer
and will mention it to him in a few days. Booth Gray, to
whom I wrote about Brown, is silent. *Duane was so till this
morning,* when he sent me a note that he had been ill and could
not visit the Tythes of Newhaven till September. Your projects
are vast ; but the essential thing seems to be a *present* decent
increase of rent for Aunt Gibbon.

I approve of the *fall* rather than *decline* of the Sussex
society.

                                                              E. G.

                                 259.

                        To J. B. Holroyd, Esq.

                             Bentinck Street, August 1st, 1775.

*Your apprehensions of a precipitate work, &c., are perfectly
groundless. I should be much more addicted to a contrary
extreme. The *head* is now printing? true, but it was wrote last

---

[1] General Fraser (1726–1782), the eldest son of the Simon, Lord Lovat, who
was executed in 1747, was himself included in the Act of Attainder for his
share in the '45. Pardoned in 1750, he raised a regiment of Highlanders
(afterwards the 78th), and commanded it in Canada during the Seven Years'
War. He became a major-general in 1771. Three years later, the estates
which his father's treason had forfeited were restored to him, in consideration
of his services in the late war. He was M.P. for Inverness from 1761 to 1782.
He married Miss Catherine Bristow, who survived him many years.

[2] Charles James Fox was Clerk of the Pells in Ireland. The place was
purchased from him by the Government, who conferred it upon Charles
Jenkinson in order that the latter might vacate his office of Vice-Treasurer
of Ireland in favour of Henry Flood.

year and the year before, the first Chapter has been composed *de nouveau three times*; the second *twice*, and all the others have undergone reviews, corrections, &c.   As to the tail, it is perfectly formed and digested (and were I so much given to self-content and haste), it is almost all written.   The ecclesiastical part, for instance, is written out in fourteen sheets, which I mean to *refondre* from beginning to end.   As to the friendly Critic, it is very difficult to find one who has leisure, candour, freedom, and knowledge sufficient.   However, Batt and Deyverdun have read and observed.   After all, the public is the best Critic.   I print no more than 500 copies of the first Edition ; and the second (as it happens frequently to my betters) may receive many improvements.   So much for Rome.*   Now for Ireland.   I am desired to consult you about Lord Ely[1] who (between ourselves) pays his court to a niece of Eliot's.   His fortune is very large, he is a widower, and as we hear behaved well in his first place ; but we wish to get an impartial account of his general character, manners, inclinations, virtues and defects.   Can you give or procure it ?

*We have nothing new from America.   But I can venture to assure you, that administration is now as unanimous and decided as the occasion requires.   Something will be done this year ; but in the spring the force of the country will be exerted to the utmost.   Scotch highlanders, Irish papists, Hanoverians, Canadians, Indians, &c. will all in various shapes be employed. Parliament meets the first week in November.   I think his Catholic Majesty may be satisfied with his summer's amusement. The Spaniards fought with great bravery, and made a fine retreat ; but our Algerine friends surpassed them as much in conduct as in number.[2]   Adieu.

The Dutchess[3] has stopped Foote's piece.   She sent for him

---

[1] Lord Ely married, on September 18, 1775, the daughter of the late Captain Hugh Bonfoy, R.N., and Mrs. Bonfoy (*née* Anne Eliot).

[2] A great expedition against the Barbary States was organized by the Spaniards, and on July 2, 1775, a powerful fleet landed their army at Algiers. After a fight of thirteen hours the Spaniards were obliged to retreat.

[3] The famous Duchess of Kingston, formerly Miss Chudleigh, married the Duke of Kingston, while her first husband, Augustus Hervey, then a lieutenant in the navy, afterwards (1775) Earl of Bristol, was living.   She was tried for bigamy and convicted in 1776.   Foote proposed to tell her story in a play called *A Trip to Calais*, and to introduce her under the name of "Kitty Crocodile."   Lord Hertford, as Chamberlain, interdicted the piece, which Foote brought out in 1777 as *The Capuchin*.

to Kingston house and threatened, bribed, argued, and wept for about two hours. He assured her that if the Chamberlain was obstinate, he should publish it with a dedication to her Grace.*

260.

To J. B. Holroyd, Esq.

Bentinck Street, August 4th, 1775.

A *vue de pays*, I should have reached S. P. the first week in September. If you visit Sir John [Russell] about that time, you and My Lady will of course lodge in Bentinck Street, and in your return I may condescend to accompany you. *Gage is recalled.*[1] Good men rejoice. Patriots murmur. Adieu.

E. G.

A quadrille party in the next room, Mrs. Bonfoy, Lady Ely,[2] &c.: we are impatient.

You have acted like yourself about Newhaven.

261.

To J. B. Holroyd, Esq.

Bentinck Street, August 15th, 1775.

I have not time to hold a long conversation with you: but I want to settle the *plan of our visit* (Aunt and self) to S. P. According to our last it seemed that you were to go into Bucks *the first week in September*, and that it would suit us all to *attend your return* into Sussex. But as I was pacing along the Strand last week, the Baronet arrested me with a friendly laugh and *a hearty shake*, and told me, among other curious and interesting particulars, that your visit to him would not *take place before the* 18*th:* an awkward period, as it intersects the time that we could bestow upon you. Suppose you *were to defer it till the first week in October*. We could then give you the whole month of September, and come up with you. *Siquid novisti rectius istis, candidus imperti, sinon*—— I have nothing to add about the

---

[1] After the battle of Bunker's Hill (June 17, 1775) General Gage was recalled, and General Howe appointed to the chief command in America.

[2] Gibbon speaks of Miss Bonfoy, the *future* Lady Ely.

enclosed. Palmer is out of town, and Lovegrove and Matthews appear wonderfully nonchalant. Eliot is stepped down into Gloucestershire. I shall communicate the Lord's portrait,[1] and I think it will please and suit them.

262.

To his Stepmother.

London, August 18th, 1775.

DEAR MADAM,

Will you excuse my present litterary business as an excuse for my not writing? I think you will be in the wrong if you do; since I was just as idle before. At all events, however, it is better to say three words, than to be totally a dumb dog. A propos of dog, but not of dumb, Bath (a foolish name enough) is the comfort of my life; pretty, impertinent, fantastical, all that a young Lady of fashion ought to be; I flatter myself that our passion is reciprocal. Have you seen Mr. Eliot very lately? He left us about ten days ago to make a visit in Glostershire, and perhaps may have looken upon you at Bath: we expect him again very soon, and shall live together as we did before in a very pleasant society for the time of year. Next month I believe Mrs. P. and myself shall pay a short visit to Sheffield place. Deyverdun, from whom I heard the other day, desires his Compliments and best wishes to you.

You will be surprized and concerned to hear, as I did last week by a letter from Mr. Dawkes at St. Omers, that poor Pitman is dead. I know no other particulars about it. Adieu.

Dear Madam,

Ever yours,

E. G.

263.

To J. B. Holroyd, Esq.

Saturday Night, August 26th, 1775.

I think that, through the dark and doubtful mist of futurity, I can discern some faint probability that the Gibbon and his Aunt will arrive at S. P. before the Sun, or rather the Earth, has

---

[1] Doubtless a reference to Mr. Holroyd's character of Lord Ely.

accomplished eight diurnal Revolutions. A Caledonian Hero, who commands the warriours of the Fraserian tribe, seemed likewise to threaten an invasion about the same period. Adieu.

Lord Ely has given great satisfaction. The business is concluded.

264.

To J. B. Holroyd, Esq.

Saturday, ten o'clock in the Evening, Spinham lands, 1775.

I arrived in town about one, and calling on the Eliots found they received yesterday a letter from their sister at Bath, that Mrs. G.'s small-pox is of a very bad confluent sort. I got out of town about half an hour after three (too much hurried to write), have travelled till the Moon failed me, propose being at Bath about noon to-morrow. Shall write to-morrow evening.

265.

To J. B. Holroyd, Esq.

Bath, October 2nd, 1775.

To continue my journal, I departed from Spinham lands about five o'clock on Sunday morning, and arrived here at eleven. Caplin, whom I had sent on before, met me at the town's end, and agreeably surprised me with the most favourable account. Miss Eliot had too rashly taken the alarm, as Mrs. G.'s sort, though confluent, was a very good one. It has turned, in the best manner possible, the ninth day, and she has at present, but in the slightest degree, the secondary fever. Dr. Delacour assures me that she is perfectly out of all danger : but hesitates about acquainting her of my arrival these three or four days. He knows not the value of time when the fate of an Empire depends upon it. Without disclosing my motives, I urge business : and at all events talk of setting out Thursday. Even if I should not see her, the attention would be all the same. I ought to have acquired some merit at the expence of infinite hurry, twenty pounds (for I rattled with four horses and two servants for the sake of sending Caplin forwards), and above all of a week's loss of time. I am impatient on all accounts to get away ; notwithstanding the agreeable society of Mrs. Cochran, Misses Sharp, Major

Matthews, and Bresboro the conjuror.————After separating them by a very long dash, I shall mention that I saw Breck Street last night; Sally looks very poorly, and Mr. H. made me melancholy by his desponding way of talking of himself. I have likewise seen Foster, the father of Harry, who inquired much after Jack Holroyd. Methinks he has something of the Brogue upon the tip of his tongue now. How do you relish solitude? Can you endure so many severe strokes which were inflicted in one day? My adorations wait on My Lady, nor do I forget the infant Spinny. Have you had any more *Desserts à la Francaise?* Depend upon it you will always be properly opposed in such arbitrary measures.

E. G.

266.

To J. B. Holroyd, Esq.

Bentinck Street, October 14th, 1775.

Yes, yes, I am safe enough in town, and so comfortably in mine own dear Library, and mine own dear Parlour, that I thought I might as well give myself a few Holydays from any Epistolary cares. Aunt Hester starts Monday or Tuesday *certainly.* It is *needless to say much of Bath,* from whence you receive weekly folios. You have been *informed how artfully the conspiracy was carried on,* and how I arrived eight and forty hours after I came. Since my return (I will not tell you what day) I have had regular and favourable despatches from Mrs. Gould, and this day for the first time an Epistle from Mrs. Gibbon herself, full of health, good spirits, and expressions of gratitude. She is much concerned that I had the trouble of coming to Bath, but if I know her, would have been much *more concerned if I had* not come. So much for that business, which has proved no inconsiderable interruption.

As to my domestic War, *Madox and the Solicitor-General* are enlisted; they have each of them received a Guinea to drink my health. Newton wanted likewise the Attorney-General; I hesitated, and asked if it was necessary to employ three great Lawyers to puzzle our plain case. A peremptory message was sent at the same time to Matthews to demand his ultimate answer. He replied by the next post that he would write as soon as he had seen Lovegrove, who was then from home. Unless they are at once subdued by the terror of my arms, I much fear that our dispute will last as long as the American Contest.

Apropos of that Contest, *I send you two pieces of intelligence from the best authority, and which, unless you hear them from some other quarter, *I do not wish you should* talk much about. 1st, When the Russians arrive,[1] (if they refresh themselves in England or Ireland,) will you go and see their Camp? We have great hopes of getting a body of these Barbarians. In consequence of some very plain advances, George, with his own hand, wrote a very polite Epistle to sister Kitty, requesting her friendly assistance. Full powers and instructions were sent at the same time to Gunning, to agree for any force between five and twenty thousand men, *Carte blanche* for the terms; on condition, however, that they should serve, not as Auxiliaries, but as Mercenaries, and that the Russian General should be absolutely under the command of the British. They daily and hourly expect a Messenger, and hope to hear that the business is concluded. The worst of it is, that the Baltic will soon be froze up, and that it must be late next year before they can get to America. 2nd. In the mean time we are not quite easy about Canada;[2] and even if it should be safe from an attack, we cannot flatter ourselves with the expectation of bringing down that martial people on the back settlements. The priests are ours; the Gentlemen very prudently wait the event, and are disposed to join the stronger party; but the same lawless spirit and impatience of Government which has infected our Colonies, is gone forth among the Canadian Peasants, over whom, since the Conquest, the Noblesse have lost much of their ancient influence. Another thing which will please and

----

[1] George III. negotiated ineffectually with the Empress Catharine for the hire of twenty thousand Russian mercenaries for service in America. Sir Robert Gunning (1731–1816), the British envoy at St. Petersburg, was at first led to believe by both Panin, the Russian Foreign Minister, and the empress herself, that the troops would be provided. The negotiations were broken off on the ground that the Russian officers could not take the required oath of allegiance to George III.

[2] In May, 1775, Ethan Allen and Benedict Arnold surprised the Forts of Ticonderoga on Lake George and Crown Point on Lake Champlain. General Carleton, the Governor of Canada, was in command of very inadequate forces, and it was feared that the province would join the Colonists against the British.

surprize, is the assurance I received from a Man who might tell me a lye, but who could not be mistaken, that no arts, no management whatsoever have been used to procure the *Addresses which fill* the Gazette,[1] and that Lord N[orth] was as much surprized at the first that came up, as we could be at Sheffield. We shall have, I suppose, some brisk skirmishing in Parliament, but the business will soon be decided by our superior weight of fire. *A propos*, I believe there has been some vague but serious conversation about *calling out the Militia.* The new Levies go on very slowly in Ireland.[2] The Dissenters, both there and here, are violent and active.[3] Adieu. I embrace My Lady and Maria.* *Bath* not Batt, *Qui croit et s'embellit*, sends you his best Compliments, and expresses great satisfaction at the hope of visiting S. P. next summer.

267.

To his Stepmother.

Bentinck Street, October 16th, 1775.

DEAR MADAM,

Though I am always pleased to hear from you, I can assure you no letter ever gave me so much satisfaction as your last. You have now completely got over a very serious disorder, and without being a prophet, I will venture to assure you, that you are armed against it for the remainder of your life. I understand that your Doctor has made a general confession of all his tricks; and indeed no Christian ever lyed on a proper occasion with more zeal and humanity than that honest Jew has done. At present he will, I hope, assure you with as much regard but with more truth, that your constitution in the late

---

[1] Addresses from the principal trading towns of England poured in, asking the king to prosecute the war with vigour. Walpole (*Journal of the Reign of George III.*, 1771-83, vol. i. pp. 501, 502, Dr. Doran's edition) says that the addresses were bought.

[2] The Government endeavoured to raise a regiment of Irish Catholics; but these, says Walpole, "would not list, nor could they in the whole summer get above 400 recruits in England" (*Journal of the Reign of George III.*, vol. i. p. 500).

[3] Dr. Wesley, on the other hand, published, in 1775, his *Calm Address to our American Colonies*, in which he urged arguments similar to those of Dr. Johnson in his *Taxation no Tyranny.*

attack, has shewn its strength, thrown off the incumbrance
and taken a new and a long lease, of many, and I flatter myself,
of happy years. We must soon talk of your finishing your
recovery by breathing the pure and healthy air of Mary-le-Bone.
In the meantime take care of yourself, and present my most
hearty thanks to Mrs. Gould for the kind and friendly part
she has acted in the whole course of this once alarming but now
agreeable transaction.

I am, Dear Madam,

Most truly yours,

E. G.

268.

To J. B. Holroyd, Esq.

31st October, 1775.

In the midst of Avocations, Litterary, Parliamentary and
Social, which now on all sides overwhelm me, you must not
expect any regular correspondence. Sayer's [1] business (you must
know it by this time) is foolish beyond description. *He* was
a fool! Richardson a busy knave, and Lord R. acting Justice
of the Peace who was obliged to take the information. You
will see by the numbers that last Thursday we had an easy,
but it was a languid, victory. We have a warm Parliament
but an indolent Cabinet. The *Conquest* of America is a *great*
Work : every part of that Continent is either lost or useless.
I do not understand that we have sufficient strength at home :
the German succours are insufficient, *and the Russians are no
longer hoped for.*[2] *When do you come up ?* I dined and lay

---

[1] Mr. Stephen Sayer, a London banker, and one of the sheriffs of the
City, was accused by one Richardson, a young American officer in the
Guards, of a plot to seize the Tower, and attack the king as he went to open
Parliament. The guards were trebled, and Sayer, brought before Lord
Rochford, Secretary of State for the Southern Department, was committed
to the Tower. Another "mad enthusiast for liberty" and "one or two dis-
senting Divines " were also apprehended. The meeting of Parliament, however, passed off quietly, and the temporary panic subsided. On October 28,
1775, Sayer was brought before Lord Mansfield on a *Habeas Corpus*, and
admitted to bail. On December 13 he was discharged from his recognizances.

[2] The negotiations with Russia failed. But the Landgrave of Hesse,
the Duke of Brunswick, and other petty German potentates supplied
seventeen thousand mercenaries.

at Twickenham, Sunday. Batt was there—Govr. Lyttleton seconded the Address,[1] matter good, manner ridiculous. Adieu. I delivered yours to C.

269.

To his Stepmother.

London, December 4th, 1775.

DEAR MADAM,

I am still alive, and in spite of the influenza perfectly well. But why have you not at least written *one* line in so very long a space of time? All that I can say on the subject is to declare with the utmost sincerity that not a single morning has arisen without my forming the resolution to write before the evening, and that not a single evening post-bell has rang without sounding the alarm to my conscience. In the mean time, days, hours and weeks have imperceptibly rolled away: a perpetual hurry and long days of Parliamentary business, the whole world coming to town at once, and a great deal of occupation at home relative to my History, which will come out some time after Christmas. In a word, I do not like to write to you, but I want very much to see you. Have you totally forgot your promise of making me a visit in town? I can lodge you, &c., without the smallest inconveniency, and I am sure that after getting the better of so formidable an enemy as you have done, nothing would be so likely to give the last polish as a change of air, of situation and of company. Be so kind as to send me an *answer* and not a compliment, on this subject.

Mrs. Porten is still well and young. Her sister-in-law has got and lost a child. The former wishes to be remembered to you. You see the honour which Mr. Eliot[2] has acquired. I am amazed

---

[1] The address was moved on October 26, 1775, by Mr. Acland (eldest son of Sir Thomas Acland), and seconded by the Hon. William Lyttleton. M.P. for Bewdley, formerly Governor of Jamaica, and minister at Lisbon. An amendment proposed by Lord John Cavendish, demanding the fullest information on the subject of America, was rejected by 278 to 108.

[2] Mr. Eliot, on the death of Sir J. Molesworth, was elected M.P. for Cornwall. Miss Burney, in 1781, speaks of meeting "Mr. Eliot, knight of the shire of Cornwall, a most agreeable, lively, and very clever man." He was one of the pall-bearers at the funeral of Sir Joshua Reynolds. He was also a friend of Johnson, to whom he lent Defoe's *Memoirs of Captain Carleton*, a book which the Doctor had never seen (Boswell's *Life of Johnson*, ed. G. B. Hill, 1887, vol. iv. pp. 334-344).

how he condescended to accept of it. The Member of St. Germans might lurk in the country, but the knight of Cornwall must attend the House of Commons.—I salute from a distance all Bath friends : and particularly the Colonel,[1] Mrs. G[ould], Fanny, Birds, dogs, &c., &c.

I am, Dear Madam,

Ever yours,

E. Gibbon.

270.

To his Stepmother.

December 24th, 1775.

My dear Madam,

Inclosed I send the ordinary draft. As you have never had reason to doubt my sincerity, you will believe me, when I say that I feel myself ashamed of my *real* and *apparent* negligence, and deeply concerned at the subject of your last letter. That subject is of such melancholy and weighty import, that though I fear I cannot say anything very satisfactory, I must beg leave to defer, two or three posts longer, the taking any farther notice of it. Allow me only to explain, what I mean by my *apparent* negligence. Your *former* letter was delivered to me while I was abroad at dinner, and when I returned home very late at night, I locked it up without having examined the contents. The next morning it was impossible for me to find it or to recollect how I had disposed of it : and I vainly and indolently delayed writing from post to post, in hopes that I might accidentally stumble upon it.—Mr. H. is probably *at* or *near* Bath. I am sorry to hear so indifferent an account of Mrs. H.

I am, Dear Madam,

Most truly yours,

E. Gibbon.

If there was anything in your former which you have not said in your last letter, may I beg you to repeat it. I am perfectly well, and shall pass my holidays in town.

---

[1] Colonel Gould.

271.

To his Stepmother.

Bentinck Street, 3rd January, 1776.

DEAR MADAM,

Had I not been engaged in hastening and finishing the Impression, I would with great pleasure have made you a Christmas visit. I may truly say to you and not to Bath, for I have never much relished the style and amusements of that seat of idleness which so many people are fond of ; and I am much inclined to think that if you fixed your residence in any other part of the Kingdom, I might pass the remainder of my life without ever seeing Bath again. Since I have mentioned my book, let me add that it will probably make its appearance about the middle or end of February : and that one of the very first copies of it shall be carefully transmitted to Charles Street. The Public, I know not why, except from the happy choice of the subject, have already conceived expectations, which it will not be easy to satisfy : the more especially as lively ignorance is apt to expect much more than the nature and extent of historical materials can enable an author to produce. However, if the first volume is decently received in the world, I shall be encouraged to proceed ; and shall find before me a stock of labour and of amusement sufficient to engage my attention for many years. The prosecution of some scheme is in my opinion the circumstance the most conducive to the happiness of life, and, of all schemes, the best is surely that, the success of which chiefly depends on ourselves. Parliamentary business, and agreeable society fill the eye, the intervals of my time, and my situation would in every respect be a comfortable one, if I could only put an end to my Buckinghamshire sale, which is still attended with many difficulties, and will hardly be decided without the interposition of Chancery. You will not wonder that I lose time and catch at every hope, rather than involve myself in that labyrinth of Chicane and expense.

I say nothing of public affairs. Never did they wear a more melancholy aspect. We much fear that Quebec [1] will not hold out

---

[1] On November 14, 1775, Benedict Arnold made an unsuccessful attempt to capture Quebec by surprise. Reinforced by a considerable body of troops under General Montgomery, he renewed his attack on December 31. Montgomery was killed, Arnold wounded, and the assault repulsed. The siege

the Winter.   The Provincials have everywhere displayed courage and abilities worthy of a better cause ; and those of my Ministerial friends who are the best acquainted with the state of America, are the least sanguine in their hopes of success for next year.

An odd discovery is just now made.   At a sale in the country, an old cabinet was going to be knocked down for twenty shillings, when the curiosity of some people present urged them to examine it more closely.   Two private drawers were found ; one of which contained bank-notes to a very large amount, the other held an older and more valuable curiosity ; the individual ring of Queen Elizabeth, the Earl of Essex, Lady Nottingham, &c.: you remember the story.[1]   It was in a very fine purse embroidered with pearls ; and is authenticated by a writing, found in the same purse, of an old Lady Cook who attended the Queen in her visit to the Countess, and picked up the ring when her Majesty threw it from her with horror and indignation.   I have seen the purse and ring (a yellow kind of diamond) at Barlow's, a silk-mercer in King Street, Covent Garden, who affirms that he has read the paper, but the mystery which is made about the place of sale, and the name of the present proprietor, leaves room for suspicion.   Horace Walpole is determined, if possible, to get to the bottom of the affair.

I hope, dear Madam, that not only your health, but your beauty likewise, are perfectly restored, but I must desire an explicit and *satisfactory* answer about your promised visit to London.   The air will, I am sure, be of the greatest service to you, and as the Spring will soon advance upon us, you may easily connect London with Essex, Sussex or any other part of the Kingdom, where you have any visits to make or promises to fulfill.

I am, Dear Madam,

Most truly yours,

E. GIBBON.

was, however, continued, and it was not till May, 1776, that General Carleton was able to assume the offensive and drive the Americans out of Canada.

[1] Gibbon alludes to the story, that the Countess of Nottingham kept back a ring which Essex, before his execution, sent by her hand to Elizabeth. The ring, which had formerly been worn by the queen, is probably now in the possession of Mr. Francis Thynne, to whom it descended through Lady Mary Devereux.   It is a cameo head of Elizabeth, cut in a sardonyx, and set in a gold ring, enamelled at the back.   It has been enlarged with *soft* solder, as though Essex had only trusted it to a jeweller working in his presence.   Walpole makes no allusion to the alleged discovery.

Bentinck Street, January 3rd of the
New Year 1776. May you find it an agreeable introduction
to many happy ones.

P.S.—Messrs. Gosling and Clive will honour your order whenever you chuse to draw for the last half year, and on every future
occasion I will take care that it shall be ready for your draught,
which I think, once for all, will be the best way of settling it.

271.

To J. B. Holroyd, Esq.

London, January 18th, 1776.

*How do you do ? Are you alive ? Are you buried under
mountains of snow ? I write merely to triumph in the superiority
of my own situation, and to rejoice in my own prudence, in not
going down to S. P., as I seriously but foolishly intended to do
last week.* Hugonin by appointment came to town, but we soon
agreed that the expedition (on his side at least) must be deferred
till next summer ; for which time he made a very solemn and, as
I believe, a very serious engagement. We talked over Horn
farm, which will be let next month by auction, and I am only
afraid of getting too much money for it. Chalk woods, &c.,
settled to admiration, and every thing goes well except the
d——d Lovegrove. However I have had the arrears of rent
paid into Fleet street : which leaves a very moderate balance of
interest against me.

*We proceed triumphantly with the Roman Empire, and
shall certainly make our appearance, before the end of next
month. I have nothing public. You know we have got 18,000
Germans from Hesse Brunswick and Hesse Darmstadt. I think
our meeting will be lively ; a spirited Minority, and a desponding
Majority. The higher people are placed, the more gloomy are
their countenances, the more melancholy their language. You
may call this cowardice, but I fear it arises from *their knowledge*
(a late knowledge) of the difficulty and magnitude of the business.
Quebec is not *yet* taken. I hear that Carleton is determined
never to capitulate with Rebels. A glorious resolution if it were
supported with 50,000 men. Adieu. I embrace My Lady and
Maria. Make my excuses to the latter for having neglected her
birthday.*

273.

To J. B. Holroyd, Esq.

January 29th, 1776.

Hares &c. arrived safe; were received with thanks, and devoured with appetite: send more, *id est*, of hares. I believe in my last I forgot saying any thing of the son of Fergus; his letters reached him.—What think you of the season? Siberia, is it not? A pleasant campaign in America. I read and pondered your last and think that in the place of Lord G. G.[1] you might perhaps succeed; but I much fear that our Leaders have not a genius which can act at the distance of 3000 miles. By the bye the little islands of the Bermudas have just declared in favour of the Congress. You know that a large draught of Guards are just going to America, poor dear creatures! We are met; but no business. Next week may be busy; Scotch Militia &c. Roman Empire (first part) will be finished in a week or fortnight. At last I have heard Texier;[2] wonderful! Embrace My lady. The weather too cold to turn over the page. Adieu.

Since this I received your last, and honour your care of the old Women, a respectable name which in spite of My lady may suit Judges, Bishops, Generals (*Je gage que j'ai raison*) &c. Several letters directed to you and enclosed to me, have been franked. Ferguson's might be among them. I am rejoyced to hear of Maria's inoculation. I know not when you have done so wise a thing. You may depend upon getting an excellent house. Adieu.

---

[1] The Duke of Grafton resigned the Privy Seal November 9, 1775. Lord Dartmouth succeeded him, and Lord George Germain took Lord Dartmouth's place as Secretary of State for the Colonies.

[2] Horace Walpole, writing November 23, 1775, says, "A Monsieur Tessier, of whom I have heard much in France, acted an entire play of ten characters, and varied his voice, and countenance, and manner, for each so perfectly, that he did not name the persons that spoke, nor was it necessary. I cannot decide to which part he did most justice, but I would go to the play every night if I could see it so acted."

274.

To J. B. Holroyd, Esq.

Bentinck-street, February 9th, 1776.

*You are mistaken about your dates. It is to-morrow *seven-night*, the 17th, that my book will decline into the World.* I will attend to Coachman and house, though I could wish that in point of price and situation you had been a little more explicit.

I am glad to find that by degrees you begin to understand the advantage of a civilized city,—I cannot say as much as Batt and Cantab, who dined with me, Beauclerk and Lady Di.[1] Adieu. *No public business ; Parliament has sate every day, but we have not had a single debate.* There is a rumour that Quebec is taken, and Washington is said to have communicated the news to Howe, but it is not yet absolutely believed. *I think you will have *your book* on Monday. The parent is not forgot, though I had not a single one to spare.*

275.

To his Stepmother.

House of Commons, Wednesday Evening, February, 1776.

DEAR MADAM,

I write two lines to return you my thanks for what you say of my book,[2] of which you are not indeed so good a Judge as you would be of any written by another author. By a mistake you have received *two* bound books instead of one. Be so good as to return one of them by coach or wagon, and I will give an order that an unbound one shall go to-morrow to Brook Street. Your soiled one (honourable marks) you will retain. But when will you flatter me in person in Bentinck Street ? March approaches.

I am, Dear Madam,

Ever yours,

E. GIBBON.

---

[1] Topham Beauclerk and Lady Diana Beauclerk (see note to Letter 47).

[2] *The History of the Decline and Fall of the Roman Empire*, by Edward Gibbon, Esq. Vol. i., London, 1776, 4to, was published by W. Strahan and T. Cadell in February.

276.

To his Stepmother.

London, March 26th, 1776.

DEAR MADAM,

Lazyness is ingenious; but on this occasion mine was provided with too good an excuse, I mean your own silence. From post to post I have expected a letter to fix the time and manner of your Journey to London. I now begin to despair, and am almost inclined to think that your sedentary life has rivetted your chains, and cut off your wings. I must therefore try (though a very sedentary animal myself) whether I cannot visit you at Bath, and as the Easter vacation seems to promise me the most convenient leisure that I am likely to enjoy in the whole year, I entertain some thoughts of running down to you for a few days. The Eliots, who with great difficulty have existed in town about two months, seem to intend moving towards that place about the same time. The Holroyds are likewise in town: they have inoculated their girl, and I understand with the greatest pleasure that there are some hopes of an increase of family. —As to myself, I have the satisfaction of telling you that my book has been very well received by men of letters, men of the world, and even by fine feathered Ladies, in short by every set of people except perhaps by the Clergy, who seem (I know not why) to shew their teeth on the occasion. A thousand Copies are sold, and we are preparing a second Edition, which in so short a time is, for a book of that price, a very uncommon event.

I am, Dear Madam,

Ever yours,

E. GIBBON.

277.

To J. B. Holroyd, Esq.

Bath, April 11th, 1776.

I write two lines to signify my arrival at this place. Beauclerck's heart failed him, and he left me in the lurch; but he had made me take such steps of giving notice, &c., that the journey was become unavoidable. I propose staying till this Day sen'night and shall return for the Budget. This morning I saw *Pater*, and do not think him worse than he has been for these two or three years past. *Soror* is actually above stairs with Mrs. G. and other Ladies. Though I had not the opportunity of a whisper, I suppose she desires Compliments. The place appears full, and they say is lively, but you know how little its kind of pleasures have the happiness of charming me. I long to get back to the Library in Bentinck Street, where I shall speedily but not hastily undertake the second Volume. The Ladies here do *me* the honour of admiring me.

278.

To his Stepmother.

London, April 26th, 1776.

Dear Madam,

Though you may censure my silence for two or three posts, you must allow that my taking up my pen while your daughter-in-law is sitting close to me is an instance of no vulgar complaisance. I am a good deal taken up with the Neckers.[1] We are vastly glad to see one another, but she is no longer a Beauty. How is Colonel Gould ? I am well.

I am, Dear Madam,

Ever yours,

E. GIBBON.

279.

To J. B. Holroyd, Esq.

27th April, 1776.

Lest you should growl, I write, though I have nothing to say, for the Dutchess alias *Countess*[2] is not an object worthy of our attention. I rejoyce to hear of your approaching arrival, and *hope* that by that time Newton may have something to say.

---

[1] Madame Necker, formerly Suzanne Curchod (see note to Letter 26), and her husband were at this time in London. "M. et Madame Necker se préparent à un voyage en Angleterre; ils partiront la semaine de Pâques, et ils m'assurent qu'ils seront ici de retour à la fin de mai" (Madame du Deffand to Walpole, March 17, 1776).

[2] The Duchess of Kingston was Countess of Bristol, her previous marriage with Augustus Hervey (afterwards Earl of Bristol) having been declared legal. See note to Letter 259.

Your letter to Foster is not forgot: nor was the visit to his namesake of Orchard Street. When will you send me up the lease for Mrs. Gibbon, who will soon complain of my delay by a thundering Epistle? At Bath all were well, *Pater* not worse, I think, than last year, and Soror in much better looks and spirits. You probably know that poor Lady Russel[1] is brought to bed of a dead child. Great is the desolation of all branches of the family. I write with three or four very fine Ladies round me. Therefore— Adieu.

E. G.

280.

To J. B. Holroyd, Esq.

London, May 20th, 1776.

*I am angry, that you should impede my noble designs of visiting foreign parts, more especially as I have an advantage which Sir Wilful had not, that of understanding your foreign lingos. With regard to Mrs. Gibbon, her intended visit, to which I was not totally a stranger, will do me honour, and though it should delay my emigration till the end of July, there will still remain the months of August, September and October. Above all abstain from giving the least hint to any Bath Correspondent, and perhaps, if I am not provoked by opposition, the thing may not be absolutely certain. At all events you may depend on a previous visit. At present I am very busy with the Neckers. I live with her just as I used to do twenty years ago, laugh at her Paris varnish, and oblige her to become a simple reasonable Suissesse. The man, who might read English husbands lessons of proper and dutiful behaviour, is a sensible good-natured creature. In about a fortnight I again launch into the World in the shape of a quarto Volume. The dear Cadell assures me that he never remembered so eager and impatient a demand for a second Edition.

The town is beginning to break up; the day after to-morrow we have our last day in the house of Commons to inquire into

---

[1] Sir John Russell, Bart., of Chequers, Bucks., married on October 25, 1771, Miss Carey, daughter of General Carey, and granddaughter of Lord Falkland.

the instructions of the Commissioners;[1] I like the man, and the motion appears plain. Adieu. I dined with Lord Palmerston[2] to-day; a great dinner of Catches; Sir Farby and spouse part of the company or rather of the family: I embrace My lady and the Maria.*

281.

To his Stepmother.

Almack's,[3] May 24th, 1776.

DEAR MADAM,

Shame, shame, always shame—— Yet two lines will I write in the midst of a crowd. My mornings have been very much taken up with preparing and correcting (though in a minute and almost imperceptible way) my new Edition, which will be out the 1st of June. My afternoons (barring the House of Commons) have been a good deal devoted to Madame Necker. Her husband and the rest of her servants leave this country next Tuesday, entertained with the Island, and owning that the barbarous people have been very kind to them. Do you know that they have almost extorted a promise to make them a short visit at Paris in the Autumn. But pray, Madam, when do you set out, the month of June draws near, and both myself, the Portens and the inhabitants of Sheffield Place are impatient to be informed of the time and circumstances of your intended journey. Poor Mallet![4] I pity his misfortune and feel for him

---

[1] Two commissioners, Admiral Lord Howe and his brother, General Howe, were empowered, in May, 1776, to treat with the colonists, receive submissions, grant pardons, and inquire into grievances. Lord Howe reached Sandy Hook on July 12th. On July 4 the Declaration of Independence had been adopted by Congress, and the mission was too late.

[2] Lord Palmerston was elected a member of the Catch Club in 1771.

[3] Almack's Club, in Pall Mall, surpassed White's in the extravagance of its gambling. Brooks, a money-lender and wine-merchant, took up the management of the club, which was dispersed when he opened the new premises of Brooks' Club, in St. James's Street, in 1778.

[4] Mr. Child (*The English and Scottish Popular Ballads*, part iii. p. 199, Boston, 1885) says that Mallet passed off as his own, with very slight changes, a ballad called *William and Margaret*, a copy of which, dated 1711, has been discovered. But the resemblances between the two poems scarcely seem to justify Mr. Child's criticism, though Gibbon's statement confirms it. The writer of the article on Mallet, in the *Dictionary of National Biography*, throws no doubts upon Mallet being the author of

probably more than he does for himself at present. His "William and Margaret," his only good piece of poetry, is torn from him, and by the evidence of old Manuscripts turns out to be the work of the celebrated Andrew Marvel composed in the year 1670. Adieu, dear Madam.

I am most truly yours,
E. GIBBON.

282.

To J. B. Holroyd, Esq.

'June the 6th, 1776, from Almack's, where I was chose last week.

*To tell you any thing of the change or rather changes of Governors I must have known something of them myself : but all is darkness confusion and uncertainty ; to such a degree that people do not even know what lyes to invent. The news from America have indeed diverted the public attention into another and far greater channel. All that you see in the papers of the repulse at Quebec as well as the capture of Lee[1] rests on the authority (a very unexceptionable one) of the Provincial papers as they have been transmitted by Governor Tryon from New York. Howe is well and eats plentifully, and the weather seems to clear up so fast that according to the English custom

William and Margaret, nor does the writer on Marvell, in the same series, lay any claim for Marvell to its authorship. Thomas, better known as "Hesiod," Cooke, who published his Life and Writings of Andrew Marvell in 1726, and who not only disliked Mallet, but characterised his William and Margaret as "trash," nowhere suggests that Mallet was not the author. The first stanza is taken from Beaumont and Fletcher's comedy of The Knight of the Burning Pestle, where old Merrythought sings—

" When it was grown to dark midnight,
And all were fast asleep,
In came Margaret's grimly ghost,
And stood at William's feet."

In Percy's <i>Reliques</i>, vol. iii. p. 331 (ed. Dodsley, 1759), Mallet's poem is printed with the following note : "This Ballad, which appeared in some of the public Newspapers in or before the year 1724, came from the pen of David Mallet, Esq.; who in the edition of his poems, 3 vols., 1759, informs us that the plan was suggested by the four verses quoted above * * *, which he supposed to be the beginning of some ballad now lost."

[1] The report of General Lee's capture was false. He was taken prisoner December 13, 1776.

we have passed from the lowest despondency, to a full assurance of success.

My new birth happened last Monday, 700 of the 1500 were gone yesterday. I now understand from pretty good authority that Dr. Porteous,[1] the friend and chaplain of St. Secker, is actually sharpening his goose quill against the last two Chapters.* Mrs. G. has not yet signified her intentions about the London and Sheffield expedition. I have not advanced one single step with regard to Lovegrove. Palmer will not interfere till he has seen the abstract of the title with Duane's observations, which we cannot get them to communicate even to their own friend. Adieu. I embrace My lady and the Maria.

283.

To J. B. Holroyd, Esq.

Almack's, June 29th, 1776.

*Yes, yes I am alive and well ; but what shall I say ? Town grows empty and this house, where I have passed very agreable hours, is the only place which still unites the flower of the English youth. The style of living though *somewhat* expensive is exceedingly pleasant and notwithstanding the rage of play I have found more entertaining and even rational society here than in any other Club to which I belong. Mrs. G. still hangs in suspense and seems to consider a town expedition with horror. I think however that she will be soon in motion, and when I have her in Bentinck-street we shall perhaps talk of a Sheffield excursion. I am now deeply engaged in the reign of Constantine, and from the specimens which I have already seen, I can venture to promise that the second Volume will not be less interesting than the first. The 1500 Copies are moving off with decent speed, and the obliging Cadell begins to mutter something of a third Edition for next year. No news of Deyverdun or his French translation. What a lazy dog ! Madame Necker has been gone a great while. I gave her *en partant* the most solemn assurances of following her *paces* in less than two months, but the voice of indolence begins

---

[1] Beilby Porteus, Bishop of Chester, afterwards Bishop of London, had been chaplain to Archbishop Secker, whose Charges he published in 1769. He did not publish any reply to Gibbon's *Decline and Fall of the Roman Empire*.

to whisper a thousand difficulties and, unless your absurd policy
should thoroughly provoke me, the Parisian journey may possibly
be deferred. I rejoyce in the progress of * * * towards light.
By Cork Street I suppose you mean the Carters and highly
approve of the place. We are in expectation of American news.
Carleton is made a Knight of the Bath.[1] The old report of
Washington's resignation and quarrel with the Congress seems to
revive.* I shall say nothing of Lovegrove, the beast makes me
very uneasy, as I cannot devise any expedient to force, persuade,
or bribe him out of his obstinate silence. Adieu.

284.

To his Stepmother.

Almack's, July 4th, 1776.

DEAR MADAM,

    I can freely and sincerely tell you, that there is no
journey which will give me half the pleasure of staying in
Bentinck Street to receive you the latter end of next week,
which I shall expect with impatience.

I am,
Ever yours,
E. GIBBON.

285.

To J. B. Holroyd, Esq.

Saturday Night, Bentinck Street, 13th July, 1776.

Mrs. G. at last arrived. I enclose her letter. Our plan
seems to be to visit Sheffield Place towards the end of next week.
A vue de pays, Friday appears the most likely day. I have no
news public or private, and loose conversation may be deferred
till our meeting. I was deeply engaged in the decline, but this
visit and journey put a heavy spoke in the wheel. Adieu.

286.

To J. B. Holroyd, Esq.

Saturday evening, August, 1776.

*We expect you at five o'Clock Tuesday without a sore throat.
You have ere this heard of the shocking accident which takes up

<hr>

[1] Sir Guy Carleton was gazetted K.B., July 6, 1776.

the attention of the town.* Our old acquaintance poor John
Damer[1] shot himself, last Wednesday night, at the Bedford arms,
his usual place of resort, where he had passed several hours with
four Ladies and a blind fidler. By his own indolence rather than
extravagance, his circumstances were embarrassed, and he had
frequently declared himself tired of life. *No public news, nor
any material expected till the end of this or beginning of the
next month when Howe will probably have collected his whole
force.[2] A tough business indeed ; you see by their declaration
that they have now passed the Rubicon and rendered the work
of a treaty infinitely more difficult : You will perhaps say, so
much the better ; but I do assure you that the *thinking* friends of
government are by no means sanguine.* Mrs. G. seems likely to
expect your arrival. She has had no answer out of you. I am
pretty much a prisoner except about *one* hour in the evening : but
as she dines to-morrow with Mrs. Ashby, *I take the opportunity
of eating turtle with Garrick at Hampton.* Adieu.

287.

To his Stepmother.

London, September 2nd, 1776.

DEAR MADAM,

Yesterday afternoon about half an hour past five a
young *Lady*[3] was introduced into the world, and though her
sex might be considered an objection, she was received with
great politeness. She is perfectly well, as likewise My Lady,
who eat a whole chicken for her dinner to-day. How do you
like Essex ladies ? Have they resisted the attacks of two and
twenty years ? I hope they will not detain you from Bentinck
Street much longer, and I rather consider my having no letter
to-day as a good sign.

I am, Dear Madam,
Most truly yours,
E. GIBBON.

[1] The Hon. John Damer, son of Lord Milton, shot himself, August 15, 1776.
To his widow, the daughter of General Conway, Horace Walpole left Straw-
berry Hill for her life.
[2] On August 27, 1776, General Howe defeated the Americans at the
battle of Brooklyn or Long Island.
[3] Louisa, second daughter of Mr. and Mrs. Holroyd.

288.

To his Stepmother.

25th September, '76.

At a large Meeting of the most considerable Wits of the two Islands, it was agreed that Rouen Ducks have white feathers, but this is not the whole business of this letter. The Gibbon has so often declared an intention of letting Mrs. Gibbon know that he is well without so doing, that it is just determined to acquaint her he exists. Moreover Mrs. H. and the Brat are quite well, and Mrs. H. wishes for an opportunity of promoting eloquence in Mrs. Gibbon on Gothic Architecture.

It is a certain fact that the Gibbon exists, and that his resolutions have been as usual much better than his intentions. He looks back with pleasure and regret on the time with Mrs. Gibbon, and most sincerely hopes that as she has now conquered all the Lyons upon the road, she will no longer entertain any apprehensions of the Journey. Mrs. Porten is well, and I believe has written. The other day I told her that there was an Irish edition of the Decline. Her question amused me. " Do you understand it ? " She supposed it was published in the Irish language. The natives have printed it very well, and the notes at the bottom take up much less space than I could have imagined.

Ever yours,
E. Gibbon.

289.

To J. B. Holroyd, Esq.

Saturday, ¾ past eleven, 19 Oct. 1776.

I have waited so long that the bell is tolling in my ear, but I know you would swear——

By the enclosed you will see Sir Hugh's impediments, and if the rest of his letter requires any answer you may amuse yourself with scratching it out.

*For the present I am so deeply engaged that you must renounce the hasty apparition at S. P. ; but if you should be very impatient I will try (after the meeting) to run down between the friday and monday, and bring you the last Editions of things. —At present *nought* but expectation. The attack on me is

begun, an anonymous eighteen-penny pamphlet, which will get
the author more Glory in *the next World* than in this. The
Heavy troops, Watson[1] and another, are on their march. No
news from Richard Way. Adieu.*

290.

To his Stepmother.

Ampthill Park, Oct. 24th, 1776.

Dear Madam,

I hardly dare recollect how long I have been without
writing to you, but you know my sentiment and my laziness ;
so I will say no more on that threadbare subject. I have been
some days at this place and have spent them very agreeably.
Luckily the weather has been bad, which in a great measure
has secured me from excursions, and confined us to an excellent
house, conducted on an easy plan, and filled with a comfortable
society in which the principal part was performed by Mr. Garrick.
I return to town to-morrow. By-the-bye, you will be so good
as not to mention this Bedfordshire journey to Miss Holroyd :
it might get round to Sheffield Place which I have cheated of
a promised visit. In a few days our Parliamentary campaign
will open, and the beginning of success which we have tasted in
America will enliven our countenances, if they should not be
clouded again by the apprehensions of a French war, which seem
to increase every day. With regard to another great object
of hostilities,—*myself*,—the attack has been already begun by an
anonymous Pamphleteer, but the heavy artillery of Dr. Watson
and another adversary are not yet brought into the field. I was
afraid that I should be hurt by them, but if I may presume of
my future feelings from the first tryal of them, I shall be in every
sense of the word *invulnerable*.

My long depending and troublesome business with Lovegrove
is at length, by the strenuous interposition of Holroyd, not

---

[1] *An Apology for Christianity, in a Series of Letters to Edward Gibbon,
Esq.*, by Richard Watson, D.D. (afterwards Bishop of Llandaff). Gibbon
had a great respect for Dr. Watson, at this time Professor of Divinity at
Cambridge, as " a prelate of a large mind and liberal spirit." He writes
(November 2, 1776) to " express his sense of the liberal treatment which he
has received from so candid an adversary."

concluded, but broke off. The fellow wanted either power or inclination to compleat his agreement, and after weighing all the difficulties and delays of Chancery, it was judged most expedient to consent to a mutual discharge. By this transaction I have lost a great deal both of time and money, and am now to begin the sale again. It has occasioned me much vexation, but Holroyd assures me that I have been guilty of no fault, and that I may still entertain very fair hopes. The subject was grown so odious to me, that I could not bring myself even to talk to you about it. Adieu, Dear Madam. Remember that by your summer excursions you gain health and give pleasure. This doctrine is true and I hope that another year you will draw some practical inferences from it.

I am,

Ever yours,

E. GIBBON.

291.

To J. B. Holroyd, Esq.

November the 4th, 1776.

I hope you bark and growl at my silence : growl and bark. This is not a time for correspondence. Parliament, visits, dinners, suppers, and an hour or two stolen with difficulty for the Decline leave but very little leisure. I dare say you admire the Howes ; so do I ; and I firmly believe that whatever force can effect will be performed by them. *I send you the Gazette and have scarcely any thing to add except that about five hundred of them have deserted to us, and that the New York incendiaries were immediately and very justifiably destined to the Cord.[1] Lord G[eorge] G[ermain] with whom I had a long conversation last night was in high spirits and hopes to reconquer Germany and America.[2] On the side of Canada he only fears Carleton's *slowness*,

---

[1] On September 15 General Howe occupied New York, which had been evacuated by the American troops ; a few days later a great part of the city was destroyed by incendiaries.

[2] Lord Chatham boasted that he had conquered America in Germany. Wilkes, in March, 1776, had said, alluding to Lord G. Germain's misconduct at Minden and Chatham's boast, that Lord George might conquer America, though, he believed, it would not be in Germany. Gibbon apparently refers to this remark, and to Lord George's hope that he might recover his lost reputation by the reconquest of America.

but entertains great expectations that the light troops and Indians under Sir William Johnson, who are sent from Oswego down the Mohawk River to Albany, will oblige the Provincials to give up the defence of the lakes for fear of being cut off.—The report of a foreign War subsides. House of Commons dull ;[1] and Opposition talk of suspending hostilities from despair.

An anonymous pamphlet and Dr. Watson out against me : (in my opinion) feeble ; the former very illiberal, the latter uncommonly genteel. At last I have had a letter from Deyverdun, wretched excuses, nothing done, vexatious enough.— To-morrow I write to Suard, a very skilful translator of Paris, who was here in the spring with the Neckers to get him (if not too late) to undertake it.* Not a line from R. Way ! Adieu. I embrace, &c. Remember the fourteenth. I expect at least a week. What's the whim of my lady's not paying her proper respects to Bentinck Street ?

292.

To J. B. Holroyd, Esq.

Almack's, Thursday evening, November 7th, 1776.

Letters from Bourgoyne. They embarked on the lakes the 30th of September with 800 British Sailors, 6000 regulars, 3000 Canadians, and a naval force superior to any possible opposition : but the season was so far advanced that they expected only to occupy and strengthen Ticonderoga and afterwards to return, and take up their winter quarters in Canada.— Yesterday we had a surprize in the house from a proclamation of the Howes[2] which made its first appearance in the Morning post, and which nobody seems to understand. By this time My lady may see that I have not much reason to fear my antagonists. Adieu till next Thursday.

---

[1] Parliament met October 31, 1776. An amendment to the address, expressing pacific sentiments, was negatived by 212 to 87, and the address carried by 232 to 83.

[2] The proclamation, issued September 19, 1776, was addressed to the people of America, promised a revision of recent legislation, and was designed to induce separate colonies to negotiate with the commissioners independently of Congress. It was not published in the official Gazettes, which had appeared on November 4 and 5, 1776.

293.

To M. Suard.[1]

Bentinck Street, Cavendish Square, le 8 Novembre 1776.

MONSIEUR,

Quand on se propose de visiter un pays étranger où la langue que nous parlons n'est pas connue, on doit chercher les plus habiles interprètes de ses pensées. C'est pour cette raison que vous me permettrez de m'adresser à vous au sujet de mon histoire de la décadence et de la chute de l'Empire Romain.

Quand j'ai eu le plaisir ce printems dernier de vous voir à Londres avec M. et Madame Necker, je crois vous avoir dit que mon ami Deyverdun s'étoit chargé de ma traduction, et qu'il se proposoit de la faire paroître en Allemagne, où il séjourne actuellement avec ce jeune Anglois. Mais l'exactitude et la diligence ne sont pas du nombre des vertus de mon ami; et après un long silence qui n'a pas laissé de m'ettonner, je reçus hier au soir une lettre de sa part, par laquelle j'apprens que sa paresse, ses occupations et les projets de son élève l'obligent de renoncer absolument à cette entreprise qu'il avoit à peine commencée. Me voici donc à present libre mais isolé. J'ai toujours méprisé la triste philosophie qui veut nous rendre insensibles à la gloire. J'ambitionne celle d'être lu en France et dans le Continent; et je me verrois au comble de mes désirs, si la même plume qui a si bien rendu l'éloquence historique de Robertson vouloit se preter à un écrivain son inferieur à tous egards mais qui a reçu de l'indulgence de ses compatriotes un acceuil presqu'aussi favorable. Un succès si flatteur m'encourage à me livrer avec ardeur à la composition du second volume. Malgré la dissipation de Londres et les soins du Parlement j'y ai déjà fait quelque progrès et je compte avec une assurance assez bien fondée de pouvoir l'achever dans deux ou tout au plus dans trois ans. Comme je m'empresserois alors de vous envoyer les feuilles à mesure qu'elles sortiroient de la presse, il nous

[1] J. B. Antoine Suard (1733–1817), whose acquaintance Gibbon made at Paris in 1763, had translated Robertson's *History of Charles V.* in 1771, and was now at work on a translation of his *History of America*, which was published in 1778.

seroit facile de nous arranger de manière que ce volume parût en même tems dans les deux langues.

Si vous avez, Monsieur, l'inclination et le loisir de vous engager dans ce travail, je ne perçcois plus que deux obstacles, qui sont à la verité assez considerables. Le premier c'est l'objet et la nature de mes deux derniers chapitres, qui doivent paroitre moins edifians encore en France qu'en Angleterre. Je sens cependant qu'un homme d'esprit rompu comme vous dans l'art d'écrire seroit souvent en état d'adoucir l'expression sans affoiblir la pensée. Je ne craindrois pas de vous confier les droits les plus étendus pour changer et même pour supprimer tout ce qui vous paroitroit le plus propre à blesser la delicatesse de votre église et de votre police. J'irais moi-même au devant· de leurs scrupules et si par le moyen des couriers de nos ministres, vous m'envoyez les feuilles de la traduction, je vous aiderois à enlever toutes les pierres d'achoppement. Enfin si malgré toutes ces précautions l'ouvrage se trouvoit encore trop fort pour passer à la censure, ne pourroit on pas obtenir par le crédit de nos amis communs un privilège tacite qui suffiroit pour mettre votre edition à couvert de l'avidité des libraires ? L'autre obstacle se tire de la crainte que dans cet intervalle de tems perdu par la negligence de mon ami, Deyverdun, quelque main assurément moins habile ne vous ait déjà prevenu. On m'a parlé fort confusement d'une traduction entreprise par Moutard, libraire sur le quai des Augustins, mais j'ignore jusqu'à quel point elle est avancée et quelles mesures on prend pour le faire paroitre. Vous êtes à portée, Monsieur, de vous informer et je conçois que cet eclaircissement pourra influer sur vos resolutions, et j'ose vous prier de me les communiquer au plûtot.

Mes affaires ne m'ont pas permis de faire un voyage à Paris cet été. J'ai senti douleureusement cette privation dont je ne me suis consolé qu'en formant des projets pour l'année prochaine. Quand on se rappelle les momens delicieux qu'on a passés avec Madame Necker dans ce taudis de Suffolk Street, toutes nos Angloises paroissent encore plus froides et plus maussades. Ayez la bonté, Monsieur, de l'assurer que son souvenir ne s'effacera jamais de mon coeur et de presenter en même tems à Monsieur Necker mes respects les plus sinceres. Comme homme je dois applaudir à la justice qu'on rend au vrai mérite ; mais si je ne pensois qu'en Anglois je vous avoue franchement que ce n'est pas là le Ministre des Finances que je voudrois donner à la France. J'espère néanmoins que l'ami de l'humanité sera disposé à nous epargner le plus terribles de ses fleaux.

Excusez, Monsieur, ce long barbouillage dont j'ai pris la liberté de vous importuner, ou pardonnez tout à l'amour paternel. Recevez mes remerciemens en même tems pour cet excellent discours à l'Academie Françoise dans lequel vous avez mis des idées à la place de complemens. A propos nous sommes fort en colère contre votre confrère Voltaire pour les blasphemes qu'il vient d'écrire contre le Dieu du Théâtre Anglois ;[1] et qu'on a lu, dit-on, en pleine Academie dans la presence même de sa prêtresse Madame Montagu.

J'ai l'honneur d'être avec une consideration distinguée,

Monsieur,

Votre très humble et très obéissant serviteur,

E. GIBBON.

294.

To J. B. Holroyd, Esq.

Friday evening, November 22nd, 1776.

News from the Lakes. A Naval combat in which the Pro- vincials were repulsed with considerable loss.[2] They burnt and abandoned Crown point. Carleton is besieging Ticonderoga. Carleton, I say, for he is there, and it is apprehended that Bour- goyne is coming home. We dismissed the Nabobs without a division. Burke and Attorney General spoke very well. This evening a letter from Aunt Hester. She seems angry with Gilbert's accounts, and dissatisfied with her poor balance. Adieu.

¹ In a letter, dated " Ferney, July 19, 1776," and addressed to M. d'Argenteuil, Voltaire wrote strongly against a projected translation of Shakespeare. He claims that he himself had first pointed out to the French some pearls which he found on Shakespeare's "enormous dung-heap." "I little thought," he continues, "that I should help to tread under foot the crowns of Racine and Corneille, in order to adorn the head of a barbarian and a buffoon." The letter was read aloud before the Academicians. Mrs. Montague, who was present, when she heard the words "énorme fumier," exclaimed, "C'est un fumier qui a fertilisé une terre bien ingrate."

² On November 22, letters arrived from Sir Guy Carleton giving an account of the destruction of the American fleet on Lake Champlain, October 11-13, 1776. Arnold, after destroying Crown Point, retired to Ticonderoga. General Burgoyne returned to England on December 9, 1776.

295.

To J. B. Holroyd, Esq.

Saturday Evening, 23rd Nov., 1776.

You will receive this post a large parcel which came last night from Northamptonshire and to which you must return an immediate answer, as the old Lady seems impatient. Her wanting me to lend her money in contradiction to all rules established between Aunts and Nephews is a very *ugly* circumstance. I do not like to borrow money to purchase land ; nor to lend money without being able to call for either principal or interest. Yet she might in various ways be offended at my declining it. Therefore if the Tythes can be dispensed with, give an opinion against them. I do not like Gilbert ; he says that Martin has a long lease of land two miles from Newhaven, and that he could distress us by taking in kind. Consider, and if there is doubt enquire.

Examine in your library an old translation of Tacitus by Sir Henry Saville : if it contains the life of Agricola, send up the book for the use of the Sollicitor General.

I embrace, &c.

296.

To his Stepmother.

London, Nov. 29th, 1776.

Dear Madam,

Let me just write a line to ask how you do and to tell you that I am very well—very well, and I think unhurt amidst as hot a cannonading as can be pointed against Washington. Two answers (which you perhaps have seen), one from Mr. Chelsham[1] of Oxford, the other from Dr. Watson of Cambridge, are already born, and I believe the former is choleric, the latter civil, and both too dull to deserve your notice ; three or four more are expected, but I believe none of them will divert me from the prosecution of the second volume, which will be much more laborious for me, but not less entertaining to the reader than the first. I shall be pretty much fixed in town, though I have been

---

[1] *Remarks on the Two Last Chapters of Mr. Gibbon's History of the Decline and Fall of the Roman Empire,* by James Chelsum, D.D. London, 1776. 8vo.

forced into a kind of promise for S. P. and tempted into another for Ampthill.[1] I understand and remember your question. *She* was in London, and I see her much less than formerly, as Beauclerc and Lady Dy are at Bath. *My lace.*

I am entirely yours,

E. G.

297.

To J. B. Holroyd, Esq.

Atwood's, Saturday Evening, Dec. 7, 1776.
Just going to supper.

This day a dispatch arrived from Northamptonshire. Mrs. G. is extremely satisfied with my diligence and prolixity ; but seems to wish that *we* would settle her account with Gilbert. I have not her letter about me, but will send it next post. I expect to receive from you some plan for the disposal of Lenborough, the great thorn which sticks in the side of my happiness. Lord G. G. who is playing at Whist says there is not any news, though great hopes.—This morning I received by the *post* (charged two guineas and a half) a first volume of a French translation containing only the seven first chapters, but to be continued. I did not however regret the money, as it is admirably well done by M. de Septchenes[2] (Sevenoaks), a young man who has been lately in England, and who sent me a very pleasant dose of flattery on the occasion.

I mean to eat my Christmas dinner with you, and think Sir Hugh will accompany me. I believe in the meantime I shall run down to Bath and pay a charitable visit to poor Beauclerck.

298.

To M. de Septchênes.

Bentinck Street, le 10 Decembre 1776.

Le paquet interessant que vous m'avez addressé, Monsieur, par la poste, m'a été rendu le 7me de ce mois : et c'est avec empressement que je saisis le premier instant pour rassurer votre modestie

---

[1] With Lord and Lady Ossory.

[2] The translation, commenced by M. Le Clerc de Septchênes, and completed by other hands, passed through numerous editions in France. It was the foundation of an Italian version published at Pisa in 1779–86.

et pour vous témoigner les sentimens auxquels vous avez acquis les droits les plus légitimes. Representez-vous les inquiétudes d'un père pour le sort d'un enfant cheri, égaré sans guide du milieu de Paris et exposé au danger de déshonorer par des liaisons honteuses le nom qu'il portoit. S'il apprenoit donc, d'un coup, qu'une main secourable retirant son fils d'un état aussi triste l'avoit présenté dans les meilleures compagnies de Paris avec un éclat et des avantages qu'il ne tenoit point de sa naissance, jugez, Monsieur, des sensibilités de ce Père envers son ami et son bienfaiteur. L'estime seroit augmentée par la reconnoissance et leur affection commune pour l'objet de leurs soins deviendroit peut-être le lien le plus étroit de leur amitié. Pour parler sans figure de votre traduction de l'histoire de la décadence de l'Empire Romain, je l'ai lu, Monsieur, avec autant de plaisir que d'avidité. Je crains de trop louer une production à laquelle j'ai moi-même fourni les materiaux, mais cette crainte ne doit pas m'interdire d'accorder des justes éloges qui sont dus à votre parfaite intelligence de l'original Anglois, et à la fidelité, aussi bien qu'à l'elegance, avec laquelle vous l'avez transporté dans votre langue. Si dans un petit nombre d'endroits j'ai été moins content de la traduction, ce ne sont que de legères meprises presqu'inevitables dans un ouvrage de longue haleine et auxquelles l'obscurité du texte peut quelquefois avoir donné lieu. Je prendrai la liberté de vous envoyer à la première occasion les observations qui se sont presentées à mesure que je lisois votre ouvrage ; vous en ferez l'usage que vous jugerez le convenable. J'attens avec une vive impatience la suite de la traduction, et si le succès de la première partie ne vous encourage pas à la continuer, je déclare d'avance que ce ne sera point votre faute mais celle de l'original. Au cas que vous ne renonciez pas à cette enterprise, je serois charmé que vous voulussiez bien m'envoyer les épreuves, au sortir de la presse, je les examinerai avec toute l'attention de l'amour propre, et comme vous avez déjà gagné de vitesse sur vos concurrens, le délai de quelques jours seroit d'une assez petite importance. A propos, Monsieur, quel parti prendrez vous à l'égard des deux derniers chapitres ? En Angleterre même ils ont excité, je ne sais pourquoi, du scandale parmi nos Ecclesiastiques, et malgré toutes vos précautions j'ai de la peine à concevoir comment ils pourront soutenir la censure sévère de votre Eglise et de votre police. Mais nous avons du tems pour y songer ; car je pense que dans tous ces chapitres, qui forment votre 2ᵉ partie, il n'y a rien, dont la delicatesse la plus scrupuleuse puisse se formaliser.

Je regrette sincèrement de n'avoir pas eu le plaisir de vous connoître dans votre dernier voyage: mais comme le Libraire Elmsley m'assure que vous aimez ce pays et que vous le visitez souvent, je ne desespère pas de trouver une occasion favorable pour reparer mes pertes. D'ailleurs j'ai quelque idée moi-même de faire une course à Paris ce printems prochain. En ce cas-là ma première demarche seroit de vous chercher, Monsieur, pour vous réitérer les assurances de l'estime et de la consideration avec laquelle j'ai l'honneur d'être

Votre très humble et très obéissant serviteur,

E. GIBBON.

P.S.—Votre paquet m'a couté deux Guinées et demi. Il vaut bien son prix: mais il faut toujours eviter les despenses inutiles. Si vous addressez vos lettres To Sir Stanier Porten, Under Secretary of State, Cleveland Row, London, Elles me parviendront avec sureté et sans frais.

299.

To J. B. Holroyd, Esq.

Thursday Evening, 19th Dec., 1776.

Believe me when I say *upon my honour*, that a particular business of serious importance has just arisen, which, as long as it is in agitation, will not allow me to quit town for a day. I still think however that I shall see S. P. before the close of the year. You may say in general in the family (if any should bark) that you are satisfied with my conduct, and order them to shut their trap.

Confused news from New York, the Howes' dispatches are not arrived; but it appears from some officers' letters which I have seen, that we attacked and carried a post ill defended by 6000 men, upon which they evacuated Kingsbridge, though they still occupy Fort Washington on the Island of N. Y.[1] They

---

[1] After the battle of Brooklyn, Washington withdrew his troops to the heights of Haarlem. General Howe, towards the end of October, engaged in several skirmishes with the Americans, but made no effort to bring them to a decisive engagement. On November 16, 1776, Fort Washington was

shew little courage or conduct, but the ground is incredibly
strong, and it seems running into a War of posts.—I shall write
to Mrs. G. Is the historian of the Roman Empire to write out
twenty copies himself of a few acres in Bucks. I should like to
have them transcribed or even printed. Why not? Adieu.

300.

To his Stepmother.

London, December 25th, 1776.

DEAR MADAM,

Next week I go for a fortnight to Sheffield Place, not
from any weariness of an empty town, for in its most deserted
state I still prefer it to the most agreeable rural scene, but the
little man is so pressing, that I was obliged to sacrifice to his
commands an invitation to Ampthill Park, accompanied with all
that could render the visit desirable. Your silence gives me
reason to hope that you have now dismissed your indisposition
which had made me a little uneasy. I hear the most favourable
accounts of Beauclerc's recovery. Adieu, Dear Madam. Messieurs
Gosling and Clive are instructed to obey your commands whenever you please to send them.

I am,
Most truly yours,
E. GIBBON.

301.

To Mrs. Holroyd.

Downing Street, January 16th, 1777.

Inconstant pusillanimous Woman!

Is it possible that you should so soon have forgot your solemn
vows and engagements, and that you should *pretend* to prefer the
dirt and darkness of the Weald of Sussex to the splendid and
social life of London? Before the reception of your Lord's epistle,
Downing Street[1] and Bentinck Street were ready to engage in

taken by the British, and 2600 of the American troops, exclusive of officers,
surrendered as prisoners of war. Following up his advantage, Howe
advanced into New Jersey, Washington retreating beyond the Delaware.

[1] General Fraser lived in Downing Street, and died there, February 8,
1782.

a Civil War.   They have now suspended their hostilities and
united their interests, and they both, jointly and separately, insist
on your appearance with or without your mate on the appointed
Saturday the 25th instant, to remain a hostage in our hands till
we think proper to dismiss you. Donna Catherina[1] will undertake
to dress you, as human and female creatures are usually dressed.
A proper application of rouge will conceal the variety of colours,
and the deficiency of hair may be supplied by a fashionable peri-
wig. Adieu.

DONNA CATHERINA. MOUNTAINEER.[2] LE GRAND GIBBON.

302.

To J. B. Holroyd, Esq.

Bentinck-street, January the 18th, 1777.

*As I presume, My Lady does not make a practise of tumbling
down stairs every day after dinner, by this time the colours must
have faded, and the high places (I mean the temples) are reduced
to a proper level. But what, in the name of the great prince, is
the meaning of her declining the urban expedition ? Is it the
spontaneous result of her own proud spirit ? or does it proceed
from the secret machinations of her domestic tyrant ? At all
events, I expect you will both remember your engagement of
next Saturday in Bentinck Street, with Donna Catherina, the
Mountaineer, &c.

Things go on very prosperously in America. Howe is himself in the Jerseys, and will push at least as far as the Delawar
River. The Continental (perhaps *now* the rebel) Army is in
a great measure dispersed, and Washington, who wishes to
cover Philadelphia, has not more than 6 or 7 thousand men
with him. Clinton designs to conquer Rhode Island in his
way home. But what *I* think of much greater consequence, a
province has made its submission, and desired to be reinstated in
the peace of the King. It is indeed only poor little Georgia, and
the application was made to Governor Tonyn of Florida ; some
disgust at a violent step of the Congress, who removed the
President of *their* provincial assembly, a leading and popular
man, co-operated with the fear of the Indians, who began to

---

[1] Mrs. Fraser.   [2] General Fraser.

amuse themselves with the exercise of scalping on their back settlements.

The measures for Leuborough are in train, but we must wait for our turn in the papers. Adieu. Town fills, and we are mighty agreeable. Last year, on the Queen's birthday, Sir G. Warren had his diamond star cut off his coat ; this day the same accident happened to him again, with another star worth £700. He had better compound by the year."

　　　　　　　　　　　　　　　　　　　　　E. G.

303.

To Mrs. Holroyd.

　　　　　　　　　　　　　　　　　　　January 21st, 1777.

The Bristol fire is universally imputed to design and patriotic virtue.[1]

What creatures women are ! They talk of the art and management of the Highlander in every point which he has a mind to carry. But Donna Catherina, with all her seeming naiveté, exceeds him many a degree.

By suggesting the Ab of Ab,[2] for whom I cannot squeeze out a bed without obliging her to pig with Caplin, she has compelled me to consent to your emigration into Downing Street. *Bien entendu*, however, that, when you are less *fine* and can appear in town accompanied only by your own charms, Bentinck Street shall be restored to its ancient rights. You puzzle us all by the mention of the 26th, which is Sunday. Had you forgot the engagement *to dinner* in B. S. for Saturday the 25th, which still holds if you can move that day ? Otherwise it stands for the 27th, as I am engaged Sunday. An answer to this by the return. I kiss your fair hands and party-coloured face.

　　　　　　　　　　　　　　　　　　　　　E. G.

---

[1] On December 7, 1776, a fire broke out in Portsmouth Dockyard, and in the hemp warehouse a quantity of combustibles were found ; at Plymouth an attempt to set the dockyard on fire was discovered ; at Bristol several houses close to the quay were set on fire. The incendiary was "John the Painter," whose real name was Aitken. He confessed his guilt, and asserted the complicity of Silas Deane, the American agent at Paris. He was tried at Winchester Assizes, convicted, and hanged at Portsmouth.

[2] *I.e.* probably the Abigail of Mrs. Abigail Holroyd.

304.

To his Stepmother.

London, February the 10th, 1777.

DEAR MADAM,

Your lace arrived safe, and now it is put on a fashionable frock makes a very handsome figure. The Taylor tells me it would be impossible to get such stuff from the shops.

Though the memorandum is quite superfluous, it will often put me in mind of the creator. The Holroyds are just gone, not from me but from General Fraser's, where they spent a fortnight. The town is now full and pleasant, though my usual hurry is increased by a daily attendance on Dr. Hunter's Anatomy lectures,[1] which amuse me beyond any I ever studied. My compliments to Mrs. Gould, she shall not wait long for her franks. I am sorry to hear of young Gould. Adieu.

Sincerely yours,

E. G.

305.

To J. B. Holroyd, Esq.

Feb. 15, 1777.

*You deserve, and we exult in, your weather and disappointments. Why would you bury yourself? I dined in Downing-street Thursday last; and I think Wedderburne was at least as agreeable a companion as your timber-surveyor could be. Lee is certainly taken, but Lord North does not apprehend he is coming home. We are not clear whether he behaved with courage or pusillanimity when he surrendered himself; but Colonel Keene told me to-day, that he had seen a letter from Lee since his confinement. "He imputes his being taken, to the alertness of Harcourt, and cowardice of his own guard; hopes he shall meet his fate with fortitude; but laments that freedom is not likely to find a resting-place in any part of the globe." It is said, he

---

[1] John Hunter (1728–1793) began his Anatomy Lectures in 1773. Originally delivered to his pupils, they were afterwards thrown open to the public on payment of a fee of four guineas. They were delivered annually from October to April, on alternate evenings at 7 to 8 p.m.

was to succeed Washington. We know nothing certain of the
Hessians ; ¹ but there *has* been a blow. Adieu.*

306.

To J. B. Holroyd, Esq.

Almack's, Wednesday evening, March 5, 1777.

*In due obedience to thy dread commands I write. But what
shall I say ? My life, though more lively than yours, is almost as
uniform ; a very little reading and writing in the morning, bones
or guts from two to four, pleasant dinners from five to eight, and
afterwards Clubs, with an occasional assembly, or supper. As to
Lenborough the bait is in the water, but I have not heard of any
fish biting. America affords nothing very satisfactory ; and
though we have many flying reports, you may be assured that we
are ignorant of the consequences of Trenton, &c. Charles Fox is
now at my elbow, declaiming on the impossibility of keeping
America, since a victorious Army has been unable to maintain
any extent of posts in the single province of Jersey. Lord North
is out of danger (the animal is so gross that we trembled for its
important existence). I now expect that *My Lady* and you
should fix the time for the proposed visitation to Bentinck Street.
March and April are open—chuse. Adieu.*

307.

To his Stepmother.

London, March the 29th, 1777.

DEAR MADAM,
        Instead of inventing any artificial excuses for my natural
and original sin of indolence, I believe my most prudent method
would be to quarrel with you for the provoking patience with
which you have endured my long and scandalous silence. Even
in the midst of the dissipation of this town I might have found
a few moments to tell you that I have been perfectly well this
winter, and to enquire after your health, your spirits and your

¹ Washington crossed the Delaware on Christmas Day, 1776, surprised
two regiments of Hessians at Trenton, and in the following January again
reduced the Jerseys, while Howe remained inactive at New York.

amusements. Lady Dy. tells me that she was once in your company at Dr. Delacour's, for whom both she and Beauclerc express a veneration almost equal to your own. As little or no conversation passed between you, she had only an opportunity of admiring the harmony of your voice and the beauty of your teeth, on which she bestows the most lavish enconiums. They mean to visit Bath again this spring, and I am very desirous that you should be better acquainted with her. You will find her one of the most accomplished women in the World, and she will soon discover in you qualities more valuable than those which are now the objects of her enconiums.

The decline of the Roman Empire does not yet decline, the clamour subsides, the sale continues, and we are now printing a third edition in quarto of 1000 copies (in all 3500) with the notes at bottom. I am often pressed about the second volume, which advances very slowly indeed. Last year was allowed for repose and preparation, the usual distractions of the winter have been increased by a constant daily attendance of two hours *every day* to Dr. Hunter's Anatomy Lectures, which have opened to me a new and very entertaining scene within myself. This summer I propose passing at Paris, as I must not lose any time if I wish to catch my friends the Neckers[1] in their brilliant and precarious situation of Ministers. As soon as we have paid the King's debts I intend (about the end of next month) to set forward on an expedition in which I promise to myself very great and various entertainment. You need not in any respect be allarmed at my design. My seat at Westminster is a full security for my return in four or five months ; the supplies for the journey will be paid by the Roman Empire, and my business (particularly in Bucks) will be entrusted to the safeguard and active hands of the Lord of Sheffield. Adieu, Dear Madam,

I am,

Ever yours,

E. GIBBON.

Mrs. Porten is as young as ever. I understand that the giddy girl has neglected writing to you.

---

[1] In June, 1776, after the fall of Turgot, Necker was associated with Taboureau des Réaux, the Controller-General, in the management of the finances of France, and given the title of *Directeur du trésor*. In June, 1777, he succeeded Taboureau des Réaux, but, because of his religion, only received the title of *Directeur Général*.

308.

To J. B. Holroyd, Esq.

Saturday night, April 12th, 1777.

Your dispatch is gone to R. Way, and I flatter myself that by your assistance I shall be enabled to lose £1000 upon Lenbourough before my return from Paris. The day of my departure is not absolutely fixed; Sunday sen-night, the 27th instant, is talked of: but if any India business should come on after the Civil list, it will occasion some delay. Otherwise things are in great forwardness, a livery servant is provided, a Swiss who speaks French and English. I take my own chaise, and begin to think of settling my credit. Pray if I can save four pr. cent. by it, may I not decline Fleet Street, who are very indifferent, I believe, about that sort of business? *Mrs. G. is an enemy to the whole plan; and I must answer, in a long letter, two very ingenious objections which she has started; 1st, that I shall be confined, or put to death by the priests, and, 2ndly, That I shall sully my *moral* character, by making love to Necker's wife. Before I go, I will consult Newton, about a power of Attorney for you. By the bye, I wish you would remember a sort of promise, and give me one day before I go. We talk chiefly of the Marquis de la Fayette,[1] who was here a few weeks ago. He is about twenty, with 130,000 Livres a year; the nephew of Noailles, who is Ambassador here. He has bought the D. of Kingston's Yacht, and is gone to join the Americans. The Court *appear* to be angry with him. Adieu.*

E. G.

[1] The Marquis de la Fayette, born 1757, married the second daughter of the Duc d'Ayen, eldest son of the' Maréchal de Noailles, and brother of the Marquis de Noailles, the French ambassador. La Fayette came to London on a visit to his wife's uncle early in 1777, and was presented to George III. A few days later he returned to Paris, sailed from Passages with several young Frenchmen for America, landed in June, and immediately received the rank of major-general in the American army. A *lettre de cachet* was sent after him to Bordeaux; but he avoided it by crossing into Spain.

309.

To his Stepmother.

Bentinck Street, April the 14th, 1777.

DEAR MADAM,

I will freely acknowledge that I was not a little surprized and even vexed at finding by your last letter, that you had conceived so strong a dislike to my intended journey. But I must add at the same time that I was equally sensible of the obliging frankness with which you communicate your objections. The less foundation I can discover for your apprehensions, the more I am convinced of the delicacy of your regard. True love is of very timid and even pusillanimous nature, and can easily transform the most harmless objects into horrid phantoms which appear to threaten the happiness of those who are dear to us. But when you have indulged the exquisite sensibility of friendship, you will, I am sure, make a proper use of your excellent understanding, and will soon smile at your own terrors. The constancy and danger of a twenty years' passion is a subject upon which I hardly know how to be serious. I am ignorant what effect that period of time has produced upon me, but I do assure you that it has committed very great ravages upon the Lady, and that at present she is very far from being an object either of desire or scandal. As a woman of talents and fortune she is at the head of the literature of Paris, the station of her husband procures her respect from the first people of the country, and the reception which I shall meet with in her house will give me advantages that have fallen to the share of few Englishmen. When I mention her *house*, I must remove the misapprehension which seems to have allarmed you. I shall *visit* but not *lodge* there. I have not the least reason to believe that they think of offering me an apartment, but if they do, I shall certainly refuse it, for the sake of my own comfort and freedom: So that the husband will be easy, the world will be mute, and my moral character will still preserve its immaculate purity.

A moment's reflection will satisfy you that I have as little to fear from the hatred of the priests as from the love of Madame N. Whatever might be the wishes of the French Clergy, the wisdom of the Government and the liberal temper of the Nation have rendered those monsters perfectly inoffensive. Their own subjects (Voltaire for instance, who resides near Geneva, but in France) think, converse and write with the most unbounded freedom : and can you imagine that an English Protestant, a member of the British Legislature, living at Paris under the protection of his Minister, and in Society with their own, will be exposed to the smallest possible danger or even trouble for having published a profane book in a foreign language and country ? When David Hume (the name, the most abhorred by the Godly) was at Paris, he was oppressed only with civilities ; and the recent fame of my book is perhaps the circumstance which will introduce me with the most favour and eclat.

The scheme of passing some months at Paris (though I have patiently waited till I could execute it with prudence and propriety) has been formed many years ago.   I cannot persuade myself without any reason that strikes my understanding to renounce an expedition which promises so much entertainment and information : but it will be a very considerable alloy to my satisfaction if I leave any uneasiness or apprehension on your mind.   I could very much have wished to fulfil my promise of an Easter visit ; but I imagined that I had already explained how closely I was confined in town by my daily attendance on Dr. Hunter's lectures.   They prevent my setting out for Paris till after the 25th instant, by which time I hope we shall have paid the King's debts.[1]   You may depend on receiving regular though concise intelligence of my motions.

I am, Dear Madam,
Most truly yours,
E. GIBBON.

310.

To J. B. Holroyd, Esq.

Atwood's, Saturday night, [April 19th, 1777].

*It is not possible as yet to fix the day of my departure.   That circumstance depends on the state of India, and will not be

---

[1] On April 9, 1777, a message from the king was delivered to both Houses, asking for the payment of his debts, which amounted to £600,000.   At the same time a Bill "for the better support of the Royal Household" was introduced, to increase his revenue by £100,000 a year.   A motion for a committee to inquire into the accounts was rejected; the king's debts were discharged, and the Government Bill carried.

determined till the general court of next Wednesday. I know from the *first* authority, if the violence of the Proprietors about the Pigot[1] can be checked in the India house by the influence of a Government Majority, the Minister does not wish to exert the omnipotence of Parliament; and I shall be dismissed from hence time enough to set forwards on Thursday the first of May. On the contrary, should we be involved in those perplexing affairs, they may easily detain me till the middle of next month. But as all this is very uncertain, I direct you and My Lady to appear in town to-morrow sennight. I have many things to say.* You mistake about the dear inseparable Caplin. He rides at his ease in the Chaise with his master, while the Swiss, who will condescend to put on a livery at Paris, will mount on horseback. *We have been animated this week, and, notwithstanding the strict œconomy recommended by Charles Fox and John Wilkes, we have paid the Royal debts.*

E. G.

311.

To J. B. Holroyd, Esq.

Monday night, [April 21st, 1777].

Bad news from Hampshire.———Support Hugonin, comfort me, correct or expell Winton, sell Lenborough, and remove my temporal cares. When do you arrive?

---

[1] Lord Pigot, Governor of Madras, was arrested in April, 1776, by the Madras Council for his support of the Rajah of Tanjore against the Nabob of the Carnatic, and his opposition to an iniquitous claim upon the Rajah's revenue made by Paul Benfield. He died while still under arrest, in May, 1777. The Court of Proprietors voted by a large majority for his release and restoration to his governorship. The Directors were almost equally divided upon the question. Meanwhile the Government exercised all its influence to carry through the Court of Proprietors three resolutions—one recalling Lord Pigot, a second ordering home his friends in the council, a third ordering home his enemies. These resolutions were carried. Lord Pigot's case was then taken up in Parliament, and on May 22, 1777, Governor Johnston moved several resolutions approving Lord Pigot's action, and condemning the Madras Council. The resolutions were rejected by 90 to 67. See note to Letter 371.

312.

To J. B. Holroyd, Esq.

Wednesday night, [April 23rd, 1777].

*It is uncertain whether India comes to Westminster this year, and it is certain that Gibbon goes to Paris next Saturday seunight. Therefore Holroyd must appear in town the beginning of next week. Gibbon wants the cordial of his presence before the journey. My Lady *must* come.*

313.

To his Stepmother.

May the 3rd, 1777.

DEAR MADAM,

After some public delays which have tryed my patience, I at length resolved to wait no longer for the Budget. I set forwards Monday, and hope to breakfast at Calais Tuesday and to dine at Paris either Friday or Saturday; the alternative depends on my stepping out of my way to Lisle. You may be assured of receiving immediate notice of my effecting my landing on the Continent.

I am, Dear Madam,
Most truly yours,
E. G.

You will find Fleet Street instructed to obey your Midsummer Order.

314.

To J. B. Holroyd, Esq.

Dover, Tuesday evening, May 6th, 1777.

*My expedition does not begin very auspiciously. The wind, Which for some days had been fair, paid me the compliment of changing on my arrival; and, though I immediately secured a vessel, it has been impossible to make the least use of it during the whole course of this tedious day. It seems doubtful, whether I shall get out to-morrow morning; and the Captain assures me, that the passage will have the double advantage of being both long and rough. Last night a small Privateer, fitted out at Dunkirk, with a commission from Dr. Franklin, attacked, took, and has carried into Dunkirk road, the Harwich Pacquet.[1] The King's Messenger had just time to throw his dispatches overboard : he passed through this town about four o'clock this afternoon, in his return to London. As the alarm is now given, our American friend will probably remain quiet, or will be soon caught ; so that I have not *much* apprehension for my personal safety ; but if so daring an outrage is not followed by punishment and restitution, it may become a very serious business, and may possibly shorten my stay at Paris.

Adieu. I shall write by the first opportunity, either from Calais or Philadelphia.* I wrote last Friday to Hugonin, and announced an Epistle of instructions from you. I embrace My lady. Did your Lord and Colonel disappoint you ?

315.

To J. B. Holroyd, Esq.

Calais, Wednesday, May the 7th, 1777.

Post nubila Phœbus. A pleasant passage, an excellent house, a good dinner with Lord Coleraine, whom I found here. Easy Custom-house Officers, fine Weather, &c. I am detained to-night by the temptation of a French Comedy, in a Theatre at the end of Dessaint's Garden ; but shall be in motion to-morrow early, and hope to dine at Paris Saturday. Adieu. I think I am a punctual Correspondent ; but this beginning is too good to last.*

316.

To his Stepmother.

Calais, May the 7th, 1777.

DEAR MADAM,

I am this moment (about one o'clock in the afternoon) landed after a very pleasant passage. I already feel my mind expand with the unbounded prospect of the Continent. But notwithstanding my love of freedom you may rest assured that

---

[1] The *Prince of Orange*, packet from Harwich to Helvetsluys, was captured by the *Surprise*, an American privateer commanded by Captain Cunningham, carrying four guns and ten swivels.

in due season, I shall return without reluctance to my cage in Bentinck Street.

I am, Dear Madam,
Most truly yours,
E. GIBBON.

317.

To his Stepmother.

Paris, May 12th, 1777.

DEAR MADAM,

The departure of the post only leaves me time to say that I reached this place last Saturday night, and that I already find myself as perfectly established as I ever was in London.

I am, Dear Madam,
Most truly yours,
E. GIBBON.

318.

To J. B. Holroyd, Esq.

Paris, June the 16th, 1777.

I told you what would infallibly happen, and you know enough of the nature of the beast not to be surprized at it. I have now been at Paris exactly five weeks,[1] during which time I have not written to any person whatsoever within the British Dominions except two lines of notification to Mrs. Gibbon. The Daemon of procrastination has at length yielded to the Genius of Friendship, assisted indeed by the powers of fear and shame. But when I have seated myself before my table and begin to revolve all that I have seen and tasted during this busy period, I feel myself oppressed and confounded ; and I am very near throwing away the pen and resigning myself to indolent despair. A compleat history would require a volume at least as corpulent as the decline and fall, and if I attempt to select and abridge, besides the difficulty of the choice there occur so many things which cannot properly be entrusted to paper, and so many others of too slight a nature to support the Journey, that I am almost tempted to reserve for our future conversations the detail of my pleasures and occupations. But as I am sensible that you are *rigid* and

---

[1] This letter was begun one Sunday and finished the next.

impatient, I will try to convey in a few words a general idea of
my situation as a man of the World and as a man of Letters.

You remember that the Neckers were my principal dependance,
and the reception which I have met with from them very far
surpassed my most sanguine expectations. I do not indeed lodge
in their house (as it might excite the jealousy of the husband and
procure me a letter de cachet), but I live very much with them,
dine and sup whenever they have company, which is almost
every day, and whenever I like it, for they are not in the least
exigeans. Mr. Walpole gave me an introduction to Madame du
Deffand,[1] an agreable young Lady of eighty-two years of age, who
has constant suppers and the best company in Paris. When you
see the D. of Richmond at Lewes he will give you an account of
that house, where I meet him almost every evening. Ask him
about Madame de Cambis.[2] I am afraid poor Mary is entirely

---

[1] Marie de Vichy-Chamrond (1697-1781) married, in 1718, Jean Baptiste
Jacques de la Lande, Marquis du Deffand. Separated from her husband in
1722 for her relations with the Regent duc d'Orléans, the President Hénault,
and others, she lived chiefly at Sceaux till the death of her husband in 1750.
In 1753 she opened her salon at the Convent of St. Joseph. A year later
she became totally blind. She had stayed at La Source with Lord Bolingbroke in 1721, and since then had known some of the most distinguished
men and women in France and England. But the following extracts from
her correspondence with Walpole, who had introduced Gibbon to her, show
her appreciation of the historian as a member of society:—"Je suis fort
contente de M. Gibbon; depuis huit jours qu'il est arrivé, je l'ai vu presque
tous les jours; il a la conversation facile, parle très-bien français; j'espère
qu'il me sera de grande ressource" (May 18, 1777). "Je lui crois beaucoup
d'esprit, sa conversation est facile, et forte de choses, comme disait Fontenelle;
il me plaît beaucoup, d'autant plus qu'il ne m'embarrasse pas" (May 27).
"Je m'accommode de plus en plus de M. Gibbon; c'est véritablement un
homme d'esprit; tous les tons lui sont faciles, il est aussi Français ici que
MM. de Choiseul, de Beauvau, etc. Je me flatte qu'il est content de moi;
nous soupons presque tous les jours ensemble, le plus souvent chez moi; ce
soir ce sera chez Madame de Mirepoix" (June 8). "M. Gibbon me convient
parfaitement; je voudrais bien qu'il restât toujours ici; je le vois presque
tous les jours; sa conversation est très facile, on est à son aise avec lui"
(June 22). "M. Gibbon a ici le plus grand succès, on se l'arrache; Je ne sais
pas si tous les jugements qu'il porte sont bien justes, mais il se comporte
avec tout le monde d'une manière qui ne donne point de prise aux
ridicules; ce qui est fort difficile à éviter dans les sociétés qu'il fréquente"
(September 21).

[2] Gabrielle Charlotte Françoise d'Alsace-Hénin-Liétard married, in
November, 1755, Jacques François, Vicomte de Cambis. She was the
sister of the Prince de Chimay, and niece of the Marquise de Boufflers. She
knew English well, and translated into French several of the *Portraits* of

forgot. I have met the D. of Choiseul[1] at his particular request, dined *by accident* with Franklin, conversed with the Emperor,[2] been presented at court, and gradually, or rather rapidly, I find my acquaintance spreading over the most valuable parts of Paris. They pretend to like me, and whatever you may think of French professions, I am convinced that some at least are sincere. On the other hand I feel myself easy and happy in their company, and only regret that I did not come over two or three months sooner. Though Paris throughout the summer promises me a very agreable society, yet I am hurt every day by the departure of Men and Women whom I begin to know with some familiarity, the departure of Officers for their Governments and Garrisons, of Bishops for their Dioceses, and even of country Gentlemen for their estates, as a rural taste gains ground in this Country.

So much for the general idea of my acquaintance ; details would be endless yet unsatisfactory. You may add to the pleasures of Society those of the Spectacles and promenades, and you will find that I lead a very agreable life ; let me just condescend to observe that it is not extravagant. After decking myself out with silks and silver, the ordinary establishment of Coach, Lodgeing, Servants, eating and pocket expences does not exceed sixty pounds pr. month. Yet I have two footmen in handsome liveries behind my Coach, and my apartment is hung with damask. Adieu for the present. I have more to say, but were I to attempt any farther progress you must wait another post, and you have already waited long enough of all conscience.

Let me just in two words give you an idea of my day. I am

Lord Chesterfield. Her conquest of the Duke of Richmond was well known in Paris. Gibbon himself was her victim. " Le Gibbon," writes Madame du Deffand to Walpole, April 20, 1780, " était aussi un peu épris ; elle fait plus de conquêtes à présent qu'elle n'en a fait dans sa première jeunesse ; sa coquetterie est sèche, froide et piquante ; c'est un nouveau genre qu'a sa séduction." The Vicomtesse de Cambis died at Richmond in 1808. Madame de Genlis, who disliked her, says (*Mémoires*, vol. ii. pp. 30, 31) that she was deeply pitted with the small-pox, and that "elle avoit l'air le plus dédaigneux et le plus impertinent qu'on ait jamais osé porter dans le monde."

[1] The Duc de Choiseul (1719–1785) was Minister of Foreign Affairs, and afterwards War Minister and Naval Minister, to Louis XV. during the ascendency of Madame de Pompadour. He was disgraced in 1770, when Madame du Barri became the royal favourite.

[2] Madame du Deffand describes a small party at the Neckers', where she met the Emperor Joseph II. and Gibbon.

now going (nine o'clock) to the King's Library, where I shall stay till twelve. As soon as I am dressed I set out to dine with the Duke de Nivernois,[1] shall go from thence to the French Comedy into the Princess de Beauvau's *loge grillée*,[2] and am not quite determined whether I shall sup at Madame du Deffand's, Madame Necker's, or the Sardinian Embassadress's.[3] Once more Adieu. Do not be fond of shewing my letter; the playful effusions of friendship would be construed by strangers as gross vanity.

I embrace My lady and Bambine. I shall with chearfulness execute any of her commissions.

[1] Louis Jules Mancini, Duc de Nivernois (1716–1798), was ambassador in England from 1762 to 1763. In that capacity he had given Gibbon introductions to leaders of Parisian society during his first visit to the capital.

[2] Marie Sylvie de Rohan-Chabot married, as her first husband, the Marquis de Chermont d'Amboise. Left a widow in 1761, she married in 1764, as his second wife, the Maréchal de Beauvau, fourth son of the Prince de Craon (died 1793), and was, therefore, stepmother of his daughter the Princesse de Poix. She and her husband belonged to the Liberal party, who supported the Duc de Choiseul and opposed the ascendency of Madame du Barry. For this reason she was nicknamed "la mère des Machabées." The Princesse de Beauvau, one of the most charming women of her time, wrote an *Eloge* of her husband. She died in 1807. Her own character is sketched in the *Hommage à la mémoire de Madame la princesse de Beauvau* of Madame de Luynes. "Elle étoit, a mon avis, la femme la plus distinguée de la société, par l'esprit, le ton, les manières, et l'air franc et ouvert qui lui étoit particulier" (Madame de Genlis, *Mémoires*, vol. i. p. 357).

[3] Count de Viry, the Sardinian ambassador, as Baron de la Perrière, was formerly Sardinian ambassador in England. There he married Miss Harriet Speed, a niece of Lady Cobham, and one of the heroines of Gray's *Long Story* who were sent from Lady Cobham's house to rid the country of the "wicked imp they call a poet." "My old friend Miss Speed," writes Gray to Wharton in 1761, "has done a very foolish thing; she has married the Baron de la Perrière, son to the Sardinian Minister, the Count de Viry. He is about twenty-eight years old (ten years younger than herself), but looks nearer forty." In September, 1777, Viry was recalled from Paris, and disgraced, because, as was alleged, his wife had been bribed by Lord Stormont to betray the diplomatic secrets of the court of Turin. Another account is given in Lescure's *Correspondance Secrète sur Louis XVI., Marie Antoinette, etc.*: "M. le Comte de Viry, ambassadeur de Sardaigne, est rappelé à Turin. On croit qu'il y a de la disgrace" (vol. i. p. 74). A secret treaty was signed early in 1777 between Austria, France, Spain, and Sardinia against England, and the secretary of the Comte de Viry "a vendu une copie du traité à milord Stormont" (*ibid.*, vol. i. p. 82). See also, for a third account, *Dutensiana* (Londres, 1806), pp. 216–219.

319.

To his Stepmother.

Hotel de Modene, Paris, July 24th, 1777.

DEAR MADAM,

If ever my negligence could be excused by your good natured friendship, it would be from the consideration of my present circumstances, and I am sure that your regard for me is of so pure and disinterested a character that you had much rather I should be happy without hearing from me, than if you received by every post a regular succession of complaints. Happily indeed have I passed two short months since my arrival at Paris, and every circumstance of my journey has more than answered my most sanguine expectations. My connection with the Neckers, who every day acquire more power and deserve more respect, first opened the door to me, and perhaps the reputation of a popular writer has contributed a little to enlarge the entrance. I pass my time in the society of men of letters, people of fashion, the higher ranks of *the clergy*, and the foreign Ministers, and except when I wish to steal a few moments' privacy, it seldom happens to me to dine or sup at my hotel. The vacancies of my time are filled by the public libraries in the morning, and in the afternoon by the spectacles, and as part of my acquaintance begin to disperse themselves in the environs of Paris, I have contrived, though in a most unfavourable season, to make several very pleasant excursions. Such is the general idea of my life, in which I have made many acquaintance and formed some more intimate connections, from all of which I receive civilities, amusement and information. Details would be infinite, and must be reserved for your fireside at Bath ; but I cannot forbear saying something of two or three persons whom you know.

First then you will expect to hear of Mrs. Mallet. Mr. Scott had desired me to take charge of a letter, and I delivered it to her own fair hands the second day after my arrival. She received me with a shriek of joy and a close embrace, and we sat down to talk of old and new subjects. I found her exactly the same talkative, positive, passionate, conceited creature as we knew her twenty years ago. She raved with her usual indiscretion and fury of Gods, Kings and Ministers, the perfections of her favourites and the vice or folly of every person she disliked. Unfortunately she had applied to Mr. Necker for some favour, and had not been received in a manner suitable to her importance. Her resentment was expressed in such indecent language, that after repeated but ineffectual hints of my intimate connection with the person she was abusing, I was obliged to shorten my visit with a firm resolution of never returning.

Your favourite, the Duke of Richmond, has fallen in my way infinitely more than he ever did in England, and I do assure you that the air of Paris agrees perfectly well with him. He is easy, attentive and cheerful, pays his court to young and to old women, and is extremely popular and even fashionable in the Society of Paris. I have likewise seen a great deal of the Sardinian Ambassadress whom you have formerly known with Lady Cobham, under the name of Miss Speed. She keeps a very hospitable house, and has acquired the manners of the country without losing the sentiments of her own. Adieu, Dear Madam. If you can think of any commissions for me I will execute them with care and pleasure, though I have no occasion for any memento to make me often think of you.

Sir Stanier will be so good as to forward anything to me.

320.

To J. B. Holroyd, Esq.

Paris, August the 11th, 1777.

*Well, and who is the Culprit now?—Thus far I had written in the pride of my heart, and fully determined to inflict an Epistle upon you, even before I received any answer to my former; I was very near a Bull. But this forward half line lay ten days barren and inactive, till its generative powers were excited by the missive which I received yesterday.

What a wretched piece of work do we seem to be making of it in America! The greatest force which any European power ever ventured to transport into that Continent, is not strong enough even to attack the enemy; the Naval strength of Great Britain is not sufficient to prevent the Americans (they have almost lost the appellation of Rebels) from receiving every assistance that they wanted; and in the mean time you are obliged to call out the Militia to defend your own coasts against

their privateers.[1] You possibly may expect from me some account
of the designs and policy of the French Court, but I chuse to
decline that task for two reasons : 1st Because you may find them
laid open in every newspaper ; and 2ndly. Because I live too much
with their Courtiers and Ministers to know anything about them.
I shall only say that I am not under any immediate apprehensions
of a War with France. It is much more pleasant as well as
profitable to view in safety the raging of the tempest, occasionally
to pick up some pieces of the Wreck, and to improve their trade,
their agriculture, and their finances, while the two countries are
lento collisa duello. Far from taking any step to put a speedy
end to this astonishing dispute, I should not be surprized if next
summer they were to lend their cordial assistance to England, as
to the weaker party. As to my personal engagement with the
D[uke] of R[ichmond], I recollect a very few slight skirmishes,
but nothing that deserves the name of a general engagement.
The extravagance of some disputants, both French and English,
who have espoused the cause of America, sometimes inspires me
with an extraordinary vigour. Upon the whole, I find it much
easier to defend the justice than the policy of our Measures ; but
there are certain cases, where whatever is repugnant to sound
policy ceases to be just.

The more I see of Paris, the more I like it.[2] The regular

[1] " American privateers," writes Walpole, July 17, 1777, " infest our
coasts; they keep Scotland in alarms, and even the harbour of Dublin
has been newly strengthened with cannon." On August 7 the crew of a
privateer landed at Penzance and plundered several farmers of their live
stock. It was in the following year, April, 1778, that Paul Jones first harried
the English and Scottish coasts.

[2] In *The Private Correspondence of David Garrick* (vol. ii, pp. 255, 256)
is printed a letter from Gibbon to Garrick, written from the " Hôtel de
Molène, rue Jacob, Fauxbourg St. Germain," at Paris, and dated August
14th, 1777. Gibbon begins by thanking Garrick for a kindly mention of
his name. " It is pleasant to find one's-self mentioned with friendship by
those whom posterity will mention with admiration. Foreign nations are
a kind of posterity, and among them you already reap the full reward of
your fame." " You have reason," he continues, " to envy me, for I can truly
declare that I reckon the three months which I have now passed in Paris
among the most agreeable of my life. My connection with a house, before
which the proudest of the Gallic nobles bow the knee, my familiar acquaintance with the language, and a natural propensity to be pleased with the
people and their manners, have introduced me into very good company; and,
different in that respect from the traveller Twiss, I have sometimes been

course of the Society in which I live is easy, polite, and entertaining ; and almost every day is marked by the acquisition of some new acquaintance, who is worth cultivating, or who, at least, is worth remembering. To the great admiration of the French, I regularly dine and regularly sup, drink a dish of strong Coffee after each meal, and find my stomach a citizen of the World. The Spectacles, (particularly the Italian, and above all the French Comedie) which are open the whole summer, afford me an agreeable relaxation from Company ; and to shew you that I frequent them from taste only, and not from idleness, I have not yet seen the Colisee, the Vauxhall, the Boulevards, or any of those places of entertainment which constitute Paris to most of our Countrymen. Occasional trips to dine or sup in some of the thousand Country-houses which are scattered round the environs of Paris, serve to vary the scene. In the mean while the summer insensibly glides away, and the fatal month of October approaches, when I must exchange the house of Madame Necker for the house of Commons.

I regret that I could not chuse the winter, instead of the Summer, for this excursion : I should have found many valuable persons, and should have preserved others whom I have lost as I began to know them. The Duke de Choiseul, who deserves

invited to the same houses a second time. If besides these advantages your partiality should ascribe any others to your friend, I am not proud enough entirely to disclaim them. I propose to stay at Paris about two months longer, to hook in (if possible) a little of the Fontainebleau voyage, and to return to England a few days before the meeting of Parliament, where I suppose we shall have some warm scenes. You cannot surely be satisfied with the beginning, or rather no beginning, of the American campaign, which seems to elevate the enemies as much as it must humble the friends of Great Britain.

" At this time of year, the society of the Turk's-head" (in Gerrard Street, where the Literary Club met) " can no longer be addressed as a corporate body, and most of the individual members are probably dispersed; Adam Smith in Scotland; Burke in the shades of Beaconsfield; Fox, the Lord or the devil knows where, &c., &c. Be so good as to salute in my name those friends who may fall in your way. Assure Sir Joshua, in particular, that I have not lost my relish for *manly* conversation and the society of the brown table. I hope Colman has made a successful campaign. May I beg to be remembered to Mrs. Garrick ? By this time she has probably discovered the philosopher's stone; she has long possessed a much more valuable secret,— that of gaining the hearts of all who have the happiness of knowing her.

" I am, dear Sir, most affectionately yours,

" E. GIBBON."

attention both for himself, and for keeping the best house in Paris, passes seven months of the year in Touraine ; and though I have been tempted, I consider with horror a journey of sixty leagues into the Country. The Princess of Beauvau* (by the bye Beauveau, fine calf, is an orthography worthy of a Sussex farmer), the Princess of Beauvau, *who is a most superior Woman, has been absent above six weeks, and does not return till the 24th of this month. A large body of Recruits will be assembled by the Fontainbleau journey ; but in order [to] have a thorough knowledge of this splendid Country, I ought to stay till the month of January ; and if I could be sure that opposition would be as tranquil as they were last year—

I think your life has been as animated, or, at least, as tumultuous, and I envy you Lady Payne,[1] and Lady Dy, &c. much more than either the Primate,[2] or the Chief Justice.[3] Let not the generous breast of Mylady be torn by the black serpents of envy. She still possesses the first place in the sentiments of her slave : but the adventure of the fan was a mere accident, owing to Lord Carmarthen. Adieu. I think you may be satisfied. I say nothing of my terrestrial affairs.* Good works are unnecessary, as I can only hope to be justified by my faith in the merit of my Redeemer John Holroyd.

321.

To his Stepmother.

Hotel de Modene à Paris, September the 1st, 1777.

DEAR MADAM,

I must either write ten lines or twenty pages, and you will easily judge which I shall prefer. The various sets of company with whom I pass my time are so completely strangers

---

[1] Françoise Lambertine, daughter of Baron Kolbel, married, September 1, 1767, "a rich West Indian," Ralph Payne (knighted in 1771), a son of the Governor of St. Christopher's, and himself Governor of the Leeward Islands (1771-75). Sir Ralph represented various constituencies in Parliament from 1768 to 1799, and, with his wife, was prominent in London society. He was created Viscount Lavington. Lady Lavington survived her husband, who died in 1807, as Governor of Antigua and a bankrupt.

[2] The Hon. Fred. Cornwallis, Archbishop of Canterbury.

[3] Lord Mansfield, Chief Justice of the Court of King's Bench.

to you, that before I mentioned any person of my acquaintance I must introduce them with a very tedious yet imperfect account of their birth, parentage, education and character. After all, what would principally interest the curiosity of friendship may be dispatched in two words—*I am well and happy.* Mr. Necker has not yet discovered any signs of jealousy, and I supped last night between two Arch-bishops who, I am persuaded, have not the least intention of solliciting a *lettre de cachet* to send me to the Bastille. I only regret that it was not possible to choose another season of the Year for my Expedition. In summer Paris is very far from being a desert like London, and I have the daily pleasure of living in a very numerous and agreeable Society, yet as there is always a considerable emigration into the provinces I am sensible that many valuable acquisitions have escaped me. In the first or second week of October the Court goes to Fontainebleau, and as it is never so full and splendid as in that place, I propose passing a few days there. I must afterwards allow myself a little space to thank and embrace my Paris friends : and shall return by the first of November to a very different scene of things in London.

You will not be sorry to hear that, though I love the French from inclination and gratitude, I have by no means lost my relish for my native country. I have spent so much time in gay dissipation, that I must set myself in good earnest to work ; but you may depend on my desire to steal a few days of the Christmas recess for a Bath expedition. I fancy we shall have a busy Session of Parliament, and unless Howe has very decisive success we shall be less unanimous for the design of conquering America. I will not trouble you with politics, but will only venture to assure you, that, in the present moment, the French Counsels are seriously inclined for peace. My friend Necker (for I now esteem and love him on his own account) is declared principal minister of the finances, and though he has great obstacles to contend with, his knowledge, his firmness, and the purity of his intentions ought to make us wish for his disgrace.

I am, Dear Madam,

Ever yours,

E. GIBBON.

322.

To J. B. Holroyd, Esq.

Bentinck Street, Nov. 4th, 1777.

I arrived last night, laid up with the gout in both my feet. I suffer like one of the first Martyrs, and possibly have provoked my punishment as much. If you wish to see me, come to town before the meeting. I hope my Lady will not laugh.

323.

To his Stepmother.

Bentinck Street, November 4th, 1777.

DEAR MADAM,

When you hear the reason, you will excuse my telling you in two words that I arrived last night. I am laid up with a very painful fit of the gout in both my feet. I came over from Calais with some difficulty; yet I rejoice that I am in my own library, and three hundred miles nearer *you* than I was a week ago. I think it cannot last long.

I am, Dear Madam,
Most truly,
E. G.

324.

To J. B. Holroyd, Esq.

[Bentinck Street,] Saturday, [November, 1777.]

Had you four horns as well as four eyes and four hands, I should still maintain that you are the most unreasonable Monster in the Creation. My pain is lively, my weakness excessive, the season cold, and only twelve days remain to the meeting. Far from thinking of trips into the Country, I shall be well satisfied if I am on my legs the 20th, in the medical sense of the word. At present I am a Corpse, carried about by four arms which do not belong to me. Yet I try to smile : I salute the hen and chickens. Adieu. Writing is really painful.

325.

To his Stepmother.

Bentinck Street, Nov. 13th, 1777.

DEAR MADAM,

As my disorder was perfectly free from danger, I thought it needless to repeat *every* post, that I was in a good deal of pain : but I seize the first opportunity of telling you that the enemy appears to be raising the siege, and that he makes a regular and gradual retreat : the pain is gone, the swellings diminished, my strength is returning ; this morning for the first time I enjoyed the luxury of using crutches, and I aspire to the superior luxury of throwing them away. In the course of my recovery you may depend on my prudence. Adieu ! dear Madam, I sincerely envy your loving couple : but be pleased to remember that *they* are only twenty.

I am

Most truly yours,

E. GIBBON.

326.

To J. B. Holroyd, Esq.

Friday, November 14th, 1777.

I do not like this disorder on your eyes: and when I consider your temperance and activity, I cannot understand why any spring of the machine should ever be deranged. With regard to myself, the Gout has behaved in a very honourable manner ; after a compleat conquest, and after making me feel his power for some days, the generous Enemy has disdained to abuse his victory or torment any longer an unresisting victim. He has already ceased to torture the lower extremities of your humble servant ; the swelling is so amazingly diminished that they are no longer above twice their ordinary size. Yesterday I moved about the room with the laborious majesty of crutches ; to-day I have exchanged them for a stick ; and by the beginning of next week, I hope, with due precaution, to take the air and to inure myself for the interesting representation of Thursday. How cursedly unlucky ! I wanted to see you both ; a thousand things to say and to hear, and every scheme of that kind broke to pieces. If you are not able to come to Bentinck Street, I must contrive to steal three or four vacant days during the Session, and run down to Sheffield. The town fills, and I begin to have numerous levers and couchers, more properly the latter. We are still in expectation, but in the mean while we believe (I mean Ministers) that the news of Howe's victory and the taking of Philadelphia are true.[1] Adieu.

327.

To J. B. Holroyd, Esq.

Saturday Night, 30th November, 1777.

Your feaver, rhumatism, confinement and the use of a strange hand make me very uneasy. If I thought I could be of any use, I would in spite of Parliament[2] immediately run down ; but I do most heartily advise, beg and intreat that, as soon as you are fit for motion, you would come to town, and consult about the best method of putting an end to this tedious complaint. For myself, I have almost forgot the gout. No alteration as to the public : Much debating, little hopes and no news. Your Inn business I will skilfully manage either in person, or by my faithful Minister, and you may depend on the earliest account of it. You asked about the Highlander : he is still in his mountains. I fear Mrs. G. expects me at Christmas, but I *really* prefer Sheffield, and will try to defer the Bath journey till Easter. Do not however reckon upon my success. Adieu.

328.

To J. B. Holroyd, Esq.

Monday night, December, 1777.

*I congratulate your noble firmness, as I suppose it must arise from the knowledge of some hidden resources which will enable us to open the next Campaign with new armies of 50 or 60,000 men. But I believe you will find yourself obliged to carry on this glorious War almost alone. It would be idle to dispute any

---

[1] General (afterwards Sir William) Howe defeated Washington at Brandy-wine on September 11, 1777, and took possession of Philadelphia on the 27th.

[2] The Parliamentary session opened on November 18.

more about politics, as we shall so soon have an opportunity of a personal combat. Your journey gives me some hopes that you have not entirely lost your reason.* Your bed shall be ready. Caplin has conversed with your Tenant, but his demands were certainly excuses, as he has given over all thoughts of the enterprize: possibly you may be more successful. Adieu. I do not embrace My lady, as she seems to decline accompanying you. Her conduct is shameful and unnatural.

329.

To J. B. Holroyd, Esq.

December 2nd, 1777.

By the enclosed you will see that America is not *yet* Conquered. Opposition are very lively,[1] and though in the house we keep our numbers, there seems to be a universal desire of peace even on the most humble conditions. Are you still fierce?

330.

To J. B. Holroyd, Esq.

House of Commons, Thursday, Dec. 4th, 1777.

Dreadful news indeed. You will see them partly in the papers, and we have not yet any particulars. An English army of nearly 10,000 men laid down their arms and surrendered prisoners of war, on condition of being sent to England and of never serving against America.[2] They had fought bravely, and were three days

---

[1] Lord Chatham, in the House of Lords, moved an amendment to the address, that the army should be recalled, the late Acts rescinded, and every effort used to reunite with America. The same motion was made in the Lower House. But the amendments were rejected by large majorities in both Houses. On December 2, Fox moved for a committee of the whole House to inquire into the state of the nation, including the expenses and resources of the nation, the loss of men, the state of trade, the present situation of the war, our foreign relations, and the progress made by the Commissioners in bringing about peace. Lord North accepted the motion, and the committee sat for the first time on February 2, 1778. Parliament was adjourned from December 11, 1777, to January 20, 1778.

[2] General Burgoyne, after capturing Ticonderoga, pushed forwards towards the Hudson River, intending to invade the United States from the side of Canada. His supplies began to fail. The American forces gathered at

without eating. Burgoyne is said to have received three wounds. General Frazer[1] with 2000 men, killed. Colonel Ackland[2] likewise killed. A general cry for peace. Adieu. We have constant late days.

331.

To his Stepmother.

Bentinck Street, December 16th, 1777.

DEAR MADAM,

I flatter myself that my long silence must have given you great satisfaction. You recollect that while I was under the tyranny of the Gout, I showed myself tolerably exact in sending you intelligence of my situation and improvement. From my silence therefore, you must have concluded that I am, now, as indeed I am, restored to public health, and once more engaged in the busy as well as idle dissipations of this great town. I jumped at once from a sick chair into the warmest debates, which I ever remember in my short parliamentary life. They have constantly been fed by our miserable news from America, and the Session after the holydays will be taken up by Committees on the state of the Nation, Enquiries into the conduct of Ministers and Generals, &c., which will at least serve to increase the public ferment. What will be the resolutions of our Governors I know not, but I shall scarcely give my consent to exhaust still further the finest country in the World in the prosecution of a war from whence no reasonable man entertains any hopes of success. It is better to be humbled than ruined.

Half my acquaintance, Lady Dy, Lady Payne, the Solicitor General,[3] &c., are running down to Bath for the holydays. Had

Saratoga, and after several days' fighting, surrounded the British troops, whose strength was reduced to three thousand five hundred men. On October 17, 1777, Burgoyne surrendered to General Gates.

[1] Simon Fraser had served under Wolfe at Quebec with the Fraser Highlanders, and commanded a brigade during Burgoyne's campaign. Mortally wounded on October 7, 1777, he died October 8, and was buried, under a heavy fire, in one of the British redoubts.

[2] John Dyke Acland, best known by the devotion of his wife, Lady Harriet, was wounded and taken prisoner at Saratoga (October 9). He died in October, 1778, from a cold caught at a duel on Bampton Down, in Devonshire. He was then M.P. for Callington, in Cornwall.

[3] Wedderburn.

I no other inducement I should certainly escape from the crowd, and employ that short interval of quiet in resuming my long neglected History. Those literary occupations however I would gladly sacrifice to the pleasure of seeing you, but I apprehend I shall be engaged to prefer the Sussex to the Bath journey by some reasons which I will fairly submit to your judgement.

1. Holroyd, as you must have learned from his sister, is in a very indifferent state of health. His eyes are affected, his spirits are low, he has been disappointed of other company and he entreats me in a very moving way not to abandon him on this occasion.

2. I wish to pass some time with him on my own account, and to consult him with regard to Buriton, which is, I fear, very indifferently treated by my tenant Winton.

3. I expect, without knowing the day, a French lady of quality, Madame de Genlis,[1] to whom I have very great obligations. Whenever she informs me of her arrival in London, I must instantly fly (on the wings of mere friendship) to receive and attend her : now it would be somewhat vexatious to travel an hundred and ten miles, and to be called away the next day. Determine for me, my dear friend, you have every tye upon me of promise, of gratitude and of inclination. If you are not perfectly satisfied with my positive engagement to pass the Easter recess with you, depend upon it I will break through every difficulty that detains me at present. I have a thousand things to hear and say, and I know that you will enjoy, what I could not perhaps say to others without incurring the censure of vanity. If the Goulds are at Bath, I beg to be remembered to them. I see your friend Mr. Melmoth[2] has published a translation of

---

[1] Stephanie Félicité Ducrest de St. Aubin (1746–1830) married, in 1761, the Comte de Genlis. Through her aunt, who was secretly married to the Duc d'Orléans, she became "gouvernante" to the duke's children by his first wife, a daughter of the Duc de Penthièvre,—Madame Adelaide, Louis Philippe, and three others. She was a voluminous and versatile writer. Her *Adèle et Théodore* was published in 1782. "J'eus une liaison assez intime," she says in her *Mémoires* (ii. 351), "avec M. Gibbon, auteur de la chute de l'empire romain, ouvrage anglais que nos philosophes ont beaucoup loué, parce qu'il renferme de très mauvais principes, mais qui est, à tous égards, un mauvais ouvrage, très diffus, sans vues nouvelles, et fort ennuyeux."

[2] William Melmoth (1710–1799), "Pliny" Melmoth, as Miss Burney says he was nicknamed, was an author, commissioner of bankrupts, and a good classical scholar. In 1753 he published Cicero's *Ad Familiares;* in 1773, the *De Senectute;* and in 1777, the work referred to in the letter, *De Amicitia.*

another piece of Tully: on a subject which you understand at least as well as either of them. It will be worth your reading, for the treatise is valuable and he is an elegant as well as faithful translator.

I am, Dear Madam,

Ever yours,

E. G.

332.

To his Stepmother.

Sheffield Place, December the 26th, 1777.

DEAR MADAM,

I arrived yesterday at Sheffield Place to enjoy the beauties of the country, which are displayed in a profusion of rain, snow and fogs. I think I never saw the Landlady in better looks, health or spirits. With regard to the Landlord, the principal object of this cold expedition, his eyes are somewhat better, and I flatter myself that the conversation of a friend will contribute to enliven him. I admire your fortitude, but I assure you that my despondency was not occasioned by the misfortunes of Bourgoyne and his gallant troops. It is founded on a very full consideration of a plan, the difficulties of which present themselves every day in a stronger light. What must be the means or the instruments to extricate us from this melancholy situation still remain to be considered with the most serious and dispassionate attention.

I am, dear Madam,

Most truly yours,

E. G.

The family desired to be remembered to you.

333.

To J. B. Holroyd, Esq.

Saturday night, 1778.

The Gib is *half* astounded and *half* disappointed at the Revolution. He thinks (at present) that he shall appear in person at S. P. either Monday or Tuesday next to require an explanation. London is a dead calm and delicious solitude. If some people would send for the Eliza all might be forgiven. Adieu.

E. G.

Tuesday next will certainly produce his presence or an Epistle.

334.

To J. B. Holroyd, Esq.

1778.

For *Tuesday* read *Wednesday*. I think I may reach S. P. by dinner time; but do not wait. My Lady's inconstancy disarranges me much, but it is far better that I should be disarranged, than that her gentle spirit should be grieved. Yet, why cannot she live quiet, and solitary at Brighton?

335.

To J. B. Holroyd, Esq.

Monday night, January 26th, 1778.

What can I say? No news or business. Lord G.'s great misfortune has procured him a respite.[1] We shall soon have something of a brush to-morrow on his first appearance.[2] Lord N. seems in high spirits: we hear no more of conciliatory propositions. I received to-day a huge pacquet, a Theological answer written by a *mere* Irish parson.[3] Adieu. I embrace my Lady, and wait with impatience. I hope your eyes are not the worse for a little fatigue. I love a dutiful aunt. It is now half an hour past nine. I have been hard at work since dinner, and am just setting out for Lady Payne's Assembly, with half the fine Bs at it, after which, I shall perhaps sup with Charles, &c., at Almack's.

---

[1] Lady George Germain (formerly Miss Diana Sambrooke) died of the measles, January 15, 1778.

[2] Gibbon voted against the Government (February 2) for Fox's motion, "That no more of the Old Corps be sent out of the Kingdom." The motion was rejected by 259 to 165.

[3] Probably, *A Reply to the Reasonings of Mr. Gibbon*, etc., by Smyth Loftus, M.A., Vicar of Coolock. Dublin, 1778.

336.

To J. B. Holroyd, Esq.

Feb. 23, 1778.

*You do not readily believe in præternatural miscarriages of letters ; nor I neither. Listen, however, to a plain and honest narrative. This morning after breakfast, as I was ruminating on *your* silence, Thomas, my new footman, with confusion in his looks, and stammering on his tongue, produced a letter reasonably soiled, which he was to have brought me the day of his arrival, and which had lain forgotten from that time in his pocket. To shorten as much as possible the continuance, I immediately inquired, whether any method of conveyance could be devised more expeditious than the post, and was fortunately informed of your Coachman's intentions.* In your observations on the opposition, &c., I desiderate somewhat of your usual moderation. I suppose you imagine that a reluctant effort of reason is at once to efface past errors, to command present acquiescence, and to inspire future confidence.

*You probably know the heads of the plan ; an act of parliament, to declare that we never *had* any intention of taxing America : another act, to empower the Crown to name commissioners, authorized to suspend hostilities by sea and land, as well as all obnoxious acts ; and, in short, to grant every thing, except Independence.¹ Opposition, after expressing their

¹ The Bills proposed by Lord North were : (1) " For removing all doubts and apprehensions concerning taxation by the Parliament of Great Britain in any of the Colonies ; " (2) for the appointment of five commissioners to treat with the Colonies. By the first the claim of taxation was abandoned. A third Bill, for the express repeal of the Massachusetts Charter Act, was also supported by the Government. The three Bills received the royal assent on March 11, 1778. Walpole, writing to Mason, February 18th, 1778, says, "You perhaps, who have all ecclesiastical history at your finger-ends, may recollect something approaching to the transaction of *yesterday, the 17th of February*, a day of confession and humiliation that will be remembered as long as the name of England exists. Yesterday, Feb. 17th, did the whole Administration, by the mouth of their spokesman, Lord North, no, no, not resign ; on the contrary, try to keep their places by a full and ample confession of all their faults, and by a still more extraordinary act, by doing full justice both to America and to the Opposition,—by allowing that the former are no cowards nor conquerable,—that they are no Rebels, for the new Commissioners are to treat with the Congress or anybody, and, by

doubts whether the lance of Achilles could cure the wound which it had inflicted, could not refuse their assent to the principles of conduct which they themselves had always recommended. Yet you must acknowledge, that in a business of this magnitude there may arise several important questions, which, without a spirit of faction, will deserve to be debated: whether Parliament ought not to name the Commissioners? whether it would not be better to repeal the obnoxious acts ourselves? I do not find that the World, that is, a few people whom I happen to converse with, are much inclined to praise Lord N.'s ductility of temper. In the service of next Friday,[1] you will, however, take notice of the injunction given by the Liturgy: "And all the people shall say after the *minister*, Turn us again, O Lord, and so shall we be turned."

While we considered whether we shall negociate, I fear the French have been more diligent. It is positively asserted, both in private and in Parliament, and not contradicted by the Ministers, that on the 5th of this month a treaty of Commerce[2] (which naturally leads to a war) was signed at Paris with the Independent States of America. What do you think of the tardyness of administration? Yet there still remains a hope that England may obtain the preference. The two greatest countries in Europe are fairly running a race for the favour of America;* and I fear our *Lord* has more bottom than foot. Adieu. Am not I very good? but you must not expect a repetition of such exalted Virtue. Your Eyes? I embrace My lady, &c. I have written to all: no answers. I will see Cadell.

I send you a parcel, that, as a member, I have just received.

337.

To his Stepmother.

February 28th, 1778.

DEAR MADAM,

You will think me the most impudent fellow alive: but I am really angry with *you* for not being angry with *me* on asking pardon by effects, *i.e.* the cancelling all offensive acts, and by acknowledging the independence of the 13 provinces, not *verbally* yet *virtually*."

[1] A solemn fast was kept on February 27, 1778.

[2] The treaty was also one of friendship. It was signed on February 6.

account of my long and shameful silence. We have had (I do not mean it as any excuse) the hardest work I have yet known in Parliament. You see that we are reduced to the humiliation of sueing for peace. I much fear we shall have the additional humiliation of being rejected. In the meantime a French war is every day a probable event. I have not yet seen so very black a prospect. How have you passed the winter, in health, in spirits and in amusements? For my own part I am perfectly free from the gout, and notwithstanding the hurry of business and pleasure, I steal some moments for the Roman Empire. I can assure you with the utmost truth that I look forward to Easter with such impatience I *will* write oftener.

I am, Dear Madam,

Most truly yours,

E. GIBBON.

338.

To J. B. Holroyd, Esq.

Almack's, Saturday night, [February, 28th, 1778].

I like your method of proceeding, and I am much relieved to find that after fighting so long with savage monsters, we have at length found a being not totally devoid of sense and feeling. Yet I fear the events which may happen before Michaelmas. With regard to your other schemes, I think them *hard:* but the times are so: and I must submit. Hugonin shall not be omitted.

*As to politics, we should easily fill pages, and therefore had better be silent. You are mistaken in supposing that the Bills are opposed; some particular objections have been stated, and in the *only* division I voted with Government.[1] * Yet I still repeat that in my opinion, Lord N. does not deserve pardon for the past, applause for the present, or confidence for the future. You are, however, perfectly in the right in supposing that the most able men in the Kingdom will go to America, as a proof

---

[1] Mr. Powys moved a clause to repeal expressly and by name the Massachusetts Charter Act. This clause was opposed by Lord North, and on a division was rejected. Lord North, however, supported a separate Bill for the attainment of the same object.

of which I must inform you that Lord Carlisle is certainly appointed first Commissioner.[1]

Caplin enquired about the groom. He is a drunken, worthless fellow. Adieu. I hear the bell. My Lady is a most aimiable Creature. I rejoice in her snugness.

339.

To J. B. Holroyd, Esq.

February 29th, 1778.

DEAR H.,

Last night I found a note from Gosling that he wished to see me this morning. In my reply I submitted it to him whether it might not be better to wait a few days for our common friend. He answered me that he had no objection to talking about Bucks when you came, but that my Estates being intermixed with Lord Verney's seemed to him an *insuperable* objection, So that I fear there is an end of our sheet Anchor. I wait impatiently for your arrival. What is to be done? Aubrey whispered me last night, that Sir Sampson Gideon[2] was purchasing everything in that part of Bucks. Excuse my writing meerly about my own affairs, I am really out of spirits. Monday night, if there is anything stirring, I will give you a letter of news. Adieu.

340.

To his Stepmother.

March 7th, 1778.

E. G. is alive, well, but much ashamed of himself. In two or three posts he intends to write somewhat more at large. The H.'s will come to him next Sunday.

341.

To J. B. Holroyd, Esq.

Saturday Night, ten o'clock, 14th March, 1778.

Enclosed I send Arthur Young's character. You will judge, but I should not be satisfied with it. Your polite footman

---

[1] The five commissioners, appointed on April 13, 1778, were Lord Carlisle, Lord Howe, Sir W. Howe, William Eden (afterwards Lord Auckland), and George Johnstone (ex-governor of Florida).

[2] M.P. for Cambridgeshire.

shall be sought for. This moment Beauclerck, Lord Ossory,
Sheridan, Garrick, Burke, Charles Fox and Lord Cambden (no
bad set you will perhaps say) have left me. It is reported that
M. de Noailles has signified to Lord Weymouth the treaty of
France with the united and independent States of America, with
the cold modification that it is not of a hostile character.[1] We
have had hard but dull work. Monday will be a great day,—the
enquiry and the orders given by Lord George for the Canada
expedition.[2]

Dr. Robertson is in town. I shall dine with him to-morrow.
Adieu. I have given directions for La Fontaine's fables.

342.

To J. B. Holroyd, Esq.

Almack's, Saturday night, [March 21st, 1778].

*As business thickens, and you may expect me to write
sometimes, I shall lay down one rule ; totally to avoid political
argument, conjecture, lamentation, declamation, &c., which would
fill pages, not to say volumes ; and to confine myself to short,
authentic pieces of intelligence, for which I may be able to afford
moments and lines. Hear then—The French ambassador[3] went
off yesterday morning, not without some slight expressions of
ill humour from John Bull. Lord Stormont[4] is probably arrived

---

[1] The note formally announcing the Treaty of Commerce and Friendship
between France and the United States, was delivered to Lord Weymouth on
March 13, 1778. "On Saturday," writes Sir Gilbert Elliot to Lord Malmesbury, March 20, 1778, "all the French in London were sent to the opera,
plays, clubs, coffee-houses, ale-houses, and spill-houses, to publish the intelligence, which they did with all their natural impertinence."

[2] On March 19 Fox moved three resolutions : (1) that the Canadian
expedition was ill concerted, (2) that it was impossible it should succeed,
(3) that no sufficient instructions to co-operate had been sent to General
Howe. The resolutions were lost by 164 to 44. Fox then tore up the
paper on which he had written the fourth resolution, a censure on Lord
G. Germain.

[3] M. de Noailles left London at six in the morning to avoid insults. He
and his wife were pelted by the mob as they passed through Canterbury ;
but the Government ordered a salute to be fired in his honour as he left
Dover.

[4] David, seventh Viscount Stormont, who succeeded (1793) his uncle
as second Earl of Mansfield, was at this time ambassador at Paris. In
October, 1779, he was made one of the Secretaries of State. He was afterwards
President of the Council under Pitt. He died in 1796.

to-day. No *immediate* declaration expected on our side. A Report (but vague) of an action in the bay, between La Motte Piquet and Digby ; the former has five ships and three frigates, with three large store ships under convoy ; the latter has eleven ships of the line. If the Frenchman should sail to the mouth of the Delawar, he may possibly be followed and shut up. When Franklin was received at Versailles,[1] Deane went in the same character to Vienna, and Arthur Lee to Madrid. Notwithstanding the reports of an action in Silesia, they subside ;[2] and I have seen a letter from Eliot at Berlin of the tenth instant, without any mention of actual hostilities, and even speaking of the impending War as not absolutely inevitable. Last Tuesday the first payment of the loan £600,000 was certainly made ; and as it would otherwise be forfeited, it is a security for the remainder. I have not yet got the intelligence you want, about former prices of stock in Critical times. These are surely such. *Dixi. Vale.* Send me some good news from Bucks ; In spite of the War, I must sell. We want you in town. Frazer is impatient : but if you come without Mylady, every door will be shut.

313.

To J. B. Holroyd, Esq.

Bentinck Street, March 30th, 1778.

The short delay of my answer, you must ascribe on this occasion not to lazyness but to despondency. What a melancholy prospect of public and private affairs. Excuse my saying anything of the former (indeed there is nothing fixed or certain), I am too much engaged by the latter.

What can I say about Fleet Street ? The remittance they mention from Hugonin, with another of a halfe year's rent from

---

[1] The three American deputies were presented to Louis XVI. on March 21, 1778, by M. de Vergennes, the Minister for Foreign Affairs.

[2] On December 30, 1777, the Elector of Bavaria died. With him was extinguished the male line of his house. Austria took the opportunity of occupying portions of Lower Bavaria, and the King of Prussia supported against her the claims of the elector's general heir and nearest male relation, the Elector Palatine of the Rhine. War began in July, 1778 ; but before negotiations were abandoned, Bohemia, Silesia, and Saxony were occupied by the forces of Austria and Prussia.

Bucks, will diminish though not discharge the accruing interest
which indeed must always gain upon me, unless I could live
upon air. With regard to the principal, as they are in very
affluent circumstances, I did flatter myself that instead of urging
me to dispose of the dearest part of my property, the new River
share, at the most unfavourable season, they would have allowed
me the chance of another summer to dispose of Lenborough
which would ease me at once of principal and interest. I beg
you would make that earnest request to them, I mean to Clive,
and manage it with all the zeal and dexterity of your friendship.
Let me know, whether I can second it by any steps of politeness
and propriety. I had rather write than speak.—Should they
still be inflexible and rigourously exact the immediate sale of the
New River, give me your advice and assistance. Your *advice*
whether in honour and prudence, I may dispute the point and
gain time by the dilatory and expensive resources of the law.
If I ought to yield, your *advice* as to the best method of Sale.
Sure they cannot insist on my selling it much below its value.
I fear you must run to town for two or three days. With regard
to Buriton. Hugonin has sent me a letter for you unsealed.
I have kept it some days, without having courage to read it.
Is it very bad? I was much satisfied with your conference
with Winton, but can we depend on his promises? What
security have we between this time and Michaelmas for the
intentions of an attorney and the conduct of a madman.

Adieu, my dear friend. My disposition is chearful, my wants
not extravagant, my amusements within my own power, and
connected with the amusement of many. But the scene before
me is horrid, unless you can shew me some ray of comfort. Adieu.

Mrs. G. presses me; I think of going about the 15th of next
month and staying a fortnight at Bath.—I have got a Groom
for you, but am not yet assured of his Character.

344.

To his Stepmother.

Bentinck Street, April the 6th, 1778.

DEAR MADAM,

As we can talk more in an hour than we can write in
a day, I shall only say that I propose myself the pleasure (and

a great pleasure it will really be) of waiting on you on Thursday evening the 16th inst. If anything should delay my journey two or three days later you shall certainly have timely notice.

I am, Dear Madam,

Most truly yours,

E. GIBBON.

345.

To J. B. Holroyd, Esq.

Bath, 25th April, 1778.

Here I am in close attendance of my Mama, who is better in health, spirits, &c., than I have known her for some years. Had I attempted an Easter excuse it would have been very ill received. I am vastly complaisant, *amuse* myself in Routes and private parties and play shilling Whist with the most edifying resignation. The Rooms and public places I seldom frequent, and claim some merit from a sacrifice which in reality is none at all. The Paynes are here, and I contrive to see something of them. Are you acquainted with Dr. Delacour? In truth there is much kindness in that Jew and much good sense likewise; he gives as good dinners as the superstition of the females of his family will permit, and has a proper contempt for all that a reasonable man ought to despise. I had destined and shall give a *full* fortnight to Bath, and shall return to town the latter end of next week, but as the day is not irrevocably fixed, I do not wish you to suppose me in Bentinck Street before the Monday or Tuesday of the week following. I understand with satisfaction that the Majorina[1] intends to visit the great City. I have much to say and much for you to do. You may expect to be favoured with some military instructions. Adieu. I hear from Zara[2] a very tolerable account; but my proposed visit was respectfully declined. I like the new house very well.

[1] Mr. Holroyd served as major in the Sussex Militia under the Duke of Richmond. The militia was in 1778 organized as a permanent force for the defence of the country.

[2] Miss Sarah Holroyd.

346.

To his Stepmother.

House of Commons, Wednesday Evening, ten o'clock, '78.

I arrived safe in town, and, after finding most *excellent* reasons for two or three days' delay, when I had really very little to do, I now snatch a moment from a very warm debate to tell you that I found the H.'s in town. The Major's eyes are not better, but otherwise his spirits are good, and he becomes his military character. Remember me to the sister. I sympathise in her distress at my departure. Assure all my friends, Christians but more especially Jews,[1] of my own grateful sense of their kindness, but let me say with the utmost truth, that the part of my Bath visit which I recollect with the greatest pleasure, are the moments which I spent with you and with you alone.

The H.'s (I had almost forgot) salute you. They stay till Monday.

I am, Dear Madam,
Ever yours,
E. GIBBON.

347.

To J. B. Holroyd, Esq.

Saturday Night, 16th May, 1778.

Before I received your letter, I had just heard from Bath ! I can say nothing on the occasion. Nature and Reason have their respective provinces ; and I ought not to hope either to prevent the effect of the former, or to hasten that of the latter.

I shall expect you about the end of next week, but it will be highly proper that you should give me some days either in going or returning. Notwithstanding all you may see in the Papers, you may be assured that there is not any certain intelligence of D'Estaing's squadron having passed the straights of Gibraltar.[2] A Court of Enquiry is ordered and will sit on Monday on

---

[1] Apparently an allusion to Dr. Delacour, Mrs. Gibbon's doctor at Bath.

[2] The Comte d'Estaing with the French fleet left Toulon on April 13, and arrived off Sandy Hook on July 8, 1778.

Bourgoyne;[1] but I am not certain whether he has been forbid Court. I attended Ireland with great alacrity;[2] but the business seems to be compromised. I do not exactly know in what manner or whether the Constituents on either side will be satisfied. The Inscriptions shall be considered. Adieu.

348.

To J. B. Holroyd, Esq.

Almack's, Friday, [June 12th, 1778].

R. Way's letter gave me that sort of satisfaction which one may receive from a good Physician, who, after a careful examination, pronounces your case incurable. But no more of that— I take up the pen, as I suppose by this time you begin to swear at my silence. Yet litterally (a bull) I have not a word to say. Since D'Estaing's fleet has passed through the Gut (I leave you to guess where it must have got out there) it has been totally forgot, and the most wonderful lethargy and oblivion, of war and peace, of Europe and of America, seems to prevail. Lord C[hatham]'s funeral was meanly attended,[3] and Government ingeniously contrived to secure the double odium of suffering the thing to be done, and of doing it with an ill grace. The chief conversation at Almack's is about tents, drill-Serjeants, subdivisions, firings, &c. and I am revered as an old Veteran. Adieu. When do you return? If it suits your evolutions, aunt Kitty and myself meditate a Sussex journey next week. I embrace Mylady.

---

[1] General Burgoyne was refused admission to the royal presence. The Court of Enquiry was not held, as the general officers reported that they could not take cognizance of the conduct of an officer who was a prisoner on parole to the Congress. A court-martial was on similar grounds refused. Finally, on May 26, a motion was proposed for a committee of the whole House on Saratoga, which gave Burgoyne the opportunity of defending himself. The motion was opposed by the Government and rejected.

[2] Counsel and evidence were heard on Irish trade; but, by a compromise between the opponents and supporters of the projected bills for the relaxation of the commercial code, and in consequence of the opposition of English traders, Lord North's projected concessions were reduced to the smallest proportions and carried without divisions.

[3] Lord Chatham died May 11, 1778. The body lay in state in the Painted Chamber on the 7th and 8th of June, and was buried in Westminster Abbey on June 9. Parliament was adjourned from June 3 to November 26.

349.

To his Stepmother.

London, June the 12th, 1778.

DEAR MADAM,

Inclosed I send you what you desire. Believe me I have not forgotten, how much, in every sense of the word, I feel myself indebted to you. I wish that all of us in publick and private affairs had a less melancholy prospect before us; but courage and Philosophy must assist us. Letters (I do not mean Epistles) are in every state of life an amusement, a comfort or a resource.

The Holroyds are still in Yorkshire, I expect them in about ten days; and have some thoughts with Mrs. Porten of making them a visit next month. I carry down a good deal of lumber, and shall work reasonably hard.

I am, Dear Madam,

Ever yours,

E. G..

350.

To J. B. Holroyd, Esq.

Monday Evening, 29th June, 1778.

With a trembling hand I inclose a letter from Hugonin in its pure and original state—*Return it with proper directions;* or answer it yourself, which would please me much better.—I suppose there are complaints of my silence. I am however by four and twenty hours less guilty than I seem——

I expect an account of your meeting and motions; and some encouragement might attract Aunt Kitty and myself in the course of next week——

What think you of Keppel?[1] We are pleased on the whole: yet some Ministers such as Ld. Mansfield and Wedd[erburn] affect to talk doubtfully about a War. Adieu.

[1] Admiral Keppel, who left Portsmouth early in June, fell in with two French frigates, the *Licorne* and the *Belle Poule,* on June 17, 1778. The first he captured, the second was driven ashore. This action began the war with France.

351.

To J. B. Holroyd, Esq.

Wednesday evening, July 1st, 1778.

Your plan of operations is clear and distinct ; yet, notwithstanding your zeal, and the ideas of Ducal discipline, I think you will be more and longer at S. P. than you imagine. However, I am disposed to advance my journey as much as possible. I want to see you ; my martial ardour makes me look to Coxheath,[1] necessity obliges me to think of Beriton, and I feel something of a very new inclination to taste the sweets of the Country. Aunt Kitty shares the same sentiments ; but various obstacles will not allow us to be with you before Saturday, or perhaps Sunday evening ; I say *evening*, as we mean to take the cool part of the day, and shall probably arrive after Supper. Keppel's return [2] has occasioned infinite and inexpressible consternation, which gradually changes into discontent against him. He is ordered out again with three or four large ships as reinforcement ; 2 of 90, 2 of 74, and the 50th Regiment as marines. In the mean time the French, with a superior fleet, are masters of the sea ; and our homeward-bound East and West India trade is in the most imminent danger. Adieu.

352.

To J. B. Holroyd, Esq.

Bentinck-street, July 7th, 1778.

*Expect me——when you see me ; and do not regulate your active motions by my uncertainty. Saturday is impossible. The most probable days are, Tuesday or Friday next. I live not

---

[1] Summer encampments were established at Salisbury, Bury St. Edmunds, Winchester, Warley, and Coxheath in Kent. At the last-named place were stationed the 1st battalion of Royals, 2nd, 14th, 18th, 59th, and 65th Regiments of Foot, the 1st Regiment of Dragoons, and twelve regiments of militia. Coxheath was visited by the king and queen in November, 1778.

[2] Papers captured on a French frigate showed Keppel that a fleet superior to his own lay in Brest harbour. He therefore retired to Portsmouth. "And now," writes Walpole, July 4, 1778, "Mr. Keppel is returned, we learn that the East and West Indian fleets, worth four millions, are at stake, and the French frigates are abroad in pursuit of them."

unpleasantly, in a round of Ministerial dinners ; but I am impatient to see my white house at Brighton. I cannot find that Sheffield really has the same attractions for you. Lord North, as a mark of his gratitude, observed the other day, that your Regiment would make a very good figure in North Carolina. Adieu. I wrote two lines to Mitchel lest he should think me dead.*

353.

To J. B. Holroyd, Esq.

Thursday Evening, July, 1778.

O Lord ! O Lord !—I am quite tired of Parliament and sigh for the country. I talked of being at S. P. next Saturday ; I shall think myself fortunate if I reach it that day sen'night. Many bills are sent to the Lords, the forms of their house will consume some days, the Ch.'s temper[1] may destroy more time, and the prorogation will not take place before the 17th. In the meanwhile every body is going out of town, and the danger of not getting a house will probably force me to stay, and, after all, this place is not uncomfortable. Adieu. No news. I embrace my Lady.

Adam talks of accompanying me.

354.

To his Stepmother.

Sheffield Place, July 19th, 1778.
DEAR MADAM,

Miss Holroyd who arrived here yesterday informed me that you were certain that I could not be at S. P. as you had not received any letter from me. This throws me under some difficulty, since I must either set aside your authority or distrust the evidence of my senses, which seems to tell me that I am actually at the seat of J. B. Holroyd, Major of the Sussex Militia. The aforesaid Major returned last night from his first sally, which had lasted a whole week, during which time he left me Governor of the Castle and Guardian of his fair Spouse. I acquitted myself

[1] Lord Thurlow became Lord Chancellor in June, 1778, succeeding Earl Bathurst.

of this great office in so satisfactory a manner, that I am again invested with the same dignity, as the doughty Champion moves forward to-morrow morng. on a second Expedition. The Regiment is divided between Lewes and Brighthelmstone, and the Duke of Richmond, &c., works like a Serjeant, a clerk, and a pack-horse. Their motions are irregular and uncertain, and if the Major's quarters should be fixed at Brighthelmstone, My Lady and Sarah will immediately march, and I shall follow the Camp, as it is a place where I can enjoy studious leisure in the midst of dissipation. If they are ordered to any other place I shall return to my retirement in Bentinck Street, as at all events the 'decline and fall' must proceed, which it does at present with tolerable vigour.

Mr. Eliot, whom I saw in London as frequently as I could, wished (if Plymouth and Port Eliot were not burnt down) to receive me in September to meet Lord and Lady Ely. I expressed gratitude but declined a promise. I should think the journey a very proper one ; but I must own that I neither like the expence nor the loss of time. Yet those would sound like paltry excuses after a six months' expedition to Paris.

The Major with our three Ladies, Abigail Holroyd, Sarah Holroyd, and Catherine Porten, present their compliments to you. We often talk you over, and this morning at Breakfast his honour scolded sister for not bringing you with her ; though on calmer reflection we all thought it better that your second visit to S. P. should be deferred to a more peaceable and settled time, such as it may be hoped next year will prove. Sarah looks well ; several passages yesterday of the House, &c., affected her a good deal, but I think she will grow easy and cheerful.

I am, dear Madam,
Most entirely yours,
E. GIBBON.

355.

To J. B. Holroyd, Esq.

Wednesday morn, Brighton, 1778.

You feed me royally and almost superabundantly.—Though Brighton is truly the most agreeable place in the World, I am desirous to spend three or four days at S. P., and am not unwilling to meet Lord M[ansfield]. But are you sure of a visit from that venerable Sage ? You have a formidable Rival, Gerard Hamilton,[1] who has invited me to dinner for Sunday to meet the Chief Justice whom I wish to conciliate, which your instructions will enable me to do ; but at all events if you miss the Judge you will have the Historian the beginning of next week. Adieu.

356.

To J. B. Holroyd, Esq.

Brighthelmstone, 1778, Wednesday morning, ten o'clock.

I have carefully perused the Report, and think you have considerably improved both the matter and arrangement. The remarks were as clear to my conception as they could be made without the help of maps, and the general language is easy and spirited: to render the style minutely elegant and correct would be a tedious and at the same time a very useless task. As it now stands the work must do credit to the author and may do service to the country. Adieu. We meet at Lord G.'s.

Friday morning ; I suspect that my Lady will decline the party.

357.

To J. B. Holroyd, Esq.

Tuesday evening, Sept. 20th, 1778.

The French fleet is stole back into Brest without meeting Keppel ;[2] the Fox frigate taken same day, the Captain (Windsor, Lord Plymouth's brother) killed ; others add, but doubtful, that we have lost a fleet of twelve merchantmen. There is good reason to believe that we have taken the Iphigenie, a French frigate. You

---

[1] William Gerard Hamilton ("Single-Speech"), at this time M.P. for Wareham, lived in Upper Brook Street. He was a brilliant talker. If Dr. Johnson was unwilling to part with a friend, he accompanied him down the first pair of stairs in hope of his return. With Hamilton he went as far as the street door. "Single-Speech Hamilton has been giving suppers to all the fine ladies," writes Storer to George Selwyn, April, 1779.

[2] After a fruitless search for the French fleet, Admiral Keppel returned to Portsmouth. "Admiral Keppel is very unlucky in having missed them, for they had not above twenty-five ships" (H. Walpole, October 8, 1778).

were hardly aware of the depth of ditch you tumbled into, and I have sent you the enclosed that you may see Hugonin's despair and reproaches. The money must be found by Saturday sennight ; and the only step I could think of was a fair polite letter to Clive, who came to town yesterday, stating the business, representing the probable near conclusion of the New River sale, and begging leave to draw upon him. I know his good nature, but if he hesitates you must intercede, or help me some way or other. Adieu. How do you advance in les Travaux de Mars? The advertisements have been inserted ; Hugonin has received one application from a Mr. Butler, Camberwell, Surry, to make enquiries.

358.

To J. B. Holroyd, Esq.

Saturday night, September 25th, 1778.

No news from the fleets ; we are so tired of waiting, that our impatience seems gradually to subside into a careless and supine indifference. We sometimes yawn, and ask, just by way of conversation, Whether Spain will joyn ?[1] I believe you may depend on the truth, not the sincerity, of an answer from their Court, that they will not support or acknowledge the independence of the Americans. But on the other hand, Magazines are forming, troops marching, in a style which threatens Gibraltar. Gib. is, however, a hard morsel ; 5000 effectives, and every article of defence in the most compleat state. We are certainly courting Russia. So much for the Republic.

I am strangely amazed and frightened about Buriton : as I had not the least suspicion of the approaching, nay impending demand of so large a sum. How could it amount to so much, and why did Hug. stipulate so near a day ? I have desired him to gain time or borrow money. They bite in the New River, and I am offered 7½, but Newton encourages me to hold out, and thinks I may get ¼ more, which is not to be despised in certain situations——

I have seen several servants, and like one who has lived with Mr. Milbank (Sir Ralph's eldest son), who desired his

[1] War was declared in June, 1779, between Great Britain and Spain.

brother to give him a very good character. On a quarrel
between him and the Swiss Valet de Chambre, both were dismissed, the one with honour, the other with ignominy. Something more in the Italian than the Swiss style had been designed
by the Valet de Chambre, but rejected by your Candidate ; yet,
as he was discharged, there is something not perfectly clear.
If you chuse it, you may write to Milbank, who is with his Militia
in the North : but send me the letter and I will forward it.
If without any farther ceremony you have a mind to try him
(I mean no harm), I can order him to quarters. I am satisfied
with his appearance, and he professes to understand what you
require. Adieu.

359.

To his Stepmother.

Bentinck Street, Sept. 29, 1778.

DEAR MADAM,

I think I grow worse and worse. I am sensible that you
are acquainted with my sentiments and my faults, and that you are
disposed to believe that the stream of my friendship is deep and
pure, though it flows *silently*, very silently indeed. Yet my conscience whispers in my ear that I ought not to abuse the confidence which you may with justice repose in me. My conscience,
likewise, informs me that as I made Sarah Holroyd the security
of my promise, she has a right to complain that she became in
some measure the accomplice of my quill. She has, I daresay,
given you a particular account of the way I spent the greatest
part of the summer ; how, in the absence of the Major, I was left
Governor of the Castle and Director of the fair females who
inhabited it, and how I behaved myself in the execution of that
important office.

I went over to Brighthelmstone, but found not much encouragement to settle, the Company was not agreeable, few of
my acquaintance except the Paynes and Beauclercs ; more difficulty and more expence than I expected in settling myself with
any degree of comfort, and great inconvenience in being so long
absent and distant from my tools. Upon mature consideration
I resolved to relinquish that plan and to retire for some time
to my rural retirement in Bentinck Street : the neighbourhood is

not very populous at present, nor am I much interrupted by visits
or invitations ; yet I find as much society as I want for relaxation ;
and motives enough to engage me to take more exercise of a
morning than I should anywhere else ; besides the occasional
Holydays which I sometimes allow myself to various friends who
dwell in villas adjacent to town. In the meantime I have the
pleasure to see the sheets of my second volume insensibly acquire
a respectable or at least a decent size ; and though my progress
gives me a clearer view of the difficulties of my undertaking, yet
I find that gentle and steady diligence will in time carry me
through it : and I still look forwards to the spring of 1780 with
hope though not with confidence.

Before I left Sussex I visited, in company with the Major,
Cox Heath Camp : where I was received as a Father of the Old
Hampshire Militia, though few officers now remain in it, with
whom I have any connection. Jolliffe was returned to his
station of Ensign, with the *Cave* of General Keppel, who would
not however see him or forgive his extravagant behaviour, which
was much worse than anything you saw in the Papers. I am
afraid you were malicious enough to rejoyce at his absurdity.
While I was in the Camp, I felt my military ardour revive ; but
I soon recollected that, notwithstanding the pleasure of passing
a part of the winter on the Down, my library is upon the whole
as agreeable as a Tent, and Almack's as comfortable as a Suttling
booth. What odd animals we are ! I have deferred from post
to post, I am afraid to think how long, a very easy and pleasing
occupation, which has now made me pass a very agreeable half
hour in conversing with the dearest and most valued of my
friends ; who will derive some pleasure from the conversation.
I positively believe I shall reform.——

Before I conclude I must add three words on a subject which
is not so entertaining. You know how little I love to talk about
business, but I ought not to omit what you will probably hear
from some other quarter. My tenant Winton had done *some*
mischief to Buriton ; he threatened to injure it much more deeply,
and I was persuaded by my Council to get rid of him, which I
have just accomplished. Till the farm is let again, which I hope
will be soon, Hugonin has undertaken the temporary administration. I have lost considerably in taking leave of my old
tenant, and fear my loss in engaging a new one will be still more

considerable, and I can ill support these extraordinary demands. Yet I should consider that, if all external circumstances were as smooth and satisfactory as the temper of my own mind, my condition would be too fortunate.

I am, Dear Madam,

Most truly yours,

E. GIBBON.

I cannot go to Port Eliot this autumn, but shall try to propose an accomodation to Madam of meeting at Bath.

360.

To J. B. Holroyd, Esq.

October 27th, 1778.

You are certainly right in your suspicions that I shall not again visit S. P. before the meeting of Parliament. I am perfectly well in wind and limb, but the time is so short, the derangement is so considerable, and I am so deeply engaged not in London but at Rome, that I can only regret and hope.—There is not any account of the French fleets in Europe or America. Sir Charles Hardy[1] is sailed chiefly to protect and convoy the East Indiamen now in Ireland. I know not what to say of your countrymen, nor have I any notion of the plan (if any) of Government. The A. G.[2] came to town last night, and I am just going to sup with him. I expect a full account of the Regiment. Adieu. Denmark[3] (inseparably connected with Russia) has behaved very handsomely in restoring two Victuallers and ordering the captor, one of Paul Jones's Squad, to quit the Harbour of Bergen. This is sure and important.

[1] Sir Charles Hardy, already over sixty years of age, as governor of Greenwich Hospital had retired from active service. He had not been to sea for many years, till he was now placed in command of the fleet.

[2] Wedderburn succeeded Thurlow as Attorney-General when the latter was made Chancellor (June, 1778).

[3] "The court of Denmark, when they gave orders for the release of our ships taken by Paul Jones, were very explicit in their declaration in our favour against America" (C. Townshend to G. Selwyn, October, 1778).

361.

To J. B. Holroyd, Esq.

Tuesday night, November, 1778.

*You sometimes complain that I do not send you early news ; but you will now be satisfied with receiving a full and true account of all the parliamentary transactions of *next* Thursday. In town we think it an excellent piece of humour (the author is one Tickell) [1] Burke and C. Fox are pleased with their own Speaches, but serious Patriots groan that such things should be turned to farce. We seem to have a chance of an additional Dutch War : [2] you may depend upon its being a very important business, from which we cannot extricate ourselves without either loss or shame. *Hugonin was in town last week about his eyes. I have given him full powers, and still hope that he will agree with Hearsay on tolerable terms. Say something to Beauclerc and Lady Dy. I pity them both, and I pity you too, for at this time of year Brighton must be a damned place. I shall now be immersed in politics. Society and study and hardly a moment be ever found for Epistolary Commerce. Therefore be patient. *Vale.*

[1] Parliament met November 26, 1778. Gibbon refers to a pamphlet called *Anticipation*, which appeared the day before the opening of Parliament, and gave a summary of what would be said by the chief speakers. The author was Richard Tickell, grandson of Addison's contemporary, and a dependent of Lord North.

[2] The outbreak of a war with Holland at this time seemed probable. At the close of 1778 a number of petitions were presented from Dutch merchants to their High Mightinesses the States-General of the United Provinces, protesting against the right of search for contraband of war which was exercised by the British ships. In September, 1780, an American packet was captured, on board of which was Mr. Laurens, President of the Congress. A box of letters, which he threw overboard, floated, and was found to contain a draft treaty between the United States and Holland, and various letters from the "patriotic party," showing that Amsterdam at least wished for alliance as early as August, 1778. A memorial reciting these letters was delivered to the States-General in November, 1780, but no answer was returned. In December the British ambassador was recalled, and the Dutch ambassador left London, December 30, 1780.

362.

To J. B. Holroyd, Esq.

Wednesday Night, December, 1778.

Good news from India, a revolution has happened among the Marattas ; the French interest is destroyed, Ragged boy [1] (or some such name) is placed on the throne of that warlike people, and we have now more to hope than to fear from them. According to the Orders sent out in the Spring it is not impossible that Pondicherry,[2] feebly garrisoned, may at this moment be in our hands. The West Indies [3] are tolerably secure by the land and sea force which went from New York, and our operations in that part of the World may be offensive. In several places the Sky clears a little, and if we could be secure from Spain we may promise ourselves some success. You see I am less desponding than usual. But we must depend more on arms and policy than upon idle threats, which may do mischief and cannot do good. We must likewise remove a Secretary of State so universally odious to the Army,[4] &c.

Our Admirals [5] have had a spar or two, and Sir H. P.,

[1] Ragoba or Ragonaut Ráo, an exiled Peshwah of Poonah, was supported by the English, and an expedition to reinstate him was despatched by Warren Hastings in the autumn of 1778.

[2] Pondicherry had already (October 17, 1778) surrendered to Sir Hector Munro, and Chandernagore had also fallen.

[3] Sir Henry Clinton, who had succeeded Sir W. Howe in the chief command in America, had sent five thousand men in October, 1778, to the Indies with Commodore Hotham.

[4] William Wildman, second Viscount Barrington (1717-1793), was succeeded as Secretary at War by Charles Jenkinson in December, 1778.

[5] The Admirals referred to were Sir Hugh Palliser and Admiral Keppel, both members of Parliament; Keppel being a Whig and opposed to Lord North, Palliser a staunch supporter of the Government. The dispute arose over the battle of Ushant. The English fleet under Keppel had met the French fleet under Count d'Orvilliers off Ushant on July 27, 1778. An indecisive engagement was fought. Keppel signalled to Sir Hugh Palliser to come up and renew the battle next morning; but Sir Hugh, whose own ship had suffered severely, was unable to do so. The French retired on the 29th to Brest, and Keppel to Portsmouth. Palliser made charges against Keppel, which led to a court-martial on the latter. The charges against him were pronounced to be malicious and ill founded, and his conduct was declared to have been that of a brave and experienced officer. Similar

finding that K. did not apply for a Court Martial upon him, has this day lodged a charge of six Articles in the Admiralty and has made himself the accuser of his Commander.

363.

To J. B. Holroyd, Esq.

Saturday Night, 1778.

Our East India Revolution has not succeeded, and Raggaboy is no longer at the head of the Marattas.[1] In the West we much fear that D'Estaing is run down to the Islands.[2] Black again. The Court Martial would furnish volumes of opinions, but not a line of fact. In private life you see we open a lively campaign of Marchionesses, Countesses, &c.—I am sorry to find that you are so firm about Buriton. Consider the bad condition and growing expence which I am so little able to bear. The option of the term of years cannot perhaps be admitted, but otherwise I am much disposed to accept the hard conditions of Hearsay, and almost fear that our delay will lose the opportunity. I am transported to hear that you will call at Buriton in your way to Bath, and only beg, that considering my situation rather than your spirit, you will not leave the place without deciding the business. How long do you stay at Bath? Shall you not return through town? I want to see you about some things which I cannot trust to paper. Adieu.

364.

To J. B. Holroyd, Esq.

Almack's, Wednesday evening, 1778.

*I delayed writing, not so much through indolence as because I expected every post to hear from you. The supplies are raised. Clive and Gosling allow me (very handsomely) to draw for the

charges were made by the Comte d'Orvilliers against the Duc de Chartres, who commanded the Blue Squadron of the French fleet, and did not obey the signal of his superior officer.

[1] The expedition against Poonah failed. The English were surrounded, and the Convention of Wargaum restored to the Mahrattas all territory acquired since 1756, and Ragoba was given up to Scindiah (January, 1779).

[2] In November, 1778, the French fleet sailed for the West Indies. But St. Lucia was successfully defended by the British forces.

Barbarian tribute, and the New river (unless one of the Suitors retreats) is gone, alas gone for ever, for £7550. The state of Buriton is uncertain, incomprehensible, tremendous. It would be endless to send you the folios of Hugonin, but I have enclosed you one of his most pictoresque Epistles, on which you may meditate. Few offers; one, promising enough, came from a Gentleman at Camberwell: I detected him, with masterly skill and diligence, to be only an Attorney's clerk, without money, credit, or experience. I wrote as yet in vain to Sir John Shelley, about Hearsay; perhaps you might get intelligence about him.

I much fear that the Buriton expedition is necessary; but it has occurred to me, that if I *met*, instead of *accompanying* you, it would save me a journey of above one hundred miles. That reflection led to another of a very impudent nature; *viz.* that if I did not accompany you, I certainly could be of no use to you or myself on the spot; that I had much rather, while you examined the premises, pass the time in a horse-pond; and that I had still rather pass it in my library with the ' decline and fall.' But that would be an effort of friendship worthy of Theseus or Perithous : modern times would hardly credit, much less imitate, such exalted virtue.

No news from America, yet there are people, large ones too, who talk of conquering it next summer with the help of 20,000 Russians. I fancy you are better satisfied with private than public War. The Lisbon Packet in coming home met about forty of our privateers. Adieu. I hardly know whether I direct right to you, but I think S. P. the surest.*

365.

To his Stepmother.

Bentinck Street, Jan. 7th, 1779.

DEAR MADAM,

You will pity rather than blame me when I tell you that all last week I have been a good deal indisposed. The changes of weather brought a severe cold, accompanied with some degree of fever. I was confined to my room several days, and the state of my spirits as well as that of my health would have rendered the effort of writing very painful to me. The effort would have been still more painful with regard to the subject of your two last letters. I feel your happiness so much connected with mine, that the account of your sentiments and situation must disturb the enjoyments and encrease the anxiety of my own life. I feel it the more deeply as I am sensible that it is not in my power to remove the two causes of your present uneasiness.

I know not how to offer advice, and I am incapable of giving any efficacious help. I have easily perceived in my successive visits to Bath that a dislike of the place, of public life, and of mixed Society was insensibly gaining ground in your mind : and as I know that our happiness must always depend on our opinions and habits, I never presumed to prescribe for the constitution of another. Business and pleasure, Society or no Society, town or country, have undoubtedly their respective merits, and every one must on those subjects think and judge and act for themselves. The gay hurry of Bath or the silent retirement of Mrs. Massey's in Essex may alike be enjoyed by the mind to which they are adapted, and the only advice which I could think of offering, would be, not to engage yourself rashly in a connection of which you might afterwards repent. I have always considered marriage as a very serious undertaking, and the agreement of any friends to live together in the same house is a sort of marriage. If they have passed several years in different modes of life, their manners, their opinions, their sentiments on almost every subject must have contracted a different colour, and every little circumstance of hours, &c., will prove the cause of mutual restraint or mutual dissatisfaction.

But I now find, what indeed I have sometimes feared, that your design of retiring from Bath is not entirely the effect of choice and inclination ; that a stronger power, the power of necessity or at least of prudence, urges you to take that resolution, and that in a word you find the place too expensive. You do not explicitly say what income would support your present establishment, and I am not so stupid or so ungrateful as not to feel the generous delicacy of your behaviour. If my own circumstances were affluent, the obligations and friendship of twenty years would instantly prompt me to gratify my own inclinations in the performance of sacred duty. I am not insensible that in my present situation, you have a substantial and even legal claim upon me to a very considerable amount, and while I feel the value of your tenderness on this occasion, I must lament that it is not in my power to attain even the humble though indispensable virtue of Justice.

Without recurring to any recollections which would be painful to us both, I may appeal to the anxious regard which you have always felt and expressed for my interest. You know the distressed embarrassed situation in which my affairs were left, and though I have always been directed by the advice of Mr. H., I have hitherto been disappointed in every attempt to extricate myself by the sale of Lenborough Estate. The prospect of public affairs and the universal want of money forces me at present to suspend every idea of a sale, and all credit is so compleatly dead, that in the most pressing exigency I should be at a loss how to borrow a thousand pounds. In the mean time I have been paying five per Cent. interest on a Estate which hardly produced three per Cent.; and in the very moment when I could the least afford it, the madness of my Buriton tenant has involved me in new scenes of vexation and expence. My desires have always been moderate and my domestic economy has been conducted with tolerable prudence. Yet my income has never been quite adequate to my expences, and those expences, unless I retired from Parliament—from London and from England— it would be impossible for me to retrench. When I look back I cannot find much to censure or regret in my own conduct, but when I look forwards, I am sometimes alarmed and perplexed. I should indeed find room to despond, if my spirits were not supported by the resources which I derive from my litterary character, and by the well grounded hopes which I build on the assistance of a tried and powerful friend.

I cannot on *this* head explain myself more particularly by letter, but I have the strongest reasons to believe that the year which we have just begun will not end without producing a material improvement in my situation. If you have not already taken any decisive steps about leaving Bath, I could wish that you would suspend them till I can have the pleasure of conversing with you in the Easter holidays. If you still persist in your design, why should you bury yourself at Mrs. Massey's? Some pleasant village retirement at a moderate distance from London, where I could frequently visit you, might be consistent with your plan of expence, and you might there find yourself at once delivered from the costly and tasteless vanities of a fashionable

life. Whatever resolution you adopt, let me hear from you soon,
and always believe me with the most unalterable affection,

Ever yours,

E. G.

I can say nothing of public affairs. Men of all parties—
Ministers themselves—think them bad enough; but I do assure
you that I have not any claims to the injurious epithet of 'a
Patriot.' The apprehension of a Dutch War, though it is now
blown over, was real and serious.

366.

To his Stepmother.

London, January the 26th, 1779.

DEAR MADAM,

As we are mutually convinced of each other's sentiments,
words, compliments, assurances would be as idle as they are
useless : yet it would be incumbent on me to employ them, if
they became either of us ; since I am so unfortunate as to be
reduced to those equivocal marks of regard, whilst I receive from
you the most solid and substantial proofs of that friendship and
real affection which I have invariably experienced above twenty
years.—You ask me why I should wish you to wait till Easter,
and you seem desirous of an explanation of the latter part of my
letter. It is for that very purpose of an explanation that I
desired that delay, as it includes a variety of circumstances which
I ought not to trust to paper or to the post. I can only say in
general that from the assistance of a very powerful friend I have
room to hope that I may soon be placed in an honourable and
advantageous post[1] either at home or abroad, which would enable

---

[1] Gibbon was on July 1, 1779, made a Lord Commissioner of Trade and
Plantations—a place which he retained until 1782, when the Board was
abolished, the work being transferred to the Secretaries of State. He had at
one time hoped to obtain the Secretaryship to the Embassy at Paris (see
Letter 476). The following lines were written on his acceptance of the
Commissionership by, it is said, Charles Fox :—

" King George, in a fright
Lest Gibbon should write
The story of England's disgrace,
Thought no way so sure,
His pen to secure,
As to give the historian a place.

me to satisfy my duty as well as inclination by making your residence at Bath easy and comfortable to you in the manner you yourself have calculated your expences. I am not of a sanguine temper, and I am very sensible that besides the usual grounds of doubt and distrust, there are many circumstances which it is impossible for me to explain, that may either forward or delay or entirely disappoint the most rational expectations. Last week things seemed to draw so very near a crisis that I suspended my letter in hopes of making it more satisfactory to you and to myself. At present they are rather thrown back, and for aught I know the present Session of Parliament may end in darkness and uncertainty. Yet, I think the chance is worth waiting for a few months, perhaps somewhat longer; the difference of your income and expence cannot be very important, and if you do not wish me to make a difficult effort, I cannot see any great mischief in your eating a little deeper into your principal. I am the more anxious that you should not hastily quit a place which upon the whole must suit you better than any other; not only because I hope it will not be necessary, but as I am sure in your indifferent state of health, the unpleasant removal would be attended with fatigue of body and anxiety of mind which might be very prejudicial to you.

I am much flattered by your approbation of my pamphlet.[1]

> " But the caution is vain,—
> 'Tis the curse of his reign
> That his projects should never succeed ;
> Though he wrote not a line,
> Yet a course of decline
> In the author's example we read.

> " His book well describes
> How corruption and bribes
> O'erthrew the great empire of Rome ;
> And his ratings declare
> A degeneracy there,
> Which his conduct exhibits at home."

[1] In 1778 appeared *An Examination of the Fifteenth and Sixteenth Chapters of Mr. Gibbon's History*, etc., by Henry Edward Davis, M.A., of Balliol College, Oxford. The author charged Gibbon with inaccuracy and plagiarism. He replied early in 1779 with his *Vindication of some Passages in the Fifteenth and Sixteenth Chapters of the History of the Decline and Fall of the Roman Empire*. Walpole calls it "the quintessence of argument, wit, temper, spirit, and consequently of victory."

It was a disagreeable but a necessary step, after which I take my
absolute and final leave of controversy.   My second volume
advances, and I hope will be finished within the *ensuing* year
(1780).   You were right as to the benefit I have derived from
the first ; under the pressure of various difficulties, it proved a
seasonable and useful friend ; but if it supported, it did not enrich
its author.   I did not send a copy of my vindication to Port
Eliot, nor indeed to any person except to yourself.   Eliot must
be in town in a fortnight to a very severe call of the House.
I have meditated a letter to him, or rather to Mrs. E., above
three months without success.

I am, Dear Madam,

Ever yours,

E. GIBBON.

367.

To J. B. Holroyd, Esq.

February 6th, 1779.

"You are quiet and peaceable, and do not bark, as usual, at my
silence.   To reward you, I would send you some news ; but we
are asleep ; no foreign intelligence, except the capture of a
frigate ; no certain account from the West Indies ; and a dissolution of parliament, which seems to have taken place since
Christmas.   In the papers you will see negociations, changes of
departments, &c. and I have *some* reason to believe, that those
reports are not entirely without foundation.   Portsmouth is no
longer an object of speculation ; the whole stream of all men, and
all parties, runs one way.   Sir Hugh is disgraced, ruined, &c. &c. ; [1]
and as an old wound has broke out again, they say he must have

<hr>

[1] The court-martial held at Portsmouth entirely acquitted Admiral
Keppel on February 11.   The news reached London that night.   It was
treated as a triumph for the Opposition.   Ladies appeared at the opera in
caps *à la Keppel*, and blue cockades bearing the Admiral's name were worn.
His "Head" became a favourite alehouse sign.   Houses were illuminated ;
guns discharged ; bells rung ; the windows of the houses of Sir H. Palliser,
Lord North, Lord G. Germain, and Lord Sandwich were broken.   Sir H.
Palliser resigned his seat for Scarborough as well as all his employments,
and asked for a court-martial, which acquitted him from any charge of
misconduct.   He underwent the operation to which Gibbon alludes.   "Here
are the exact, and all the words which the King said to him, the first time
he was at Court afterwards—'Sir Hugh, how does your leg do?'" (Warner
to Selwyn, May, 1779).

his leg cut off as soon as he has time. In a night or two we shall be in a blaze of illumination, from the zeal of Naval Heroes, Land Patriots, and Tallow-Chandlers ; the last are not the least sincere. I want to hear some details of your military and familiar proceedings. By your silence I suppose you admire Davis, and dislike my pamphlet ; yet such is the public folly, that we have a second Edition in the press ; the fashionable style of the Clergy, is to say they have not read it. If Maria does not take care, I shall write a much sharper invective against her, for *not* answering my Diabolical book. My lady carried it down, with a solemn promise that I should receive an *unassisted* French letter. Yet I embrace the little animal, as well as Mylady, and the *spes altera Romæ.* Adieu.

E. G.

There is a buz about a peace, and Spanish Mediation.*

368.

To J. B. Holroyd, Esq.

March 16th, 1779.

You use me very ill.—Will you never condescend to abuse, curse, damn me for not writing ? There is no bearing such treatment. Yet I have not anything particular to write except to acquaint you with the *certain* intelligence of the taking of Pondicherry, which arrived this day. You will soon hear the particulars, but the essential is that the French have not any place of arms in the East Indies. With regard to the West, there is a strong rumour of action in our favour : but at all events we are safe, and possibly successful. We have had and are like to have Parliamentary storms. There are no questions which my opposition friends think stronger, and which I think weaker than their Naval Operations.[1] I hardly know your opinion about them. I want to hear some account of your military state and progress, but much about my Lady, Maria, &c. &c., which interest me more nearly than the Grenadier or Light Infantry

---

[1] The Opposition used every effort to make political capital out of the dispute between Keppel and Palliser. Motions were proposed by them on December 11, 1778, for the trial of Sir Hugh Palliser; on February 19, 1779, for the dismissal of Sir H. Palliser from the Navy; March 3, for a censure on the Admiralty for sending out Admiral Keppel with too small a force; on April 19, for the removal of the Earl of Sandwich from the Admiralty.

Companies. I was obliged to you about your friendly hint from Bath. I had not been deficient, but from a sort of delicacy, I had satisfied myself with icorresponding with Mrs. Gould and Dr. Delacour, and desired that Mrs. G. might not be informed of it. However, since your letter she is in a less dangerous way, several letters have passed between us, and we are now come to a tolerable understanding. Do you recollect that you promised me a Visit of Inspection to my Aunt? She wrote to me some time ago, I promised an account, and by this time she may be grown impatient again.

E. G.

I expect you (without a blush) to write soon.

369.

To his Stepmother.

Bentinck Street, 21st March, 1779.

Dear Madam,

If your former letters made me uneasy, your last note, which I received yesterday after the hour of the post, made me quite unhappy for many reasons; but most of all because I found that you were so yourself. The delay in my answer which has given you so much pain, was not occasioned by any avocations of business, for there could be no business which interested me half so much; nor by any carelessness or forgetfulness, for I can say with truth that there has not been any hour in the day and very few in the night in which the idea was not uppermost in my mind. Much less did it arise from any degree of resentment at any part of your behaviour. I had expressed myself with some warmth, I wrote from my feelings, and I was apprehensive of some alteration in your sentiments towards me. Had I been cold and indifferent myself, I should probably have been more cautious and respectful.

Yet unless I totally forget the language of my letter, I did not, I could not, disapprove of your consulting your own happiness, and of calling on me after so long a respite to fulfil some part of the most equitable obligation. The cause of my delay was a strong, an unjustifiable repugnance to write on a subject so foreign to our ordinary conversations. I dreaded and I delayed too long so painful an effort. As I am now sensible

how uneasy that delay has made you, I have taken the shortest
method of sending, that of the coach. Forgive this seeming
inattention, and believe me when I say that the affectionate
regard, the tender solicitude which you express, have made an
essential part of the happiness, and will always contribute to the
consolation of my life.

I find that I must have stated rather too strongly the difficulties of my situation so as to alarm and terrify you, both on
your account and on my own. I will endeavour to represent
them more clearly. I have never been extravagant; nor have
I made as yet any *considerable* addition to the load of debt contracted by my father: but I have not been able to discharge it.
The unhappy accidents which retarded the sale of Lenborough,
have been attended, from the general hardships of the times,
with the most fatal consequences, as land cannot at present be
sold even on the most disadvantageous terms. In the course of
seven or eight years interest has been much higher than rent, my
Expences (notwithstanding the supply of some hundred pounds
from my book) have inevitably exceeded my income.

You are sensible from your own experience that any plan of
economy must be regulated by place and circumstances. As long
as I am in London and in Parliament, a house in Bentinck
Street, a coach, such a proportion of servants, clothes, living, &c.,
are almost necessaries. But they are only necessaries in that
situation, and I am not ignorant that a prudent man should
adapt his arrangements to his fortune. Other countries of a less
expensive cost, France, Switzerland, or perhaps Scotland, may
afford an humble Philosophical retreat to a man of letters, nor
should I suffer any accidental change of fortune, any fall in the
World to affect my spirits or ruffle my tranquility. I have more
than once balanced in my own mind the propriety, or indeed the
necessity of such a resolution. The reason which induces me to
suspend such an important and decisive measure arises from a
hope which I could only insinuate and which I can at present
only imperfectly explain. I can only mention that I am particularly connected with the present Attorney General, that he
solicited my friendship, and offered me his services; and that if
some arrangement should take place which would raise him to
a much higher station, I may depend on a seat at one of the
boards with an additional income of £1000 a year, which would

remove every difficulty and supply every want. Without building on a doubtful foundation, inclination and even prudence recommend that I should wait some time for the event of this hope : and my only request is that you would on your side suspend any resolution of leaving Bath for some months, perhaps for a year. The difference of the expence in a year would not exceed £100, which you may command whenever (with a few days' notice) you will draw upon me.

If my expectations should deceive me (and I am never sanguine) my party is taken. I feel with gratitude and confusion your kind offer of retiring for my sake : but independent of every other consideration, it is far more proper that the unpleasant circumstances of such a removal should fall on the person who has health and youth and spirits to support them. With regard to any further *security*, I should have imagined that in the ordinary course of credit, my Bond was a very good security to the amount of the sum : but I am ready to consent to any act which you may consider as conducive to your interest or happiness.—I much fear that the agitation of mind may have injured your health before its perfect recovery from your late accident, and if a single word which I have written has tended to produce that effect, I shall not easily forgive myself. Though I cannot bear the thought of your quitting Bath against your inclinations, I should imagine that in the summer months, the air of the country would be beneficial to you. Whether you choose Port Eliot, Sheffield, Essex or any other place, I will, if my company can be any pleasure or relief to you, lay aside every other occupation to accompany you.

I am, Dear Madam,

Most truly and affectionately yours,

E. GIBBON.

370.

To J. B. Holroyd, Esq.

Wednesday night, April, 1779.

I am glad you have exerted some diligence about Mrs. G.'s Estate, but I wish you could have prevented a letter which I have just received, and which like a true coward I send you unopened. I fear it contains sharp or dry reproach for my

neglect and silence. On this occasion you must step in to my
assistance and in a proper letter exculpate me, and take the *whole*
of the blame upon yourself. Whatever *you* do, you are always
entitled to her gratitude, and cannot be afraid of her displeasure.
No time should be lost, therefore return her Epistle with the
aforesaid ostensible letter. I do not go to Bath this Easter ; and
Mrs. Gibbon is now satisfied with my conduct and correspondence.
Some journey or arrangement to see her must be thought of in
the course of the summer, but at present it would be highly
inconvenient, our respite is little more than a week, and besides
the approaching hurry of Parliamentary business, of which there
is a large provision, I am now deeply and not unsuccessfully
engaged in the decline and fall ; and I *do not totally despair* of
bringing out the second Volume next Winter. So that upon the
whole (as you do not interfere either with History or Parliament)
I am ready to receive you when you please : but had much rather
you would bring My Lady with you, as I very much like that
sort of taste of Matrimonial life. I am not perfectly well. So—
Adieu.

E. G ibbon.

371.

To J. B. Holroyd, Esq.

Friday Evening, 1779.

When do you come to town ? You gave me hopes of a visit,
and I want to talk over things in general with you, before you
march to the extremities of the West, where the Sun goes to
sleep in the Sea. Mrs. Trevor told me your destination was
Exeter ;[1] and I suppose nothing but truth can proceed from a
pretty mouth. I have been, and am still very diligent ; and,
though it is a huge beast, (the Roman Empire,) yet, if I am not
mistaken, I see it move a little. You seem surprized that I
was able to get off Bath : very easily, the extreme shortness of
our Holydays was a fair excuse ; her recovery of health, spirits,
&c. made it less necessary, and she accepted my Apology, which
was however accompanied with an offer, if she chose it, in the
prettiest manner possible. A load of business in this house, (I
write from it,) will be the amusement of the Spring ; Motions,

---

[1] The Sussex Militia were ordered to Exeter.

Enquiries, taxes, &c. &c. We are now engaged in Lord Pigot's affair, brought on by a motion from the Admiral,[1] that the Attorney General should prosecute Mr. Stratton[2] and Council;[3] all the Masters, Charles, Burke, Wedderburne, are of the same side, for it; Lord North seems to make a feeble stand, for the pleasure of being in a Minority. The day is hot and dull; will be long: some curious Evidence; one Man who refused three Lacks of Rupees, (£37,500,) merely not to go to Council; our mouths watered at such Royal corruption; how pitiful is our Insular bribery! A letter from aunt Hester. Adieu.

372.

To his Stepmother.

House of Commons, April 16th, 1779.

DEAR MADAM,

We are now, after a very short recess, engaged in a great hurry of business, which will probably last a great while. I find however time, and a good deal of time (without fatiguing myself too much), for the occupation which after all is the pleasure, and I hope, the honour of my life. In your last letter you ask whether your remaining at Bath is necessary to my tranquility. I can answer that question in the clearest manner, and, while I answer it, I must feel with gratitude how kindly it is proposed. It *is* necessary for my happiness that you should not be *forced* to leave Bath by any difficulties which it would be my duty to remove: nor could I enjoy the comfort of any situation which was purchased at the expence of your ease and happiness. But if your retiring from Bath was the effect of your own inclination, it is impossible that I could be hurt at your leaving a place which I should never visit but on your account; and I should visit you with at least as much pleasure in a

---

[1] Admiral Pigot, M.P. for Bridgnorth, brother of Lord Pigot. See Letter 311.

[2] Mr. Stratton was a member of the Madras Council, by which Lord Pigot was arrested.

[3] The House resolved on an address to the Crown for the prosecution of Stratton and other members of the Council. The case was tried in the Court of King's Bench, before Lord Mansfield, Wedderburn being for the prosecution and Dunning for the defence. The jury convicted (December 20, 21), and on February 10, 1780, Messrs. Stratton, Brooke, Floyer, and Mackay were fined £1000 apiece.

country retirement as in that scene of (what has always appeared to me) very awkward gaiety. But surely it is better to suspend any decisive resolution for the present. I was happy to hear from General Frazer, a very favourable account of your health & spirits.

I am, Dear Madam,
Ever yours,
E. G.

373.

To Mrs. Holroyd.

April 30th, 1779.

You easily conceive my reasons for not answering your Epistle. The Major is with me as I believe ; I say—as I believe, because the House of Commons takes me up so entirely that we have scarcely seen each other. He is as usual hurried, flurried, taken up with innumerable business and wishing to be quiet. He looks better than I expected, but he complains of heat, and want of sleep, and I have persuaded him to consult Heberden.—What does your Ladyship mean by preferring the Regiment to Bentinck Street ? It is my intention before you march into the West, you should take a moderate taste of the amusements of the Civilized World. I am glad to hear a favourable account of the Infants : but am much at a loss to understand how Maria can so far forget her I. S. as to break her engagement of sending me a French letter. Yet I embrace her as well as her Mama. Adieu.

374.

To J. B. Holroyd, Esq.

Saturday night, May, 1779.

*Alas ! alas ! fourteen Ships of the line :[1] you understand by this time that you have not got a single long-boat. Ministry are more crestfallen than I ever knew them, with the last intelligence ; and I am sorry to say, that I see a smile of triumph

---

[1] In the daily papers of May 15, 1779, it was announced that " fourteen ships of the line " had sailed from Brest to attack Admiral Arbuthnot, who lay with a much smaller force at Torbay. Orders were sent to Portsmouth to fit out every available ship for his support.

on some opposition faces. Though the business of the West Indies may still produce something, I am much afraid that we shall [have] a campaign of immense expence, and little or no action. The most busy scene is at present in the House of C.; and we shall be involved, during a great [part] of next month, in tedious, fruitless, but, in my opinion, proper Enquiries.

You see how difficult it would be for me to visit Brighton ; and I fancy I must content myself with receiving you on your passage to Ireland. Indeed, I much want to have a *very serious* conversation with you. Another reason, which must in a great measure pin me to Bentinck-street, is the decline and fall. I have resolved to bring out the *suite* in the course of next year ; and, though I have been tolerably diligent, so much remains to be done, that I can hardly spare a single day from the Shop. I can guess but one reason which should prevent you from supposing that the picture of Leicester Fields was intended for Sheffield library ;[1] *viz.* my having told you some time ago that I was under a formal engagement to Mr. Walpole. Probably I should not have been in any great hurry to execute my promise, if Mr. Cadell had not strenuously urged the curiosity of [the] public, who may be willing to repay the exorbitant price of *fifty* Guineas. It is now finished, and my friends say, that, in every sense of the word, it is a good head. Next week it will be given to Hall the Engraver, and I promise you a first Impression. If I were a rich man you should have a similar picture. Adieu. I embrace my lady, and infants.[*]

E. G.

375.

To his Stepmother.

May 31st, 1779.

DEAR MADAM,

It is almost ridiculous for so hardened a sinner as myself to assign any particular reason for his silence and negligence : Yet I can say with truth that I do not remember the time when I have been more fully engaged. The attendance of the House of Commons on our fruitless, hopeless enquiries is really severe at this unseasonable time of year, and my literary

---

[1] Sir Joshua Reynolds, in May to July, 1779, painted a portrait of Gibbon. But the picture here referred to is probably that by Wharton.

business, though much more pleasing, engrosses a still larger share of my time and attention.   On every account both of fame and interest, it will be highly expedient that the continuation of my history should appear about this time twelvemonth ; much is already done, much remains to do ; I am well satisfied that by a course of steady temperate diligence, the object may be accomplished ; but I shall not be able to lose a week, and hardly a day.

I most sincerely rejoice at the visible improvement in your health and spirits, and am convinced amusement and change of air will produce the most salutary effects.   I conceive and I wish I could partake the happiness you enjoy with Mrs. Eliot and her sons : I beg you would communicate to them the expression of my most sincere and lively regard.   Has Mrs. Eliot totally renounced London ?   She herself may be happy in a Solitude, but she might diffuse happiness among a larger circle of her friends.   For myself I cannot say anything very positive or indeed very pleasing on the subject of my hopes : but I have weighed every circumstance and am prepared for every possible event.   I only beg you to have patience a few months longer, and I give you *my honour* that I will make such arrangements as shall enable you to reside at Bath.   I will likewise add, what I know is material to your feelings, that I shall enjoy myself a very comfortable if not desirable plan of life.   I should be glad to provide for Will Budd, but the sort of place which you described to me some time ago, hardly exists in any family. However I shall not forget him.

I am, Dear Madam,
Ever yours,
E. G.

376.

To J. B. Holroyd, Esq.

Friday evening, July, 1779.

The inclosed will inform you of an event, not the most disagreeable of those which I have lately experienced.   I have only to add, that it was effected by the firm and sincere friendship of the A[ttorney] G[eneral].   So many incidents have happened, that I hardly know how to talk of news.   You will learn that the Lords have strangely castrated the new Militia Bill.[1] The Ferrol Squadron, 8 or 9 ships, have joined the French. The numbers stand on our side 32, on their's 37 ; but our force is at least equal, and the general consternation much dispelled. If you do not Hibernize, you might at least Bentinckize. I embrace, &c. Parliament will be prorogued to-morrow.

377.

To his Stepmother.

Bentinck Street, July the 3rd, 1779.

DEAR MADAM,

I have the pleasure of acquainting you, that I am now appointed one of the Lords of Trade in the room of Bamber Gascoyne ;[2] Andrew Stuart[3] has succeeded at the same time to the place of Jolliffe, and our new Colleagues[4] do us the honour of saying that in both instances they have gained by the exchange. As the salary of this place will secure and improve my own situation, so I really set much more value upon it, as it will enable me to discharge a small part of my debt of duty and gratitude towards you. For the future you may depend on receiving the interest of the Bond (at 5 per cent.) which will make the two half yearly payments £150 instead of £100 each ; and will I hope be sufficient to support your establishment at Bath in a manner more agreeable to you. I have only to beg a short respite, and that you would be satisfied with the usual draught at present and the double (£200) at next Christmas. At the moment my increase of fortune encreases my actual poverty. Sir Francis Wronghead[5] was perfectly in the right

---

[1] On June 21 Lord North proposed a Bill for doubling the militia. The Bill was read a third time on June 24. The Lords (June 30) threw out the second clause, which empowered his Majesty " to direct the number of private men to serve in the militia to be doubled." On recommitment to the Commons, it was argued that the amendment was a breach of privilege, as the Bill was a Money Bill. Eventually the amendment was accepted, and the Bill, as amended, received the royal assent on July 3.

[2] Bamber Gascoyne, M.P. for Truro, was made a Commissioner of the Admiralty.

[3] M.P. for Lanarkshire.

[4] His colleagues were Soame Jenyns, Lord R. Spencer, Hon. Charles Greville, William Eden, and Thomas de Grey.

[5] Sir Francis Wronghead, of Bumper Hall, M.P. for Guzzledown, in *The Provoked Husband; or, A Journey to London* (Vanbrugh and Cibber).

when he said, "Mayhap I may not receive the first quarter of
my salary this halfe yeare :" he might have added that the heavy
fees of offices eat up the greatest part of it, and that a space
of some months must elapse before the stream begins to flow
regularly and beneficially. I am not insensible that this addition
of income is of a very precarious nature, and that the event of an
hour or the caprice of a man may throw me back into my former
anxiety, but the alteration shall never affect your happiness or
situation, and the plan of retirement into Switzerland with my
friend d'Eyverdun which I had perfectly considered and digested
will be a resource not unworthy of a Philosopher, which I shall
always have it in my power to command.

I am now going to resume my literary employments, which
have suffered a short interruption, and I shall resume them, if
not with more tranquility at least with more cheerfulness of mind.
I find myself however under a difficulty of reconciling two plans
for this year, each of which is equally recommended by my
interest, my duty and my inclination. On the one hand I
anxiously desire to publish the continuation of my history about
this time twelvemonth. Though much is already done, much
still remains to do, and I should almost despair of being able
to finish so large a task, unless I steadily proceed without losing
a day, or unless I compensate any intervals of negligence by
extraordinary and improper efforts of industry. This important
object seems to confine me to Bentinck Street and my Library :
but on the other hand I am desirous and even impatient to visit
you at Bath ; to carry you down to Port Eliot, where I am sure
the air and society would be your best Physician, to see Mrs.
Eliot, and to convince *him* of the grateful sense that I entertain
of his behaviour in consenting to my re-election,[1] which I know
was highly unpleasant to him. I shall endeavour to concert
measures in such a manner as to reconcile those opposite views :
but I foresee that the execution of such a scheme can only
become practicable towards the Autumn.

I ought to make some apology for leaving some days in
anxious suspence. I can only say, that I was myself in the same
condition. Every morning I expected the event of the evening,
and every evening the return of the morning. Till the business
was absolutely finished, a hundred accidents might have dashed

---

[1] *I.e.* as a Commissioner of Trade.

the cup from my lips, and I was afraid of raising your hopes only
to embitter the melancholy news which might have followed.

I am, Dear Madam,

Ever yours,

E. G.

378.

To his Stepmother.

Bentinck Street, September 17th, 1779.

DEAR MADAM,

*I am well and happy ; two words which you will accept
as the substance of a very long letter ; and even as a sufficient
excuse for a very long silence. Yet I really do intend to behave
better ; and to prevent the abominable consequence of hours
and days and posts stealing away, till the sum total amounts to
a formidable account, I have a great mind to enter into an
agreement, of sending you regularly every month, a *miniature*
picture of my actual state and condition on the first day of the
aforesaid month.

I am happy to hear of the very beneficial effects you have
derived from your recent friendship with the Goats ;[1] and as
I cannot discover in what respect this poor Country is more
prosperous or secure than it was last year, I must consider your
present confidence as a proof that you view the prospect through
a purer medium, and a glass of a more cheerful colour. I find
myself so much more susceptible of private friendship than of
public spirit, that I am very well satisfied with that conclusion.
My summer has been passed in the town and neighbourhood,
which I still maintain to be the best society, and the best
retirement ; the latter, however, has been sometimes interrupted
by the Colonel of Dragoons[2] with a train of Serjeants, Trumpets,
Recruits, &c. &c. My own time is much and agreeably employed
in the prosecution of my business. After doing much more than
I expected to have done within the time, I find myself much
less advanced than I expected : yet I begin to reckon, and as
well as I can calculate, I believe, that in twelve or fourteen

---

[1] Mrs. Gibbon had recently paid a visit to Abergavenny.

[2] Major Holroyd had raised a regiment of horse, called the Sussex, or
22nd Regiment of Light Dragoons, of which he was colonel.

months I shall be brought to bed, perhaps of twins. May they live, and prove as healthy as their eldest brother.

With regard to the little foundling which so many friends or enemies chose to lay at my door, I am perfectly innocent, even of the knowledge of that production; and *all* the faults or merits of the History of Opposition must, as I am informed, be imputed to Macpherson, the Author or translator of Fingal.* I am much at a loss what to say about Mr. Eliot; he is certainly very far from being in a good state of health or spirits, but I am not Physician enough to distinguish between the influence of the body and that of the mind : he feels for the public with the most exquisite sensibility, and all his sentiments are of the painful kind. He still loiters in town, which I dare say he will not leave till near the meeting of Parliament, and will go about the month of November to pass the *Summer* in Cornwall. His delay has disconcerted my measures, as I had resolved (however inconvenient it might be) to make an Expedition this year to Port Eliot; and had proposed myself the pleasure of passing some days at Bath on my way. Cornwall must be deferred till next summer, which will arrange indeed much better with my litterary projects; but I cannot refuse myself the satisfaction of seeing you either before the meeting of Parliament or in the Christmas recess.

I am, Dear Madam,

Most truly Yours,

E. GIBBON.

379.

To Colonel Holroyd.

September, 1779.

I do not despair of passing some days at S. P. before the meeting of Parliament; but unless I should totally interrupt my business in a very Critical moment, it is impossible to fix any time which must undoubtedly be at a *considerable* distance. No news of Sir John Ross; Lord Mackartney[1] has written to Lord

---

[1] Lord Macartney (1737–1806) was at that time Governor and Captain-General of the Caribbee Islands, and was at his post at Grenada in July, 1779, when that island was attacked, and, after a gallant defence, was captured by the French. Macartney was carried as prisoner of war to France, but

George [Germain] from Rochelle ; the insolence of d'Estaing's terms made him rather chuse to surrender at discretion, but he has since received assurance that private property will be respected.

Lady Spencer, Lady Harriet and D[uchess] of Devonshire behaved like heroines in the Engagement[1] which they saw very distinctly ; the latter exposed herself to save them. I perfectly approve of Neville for eldest Captain, and think that Wedderburne cannot be offended. I am curious to see your Colonel's letter, but you must answer it. I embrace My Lady ; did you scold her very much ? She was, as on most occasions, quite in the right.

380.

To Colonel Holroyd.

October 6th, 1779.

I am always in the right, I knew the journey would be of service to me, and I eat my Pheasant at dinner with a degree of appetite which I have not known for some days. As to the majestic complaint of the foot, the event will probably be decided by to-morrow morning, but as it seems to be better notwithstanding the jolting of the Chaise, I begin to hope that it may go off without further trouble. In spite of the Divine Billy Burrel it is certain that Dr. Turton *is* in town, and that I shall see him to-morrow. If I am well enough to go out I must attend a board of trade for which I have found a summons. You think we are idle—— Embrace my Lady in my name and respectfully salute Miss Cooke, Major Price, &c. By the enclosed you will see that there is not any authentic news.

was soon exchanged.   Count d'Estaing's terms were that he should hold Macartney personally responsible for all the consequences of his refusal to surrender.   Such of the inhabitants as were taken in arms would irrecoverably lose their estates and properties, and the free coloured people would be reduced to slavery.

[1] The ladies, returning from Spa, embarked at Ostend on the *Fly* sloop for Calais. On the voyage the sloop was attacked (September 17) by two French cutters. After a long engagement the French were beaten off.

381.

To his Stepmother.

Bentinck Street, October the 27th, 1779.

DEAR MADAM,

Whenever you have desired an immediate answer you have not found me very negligent; it is therefore incumbent on me to explain my *apparent* tardiness which was occasioned by a visit to Tunbridge. Your letter was sent there the day after I left it, and by some delay and some circuits it did not reach my hands till Monday last, and I had firmly resolved before I received your second Epistle to write by to-night's post.

The officious intelligence which was communicated, I suppose, from Sheffield Place to Bath, alarmed your tenderness much more than was necessary about the state of my health. A Derangement in my stomach which seemed of the bilious kind determined me to return to town in search of advice. Turton was divided for two or three days between the probability of Jaundice and Gout, but either Nature or his skill preserved me from both; and I am now perfectly free from all complaints and apprehensions whatsoever. It will be an addition to my happiness if you are able to make the same declaration.

I hope you are perfectly satisfied that I had no hand in the History of the Opposition, but you will receive by the Coach (directed for fear of a mistake to Dr. Delacour's) a French pamphlet which I have not the same right to disclaim.[1] In the summer the Chancellor and Lord Weymouth were desirous of answering a very weak Manifesto of the Court of Versailles, and very politely requested me to undertake the task. Though I will never make myself the Champion of a party, I thought there was

---

[1] In 1779 a *Mémoire Justificatif* was put forth both at Paris and Madrid to explain the zeal of two despotic monarchies for the new-born republic of the United States. Gibbon was requested by the Lord Chancellor and Lord Weymouth, then Secretary of State, to vindicate, against the French manifesto, the justice of the British arms. His *Mémoire*, written in French, was approved by the Cabinet, and delivered as a State Paper to the courts of Europe. The *Mémoire* is published in English in the Annual Register for 1779 (pp. 397-412), preceded by translations of the Spanish and French manifestoes. Beaumarchais wrote a reply to the *Mémoire*, which he attributes to Lord Stormont (*Observations sur le Mémoire Justificatif de la cour de Londres. Œuvres de Beaumarchais.* Edition 1809, vol. v. pp. 1-50).

no disgrace in becoming the Advocate of my Country against a foreign enemy, and the *memoire Justificatif* which you may read was the result of that opinion. The publication was delayed for various reasons ; but it has now been communicated as a State paper and in the King's [name] to all the Ministers and Courts in Europe, and as far as I can understand it has been received with some degree of approbation. Elmsley the bookseller desired to print a new Edition which he has swelled by the addition of the French Manifesto. You will easily suppose that I rather expect by such a work to *procure friends* than fame: but it may very possibly be abused in some shape or other in the approaching Session of Parliament, which will be loud and turbulent.[1]

　　　　　I am, Dear Madam,
　　　　　　　Most affectionately yours,
　　　　　　　　　　E. GIBBON.

　　　　　　382.

　　　　　To his Stepmother.
　　　　　　　　　London, Oct. 29th, 1779.
DEAR MADAM,

　　This day I dined in Conduit Street, a well-furnished house, good table, proper attendance, &c. Thus far you will say there was nothing very extraordinary. But the Lady of the house was Mrs. Williams, alias Bell Mallet. Her aunt Elstob is just dead, and has left her that house, furniture, plate, &c., with a fortune (as Mr. Scott tells me) of £14,000 chargeable only with an Annuity of £100 a year to her sister during her mother's life. She is in high spirits, as she well may be, very French, but really agreeable and even handsome. She talks of settling her affairs and returning to France. Her husband is at New York much esteemed in his profession, and she may be very happy if he does not *now* recollect his wife, though Mrs. Elstob, by appointing Trustees, George Scott and Mr. Waller, has taken every possible measure to secure her fortune from him. I thought you would not be sorry to hear something of that little animal, who came to town only Saturday and sent to me only last night.

　　　　　I am,
　　　　　　　Most truly yours,
　　　　　　　　　　E. GIBBON.

---

[1] Parliament met November 25, 1779.

383.

To his Stepmother.

Bentinck Street, Dec. 10th, 1779.

DEAR MADAM,

Nothing has given me for a long while more real uneasiness than the doubt, which I am now obliged to express, whether it will be in my power to pass my Holydays at Bath. After so long a delay and such repeated disappointments, I had promised myself much pleasure, I may say happiness, in spending some few days with you at a time when every disagreeable circumstance was removed and our domestic prospect was become more cheerful. But the advantages of office must be accepted with some inconveniences. You know how much the Irish business engages our attention and fears at this moment, and you will see by the papers that Lord North has proposed some very important alterations with regard to the commerce of that country.[1] The bills for that purpose will pass in Parliament, but there still remains a great number of subordinate circumstances, though highly essential to be regulated, and which in some form will be referred to the Board of Trade. We shall be forced to sit almost every day during the Recess, and the absence of a *new Lord* on the occasion would be thought peculiarly improper.

There is even another motive which I cannot explain, which will I hope make my attention to this business of some future benefit to the public or at least to myself. These reasons will satisfy the delicacy of your friendship, but I beg you would keep them to yourself, as I abhor and despise above all things the seeming affectation of official importance. Only be persuaded that I feel the delay (as I fear it must prove) of my visit, not less disagreeably than you do yourself.

I have seen very little of Mrs. Williams, and am sorry, and

---

[1] On December 1, Lord Shelburne in the Lords, and, on December 6, Lord Ossory in the Commons, moved a vote of censure on the Government for their conduct in Ireland. The Volunteer movement spread rapidly; a French invasion was dreaded; the cry for "free trade" rose higher and higher; a non-importation agreement was entered into; and the relief of Dissenters from the sacramental test was demanded. In consequence of this pressure, Lord North (December 13, 1779) proposed and carried a series of resolutions granting free export trade to Ireland.

indeed surprised to hear so bad an account of a little coquette
to whom I only imputed the venial faults of vanity and affectation. I understand she is already on the Wing. Mr. Eliot
is still in town: we all try to push him down to Bath; he
seems immoveable; but he appears in somewhat better health
and spirits. He deplores the state of public affairs, past, present
and future. With regard to the last, though from different
principles, I am afraid that his apprehensions are not imaginary,
and the impending dangers from war and faction are most
alarming. I never knew anything equal to the violence of this
Session of Parliament, which has not left me a moment of
peace or leisure. Adieu! dear Madam, I do most seriously
intend to write again very soon. Your *ordinary* remittance shall
reach you on Christmas-day, and I hope that I shall be able to
add the *extraordinary* or rather the new one. But my own
supplies, both from Hampshire and from the Exchequer, come
in so very slowly that I may be obliged to defer the second £100
till the end of January in case it should not be inconvenient
to you.

> I am,
> Most truly yours,
> E. GIBBON.

384.

To his Stepmother.

December 25th, 1779.

DEAR MADAM,

Inclosed you will receive two draughts for two different
terms, which will each be ready for your commands.—I must
delay the pleasure of seeing you; but *hope* I shall write oftener
than usual. I wish you joy of the fair ending of the Year. May
1780 be still more propitious for public and private happiness.

> I am,
> Most truly yours,
> E. GIBBON.

385.

To Colonel Holroyd, at Coventry.

London, Monday, February 7th, 1780.

*When the A. G. informed me of the Express he had just sent down to Coventry,[1] I had not the least doubt of your embracing the bolder resolution. You are indeed obliged to him for his real friendship, which he feels and expresses warmly ; on this occasion, I hope, it will be successfully, and that in a few days you will find yourself among us at St. Stephen's in the heat of the battle. But you know that I am a dastardly, pusillanimous spirit, more inclined to fear than to hope, and not very eager in the pursuit of *expensive* Vanity. On this vacancy the celerity of your motions may probably prevent opposition ; but at the general election, your enemy, the Corporation, will not be asleep, and I wish, if it be not too late, to warn you against any promises or engagements which may terminate in a defeat, or at least a Contest of ten thousand pounds. Adieu. I could believe (without seeing it under her paw) that my lady wishes to leave Coventry. No news ! foreign or domestic. I did not forget to mention the *Companies*, but find people, as I expected, torpid. Burke makes his motion Friday ; but I think the rumours of a Civil War subside every day :[2] petitions are thought less formidable ; and I hear the Sussex protest[3] does not gather signatures in the country.*

[1] "The character of my friend (Mr. Holroyd)," says Gibbon in his autobiography, "had recommended him to a seat in Parliament for Coventry, the command of a regiment of light dragoons, and an Irish peerage." The seat for Coventry was vacant by the death of Walter Waring, M.P.

[2] Towards the end of 1779, and in January, 1780, Yorkshire, Middlesex, Hampshire, and many other counties petitioned the House of Commons to grant no more taxes till the expenses of Government were reduced and sinecure places abolished. The tone of several of these county meetings seemed almost to threaten Civil War. Devonshire is said to have voted a fund for buying arms. The Yorkshire petition was presented by Sir George Saville, February 8, 1780.

[3] In Lord Sheffield's edition of this letter (Gibbon's *Miscellaneous Works*, vol. ii. p. 239), the words are given as "I hear your Sussex protest gathers signatures in the country." The protest was suggested and promoted by Colonel Holroyd.

386.

To Colonel J. B. Holroyd.

Brookes's,[1] Saturday Night, February (12th), 1780.

I rejoyce in the successful progress, and am convinced that for the *present* at least the catastrophe will be happy. Your last was safely conveyed to Lord Charles Spencer in the few hours that he happed to be in town. Though I hate to go out in the morning I will be at the Admiralty with Lord Mulgrave, Lord Lisburn and Penton to-morrow at ten o'clock.

Burke[2] opened his ingenious partial scheme of public economy yesterday, but I cannot give you a speech of three hours in three lines, and you will hear and see enough about it. What is of much more consequence than this Parliamentary prattle (I talk to you now as a free mason) is the business of which we have received to-day the certain though not official information. Rodney encountered the Spanish Fleet off Cape St. Mary's;[3] the Commodore (90 guns) blew up, three line of battle-ships taken, two more

---

[1] Brooks's Club, originally in Pall Mall, was moved to 60, St. James's Street, in 1778. Gibbon, proposed by Mr. St. John, was elected in 1777. In Richard Tickell's verses celebrating the Hon. John Townshend's return for Cambridge in 1780, occur the following lines:—

"And, know, I've bought the best champagne from Brookes.
From liberal Brookes, whose speculative skill
Is hasty credit, and a distant bill;
Who, nursed in clubs, disdains a vulgar trade,
Exults to trust and blushes to be paid."

[2] On February 11, Burke brought forward his scheme for securing the independence of Parliament, and for Economical Reform, in a speech which Lord North said was "such as no other member could have made." Besides other reductions of expense, he proposed to abolish altogether the Board of Trade, the Civil Branch of the Ordnance, and the third Secretaryship of State. Lord North allowed the Establishment Bill to be brought in, the only member who opposed its introduction being Lord George Gordon. The House of Commons went into Committee on the Bill, March 8, 1780.

[3] On January 16, 1780, Rodney encountered the Spanish Admiral Langara off Cape St. Vincent, won a complete victory, relieved Gibraltar, supplied Minorca, and proceeded to the West Indies. The *San Domingo* (70 guns) blew up; the flagship *Phœnix* (80 guns), and three other ships of 70 guns, were taken. The *San Julian* (70 guns), after her prize crew was put on board, ran ashore. Another ship, after her officers were shifted, was totally wrecked. Four, more or less damaged, escaped into Cadiz.

likewise taken, but so much shattered and dismasted, that they were separated and forced by an unlucky gale of wind into the Port of Cadiz. The letters from thence express despondency and fears (which for us are hopes) of several other ships. Patriots very dull, the Duke of Grafton who is now standing by the fire, looks blacker than usual. I dined with Wedderburne (at Lord Carlisle's), who was to see one of your Agents to-night ; he is earnest and sanguine—God send a good deliverance to the Colonel and Secretary.

387.

To his Stepmother.

Bentinck Street, March 10th, 1780.

DEAR MADAM,

*When you awakened me with your pen, it was my intention to have shown some signs of life by the next post. But so uncertain are all human affairs, that I found myself arrested by a mighty unrelenting Tyrant, called the Gout ; and though my feet were the part on which he chose to exercise his cruelty, he left me neither strength nor spirits to use my hand in relating the melancholy tale. At present I have the pleasure of informing you, that the feaver and inflammation have subsided ; but the absolute weakness and monstrous swelling of my two feet confine me to my chair and flannels ; and this confinement most unluckily happens at a very *nice* and important moment of Parliamentary affairs. Col. Holroyd pursues those affairs with eager and persevering zeal ; and has the pleasure of undertaking more business than any three men could possibly execute.* He is much obliged to you for your kind congratulation. Mrs. Eliot is in town ; but I am quite ignorant (not more so than they are themselves) of their intentions. I will write again very soon.

I am, Dear Madam,

Most truly yours,

E. GIBBON.

388.

To his Stepmother.

Bentinck Street, ½ hour past nine,
Saturday Evening, March, '80.

Dear Madam,

If I had written as I intended three or four posts ago, I should have informed you that Turton and myself were very well satisfied with the proceedings of the Gout, that he had behaved like a fair and honourable enemy, and that after making me sensible of his power, he was taking leave in a gentle and orderly manner. I cannot send you at present quite so favourable an account; the Gout has seriously returned into one of my feet; the pair kept me sleepless last night; and I have been low and weak all day. I can easily understand this alteration, and you will not be surprized when you hear that I was forced to go out rather too soon, and to sit up two whole nights in the House of Commons. You will see by the Papers, that a Vote has passed against the Board of Trade,[1] but I can assure you that it has not disturbed my tranquility. It will probably be rejected by the House of Lords; and at all events I have reason to expect some equivalent. I hope I am falling asleep.

I am, Dear Madam,
Most truly yours,
E. Gibbon.

389.

To his Stepmother.

April 3rd, 1780.

Dear Madam,

I have now the pleasure of informing you that the gout has quite left me, and from the general state of my health and spirits, I am much inclined to believe many of the things that are reported in its favour. I wish it were in my power to embrace

[1] On March 13, 1780, the Board of Trade was declared to be useless by 207 to 199. Burke alluded to the literary value of the Board, which had its separate professor for every department of literature, and paid a sneering compliment to the "historian's labours, the wise and salutary results of deep, religious researches." As an Academy of *Belles Lettres* he held the commissioners hallowed; as a Board of Trade he wished them abolished.

your scheme of Lord Mulgrave's lodging : but my two great chains the *press* and the *house* chain me by either foot.

I am,

Most truly yours,

E. GIBBON.

390.

To his Stepmother.

Bentinck Street, Monday Evening, April, '80 (?).

DEAR MADAM,

I should not have left you in suspense, if the Gout had not treated me exactly in the same manner. My journal (had I sent one every post) could only have specified its irregular motions from one place and from one foot to another ; swelling, inflammation, weakness, pain increasing, diminishing, shifting, &c. : and the alternative of good and bad nights ; sometimes forcing myself out of doors and sometimes nursing myself at home. However the real violence of the fit such as it was during the first week or ten days has never returned, there has not at any time been the slightest symptom or most distant hint in any part except the feet, and I now hope that it is seriously and finally going away. The short interval of the holidays (short indeed, for Parliament meets again to-morrow Sennight) may give me strength and spirits to support a scene which I am heartily tired of. We must again submit to our common disappointment, and if the decline and fall make you any amends you will be glad to hear that the continuation (two quarto volumes) goes to the press in May and will certainly appear next winter.

I am, dear Madam,

Ever yours,

E. G.

391.

To his Stepmother.

May the 15th, 1780.

DEAR MADAM,

Your kind epistle gave me much more pleasure than pain ; for I am grown callous to shame, but am not insensible of gratitude and friendship.

I have heard of you by Mrs. Sarah Holroyd, and was much

pleased and edified by the zeal with which you communicated to
your family the Colonel's first spirited Oration.[1] He instantly
exclaimed, 'Those are the friends I like to have.' He has not
spoke since, but he is, as you may well suppose, indefatigable and
eager, and it will not be long before he feels a second inspiration.
I can only condole with you that a person, in whose fate and
reputation you are perhaps more deeply interested, should still
continue a dumb dog. He has indeed the grace to acknowledge
his infirmity, and if my seat in the House of C. had not some
remote connection with a more valuable seat, I should retire
without any regret from that scene of noise, heat and contention.
A dissolution of Parliament, though it may be delayed many
months, is by many expected every hour: and I am totally
ignorant of the designs of the Electors of Liskeard. My great
constituent grows warmer in patriotism, but he still expresses the
same regard for me, and though I have no motives for confidence,
I have not any reasons for fear. He is perfectly silent on the
subject, and I am prepared for the worst. I saw my young friend
John in his passage, and was indeed astonished by the sense and
propriety of his behaviour without embarrassment and without
forwardness. Mrs. Eliot is not in the least altered.

I am, Dear Madam,

Most truly yours,

E. Gibbon.

392.

To his Stepmother.

June 6th, 1780.

Dear Madam,

  *As the old story of Religion has [raised] most *formidable*
tumults in this town,[2] and as they will of course seem much more
formidable at the distance of an hundred [miles], you may not
be sorry to hear that I am perfectly safe and well : my known

---

[1] In the debate on the Army Estimates and the new Levies (April 5,
1780), Fox commented on the manner in which Colonel Holroyd had raised
his Regiment of Horse. It is to Holroyd's reply, and his explanation that
the regiment was raised by him for active service, and not as a "fencible
corps," that Gibbon refers.

[2] On June 2, 1780, Lord George Gordon presented the petition of the
Protestant Association against the relaxation of the Penal Laws against the
Roman Catholics. The "No Popery" riots took place on the 6th and 7th,
when London was for some hours in the hands of the mob.

attachment to the Protestant Religion has most probably saved me. Measures, and effectual measures, are taken to suppress these disorders, and every street is filled with horse and foot. Mrs. and Mrs. Sarah H. went out of town yesterday morning. The Colonel shews his usual spirit.*

I am sincerely Yours,
E. GIBBON.

393.

To his Stepmother.

London, June 8th, 1780.

DEAR MADAM,

As a M. of P., I cannot be exposed to any danger, as the H. of C. has ajourned to Monday sen'night ; as an individual, I do not conceive myself to be obnoxious. I am not apt, without duty or of necessity, to thrust myself into a Mob : and our part of the town is as quiet as a Country Village. So much for personal safety ; but I cannot give the same assurances of public tranquillity ; forty thousand Puritans, such as they might be in the time of Cromwell, have started out of their graves ; the tumult has been dreadful ; and even the remedy of military force and martial law is unpleasant. But Government with 15,000 Regulars in town, and every Gentleman (but one) on their side, must extinguish the flame. The execution of last night was severe ; perhaps it must be repeated to-night : Yet upon the whole the tumult subsides. Col. H. was all last night in Holbourn among the flames, with the Northumberland Militia, and performed very bold and able service.[1] I write again in a post or two.

I am, Dear Madam,
Ever Yours,
E. G.

---

[1] On Wednesday night, June 7, the riot was quelled by military force. The Northumberland Militia, which reached London on June 7 by a forced march of twenty-five miles, were led by Colonel Holroyd into the thick of the riot at High Holborn, to prevent the mob advancing westward, and to protect, if possible, Mr. Langdale's distillery. By Thursday morning the tumult was entirely suppressed. "To Colonel Holroyd, since deservedly raised to the British peerage as Lord Sheffield, the Country was eminently indebted for repelling the fury of the Mob at the Bank" (Wraxall's *Historical Memoirs*, 3rd edit., vol. i. p. 351).

394.

To his Stepmother.

June 10th, 1780.

DEAR MADAM,

I should write with great pleasure, to say that this audacious tumult is perfectly quelled; that Lord G[eorge] G[ordon] is sent to the Tower; and that instead of safety or danger, we are now at leisure to think of justice; but I am now alarmed on your account, as we have just got a report, that a similar disorder has broken out at Bath. I shall be impatient to hear from you; but I flatter myself that your pretty town does not contain much of that scum which has boiled up to the surface in this huge Cauldron.

I am, Dear Madam,
Most sincerely Yours,
E. G.

395.

To his Stepmother.

Bentinck Street, June 27th, 1780.

DEAR MADAM,

*I believe we may now rejoyce in our common security. All tumult has perfectly subsided, and we only think of the justice which must be properly and severely inflicted on such flagitious criminals. The measures of Government have been seasonable and vigorous; and even opposition has been forced to confess, that the military force was applied and regulated with the utmost propriety. Our danger is at an end, but our disgrace will be lasting, and the month of June 1780, will ever be marked by a dark and diabolical fanaticism, which I had supposed to be extinct, but which actually subsists in Great Britain, perhaps beyond any other Country in Europe. Our Parliamentary work draws to a conclusion;[1] and I am much more pleasantly, though laboriously engaged in revising and correcting for the press, the continuation of my history, two Volumes of which will certainly appear next winter. This business fixes me to Bentinck Street more closely than any other part of my litterary labour; as it is absolutely necessary that I should be in the midst of all the

---

[1] The session ended July 8, 1780.

books which I have at any time used during the composition. But I feel a strong desire (irritated, like all passions, by repeated obstacles) to escape to Bath.* And if the summer should pass away, the autumn shall not elapse without gratifying my wishes. As you are my sole object, it is a matter of perfect indifference whether the place is full or empty, but I should like to know your summer plan, and if you have any design to climb the Welsh mountains. I am ashamed that Midsummer day should have passed in silence, but I am not able to get a shilling from Hampshire, and the treasury, my best support, is uncommonly backward. Next week, however, you may depend on receiving the proper line from me.

I am, Dear Madam,

Most truly Yours,

E. GIBBON.

396.

To his Stepmother.

Bentinck Street, July 8th, 1780.

DEAR MADAM,

I keep my promise though I have been driven to the last verge of breaking it : but I hope you have not felt any inconvenience from the delay. The World disperses and London grows a very pleasant retire[ment]. We are now so quiet that the tumults of last month appear a very incredible dream. Colonel H. passed through town in his way to his Regiment. I understand that his spirited behaviour in London has firmly seated him at Coventry.

I am, Dear Madam,

Most truly Yours,

E. G.

397.

To Colonel Holroyd.

July 25th, 1780.

*As your motions are spontaneous, and the stations of the Lord Chief[1] unalterably fixed, I cannot perceive the necessity of your sending or receiving intelligence. However, your commands are obeyed. You wish I would write, as a sign of life. I am alive ; but, as I am immersed in the decline and fall, I shall only make

---

[1] Lord Mansfield.

the sign. It is made. You may suppose that we are not pleased with the junction of the fleets ; nor can an ounce of West India loss be compensated by a pound of East India success ; but the Circuit will roll down all our news and politics of London. I rejoyce to hear that the Sussex Dragoons are such well-disciplined Cannibals ; but I want to know when the chief Cannibal will return to his den. It would suit me better that it should happen soon. Adieu.*

398.

To his Stepmother.

July 29th, 1780.

I have not heard from Way. It will be necessary that I should be provided with a Bucks Steward to make his visit soon after Michaelmas to examine the state of things and inspect the late Harris's accounts which an Attorney (Mr. Hearne) has offered for my perusal. Such extra trouble will doubtless claim an extra allowance.

We are pleased that Clinton[1] has returned to New York, as an army on the salt water is a very helpless animal. Greaves[2] has been seen on the coast with a wind fair for the northwards. He has certainly the start of Ternay, who is still invisible. I cannot send you the least account or even conjecture of Lords to be created or Commons to be dissolved. Adieu, I shall expect you about the middle of next month ; and I find that it will suit me to visit the Castle within a few days of your return.

399.

To his Stepmother.

Reading, Six o'clock, Sunday evening, '80.

Eels, Beer and fowl.—A nasty day makes a good Inn appear still more comfortable. And now let me look back to Bath, and declare in sober truth, that I number the last three weeks among

---

[1] Sir Henry Clinton had captured Charleston, May 12, 1780. Early in June, he re-embarked on Admiral Arbuthnot's fleet and returned to New York. Sir Henry was married to Miss Harriett Carter, a first cousin of Colonel Holroyd.

[2] Admiral (or. 1794 Lord) Graves sailed, June, 1780, with six ships of the line, to reinforce Admiral Arbuthnot at Long Island, and joined him in July. The French fleet under d'Estaing was at the same time strengthened.

the happiest of my life. The best ingredient in that happiness was the satisfaction of seeing you more perfectly alive both in mind and body than I have known you for many years past. My best compliments to all friends, &c., Jews and Christians, particularly to Sarah, who was a naughty girl for not staying dinner. Pray send me with all convenient speed, the adventures of a tame Cat.

Bentinck Street—Monday half-past one.

Safely landed—I ran my time to the last moment, and find on my table some respectful complaints from Mr. Cadell, and a summons for the Board of Trade to-morrow, which particularly requires *my* attendance.

400.

To Mr. Eliot.

August 11th, 1780.

DEAR SIR,

Before you leave town, I cannot refrain from applying to you on a very interesting subject, and I trust that you will excuse either my past silence or my present importunity. The former has not been the effect of presumption, nor does the latter proceed from any want of confidence in your friendship.

It seems to be universally understood that this parliament will be dissolved in a few months and perhaps in a few days— and you are not ignorant how much the whole colour of my future life depends on your resolution. Unless I obtain a seat in the next parliament, I cannot flatter myself with a hope of remaining at the board of trade ; such is the unpleasant state of my private affairs, that I must resign with my office all prospect of living in England, and the discontinuance of your favours will therefore be a sentence of banishment from my native country. My firm assurance that your kindness will allow some weight to these personal considerations will teach me to acquiesce, whatever may be your designs, with sincere and grateful resignation. I could not even lament that I was not sooner apprized of your intention to withdraw this mark of your friendship at the time when it became the most valuable. The largest notice would not perhaps have enabled me to take any other measures for the attainment of the same object, and your silence, though it may have excited some anxious thoughts or nourished some delusive hopes, has not made any real difference in my situation.

It gives me pain at the same time to mention another topic. Various circumstances of public and private distress have hitherto prevented me from disposing of my Buckinghamshire Estate, from whence I may expect to derive a considerable supply, and I shall find myself under the necessity of soliciting your indulgence till I can discharge what I shall always esteem a very small part of my obligations.

401.

To Mrs. Holroyd.

August 31st, Bentinck Street, 1780.

The Colonel left town about seven o'clock. Could he have held a pen with each finger and each toe, at the same time, he would have found employment for them all. He therefore named me his Secretary to signify to Sheflield Place his health, duty, impatience, &c.—The *Intrigue du Cabinet* shall not be neglected. But the *Intrigue du Parlement* is now the universal pursuit. It will be dissolved to-morrow,[1] the Writs will be out Saturday night, and a few days will terminate the business. You probably receive my last frank. I have *found* reason to believe that I shall never rise again, and I submit to my fate with Philosophic composure. If any parcels or letters directed to me should arrive at Sheflield you will be so good as to return them by the Coach.—Adieu.

E. G.

402.

To his Stepmother.

Bentinck Street, Sept. 2nd, 1780.

DEAR MADAM,

In the general dissolution you will be anxious to know my fate, and I wish it were in my power to send you a more agreeable account. Mr. Eliot, actuated, as it should seem, by the Demon of Party, has renounced me.[2] I am not without resources ;

but his civil ambiguous silence, by feeding my hopes, has encreased my difficulties. I doubt whether my *real* friends will be able to serve me at so short a notice, and I think it more than probable that I shall not be in the new Parliament, at least in the beginning of it. A few days however will determine that question, and I still proceed with perfect composure to prepare for my lying-in. They will be twins, and I reckon about next February.

I am, Dear Madam,
Most truly yours,
E. G.

Col. H. who came with me Thursday from S. P. darted down to Coventry. I think he is secure.

403.

To Colonel Holroyd.

September 7th, 1780.

I shall again breathe the pestiferous air of St. Stephen's Chappel.[1]—The sagacious Eden whom I accidentally visited the day after your departure pressed and persuaded me to make a bold application to the powers above. I fairly stated my public disappointment and private difficulties, and declared to Lord N. in the most explicit terms, that notwithstanding my sincere desire to replace myself in a situation, where I may be serviceable to his Government, *small indeed* must be the effort which I shall be capable of making for that purpose, an idea which I explained to Robinson in a more familiar tone, by asking for an *almost* gratuitous seat. After some importunity and delay, I saw the Secretary yesterday ; and he communicated Lord N.'s resolution of bringing me into Parliament, either for the first meeting, or at the Re-Elections which will immediately be occasioned by the option of those who are returned for two places. He did not mention terms ; if any, they must be very light. On my return home I found a letter from Lord L[oughborough][2] worthy of

---

[1] The newly elected Parliament met October 31, 1780. Gibbon was elected, at a by-election, M.P. for Lymington, June 25, 1781.

[2] Alexander Wedderburn succeeded Sir W. de Grey (afterwards Lord Walsingham) as Lord Chief Justice of the Common Pleas, with the title of Lord Loughborough (June, 1780).

himself, and may now remain perfectly quiet and secure. Success produces good humour; and I shall be very gentle in my answer to the Port, which I do not hurry. This event, as you will easily understand, decides in a great measure the rest of my life. You will growl if I lament in some sort that it has disconcerted a very pleasant scheme, a sweet vision of *Helvetic* retirement : I know that a prudent man ought not to make himself happy.

While I steal in through a postern, you thunder at one of the great gates : knock and it shall be opened unto you. Your victory appears certain, and it will be productive of a lasting conquest. Eden is not yet returned from Woodstock; I will confabulate with him.

The Westminster battle[1] begins this morning; Rodney will be chose almost unanimously. It was imprudent to propose Lord Lincoln; he is disliked by the substantial tradesmen : but they *abhor* Fox, and the Patriot, after his appeal to the *People* of Westminster, must probably retire to the Duke of R.'s dependent voters of Chichester, where I am told Keppel[2] will make room for him.

Not a word of news. Adieu.

404.

To Mr. Eliot.

B. S., Sept. 8th, 1780.

My DEAR SIR,

I have not attempted to shake your decided resolutions nor shall I presume to arraign the consistency of the Electors of Leskeard, whom you so gravely introduce. You are undoubtedly free as air to confer and to withdraw your parliamentary favours, and I should despise my own ingratitude were I capable of forgetting my past obligations to you because you are not disposed to render them more perfect, or more permanent. I am still ignorant what will be the consequences of your refusal; but

[1] Admiral Rodney and Charles Fox were elected for Westminster, September 22, 1780, against Lord Lincoln.

[2] Admiral Keppel was returned for Surrey, after being defeated at Windsor by Portlock Powney. George III. canvassed for the latter. "The pony with the powerful rider has carried away the plate" (Warner to G. Selwyn, September, 1780).

I declare upon my honour, at the date of my last letter that they appeared to me exactly in the light in which I represented them, that I had never formed any hopes much less any claims of ministerial support, and that I never opened my lips on the subject to the noble friend whose character seems to extort the praise of his political enemies. Since your absolute refusal, I have been encouraged to hazard an application which has been kindly entertained. If it proves unsuccessful the principal difficulty will arise from the lateness of my request. I am asked why Mr. Eliot, who re-elected a placeman last year, maintained to the last moment an ambiguous silence without condescending to inform me that I must not depend on his friendship at the General Election. I confess that I am at a loss for an answer.

I am equally at a loss how to answer the part of your letter, which in polite language represents my parliamentary conduct as the cause of your displeasure. You will not expect that I should justify the grounds of every silent vote which I have given, or that I should write a political pamphlet on the eventful history of the last six years. But I may fairly rest my apology on the truth of one single assertion, that I have never renounced any principle, deserted any connection, or violated any promise. I have uniformly asserted both in private and public the justice of the American War. I have constantly supported in Parliament the general measures of Government, except at one particular crisis while it was doubtful, after Bourgoyne's defeat whether they would offer terms to the rebels. I agreed with you in a speculative opinion, almost equally rejected by both parties, that after the substance of power was lost, the name of independence might be granted to the Americans. I have often and severely censured the faults of administration, but I have always condemned the *system* of opposition : and your judgment will allow that in public life, every man is reduced to the necessity of choosing the side which upon the whole appears to him the least reprehensible. The mere acceptance of a seat at the board of trade does not surely convey any reproach or disgrace, since you yourself, my Dear Sir, have held the same disqualifying place under several successive Administrations, without any of those domestic reasons, which, if an excuse were necessary, might be alleged in my favour. You revive an old conversation between us concerning Mr. Peachey's election, which passed, if I am not mistaken, in the garret of the House of Commons. At that time I had never given a single vote against the actual measures of Government, and the indiscreet opinion which you urged me to declare must apply to your sentiments, not to my own. I thought and I still think, that, were I master of a Borough, I would not from motives of interest, elect a *stranger* whose political principles were repugnant to my own.

Thus far for my own honour, I have been forced into this unpleasant, though I hope not intemperate explanation, but I perfectly concur with your wish to avoid all future complaints or apologies. I most willingly embrace the offer of your private friendship, and I shall always cultivate a cordial intercourse with a person who is entitled to my esteem and gratitude.

I beg you would present my kindest wishes and compliments to Mrs. Eliot and the rest of your family. I suppose Mr. Edward will succeed me at Leskeard.[1]

I am, &c., &c.

405.

To Colonel Holroyd.

Sept. 15th, 1780.

I expect but cannot send news. I am passive, you are active, without the form of a letter you might dispatch every night the numbers of the poll.—Fox is victorious, and though some Enemies have been thrown out, I do not find that we gain so much as might be wished. Lord L[oughborough] is not yet arrived, but I have conversed with the future Secretary of the bog :[2] he approves and will assist your vanity. I am very sorry to hear that Batt is detained at Oxford in a bad state of health, with some symptoms of a growing dropsy. Adieu.

[1] Edward James Eliot, eldest son of Mr. Eliot, was elected for St. Germains. He was made a Commissioner of the Treasury in July, 1782.

[2] William Eden, M.P. for Woodstock, was appointed in October, 1780, principal secretary to the Lord Lieutenant and Privy Council of Ireland.

406.

To his Stepmother.

Bentinck Street, October 5th, 1780.

DEAR MADAM,

I have delayed answering your kind enquiry about my seat in Parliament, till I should be able to say something satisfactory and positive. Had Mr. Eliot been explicit some months since, another arrangement would have been made without difficulty. His silence has occasioned some delay, but I have the strongest reason to believe that I shall be again in the House of Commons before Christmas. I expect the event with the most tranquil indifference : I am heartily tired of the place, and if such indulgence were compatible with my situation and prospects I should be glad to find myself released from such troublesome attendance. Your anxiety lest any coldness should arise between Mr. E. and me will, I hope, prove groundless. I have nothing to reproach myself, I do not reproach him, and from the letters which have passed between us, I should imagine that we shall meet next winter on proper terms of friendship and civility. You see by the Gazette that Langlois[1] is dismissed ; and he himself has not received any other information from Cornwall. You may easily suppose that in my present state of suspence and attendance, it is not in my power to leave town : but I am almost offended that you are not angry ! I think I may venture to promise not you but myself, that no considerations human or divine shall prevent me from eating my Christmas dinner at the Belvedere.

I am, Dear Madam,

Most truly yours,

E. GIBBON.

We need not trouble Sir Stanier ; three shillings (no very considerable sum) pay twelve letters. The economy of the age on the subject of Franks and postage has always amazed me.

---

[1] Benjamin Langlois, M.P. for St. Germains in the last Parliament, made room for Mr. Dudley Long. He was made keeper of his Majesty's stores, ordnance, and ammunition of war in June, 1778, and was appointed a Commissioner for Trade and Plantations *vice* Soame Jenyns.

407.

To Mrs. Holroyd
(*announcing that Colonel Holroyd was created Lord Sheffield*[1]).

Bentinck Street, Nov. 27th, 1780.

Mr. Gibbon presents his respectful compliments to Lady Sheffield and hopes her Ladyship is in perfect health, as well as the Honble. Miss Holroyd, and the Honble. Miss Louisa Holroyd. Mr. Gibbon has not had the honour of hearing from Lord Sheffield, since his Lordship reached Coventry, but supposes that the election begins this day.

Be honest? How does this read? Do you not feel some titillations of vanity? Yet I will do you the justice to believe that they are as faint as can find place in a female (you will retort, or a male) heart, on such an auspicious event. When it is revealed to the Honble. Miss, I should recommend the loss of some ounces of noble blood. You may expect, every post, a formal notification, which I shall instantly dispatch. The birds, as well as I now recollect their taste, were excellent. I hope the *Voyages* still amuse. I had almost forgot to say that my seat in parliament is deferred. Stronger and more impatient rivals have stepped before me, and I can wait with chearful resignation till another opportunity. I wish the Baron's situation (and temper) were as placid as mine. No news—we are very dull. Adieu—I shall go to Bath, about the 15th of next month—But silence.

408.

To Colonel Holroyd.

Brookes's, November 28th, 1780.

*Perhaps the sheriffs, the tools of your enemies, may venture to make a false and hostile return, on the presumption that they shall have a whole year of impunity, and that the merits of your

---

[1] The *Gazette* for December, 1780, announces that the grant of the dignity of a baron of the kingdom of Ireland was conferred on John Baker Holroyd, Esq.—Baron Sheffield, of Dunamore, in the county of Meath. "I had a long conversation," writes Miss Burney in 1781, "with the new Lord Sheffield. He gave me a long account of his Coventry affairs, and of the commitment of the sheriffs to Newgate. He is a spirited and agreeable man, and, I doubt not, will make himself conspicuous in the right way."

petition cannot be heard this session.' Some of your most respectable friends in the house of Commons are resolved, (if the return should be unfavourable) to state it forcibly as a special and extraordinary case ; and to exert all proper strength for bringing on the tryal of your petition without delay. The knowledge of such a resolution may awe the sheriffs ; and it may be prudent to admonish them of the *impending* danger, in the way that you judge most advisable. Adieu. God send you a good deliverance.*

409.

To his Stepmother.

December the 7th, 1780.

DEAR MADAM,

My restoration to the character of a Senator has suffered some delay by the impatience of some strong competitors who have pushed between me and the door. I have received from the fountain head every kind of apology and assurance. I believe them to be sincere, and it is a matter of perfect indifference to me whether I enter the H. of C. the beginning or the end of the winter. My journey to Bath is not an object of indifference, and as nearly as I can calculate the business (for there is business) of the board of trade, I think I shall have the pleasure of embracing you about the 23rd or 24th of this month. You mentioned a lodging near your aerial castle (my sole object at Bath), and I shall be glad if you will secure it for that time.

Poor George Scott died this morning of the consequence of falling down a flight of stairs at Lord Bathurst's. His life was

¹ At the general election in September, 1780, Colonel Holroyd's re-election for Coventry was prevented by no return being made. After a hearing before the House, the sheriffs of Coventry were committed to Newgate, and a new election ordered. The poll began towards the end of November, and remained open for thirty days. At the close, though a large majority voted for Colonel Holroyd and Mr. Yeo, Sir Thomas Hallifax and Mr. Thomas Rogers were declared duly elected. The unsuccessful candidates petitioned against the return. The first day on which a committee could be balloted for was June 26, 1781. But on the motion of Lord Beauchamp (January 23) the petition of Lord Sheffield and Mr. Yeo was referred to a committee for February 15. The return was amended by an order of the House, dated February 27, 1781, by substituting for Hallifax and Rogers the names of Colonel Holroyd (who in the interval had been created Lord Sheffield) and Mr. Edward Roe Yeo.

long and happy, and his death was not painful. After a false alarm I was glad to hear that Dr. Delacour was not in the bosom of Abraham. The poor Colonel is fighting with the monsters of Coventry. I think he will conquer, but his victory will be dearly purchased.

I am, Dear Madam,
Ever yours,
E. GIBBON.

Young Eliot is in town and dined with me Tuesday. The kindest enquiries passed reciprocally between Port Eliot and Bentinck Street. The father does not come till after the Holydays.

410.

To J. B. Holroyd, Esq.

[Dec. 9th], Saturday Night, 1780.

Succeed—and may you say, such another victory would ruin us ! The messenger has returned from the Bog, but Lord B[uckinghamshire][1] has not yet sent the necessary forms and titles for his creatures ; it will not however be in his favour to delay, that or any other business much longer, and I wish your entrance into one house was as secure as the other.

An express has just arrived in nine days from Vienna ; the Empress is dead,[2] and the Austrian Eagle may soar.—It is confidently said that the two great fleets are in sight, and expectation is high and eager. For my own part I do not believe that there ever can be a sea-fight.

411.

To J. B. Holroyd, Esq.

Monday Night, December, 1780.

All delays are at an end—Tuesday—to-morrow the final warrant will be signed ; Friday next, you may salute the Royal paw.

Saturday the gazette will announce his Lordship, and Sunday

---

[1] Lord Buckinghamshire was Lord Lieutenant of Ireland. The reference is to Colonel Holroyd's elevation to the Irish peerage as Lord Sheffield.

[2] The Empress Maria Theresa died November 29, 1780.

(December 24th) I shall set out for Bath. Be resolute and conquer. We have forgot the fleets, but it is supposed that d'Estaing is in Brest. It is time that everybody should go to sleep for the Winter.

412.

To his Stepmother.

Bentinck Street, December 21st, 1780.

DEAR MADAM,

I am sorry to inform you that I shall be forced to trespass a few days beyond the precise term which I had fixed. The constant attendance on the board of trade almost every day this week, has obliged me to defer till next Monday a visit of inclination and propriety to Lord Loughborough (at Mitcham in Surrey). I shall not return till Wednesday or Thursday, and instead of my Christmas, I shall eat my new-year's dinner, at the Belvidere. May that new year prove fortunate to you, to me, and to this weary country, which is this day involved in a new War. I shall write again about the middle of next week with a precise account of my motions. I think the gallant Colonel, who is now Lord Sheffield, will succeed at Coventry *perhaps* on the return, certainly on the petition.

I am, Dear Madam,

Ever yours,

E. GIBBON.

413.

To Lord Sheffield.

Prophecy of the events of two years.

A profane historian will depart from Bentinck Street, London, and drink tea, sup and lye at Newbury in Berkshire. December 31st, 1780.

The same historian will gently proceed from Newbury to Bath till he reaches the aerial cell of the Fairy of the Green, or more probably the white mountain. It is apprehended that the said Fairy will not be able to dine that day before four o'clock in the afternoon. January 1st, 1781.

414.

To his Stepmother.

Bentinck Street, February 24th, 1781.

DEAR MADAM,

*As you have probably received my last letter of thirteen hundred pages,[1] I shall be very concise; Read, judge, pronounce: and believe that I sincerely agree with my friend Julian,[2] in esteeming the praise of those only who will freely censure my defects. Next Thursday I shall be delivered to the World, for whose inconstant and malicious levity I am coolly but firmly prepared. Excuse me to Sarah. I see more clearly than ever the absolute necessity of confining my presents to my own family; *that*, and that only, is a determined line, and Lord S. is the first to approve his exclusion. He has a strong assurance of success, and some hopes of a speedy decision. How suddenly your friend

[1] The second and third volumes of the *Decline and Fall of the Roman Empire.* Gibbon had presented his first volume of the *Decline and Fall* to the Duke of Gloucester. When the second volume appeared, it was, in like manner, presented to the Duke, who "received the author with much good nature and affability, saying to him, as he laid the quarto on the table, 'Another d—mn'd thick, square book! Always scribble, scribble, scribble! Eh! Mr. Gibbon?'" (Best's *Personal and Literary Memorials*, p. 68). "You will be diverted to hear," writes Walpole to Mason, January 27, 1781, "that Mr. Gibbon has quarrelled with me. He lent me his second volume in the middle of November. I returned it with a most civil panegyric. He came for more incense; I gave it, but alas! with too much sincerity; I added, 'Mr. Gibbon, I am sorry *you* should have pitched on so disgusting a subject as the Constantinopolitan History. There is so much of the Arians and Eunomians, and semi-Pelagians; and there is such a strange contrast between Roman and Gothic manners, and so little harmony between a Consul Sabinus and a Ricimer, Duke of the Palace, that though you have written the story as well as it could be written, I fear few will have patience to read it.' He coloured: all his round features squeezed themselves into sharp angles; he screwed up his button-mouth, and rapping his snuff-box, said, 'It had never been put together before'—*so well*, he meant to add—but gulped it. He meant *so well* certainly, for Tillemont, whom he quotes in every page, has done the very thing. I well knew his vanity, even about his ridiculous face and person, but thought he had too much sense to avow it so palpably."

[2] "When he ascended the throne, his pride was sometimes cruelly mortified by the reflection that the slaves who would not dare to censure his defects were not worthy to applaud his virtues" (*Decline and Fall of the Roman Empire*, vol. iii. ch. xxii.). Gibbon quotes the sentiments from the words of Julian himself (Ammianus, xxii. 10).

General Pierson[1] disappeared ! You thought him happy. What is happiness ? *

> I am, My Dear Madam,
> Ever Yours,
> E. GIBBON.

415.

To his Stepmother.

Bentinck Street, April 13th, 1781.

DEAR MADAM,

I am always obliged to you for waking me by a friendly pinch from my silent lethargy, and I think it most prudent to write before I fall asleep again.

An author must always begin on the subject of his own work, the subject always most interesting to himself, but on this occasion he may assume the privilege of friendship and justly believe that it is not less interesting to you. Your praise has afforded me real satisfaction, not only because I wish to please you, but as I do not know any person (where questions of pure learning are concerned) from whose approbation I should derive more pride. To speak frankly, I am of your opinion with regard to the improvement of the style, nor is it very surprizing that my long practice should make a workman more expert and ready at his trade. I am curious to learn what passage in Prior you have in your eye : but as the works of that agreeable Poet are not extremely familiar to me, the resemblance is more probably the effect of chance than of design. The reception of these two volumes has been very unlike that of the first, and yet my vanity is so very dextrous, that I am not displeased with the difference. The effects of novelty could no longer operate, and the public was not surprized by the unexpected appearance of a new and unknown author. The progress of these two volumes has hitherto been quiet and silent. Almost everybody that reads has purchased, but few persons (comparatively) have read them ; and I find that the greater number, satisfied that they have acquired a valuable fund of entertainment, differ the perusal to the summer, the country and a more quiet period. Yet I have reason to think, from the opinion of some judges, that my reputation has not

[1] Probably General Sir Richard Pearson, K.B., who died suddenly at Bath of gout in the stomach, February 13, 1781.

suffered by this publication. The Clergy (such is the advantage
of total loss of character) commend my decency and moderation :
but the patriots wish to damn the work and the author.

Mrs. Hester Gibbon is now in town and stays some weeks.
Her house is repairing, and her old friend Mrs. Hutchinson[1] is
just dead, without leaving her anything, at which Hester expresses
more resentment than seems becoming in the character of a Saint.
She is still healthy and sensible, refuses as formerly to enter my
house, but appears pleased with my attentions, and those of Mrs.
and Lady Porten and of Lord and Lady Sheffield, who have all
visited her in Surrey Street. She enquired civilly and even quietly
into your situation, and approved the sentiments which naturally
fell from me.—When I sent you my book I likewise despatched
another with a very polite letter to Port Eliot—A dead silence—I
accidentally called in Spring Gardens to visit the son, and heard
that the father had been three weeks or a month in town. I
instantly wrote a note to express my surprize and concern,—a
dead silence of four days terminated only by a mute, blank, formal
visit. Mrs. Eliot however (they are an odd family) has called
upon me this morning to announce her arrival ; and I shall return
her visit this evening.

My health this winter has been perfect, without the slightest
attack of the gout, and I rejoyce to hear that you revive with the
Spring. A friend like Mrs. P. was a real loss, and I think with
you that in such an intimate connection the heart is of much
more importance than the head. Embrace in my name Sara and
the tame cat. I hope the former is not offended with, and I am
persuaded that the latter adores, me, but am much disappointed
that her Bath residence has not produced any shining adventures :
a pair of small, neat horns might peep very gracefully out of a
laurel crown, which her husband well deserves, though I think
with you that his effusions are too frequent and precipitate.[2]

[1] Mrs. Hutcheson, whose maiden name was Lawrence, married as her
first husband Colonel Steward. Her second husband, Archibald Hutcheson,
M.P. for Hastings, at the time of his death (1740) commended her to the guid-
ance of William Law. She was joined by Miss Hester Gibbon, and the two
ladies, in 1743, settled at King's Cliffe, in a house belonging to Law. There
Mrs. Hutcheson founded a school for boys. She died at the age of ninety-
one, in January, 1781, and, at her own request, was buried at the feet of
Mr. Law.

[2] William Hayley (1745-1820) was a voluminous poet. Byron (*English
Bards and Scotch Reviewers*) attacks him with severity—

Adieu, dear Madam. I am still ignorant and indeed indifferent about the precise moment of my parliamentary beatification. Lord S. is chaired next Monday at Coventry ; but it is needless to mention that family, as you hear the earliest and most copious accounts of them. Once more, Adieu !

I am, Dear Madam,

Most truly yours,

E. GIBBON.

416.

To his Stepmother.

Friday, May 30th, 1781.

DEAR MADAM,

When I was called upon last February for my annual tax to the Gout, I only paid for my left foot which in general is most heavily assessed : the officer came round last week to collect the small remainder that was due for the right foot. I have now satisfied his demand ; he is retired in good humour, and I feel myself easy both in mind and body.—If I complained of your silence, though somewhat longer than usual, I should be unreasonable indeed, and I only wish to be assured that it does not proceed from want of health or spirits. I hope you do not stand in need of a Physician, but I am concerned to think that, since the Jew's departure, you have not any one who knows your constitution or in whom you repose any confidence. How do you propose to spend the summer ? do you mean to breathe the sharp air of the Welsh mountains ? If you would visit the banks of the Thames you would find a hearty welcome, and my cottage would be easily enlarged by an occasional lodging. I feel great comfort

<blockquote>
" Whether he spin poor couplets into plays,
  Or damn the dead with purgatorial praise,
  His style in youth or age is still the same,
  For ever feeble and for ever tame."
</blockquote>

In 1780 he had addressed to Gibbon *An Essay on History, in Three Epistles.* He married, in 1769, Eliza Ball, daughter of the Dean of Chichester. The marriage proved unhappy ; but it should be added that Mrs. Hayley adopted her husband's illegitimate son, who, born in 1780, afterwards became the sculptor, and treated him as her own child. In 1789 Hayley was separated from his wife, whose mind had become affected. Hayley was at this time living at Eartham, in Sussex, a property which he had inherited from his father.

in this retreat at Hampton Court, and shall now escape every week from the heat and dust of the House of Commons.

I am, Dear Madam,

Ever yours,

E. G.

417.

To his Stepmother.

June 16th, 1781.

DEAR MADAM,

I take the earliest opportunity of informing you that in the course of next week I shall be elected for the borough of Lymington in Hampshire. You may be sure of hearing from me before the end of the month.

I am,

Ever yours,

E. GIBBON.

END OF VOL. I.

LONDON: PRINTED BY WILLIAM CLOWES AND SONS, LIMITED,
STAMFORD STREET AND CHARING CROSS.